This Missal belongs to

....

Cycle B

For 1997

New *Saint Joseph*

SUNDAY MISSAL

PRAYERBOOK AND HYMNAL

This new Missal has been especially designed to help you participate at Mass . . . in the fullest and most active way possible.

How easy it is to use this Missal

- Refer to the Calendar inside the front cover for the page of the Sunday Mass (the "Proper").
- This arrow (↓) means continue to read. This arrow (→) indicates a reference back to the Order of Mass ("Ordinary") or to another part of the "Proper."
- Boldface type always indicates the people's parts that are to be recited aloud.

*The People of God together with Christ worship
the heavenly Father*

VIRGINIA BRODERICK

MASS CALENDAR FOR 1997

The Value of a Missal

"*Hand Missals which are drawn up according to the requirements of the modern liturgical renewal and which contain not only the Ordinary of the Mass but a version of all the liturgical texts approved by the competent authority are still necessary for more perfect understanding of the total mystery of salvation celebrated during the liturgical year, for drawing meditation and fervor from the inexhaustible riches of the liturgical texts, and for facilitating actual participation.*

"*This demands not only that the Word of God be proclaimed within the gathered community and attentively listened to by it, but also that the holy people respond to the Word of God which they have received and celebrate the Sacred (Mysteries) by singing or reciting the parts of the Ordinary and Proper [of the Mass], hymns and Psalms.*

[Missals are] especially necessary for . . . those who participate in daily Mass, or who desire to live and pray every day in the spirit of the liturgy; those who because of sickness or inconvenience or other similar reasons cannot assemble with their own liturgical community, so that they may be joined to their prayer more truly and intimately; children who are to be initiated progressively into the mystery of the liturgy."

Postconciliar Commission for the Implementation of the Constitution on the Sacred Liturgy.

New . . . St. Joseph

SUNDAY MISSAL

PRAYERBOOK AND HYMNAL

For 1997

THE COMPLETE MASSES FOR SUNDAYS, HOLYDAYS, and the EASTER TRIDUUM

With the People's Parts of Holy Mass
Printed in Boldface Type
and Arranged for Parish Participation

WITH THE "NEW AMERICAN BIBLE" TEXT
SHORT HELPFUL NOTES AND EXPLANATIONS
AND A TREASURY OF POPULAR PRAYERS

Dedicated to St. Joseph
Patron of the Universal Church

CATHOLIC BOOK PUBLISHING CO.
Totowa, N.J.

NIHIL OBSTAT: Francis J. McAree, S.T.D.
Censor Librorum

IMPRIMATUR: ✝ Patrick J. Sheridan, D.D.
Vicar General, Archdiocese of New York

The St. Joseph Missals have been diligently prepared with the invaluable assistance of a special Board of Editors, including specialists in Liturgy and Sacred Scripture, Catechetics, Sacred Music and Art.

In this new Sunday Missal Edition the musical notations for responsorial antiphons are by Rev. John Selner, S.S.

The Scriptural Readings and Responsorial Psalms are taken from the *Lectionary for Mass* © 1970 by Confraternity of Christian Doctrine, Washington, D.C. All rights reserved.

The prose English translations of the Sequence are taken from Joseph Connolly, *Hymns of the Roman Liturgy* (London: Longmans, Green).

English translation of the Roman Missal, Rites for Holy Week, original texts of The Alternative Opening Prayers, Invitatories, and the Penitential Rites; The Rite of Baptism for Children; The Rite of Penance; titles, responsorial psalms and alleluia verses of the Lectionary for Mass, Copyright © 1969, 1970, 1973, 1975, International Committee on English in the Liturgy, Inc. All rights reserved.

All other texts and illustrations © Copyright by Catholic Book Publishing Co., N.J.

(T-897)

PREFACE

IN the words of the Second Vatican Council in the *Constitution on the Sacred Liturgy*, the *Mass* "is an action of Christ the priest and of his body which is the Church; it is a sacred action surpassing all others; no other action of the Church can equal its efficacy by the same title and to the same degree" (art. 7). Hence, the Mass is a sacred sign, something visible which brings the invisible reality of Christ to us in the worship of the Father.

The Mass was first instituted as a meal at the Last Supper and became a living memorial of Christ's sacrifice on the cross:

"At the Last Supper, on the night when he was betrayed, our Savior instituted the Eucharistic sacrifice of his body and blood. He did this in order to perpetuate the sacrifice of the Cross throughout the centuries until he should come again, and so to entrust to his beloved spouse, the Church, a memorial of his death and resurrection: a sacrament of love, a sign of unity, a bond of charity, a Paschal banquet in which Christ is eaten, the mind is filled with grace, and a pledge of future glory is given to us.

"The Church, therefore, earnestly desires that Christ's faithful, when present at this mystery of faith, should not be there as strangers or silent spectators; on the contrary, through a good understanding of the rites and prayers they should take part in the sacred action conscious of what they are doing, with devotion and full collaboration. They should be instructed by God's word and be nourished at the

7

table of the Lord's body; they should give thanks to God; by offering the immaculate Victim, not only through the hands of the priests, but also with him, they should learn also to offer themselves; through Christ the Mediator, they should be drawn day by day into ever more perfect union with God and with each other, so that . . . God may be all in all" (art. 47-48).

Accordingly, this new Sunday Missal has been edited, in conformity with the latest findings of modern liturgists, especially to enable the people to attain the most active participation.

To insure that "each . . . layman who has an office to perform [will] do all of, but only, those parts which pertain to his office" (art. 28), a simple method of instant identification of the various parts of the Mass, has been designed, using different type faces:

(1) **boldface type** — clearly identifies all people's parts for each Mass.

(2) lightface type — indicates the priest's or lector's parts.

In order to enable the faithful to prepare for each Mass AT HOME and so participate more actively AT MASS the editors have added short helpful explanations of the new scripture readings geared to the spiritual needs of daily life. A large selection of hymns for congregational singing has been included as well as a treasury of private prayers.

We trust that all these special features will help Catholics who use this new St. Joseph Missal to be led—in keeping with the desire of the Church—"to that full, conscious, and active participation in liturgical celebrations which is demanded by the very nature of the liturgy. Such participation by the Christian people as a chosen race, a royal priesthood, a holy nation, a redeemed people (1 Pt 2, 9; cf. 2, 4-5), is their right and duty by reason of their baptism" (art. 14).

PLAN OF THE MASS

INTRODUCTORY RITES
1. Entrance Antiphon (**Proper**)
2. Greeting
3. Blessing and Sprinkling Water
4. Penitential Rite
5. Kyrie
6. Gloria
7. Opening Prayer (**Proper**)

LITURGY OF THE WORD
8. First Reading (**Proper**)
9. Responsorial Psalm (**Proper**)
10. Second Reading (**Proper**)
11. Alleluia (**Proper**)
12. Gospel (**Proper**)
13. Homily
14. Profession of Faith (**Creed**)
15. General Intercessions

(Preparation of the Gifts)
16. Offertory Song
17. Preparation of the Bread
18. Preparation of the Wine
19. Invitation to Prayer
20. Prayer over the Gifts (**Proper**)

(Eucharistic Prayer)
LITURGY OF THE EUCHARIST
21. Introductory Dialogue
22. Preface
23. Sanctus
   Eucharistic Prayer
   1, 2, 3, 4
   Children 1, 2, 3
   Reconciliation 1, 2

(Communion Rite)
24. Lord's Prayer
25. Sign of Peace
26. Breaking of Bread
27. Prayers Before Communion
28. Reception of Communion
29. Communion Antiphon (**Proper**)
30. Silence After Communion
31. Prayer After Communion (**Proper**)

CONCLUDING RITE
32. Greeting
33. Blessing
34. Dismissal

THE ORDER OF MASS

Options are indicated by A, B, C, D in the margin.

INTRODUCTORY RITES

Acts of prayer and penitence prepare us to meet Christ as he comes in Word and Sacrament. We gather as a worshiping community to celebrate our unity with him and with one another in faith.

1 ENTRANCE ANTIPHON   `STAND`

If it is not sung, it is recited by all or some of the people.

Joined together as Christ's people, we open the celebration by raising our voices in praise of God who is present among us. This song should deepen our unity as it introduces the Mass we celebrate today.

→ `Turn to Today's Mass`

2 GREETING (3 forms)

When the priest comes to the altar, he makes the customary reverence with the ministers and kisses the altar. Then, with the ministers, he goes to his seat. After the entrance song, all make the sign of the cross:

Priest: In the name of the Father, ✠ and of the Son, and of the Holy Spirit.

PEOPLE: **Amen.**

The priest welcomes us in the name of the Lord. We show our union with God, our neighbor, and the priest by a united response to his greeting.

A ————————————————————————

Priest: The grace of our Lord Jesus Christ and the love of God and the fellowship of the Holy Spirit be with you all.

PEOPLE: **And also with you.**

B ———————————— OR ————————————

Priest: The grace and peace of God our Father and the Lord Jesus Christ be with you.

PEOPLE: **Blessed be God, the Father of our Lord Jesus Christ.**

or:
And also with you.

C ———————————— OR ————————————

Priest: The Lord be with you.

PEOPLE: **And also with you.**

[Bishop: Peace be with you.
People: **And also with you.**]

3 RITE OF BLESSING and SPRINKLING HOLY WATER

The rite of blessing and sprinkling holy water may be celebrated in all churches and chapels at all Sunday Masses celebrated on Sunday or Saturday evening. See pp. 72-74.

4 PENITENTIAL RITE (3 forms)

(Omitted when the rite of blessing and sprinkling holy water has taken place or some part of the liturgy of the hours has preceded.)

Before we hear God's word, we acknowledge our sins humbly, ask for mercy, and accept his pardon.

Invitation to repent:

After the introduction to the day's Mass, the priest invites the people to recall their sins and to repent of them in silence:

A As we prepare to celebrate the mystery of Christ's love,
  let us acknowledge our failures
  and ask the Lord for pardon and strength.

B Coming together as God's family,
  with confidence let us ask the Father's forgiveness,
  for he is full of gentleness and compassion.

C My brothers and sisters,
  to prepare ourselves to celebrate the sacred mysteries,
  let us call to mind our sins.

Then, after a brief silence, one of the following forms is used.

A

Priest and **People:**

I confess to almighty God,
and to you, my brothers and sisters,
that I have sinned through my own fault

They strike their breast:

in my thoughts and in my words,
in what I have done,

and in what I have failed to do;
and I ask blessed Mary, ever virgin,
all the angels and saints,
and you, my brothers and sisters,
to pray for me to the Lord our God.

B —————— OR ——————

Priest: Lord, we have sinned against you:
Lord, have mercy.
PEOPLE: Lord, have mercy.
Priest: Lord, show us your mercy and love.
PEOPLE: And grant us your salvation.

C —————— OR ——————

Priest or other minister:

You were sent to heal the contrite:
Lord, have mercy.
PEOPLE: Lord, have mercy.

Priest or other minister:

You came to call sinners:
Christ, have mercy.
PEOPLE: Christ, have mercy.

Priest or other minister:

You plead for us at the right hand of
the Father:
Lord, have mercy.
PEOPLE: Lord, have mercy.

(Other invocations may be used as on pp. 75-77.)

Absolution:

At the end of any of the forms of the penitential rite:

Priest: **May almighty God have mercy on us,
forgive us our sins,
and bring us to everlasting life.**

PEOPLE: Amen.

5 KYRIE

Unless included in the penitential rite, the Kyrie is sung or said by all, with alternating parts for the choir or cantor and for the people:

℣. Lord have mercy.

℟. **Lord, have mercy.**

℣. Christ, have mercy.

℟. **Christ, have mercy.**

℣. Lord, have mercy.

℟. **Lord, have mercy.**

6 GLORIA

As the Church assembled in the Spirit we praise and pray to the Father and the Lamb.

When the Gloria is sung or said, the priest or the cantors or everyone together may begin it:

**Glory to God in the highest,
and peace to his people on earth.**

**Lord God, heavenly King,
almighty God and Father,
we worship you, we give you thanks,
we praise you for your glory.**

**Lord Jesus Christ, only Son of the Father,
Lord God, Lamb of God,
you take away the sin of the world:**
   have mercy on us;
you are seated at the right hand of the Father:
   receive our prayer.

**For you alone are the Holy One,
you alone are the Lord,
you alone are the Most High,**
   Jesus Christ,
   with the Holy Spirit,
   in the glory of God the Father. Amen.

7 OPENING PRAYER

The priest invites us to pray silently for a moment and then, in our name, expresses the theme of the day's celebration and petitions God the Father through the mediation of Christ in the Holy Spirit.

Priest: Let us pray.

➜ Turn to Today's Mass

Priest and people pray silently for a while. Then the priest says the opening prayer and concludes:

Priest: For ever and ever.
PEOPLE: Amen.

LITURGY OF THE WORD

The proclamation of God's Word is always centered on Christ, present through his Word. Old Testament writings prepare for him; New Testament books speak of him directly. All of scripture calls us to believe once more and to follow. After the reading we reflect upon God's words and respond to them.

As-in-Today's-Mass **SIT**

8 FIRST READING

At end of reading: Reader: The word of the Lord.
PEOPLE: Thanks be to God.

9 RESPONSORIAL PSALM

The people repeat the response sung by the cantor the first time and then after each verse.

10 SECOND READING

At end of reading: Reader: The word of the Lord.
PEOPLE: Thanks be to God.

11 ALLELUIA (Gospel Acclamation) **STAND**

Jesus will speak to us in the gospel. We rise now out of respect and prepare for his message with the alleluia.

The people repeat the alleluia after cantor's alleluia and then after the verse.

During Lent one of the following invocations is used as a response instead of the alleluia:

(a) **Praise to you, Lord Jesus Christ, king of endless glory!**
(b) **Praise and honor to you, Lord Jesus Christ!**
(c) **Glory and praise to you, Lord Jesus Christ!**
(d) **Glory to you, Word of God, Lord Jesus Christ!**

12 GOSPEL

Before proclaiming the gospel, the deacon asks the priest: **Father, give me your blessing.** *The priest says:*

The Lord be in your heart and on your lips that you may worthily proclaim his gospel. In the name of the Father, and of the Son, ✠ and of the Holy Spirit. *The deacon answers:* **Amen.**

If there is no deacon, the priest says inaudibly:

Almighty God, cleanse my heart and my lips that I may worthily proclaim your gospel.

Deacon (or Priest):

   The Lord be with you.

PEOPLE: And also with you.

Deacon (or Priest):

✠ A reading from the holy gospel according to N.

PEOPLE: Glory to you, Lord.

At the end:

Deacon (or priest):

   The gospel of the Lord.

PEOPLE: Praise to you, Lord Jesus Christ.

Then the deacon (or priest) kisses the book, saying inaudibly: **May the words of the gospel wipe away our sins.**

13 HOMILY   SIT

God's word is spoken again in the homily. The Holy Spirit speaking through the lips of the preacher explains and applies today's biblical readings to the needs of this particular congregation. He calls us to respond to Christ through the life we lead.

14 PROFESSION OF FAITH (CREED)   STAND

As a people we express our acceptance of God's message in the scriptures and homily. We summarize our faith by proclaiming a creed handed down from the early Church.

All say the profession of faith on Sundays.

——— NICENE CREED ———

We believe in one God,
  the Father, the Almighty,
  maker of heaven and earth,
  of all that is seen and unseen.

We believe in one Lord, Jesus Christ,
  the only Son of God,
  eternally begotten of the Father,
  God from God, Light from Light,
  true God from true God,
  begotten, not made, one in Being with the Father.
  Through him all things were made.
For us men and for our salvation
  he came down from heaven:
by the power of the Holy Spirit
  he was born of the Virgin Mary,   } *bow*
    and became man.
For our sake he was crucified under Pontius Pilate;
  he suffered, died, and was buried.
  On the third day he rose again
    in fulfillment of the Scriptures;
  he ascended into heaven
    and is seated at the right hand of the Father.
He will come again in glory to judge the living and
    the dead,
  and his kingdom will have no end.
We believe in the Holy Spirit, the Lord, the giver of life,
  who proceeds from the Father and the Son.
  With the Father and the Son he is worshiped and
    glorified.
  He has spoken through the Prophets.
We believe in one holy catholic and apostolic Church.

We acknowledge one baptism for the forgiveness
　　of sins.
We look for the resurrection of the dead,
　　and the life of the world to come. Amen.

OR ——————— APOSTLES' CREED ———————

*In celebrations of Masses with Children, the Apostles'
Creed may be said after the homily.*

I believe in God, the Father almighty,
　　creator of heaven and earth.

I believe in Jesus Christ, his only Son, our Lord.
　　He was conceived by the power of the Holy Spirit
　　　　and born of the Virgin Mary.
　　He suffered under Pontius Pilate,
　　　　was crucified, died, and was buried.
　　He descended to the dead.
　　On the third day he rose again.
　　He ascended into heaven,
　　　　and is seated at the right hand of the Father.
　　He will come again to judge the living and the dead.

I believe in the Holy Spirit,
　　the holy catholic Church,
　　the communion of saints,
　　the forgiveness of sins,
　　the resurrection of the body,
　　and the life everlasting. Amen.

15 GENERAL INTERCESSIONS (Prayer of the Faithful)

As a priestly people we unite with one another to pray for
today's needs in the Church and the world.

*After the priest gives the introduction the deacon or
other minister sings or says the invocations.*

PEOPLE: Lord, hear our prayer.

(or other response, according to local custom)
At the end the priest says the concluding prayer:

PEOPLE: Amen.

LITURGY OF THE EUCHARIST

Made ready by reflection on God's Word, we enter now into the eucharistic sacrifice itself, the Supper of the Lord. We celebrate the memorial which the Lord instituted at his Last Supper. We are God's new people, the redeemed brothers and sisters of Christ, gathered by him around his table. We are here to bless God and to receive the gift of Jesus' body and blood so that our faith and life may be transformed.

PREPARATION OF THE GIFTS

16 OFFERTORY SONG SIT

The bread and wine for the Eucharist, with our gifts for the Church and the poor, are gathered and brought to the altar. We prepare our hearts by song or in silence as the Lord's table is being set.

While the people's gifts are brought forward to the priest and are placed on the altar, the offertory song is sung.

17 PREPARATION OF THE BREAD

Before placing the bread on the altar, the priest says inaudibly:

Blessed are you, Lord, God of all creation.
Through your goodness we have this bread to offer,
which earth has given and human hands have made.
It will become for us the bread of life.

If there is no singing, the priest may say this prayer aloud, and the people may respond:

PEOPLE: **Blessed be God for ever.**

18 PREPARATION OF THE WINE

When he pours wine and a little water into the chalice, the deacon (or the priest) says inaudibly:

20

By the mystery of this water and wine
may we come to share in the divinity of Christ,
who humbled himself to share in our humanity.

Before placing the chalice on the altar, he says:
Blessed are you, Lord, God of all creation.
Through your goodness we have this wine to offer,
fruit of the vine and work of human hands.
It will become our spiritual drink.

*If there is no singing, the priest may say this prayer
aloud, and the people may respond:*
PEOPLE: **Blessed be God for ever.**

The priest says inaudibly:
Lord God, we ask you to receive us
and be pleased with the sacrifice we offer you
with humble and contrite hearts.

Then he washes his hands, saying:
Lord, wash away my iniquity;
cleanse me from my sin.

19 INVITATION TO PRAYER

Priest: Pray, brethren, that our sacrifice may be
acceptable to God, the almighty Father.
PEOPLE:
**May the Lord accept the sacrifice at your hands
for the praise and glory of his name,
for our good, and the good of all his Church.**

20 PRAYER OVER THE GIFTS `STAND`

The priest, speaking in our name, asks the Father to bless
and accept these gifts.

→ **Turn to Today's Mass**

At the end, **PEOPLE:** **Amen.**

EUCHARISTIC PRAYER

We begin the eucharistic service of praise and thanksgiving, the center of the entire celebration, the central praryer of worship. We lift our hearts to God, and offer praise and thanks as the priest addresses this prayer to the Father through Jesus Christ. Together we join Christ in his sacrifice, celebrating his memorial in the holy meal and acknowledging with him the wonderful works of God in our lives.

21 INTRODUCTORY DIALOGUE

Priest: The Lord be with you.

PEOPLE: And also with you.

Priest: Lift up your hearts.

PEOPLE: We lift them up to the Lord.

Priest: Let us give thanks to the Lord our God.

PEOPLE: It is right to give him thanks and praise.

21 PREFACE

As indicated in the individual Masses of this Missal, the priest may say one of the following Prefaces (listed in numerical order).

23   ACCLAMATION

Priest and **People:**

Holy, holy, holy Lord, God of power and might, heaven and earth are full of your glory.

> **Hosanna in the highest.**

Blessed is he who comes in the name of the Lord.

> **Hosanna in the highest.** `KNEEL`

Then the priest continues with one of the following Eucharistic Prayers.

EUCHARISTIC PRAYER ....Choice of nine

1 We come to you, Father ....p. 24
2 Lord, you are holy indeed............................p. 30
3 Father, you are holy indeed.........................p. 33
4 Father, we acknowledge ....p. 38
C1 God our Father, you are most holy............p. 44
C2 God our Father, we now ask you ....p. 49
C3 Yes, Lord, you are holy ....p. 53
R1 Father, from the beginning ....p. 58
R2 God of power and might ....p. 63

The Roman Canon

(This Eucharistic Prayer is especially suitable for Sundays and Masses with proper "Communicantes" and "Hanc igitur.")

[The words within brackets may be omitted.]

[Praise to the Father]

We come to you, Father,
with praise and thanksgiving,
through Jesus Christ your Son.
Through him we ask you to accept and bless
these gifts we offer you in sacrifice.

[Intercessions: For the Church]

We offer them for your holy catholic Church,
watch over it, Lord, and guide it;
grant it peace and unity throughout the world.
We offer them for N. our Pope,
for N. our bishop,
and for all who hold and teach the catholic faith
that comes to us from the apostles.
Remember, Lord, your people,
especially those for whom we now pray, N.
and N.

Remember all of us gathered here before you.
You know how firmly we believe in you
and dedicate ourselves to you.
We offer you this sacrifice of praise
for ourselves and those who are dear to us.
We pray to you, our living and true God,
for our well-being and redemption.

In union with the whole Church*
we honor Mary,
the ever-virgin mother of Jesus Christ our Lord
   and God.
We honor Joseph, her husband,
the apostles and martyrs
Peter and Paul, Andrew,
[James, John, Thomas,
James, Philip,
Bartholomew, Matthew, Simon and Jude;
we honor Linus, Cletus, Clement, Sixtus,
Cornelius, Cyprian, Lawrence, Chrysogonus,
John and Paul, Cosmas and Damian]
and all the saints.
May their merits and prayers
gain us your constant help and protection.
[Through Christ our Lord. Amen.]

Father, accept this offering*
from your whole family.
Grant us your peace in this life,
save us from final damnation,
and count us among those you have chosen.
[Through Christ our Lord. Amen.]

Bless and approve our offering;
make it acceptable to you,
an offering in spirit and in truth.
Let it become for us
the body and blood of Jesus Christ,
your only Son, our Lord.
[Through Christ our Lord. Amen.]

*See page 90 for Special Communicantes and Hanc
Igitur.*

[The Lord's Supper]

1

The day before he suffered
he took bread in his sacred hands
and looking up to heaven,
to you, his almighty Father,
he gave you thanks and praise.
He broke the bread,
gave it to his disciples, and said:

Take this, all of you, and eat it:
this is my body which will be given up for you.

When supper was ended,
he took the cup.
Again he gave you thanks and praise,
gave the cup to his disciples, and said:

Take this, all of you, and drink from it:
this is the cup of my blood,
the blood of the new and everlasting covenant.
It will be shed for you and for all
so that sins may be forgiven.
Do this in memory of me.

[Memorial Acclamation]

Priest: Let us proclaim the mystery of faith.

PEOPLE:

A **Christ has died,**
Christ is risen,
Christ will come again.

B **Dying you destroyed our death,**
rising you restored our life.
Lord Jesus, come in glory.

C **When we eat this bread and drink this cup,** **1**
   we proclaim your death, Lord Jesus,
   until you come in glory.

D **Lord, by your cross and resurrection**
   you have set us free.
   You are the Savior of the world.

[The Memorial Prayer]

Father, we celebrate the memory of Christ,
   your Son.
We, your people and your ministers,
recall his passion,
his resurrection from the dead,
and his ascension into glory;
and from the many gifts you have given us
we offer to you, God of glory and majesty,
this holy and perfect sacrifice:
the bread of life
and the cup of eternal salvation.
Look with favor on these offerings
and accept them as once you accepted
the gifts of your servant Abel,
the sacrifice of Abraham, our father in faith,
and the bread and wine offered by your priest
   Melchisedech.
Almighty God,
we pray that your angel may take this sacrifice
to your altar in heaven.
Then, as we receive from this altar
the sacred body and blood of your Son,
let us be filled with every grace and blessing.
[Through Christ our Lord. Amen.]

[For the Dead]

Remember, Lord, those who have died
and have gone before us marked with the sign
    of faith,
especially those for whom we now pray, *N.* and *N.*
May these, and all who sleep in Christ,
find in your presence
light, happiness, and peace.
[Through Christ our Lord. Amen.]

For ourselves, too, we ask
some share in the fellowship of your apostles
    and martyrs,
with John the Baptist, Stephen, Matthias, Bar-
    nabas,
[Ignatius, Alexander, Marcellinus, Peter, Felicity,
Perpetua, Agatha, Lucy, Agnes, Cecilia, Anastasia]
and all the saints.
Though we are sinners,
we trust in your mercy and love.
Do not consider what we truly deserve,
but grant us your forgiveness.
Through Christ our Lord.

Through him you give us all these gifts.
You fill them with life and goodness,
you bless them and make them holy.

Through him,   *[Concluding Doxology]*
with him,
in him,
in the unity of the Holy Spirit,
all glory and honor is yours,
almighty Father,
for ever and ever.
All reply: **Amen.** *Continue with the Mass, as on p. 66.*

(This Eucharistic Prayer is particularly suitable on Weekdays or for special circumstances)

STAND

℣. The Lord be with you.

℟. **And also with you.**

℣. Lift up your hearts.

℟. **We lift them up to the Lord.**

℣. Let us give thanks to the Lord our God.

℟. **It is right to give him thanks and praise.**

PREFACE   *[Praise to the Lord]*

Father, it is our duty and our salvation,
always and everywhere
to give you thanks
through your beloved Son, Jesus Christ.

He is the Word through whom you made the
    universe,
the Savior you sent to redeem us.

By the power of the Holy Spirit
he took flesh and was born of the Virgin Mary.

For our sake he opened his arms on the cross;
he put an end to death
and revealed the resurrection.

In this he fulfilled your will
and won for you a holy people.

And so we join the angels and the saints
in proclaiming your glory
as we sing (say):

2 SANCTUS *[First Acclamation of the People]*

**Holy, holy, holy Lord, God of power and might,
heaven and earth are full of your glory.**
> **Hosanna in the highest.**

Blessed is he who comes in the name of the Lord.
> **Hosanna in the highest.**

`KNEEL`

[Invocation of the Holy Spirit]

Lord, you are holy indeed,
the fountain of all holiness.

Let your Spirit come upon these gifts to make
    them holy,
so that they may become for us
the body and blood of our Lord, Jesus Christ.

[The Lord's Supper]

Before he was given up to death,
a death he freely accepted,
he took bread and gave you thanks.
He broke the bread,
gave it to his disciples, and said:

Take this, all of you, and eat it:
this is my body which will be given up for you.

When supper was ended, he took the cup.
Again he gave you thanks and praise,
gave the cup to his disciples, and said:

Take this, all of you, and drink from it:
this is the cup of my blood,
the blood of the new and everlasting covenant.
It will be shed for you and for all
so that sins may be forgiven.
Do this in memory of me.

[Memorial Acclamation] **2**

Priest: Let us proclaim the mystery of faith.

PEOPLE:

A **Christ has died,**
   Christ is risen,
   Christ will come again.

B **Dying you destroyed our death,**
   rising you restored our life.
   Lord Jesus, come in glory.

C **When we eat this bread and drink this cup,**
   we proclaim your death, Lord Jesus,
   until you come in glory.

D **Lord, by your cross and resurrection**
   you have set us free.
   You are the Savior of the world.

[The Memorial Prayer]

In memory of his death and resurrection,
we offer you, Father, this life-giving bread,
this saving cup.
We thank you for counting us worthy
to stand in your presence and serve you.

[Invocation of the Holy Spirit]

May all of us who share in the body and blood
   of Christ
be brought together in unity by the Holy Spirit.

2 *[Intercessions: For the Church]*
Lord, remember your Church throughout the
  world;
make us grow in love,
together with N. our Pope,
N. our bishop, and all the clergy.*

[For the Dead]
Remember our brothers and sisters
who have gone to their rest
in the hope of rising again;
bring them and all the departed
into the light of your presence.

[In Communion with the Saints]
Have mercy on us all;
make us worthy to share eternal life
with Mary, the virgin Mother of God,
with the apostles, and with all the saints
who have done your will throughout the ages.
May we praise you in union with them,
and give you glory
through your Son, Jesus Christ.

Through him,   *[Concluding Doxology]*
with him,
in him,
in the unity of the Holy Spirit,
all glory and honor is yours,
almighty Father,
for ever and ever.
All reply: **Amen.**   *Continue with the Mass, as on p. 66*

---

* *In Masses for the Dead the following may be added:*
Remember N., whom you have called from this life.
In baptism he (she) died with Christ:
may he (she) also share his resurrection.

EUCHARISTIC PRAYER No. 3

*(This Eucharistic Prayer may be used with any Preface
and preferably on Sundays and feast days)*

KNEEL

[Praise to the Father]

Father, you are holy indeed,
and all creation rightly gives you praise.
All life, all holiness comes from you
through your Son, Jesus Christ our Lord,
by the working of the Holy Spirit.

From age to age you gather a people to yourself,
so that from east to west
a perfect offering may be made
to the glory of your name.

[Invocation of the Holy Spirit]

And so, Father, we bring you these gifts.
We ask you to make them holy by the power of
   your Spirit,
that they may become the body and blood
of your Son, our Lord Jesus Christ,
at whose command we celebrate this eucharist.

[The Lord's Supper]

On the night he was betrayed,
he took bread and gave you thanks and praise.
He broke the bread, gave it to his disciples, and
   said:

Take this, all of you, and eat it:
this is my body which will be given up for you.

3 When supper was ended, he took the cup.
Again he gave you thanks and praise,
gave the cup to his disciples, and said:

Take this, all of you, and drink from it:
this is the cup of my blood,
the blood of the new and everlasting covenant.
It will be shed for you and for all
so that sins may be forgiven.
Do this in memory of me.

[Memorial Acclamation]

Priest: Let us proclaim the mystery of faith.

PEOPLE:

A Christ has died,
   Christ is risen,
   Christ will come again.

B Dying you destroyed our death,
   rising you restored our life.
   Lord Jesus, come in glory.

C When we eat this bread and drink this cup,
   we proclaim your death, Lord Jesus,
   until you come in glory.

D Lord, by your cross and resurrection
   you have set us free.
   You are the Savior of the world.

[The Memorial Prayer]

Father, calling to mind the death your Son
   endured for our salvation,
his glorious resurrection and ascension into
   heaven,
and ready to greet him when he comes again,
we offer you in thanksgiving this holy and living sacrifice.

Look with favor on your Church's offering,
and see the Victim whose death has reconciled
  us to yourself.

[Invocation of the Holy Spirit]

Grant that we, who are nourished by his body
  and blood,
may be filled with his Holy Spirit,
and become one body, one spirit in Christ.

[Intercessions: In Communion with the Saints]

May he make us an everlasting gift to you
and enable us to share in the inheritance of your
  saints,
with Mary, the virgin Mother of God;
with the apostles, the martyrs,
(Saint *N.)* and all your saints,
on whose constant intercession we rely for help.

[For the Church]

Lord, may this sacrifice,
which has made our peace with you,
advance the peace and salvation of all the world.
Strengthen in faith and love your pilgrim
  Church on earth;
your servant, Pope *N.,* our bishop *N.,*
and all the bishops,
with the clergy and the entire people your Son
  has gained for you.
Father, hear the prayers of the family you have
  gathered here before you.
In mercy and love unite all your children
wherever they may be.*

[For the Dead]

Welcome into your kingdom our departed
  brothers and sisters,

* *See p. 36 for special prayer for Mass for the Dead.*

3 and all who have left this world in your friendship.
We hope to enjoy for ever the vision of your
glory,
through Christ our Lord, from whom all good
things come.

[Concluding Doxology]

Through him,
with him,
in him,
in the unity of the Holy Spirit,
all glory and honor is yours,
almighty Father,
for ever and ever.
All reply: **Amen.**

Continue with the Mass, as on p. 66

*In Masses for the Dead the following is said:

Remember N.
In baptism he (she) died with Christ:
may he (she) also share his resurrection,
when Christ will raise our mortal bodies
and make them like his own in glory.
Welcome into your kingdom our departed brothers
and sisters,
and all who have left this world in your friendship.
There we hope to share in your glory
when every tear will be wiped away.
On that day we shall see you, our God, as you are.
We shall become like you
and praise you for ever through Christ our Lord,
from whom all good things come.
Through him, etc., *as above.*

℣. The Lord be with you.   STAND
℟. **And also with you.**
℣. Lift up your hearts.
℟. **We lift them up to the Lord.**
℣. Let us give thanks to the Lord our God.
℟. **It is right to give him thanks and praise.**

PREFACE

Father in heaven,
it is right that we should give you thanks and
    glory:
you are the one God, living and true.
Through all eternity you live in unapproachable
    light.
Source of life and goodness, you have created
    all things,
to fill your creatures with every blessing
and lead all men to the joyful vision of your light.
Countless hosts of angels stand before you to do
    your will;
they look upon your splendor
and praise you, night and day.
United with them,
and in the name of every creature under heaven,
we too praise your glory as we sing (say):

SANCTUS   *[First Acclamation of the People]*

**Holy, holy, holy Lord, God of power and might,
heaven and earth are full of your glory.**
    Hosanna in the highest.
Blessed is he who comes in the name of the Lord.
    Hosanna in the highest.

4

Father, we acknowledge your greatness:
all your actions show your wisdom and love.
You formed man in your own likeness
and set him over the whole world
to serve you, his creator,
and to rule over all creatures.
Even when he disobeyed you and lost your
    friendship
you did not abandon him to the power of death,
but helped all men to seek and find you.
Again and again you offered a covenant to man,
and through the prophets taught him to hope for
    salvation.
Father, you so loved the world
that in the fullness of time you sent your only
    Son to be our Savior.
He was conceived through the power of the
    Holy Spirit,
and born of the Virgin Mary,
a man like us in all things but sin.
To the poor he proclaimed the good news of sal-
    vation,
to prisoners, freedom,
and to those in sorrow, joy.
In fulfillment of your will
he gave himself up to death;
but by rising from the dead,
he destroyed death and restored life.
And that we might live no longer for ourselves
    but for him,
he sent the Holy Spirit from you, Father,
as his first gift to those who believe,

4

to complete his work on earth
and bring us the fullness of grace.

[Invocation of the Holy Spirit]

Father, may this Holy Spirit sanctify these offerings.
Let them become the body ✠ and blood of Jesus
Christ our Lord
as we celebrate the great mystery
which he left us as an everlasting covenant.

[The Lord's Supper]

He always loved those who were his own in the
world.
When the time came for him to be glorified by
you, his heavenly Father,
he showed the depth of his love.
While they were at supper,
he took bread, said the blessing, broke the bread,
and gave it to his disciples, saying:

Take this, all of you, and eat it:
this is my body which will be given up for you.

In the same way, he took the cup, filled with
wine,
He gave you thanks, and giving the cup to his
disciples, said:

Take this, all of you, and drink from it:
this is the cup of my blood,
the blood of the new and everlasting covenant.
It will be shed for you and for all
so that sins may be forgiven.
Do this in memory of me.

[Memorial Acclamation]

Priest: Let us proclaim the mystery of faith:

4 PEOPLE:

A Christ has died,
Christ is risen,
Christ will come again.

B Dying you destroyed our death,
rising you restored our life.
Lord Jesus, come in glory.

C When we eat this bread and drink this cup,
we proclaim your death, Lord Jesus,
until you come in glory.

D Lord, by your cross and resurrection
you have set us free.
You are the Savior of the world.

[The Memorial Prayer]

Father, we now celebrate this memorial of our
redemption.
We recall Christ's death, his descent among the
dead,
his resurrection, and his ascension to your right
hand;
and, looking forward to his coming in glory, we
offer you his body and blood,
the acceptable sacrifice
which brings salvation to the whole world.

Lord, look upon this sacrifice which you have
given to your Church;
and by your Holy Spirit, gather all who share
this one bread and one cup
into the one body of Christ, a living sacrifice of
praise.

4

[Intercessions: For the Church]

Lord, remember those for whom we offer this
    sacrifice,
especially *N.,* our Pope,
N., our bishop, and bishops and clergy everywhere.
Remember those who take part in this offering,
those here present and all your people,
and all who seek you with a sincere heart.

[For the Dead]

Remember those who have died in the peace of
    Christ
and all the dead whose faith is known to you alone.

[In Communion with the Saints]

Father, in your mercy grant also to us, your
    children,
to enter into our heavenly inheritance
in the company of the Virgin Mary, the Mother
    of God,
and your apostles and saints.
Then, in your kingdom, freed from the corrup-
    tion of sin and death,
we shall sing your glory with every creature
    through Christ our Lord,
through whom you give us everything that is good.

[Concluding Doxology]

Through him,
with him,
in him,
in the unity of the Holy Spirit,
all glory and honor is yours,
almighty Father,
for ever and ever.

All reply: **Amen.**   *Continue with Mass, as on p. 66.*

EUCHARISTIC PRAYER FOR MASSES WITH CHILDREN I

STAND

℣. The Lord be with you.
℟. **And also with you.**
℣. Lift up your hearts.
℟. **We lift them up to the Lord.**
℣. Let us give thanks to the Lord our God.
℟. **It is right to give him thanks and praise.**

God our Father,
you have brought us here together
so that we can give you thanks and praise
for all the wonderful things you have done.

We thank you for all that is beautiful in the world
and for the happiness you have given us.
We praise you for daylight
and for your word which lights up our minds.
We praise you for the earth,
and all the people who live on it,
and for our life which comes from you.

We know that you are good.
You love us and do great things for us.
[So we all sing (say) together:

Holy, holy, holy Lord, God of power and might, heaven and earth are full of your glory.
Hosanna in the highest.]

Father,
you are always thinking about your people;
you never forget us.

C 1

You sent us your Son Jesus,
who gave his life for us
and who came to save us.
He cured sick people;
he cared for those who were poor
and wept with those who were sad.
He forgave sinners
and taught us to forgive each other.
He loved everyone
and showed us how to be kind.
He took children in his arms and blessed them.
[So we are glad to sing (say):

Blessed is he who comes in the name of the Lord.
     Hosanna in the highest.]

God our Father,
all over the world your people praise you.
So now we pray with the whole Church:
with N., our pope and N., our bishop.
In heaven the blessed Virgin Mary,
the apostles and all the saints
always sing your praise.
Now we join with them and with the angels
to adore you as we sing (say):

People:
Holy, holy, holy Lord, God of power and might,
heaven and earth are full of your glory.
     Hosanna in the highest.
Blessed is he who comes in the name of the Lord.
     Hosanna in the highest.

C 1 God our Father,
you are most holy
and we want to show you that we are grateful.

KNEEL

We bring you bread and wine
and ask you to send your Holy Spirit to make these gifts
the body ✠ and blood of Jesus your Son.
Then we can offer to you
what you have given to us.

On the night before he died,
Jesus was having supper with his apostles.
He took bread from the table.
He gave you thanks and praise.
Then he broke the bread, gave it to his friends, and said:

Take this, all of you, and eat it:
this is my body which will be given up for you.

When supper was ended,
Jesus took the cup that was filled with wine.
He thanked you, gave it to his friends, and said:

Take this, all of you, and drink from it:
this is the cup of my blood,
the blood of the new and everlasting covenant.
It will be shed for you and for all
so that sins may be forgiven.
Then he said to them:
do this in memory of me.

We do now what Jesus told us to do.
We remember his death and his resurrection

and we offer you, Father, the bread that gives us
  life,
and the cup that saves us.
Jesus brings us to you;
welcome us as you welcome him.

Priest: Let us proclaim our faith:

PEOPLE:

A **Christ has died,**
    Christ is risen,
    Christ will come again.

B **Dying you destroyed our death,**
    rising you restored our life.
    Lord Jesus, come in glory.

C **When we eat this bread and drink this cup,**
    we proclaim your death, Lord Jesus,
    until you come in glory.

D **Lord, by your cross and resurrection**
    you have set us free.
    You are the Savior of the world.

Father,
because you love us,
you invite us to come to your table.
Fill us with the joy of the Holy Spirit
as we receive the body and blood of your Son.

Lord,
you never forget any of your children.
We ask you to take care of those we love,
especially of N. and N.;
and we pray for those who have died.

C1 Remember everyone who is suffering from pain or sorrow.
Remember Christians everywhere
and all other people in the world.

We are filled with wonder and praise
when we see what you do for us
through Jesus your Son,
and so we sing:

Through him,
with him,
in him,
in the unity of the Holy Spirit,
all glory and honor is yours,
almighty Father,
for ever and ever.

The people respond: **Amen.**

Continue with the Mass, as on p. 66.

℣. The Lord be with you.
℟. **And also with you.**
℣. Lift up your hearts.
℟. **We lift them up to the Lord.**
℣. Let us give thanks to the Lord our God.
℟. **It is right to give him thanks and praise.**

God our loving Father,
we are glad to give you thanks and praise
because you love us.
With Jesus we sing your praise:

All say

Glory to God in the highest.

> *or:*

Hosanna in the highest.

Because you love us,
you gave us this great and beautiful world.
With Jesus we sing your praise:

All say:

Glory to God in the highest.

> *or:*

Hosanna in the highest.

Because you love us,
you sent Jesus your Son
to bring us to you
and to gather us around him
as the children of one family.

C 2

With Jesus we sing your praise:

All say:

Glory to God in the highest.
> *or:*

Hosanna in the highest.

For such great love
we thank you with the angels and saints
as they praise you and sing (say):

All say:

**Holy, holy, holy Lord, God of power and might,
heaven and earth are full of your glory.**
> **Hosanna in the highest.**

Blessed is he who comes in the name of the Lord.
> **Hosanna in the highest.**

Blessed be Jesus, whom you sent
to be the friend of children and of the poor.

He came to show us
how we can love you, Father,
by loving one another.
He came to take away sin,
which keeps us from being friends,
and hate, which makes us all unhappy.

He promised to send the Holy Spirit,
to be with us always
so that we can live as your children.

All say:

Blessed is he who comes in the name of the Lord.
> **Hosanna in the highest.**

God our Father,
we now ask you
to send your Holy Spirit
to change these gifts of bread and wine
into the body ✝ and blood
of Jesus Christ, our Lord.

The night before he died,
Jesus your Son showed us how much you love
   us.
When he was at supper with his disciples,
he took bread,
and gave you thanks and praise.
Then he broke the bread,
gave it to his friends, and said:
Take this, all of you, and eat it:
This is my body which will be given up for you.

All say:
Jesus has given his life for us.

When supper was ended,
Jesus took the cup that was filled with wine.
He thanked you, gave it to his friends, and said:

Take this, all of you, and drink from it:
this is the cup of my blood,
the blood of the new and everlasting covenant.
It will be shed for you and for all
so that sins may be forgiven.

All say:
Jesus has given his life for us.

Then he said to them:
do this in memory of me.

C 2 And so, loving Father,
we remember that Jesus died and rose again
to save the world.
He put himself into our hands
to be the sacrifice we offer you.

All say:
We praise you, we bless you, we thank you.

Lord our God,
listen to our prayer.
Send the Holy Spirit
to all of us who share in this meal.
May this Spirit bring us closer together
in the family of the Church,
with N., our pope,
N., our bishop,
all other bishops,
and all who serve your people.

All say:
We praise you, we bless you, we thank you.

Remember, Father, our families and friends (. . .),
and all those we do not love as we should.
Remember those who have died (. . .).
Bring them home to you
to be with you for ever.

All say:
We praise you, we bless you, we thank you.

Gather us all together into your kingdom.
There we shall be happy for ever
with the Virgin Mary, Mother of God and our
  mother.

**C
2**

There all the friends
of Jesus the Lord
will sing a song of joy.

All say:
We praise you, we bless you, we thank you.

Through him,
with him,
in him,
in the unity of the Holy Spirit,
all glory and honor is yours,
almighty Father,
for ever and ever.

The people respond: **Amen.**

Continue with the Mass, as on p. 66.

℣. The Lord be with you. **STAND**
℟. **And also with you.**
℣. Lift up your hearts.
℟. **We lift them up to the Lord.**
℣. Let us give thanks to the Lord our God.
℟. **It is right to give him thanks and praise.**

Outside Easter season:

We thank you,
God our Father.
You made us to live for you and for each other.
We can see and speak to one another,
and become friends,
and share our joys and sorrows.

During Easter Season:

We thank you
God our Father.
You are the living God;
you have called us to share in your life,
and to be happy with you for ever.
You raised up Jesus, your Son,
the first among us to rise from the dead,
and gave him new life.
You have promised to give us new life also,
a life that will never end,
a life with no more anxiety and suffering.

C 3

And so, Father, we gladly thank you
with every one who believes in you;
with the saints and the angels,
we rejoice and praise you, saying:

**Holy, holy, holy Lord, God of power and might,
heaven and earth are full of your glory.**
    Hosanna in the highest.
Blessed is he who comes in the name of the Lord.
    Hosanna in the highest.

Yes, Lord, you are holy;
you are kind to us and to all.
For this we thank you.
We thank you above all for your Son, Jesus
    Christ.

Outside Easter season:

You sent him into this world
because people had turned away from you
and no longer loved each other.
He opened our eyes and our hearts
to understand that we are brothers and sisters
and that you are Father of us all.

During Easter season:

He brought us the good news
of life to be lived with you for ever in heaven.
He showed us the way to that life,
the way of love.
He himself has gone that way before us.

He now brings us together to one table
and asks us to do what he did.

C 3 Father,
we ask you to bless these gifts of bread and wine
and make them holy.
Change them for us into the body ✠ and blood
　　of Jesus Christ, your Son.

On the night before he died for us,
he had supper for the last time with his disciples.
He took bread
and gave you thanks.
He broke the bread
and gave it to his friends, saying:
Take this, all of you, and eat it:
this is my body which will be given up for you.

In the same way he took a cup of wine.
He gave you thanks
and handed the cup to his disciples, saying:
Take this, all of you, and drink from it:
this is the cup of my blood,
the blood of the new and everlasting covenant.
It will be shed for you and for all
so that sins may be forgiven.
Then he said to them:
do this in memory of me.

God our Father,
we remember with joy
all that Jesus did to save us.
In this holy sacrifice,
which he gave as a gift to his Church,
we remember his death and resurrection.

C 3

Father in heaven,
accept us together with your beloved Son.
He willingly died for us,
but you raised him to life again.
We thank you and say:

All say:
Glory to God in the highest.
(Or some other suitable acclamation of praise.)

Jesus now lives with you in glory,
but he is also here on earth, among us.
We thank you and say:

All say:
Glory to God in the highest.
(Or some other suitable acclamation of praise.)

One day he will come in glory
and in his kingdom
there will be no more suffering,
no more tears, no more sadness.
We thank you and say:

All say:
Glory to God in the highest.
(Or some other suitable acclamation of praise.)

Father in heaven,
you have called us
to receive the body and blood of Christ at this
     table
and to be filled with the joy of the Holy Spirit.

C 3 Through this sacred meal
give us strength to please you more and more.

Lord, our God,
remember *N.,* our pope,
N., our bishop, and all other bishops.

Outside Easter season:

Help all who follow Jesus
to work for peace
and to bring happiness to others.

During Easter season:

Fill all Christians with the gladness of Easter.
Help us to bring this joy
to all who are sorrowful.

Bring us all at last
together with Mary, the Mother of God,
and all the saints,
to live with you
and to be one with Christ in heaven.

Through him,
with him,
in him,
in the unity of the Holy Spirit,
all glory and honor is yours,
almighty Father,
for ever and ever.

The people respond: **Amen.**

Continue with the Mass, as on p. 66

℣. The Lord be with you. `STAND`
℟. **And also with you.**
℣. Lift up your hearts.
℟. **We lift them up to the Lord.**
℣. Let us give thanks to the Lord our God.
℟. **It is right to give him thanks and praise.**

Father, all-powerful and ever-living God,
we do well always and everywhere to give you
   thanks and praise.
You never cease to call us
to a new and more abundant life.

God of love and mercy,
you are always ready to forgive;
we are sinners,
and you invite us
to trust in your mercy.

Time and time again
we broke your covenant,
but you did not abandon us.
Instead, through your Son, Jesus our Lord,
you bound yourself even more closely to the
   human family
by a bond that can never be broken.

Now is the time
for your people to turn back to you
and to be renewed in Christ your Son,
a time of grace and reconciliation.

57

R You invite us
to serve the family of mankind
1 by opening our hearts
to the fullness of your Holy Spirit.

In wonder and gratitude,
we join our voices with the choirs of heaven
to proclaim the power of your love
and to sing of our salvation in Christ:

All say:

**Holy, holy, holy Lord, God of power and might,
heaven and earth are full of your glory.**
> **Hosanna in the highest.**

Blessed is he who comes in the name of the Lord.
> **Hosanna in the highest.**

Father,
from the beginning of time
you have always done what is good for man
so that we may be holy as you are holy.

Look with kindness on your people
gathered here before you:
send forth the power of your Spirit
so that these gifts may become for us
the body ✠ and blood of your beloved Son,
   Jesus the Christ,
in whom we have become your sons and daughters.

R 1

When we were lost
and could not find the way to you,
you loved us more than ever:
Jesus, your Son, innocent and without sin,
gave himself into our hands
and was nailed to a cross.
Yet before he stretched out his arms between heaven and earth
in the everlasting sign of your covenant,
he desired to celebrate the Paschal feast
in the company of his disciples.

While they were at supper,
he took bread and gave you thanks and praise.
He broke the bread, gave it to his disciples, and said:

Take this, all of you, and eat it:
this is my body which will be given up for you.

At the end of the meal,
knowing that he was to reconcile all things in himself
by the blood of his cross,
he took the cup, filled with wine.
Again he gave you thanks,
handed the cup to his friends, and said:

Take this, all of you, and drink from it:
this is the cup of my blood,
the blood of the new and everlasting covenant.
It will be shed for you and for all
so that sins may be forgiven.
Do this in memory of me.

R 1 Priest: Let us proclaim the mystery of faith:

PEOPLE:

A Christ has died,
Christ is risen,
Christ will come again.

B Dying you destroyed our death,
rising you restored our life.
Lord Jesus, come in glory.

C When we eat this bread and drink this cup,
we proclaim your death, Lord Jesus,
until you come in glory.

D Lord, by your cross and resurrection
you have set us free.
You are the Savior of the world.

We do this in memory of Jesus Christ,
our Passover and our lasting peace.
We celebrate his death and resurrection
and look for the coming of that day
when he will return to give us the fullness of joy.
Therefore we offer you, God ever faithful and
true,
the sacrifice which restores man to your friendship.

Father,
look with love
on those you have called
to share in the one sacrifice of Christ.
By the power of your Holy Spirit
make them one body,
healed of all division.

R 1

Keep us all
in communion of mind and heart
with *N.*, our pope, and *N.*, our bishop.
Help us to work together
for the coming of your kingdom,
until at last we stand in your presence
to share the life of the saints,
in the company of the Virgin Mary and the
    apostles,
and of our departed brothers and sisters
whom we commend to your mercy.

Then, freed from every shadow of death,
we shall take our place in the new creation
and give you thanks
with Christ, our risen Lord.

Through him,
with him,
in him,
in the unity of the Holy Spirit,
all glory and honor is yours,
almighty Father,
for ever and ever.

The people respond: **Amen.**

Continue with the Mass, as on p. 66.

℞ 2   EUCHARISTIC PRAYER FOR MASSES OF RECONCILIATION II

℣. The Lord be with you.   `STAND`
℟. **And also with you.**
℣. Lift up your hearts.
℟. **We lift them up to the Lord.**
℣. Let us give thanks to the Lord our God.
℟. **It is right to give him thanks and praise.**

Father, all-powerful and ever-living God,
we praise and thank you through Jesus Christ
    our Lord
for your presence and action in the world.

In the midst of conflict and division,
we know it is you
who turn our minds to thoughts of peace.
Your Spirit changes our hearts:
enemies begin to speak to one another,
those who were estranged join hands in friend-
    ship,
and nations seek the way of peace together.

Your Spirit is at work
when understanding puts an end to strife,
when hatred is quenched by mercy,
and vengeance gives way to forgiveness.

For this we should never cease
to thank and praise you.
We join with all the choirs of heaven
as they sing for ever to your glory:

R 2

All say:

Holy, holy, holy Lord, God of power and might.
Heaven and earth are full of your glory.
Hosanna in the highest.
Blessed is he who comes in the name of the Lord.
Hosanna in the highest.

God of power and might,   `KNEEL`
we praise you through your Son, Jesus Christ,
who comes in your name.
He is the Word that brings salvation.
He is the hand you stretch out to sinners.
He is the way that leads to your peace.

God our Father,
we had wandered far from you,
but through your Son you have brought us back.
You gave him up to death
so that we might turn again to you
and find our way to one another.

Therefore we celebrate the reconciliation
Christ has gained for us.

We ask you to sanctify these gifts
by the power of your Spirit,
as we now fulfill your Son's ✛ command.

While he was at supper
on the night before he died for us,
he took bread in his hands,
and gave you thanks and praise.
He broke the bread,
gave it to his disciples, and said:

Take this, all of you, and eat it:
this is my body which will be given up for you.

R 2 At the end of the meal he took the cup.
Again he praised you for your goodness,
gave the cup to his disciples, and said:

Take this, all of you, and drink from it:
this is the cup of my blood,
the blood of the new and everlasting covenant.
It will be shed for you and for all men
so that sins may be forgiven.
Do this in memory of me.

Priest: Let us proclaim the mystery of faith:

PEOPLE:

A Christ has died,
Christ is risen,
Christ will come again.

B Dying you destroyed our death,
rising you restored our life.
Lord Jesus, come in glory.

C When we eat this bread and drink this cup,
we proclaim your death, Lord Jesus,
until you come in glory.

D Lord, by your cross and resurrection
you have set us free.
You are the Savior of the world.

Lord our God,
your Son has entrusted to us
this pledge of his love.
We celebrate the memory of his death and resurrection
and bring you the gift you have given us,
the sacrifice of reconciliation.

R 2

Therefore, we ask you, Father,
to accept us, together with your Son.

Fill us with his Spirit
through our sharing in this meal.
May he take away all that divides us.

May this Spirit keep us always in communion
with *N.*, our pope, *N.*, our bishop,
with all the bishops and all your people.
Father, make your Church throughout the world
a sign of unity and an instrument of your peace.

You have gathered us here
around the table of your Son,
in fellowship with the Virgin Mary, Mother of
     God, and all the saints.

In that new world where the fullness of your
     peace will be revealed,
gather people of every race, language, and way
     of life
to share in the one eternal banquet
with Jesus Christ the Lord.

Through him,
with him,
in him,
in the unity of the Holy Spirit,
all glory and honor is yours,
almighty Father,
for ever and ever.

The people respond: **Amen.**

COMMUNION RITE

To prepare for the paschal meal, to welcome the Lord, we pray for forgiveness and exchange a sign of peace. Before eating Christ's body and drinking his blood, we must be one with him and with all our brothers and sisters in the Church.

24 LORD'S PRAYER **STAND**

Priest:

A Let us pray with confidence to the Father
in the words our Savior gave us:

B Jesus taught us to call God our Father,
and so we have the courage to say:

C Let us ask our Father to forgive our sins
and to bring us to forgive those who sin against
us.

D Let us pray for the coming of the kingdom
as Jesus taught us.

Priest and **PEOPLE**:

> **Our Father, who art in heaven,**
> **hallowed be thy name;**
> **thy kingdom come;**
> **thy will be done on earth as it is in heaven.**
> **Give us this day our daily bread;**
> **and forgive us our trespasses**
> **as we forgive those who trespass against us;**
> **and lead us not into temptation,**
> **but deliver us from evil.**

Priest: Deliver us, Lord, from every evil,
and grant us peace in our day.

In your mercy keep us free from sin
and protect us from all anxiety
as we wait in joyful hope
for the coming of our Savior, Jesus Christ.

PEOPLE: **For the kingdom, the power, and the glory are yours, now and for ever.**

25 SIGN OF PEACE

The Church is a community of Christians joined by the Spirit in love. It needs to express, deepen, and restore its peaceful unity before eating the one Body of the Lord and drinking from the one cup of salvation. We do this by a sign of peace.

The priest says the prayer for peace:
Lord Jesus Christ, you said to your apostles:
I leave you peace, my peace I give you.
Look not on our sins, but on the faith of your Church,
and grant us the peace and unity of your kingdom
where you live for ever and ever.

PEOPLE: **Amen.**

Priest: The peace of the Lord be with you always.

PEOPLE: **And also with you.**

Deacon (or priest):
Let us offer each other the sign of peace.

The people exchange a sign of peace and love, according to local custom.

26 BREAKING OF THE BREAD

Christians are gathered for the "breaking of the bread," another name for the Mass. In communion, though many we are made one body in the one bread, which is Christ.

Then the following is sung or said:
PEOPLE:

**Lamb of God, you take away the sins of the
     world:**
  have mercy on us.
**Lamb of God, you take away the sins of the
     world:**
  have mercy on us.
**Lamb of God, you take away the sins of the
     world:**
  grant us peace.

*The hymn may be repeated until the breaking of the
bread is finished, but the last phrase is always: "Grant
us peace."*

*Meanwhile the priest breaks the host over the paten and
places a small piece in the chalice, saying inaudibly:*

May this mingling of the body and blood of our
   Lord Jesus Christ
bring eternal life to us who receive it.

KNEEL

27 PRAYERS BEFORE COMMUNION

We pray in silence and then voice words of humility and hope
as our final preparation before meeting Christ in the
eucharist.

*Before communion, the priest says inaudibly one of the
following prayers:*

Lord Jesus Christ, Son of the living God, by the will
of the Father and the work of the Holy Spirit your
death brought life to the world. By your holy body
and blood free me from all my sins and from every
evil. Keep me faithful to your teaching, and never let
me be parted from you.

OR

Lord Jesus Christ, with faith in your love and mercy
I eat your body and drink your blood. Let it not bring
me condemnation, but health in mind and body.

28 RECEPTION OF COMMUNION

*The priest genuflects. Holding the host elevated slightly
over the paten, the priest says:*

Priest: This is the Lamb of God
   who takes away the sins of the world.
   Happy are those who are called to his supper.

Priest and **People** (once only):

**Lord, I am not worthy to receive you,
but only say the word and I shall be healed.**

Before receiving communion, the priest says inaudibly:

May the body of Christ bring me to everlasting life.
May the blood of Christ bring me to everlasting life.

He then gives communion to the people.

Priest: The body of Christ. Communicant: **Amen.**

Priest: The blood of Christ. Communicant: **Amen.**

29 COMMUNION SONG or ANTIPHON

*The Communion Psalm or other appropriate Song or
Hymn is sung while Communion is given to the faithful.
If there is no singing, the Communion Antiphon is said:*

→ Turn to Today's Mass

*The vessels are cleansed by the priest or deacon or
acolyte. Meanwhile he says inaudibly:*

Lord, may I receive these gifts in purity of heart.
May they bring me healing and strength, now and for
   ever.

30 PERIOD OF SILENCE or Song of Praise

After communion there may be a period of silence, or a song of praise may be sung.

31 PRAYER AFTER COMMUNION `STAND`

The priest prays in our name that we may live the life of faith since we have been strengthened by Christ himself. Our *Amen* makes his prayer our own.

Priest: Let us pray.

Priest and people may pray silently for a while. Then the priest says the prayer after communion.

→ `Turn to Today's Mass`

At the end, **PEOPLE:** **Amen.**

CONCLUDING RITE

We have heard God's Word and eaten the body of Christ. Now it is time for us to leave, to do good works, to praise and bless the Lord in our daily lives.

32 GREETING `STAND`

After any brief announcements (sit), the blessing and dismissal follow:

Priest: The Lord be with you.

PEOPLE: **And also with you.**

33 BLESSING

`A` Simple form

Priest: May almighty God bless you
the Father, and the Son, ✠ and the Holy Spirit.

PEOPLE: **Amen.**

On certain days or occasions another more solemn form of blessing or prayer over the people may be used as the rubrics direct.

B Solemn blessing

Texts of all the solemn blessings are given on pp. 92-99.

Deacon: Bow your heads and pray for God's blessing.

The priest always concludes the solemn blessing by adding:

May almighty God bless you
the Father, and the Son, ✠ and the Holy Spirit.

PEOPLE: Amen.

C Prayer over the people

Texts of all prayers over the people are given on pp. 99-103.

After the prayer over the people, the priest always adds:

May almighty God bless you,
the Father, and the Son, ✠ and the Holy Spirit.

PEOPLE: Amen.

34 DISMISSAL

Deacon (or priest):

A Go in the peace of Christ.

B The Mass is ended, go in peace.

C Go in peace to love and serve the Lord.

PEOPLE: Thanks be to God.

If any liturgical service follows immediately, the rite of dismissal is omitted.

RITE OF BLESSING AND
SPRINKLING HOLY WATER

When this rite is celebrated it takes the place of the penitential rite at the beginning of Mass. The Kyrie is also omitted.

After greeting the people the priest remains standing at his chair. A vessel containing the water to be blessed is placed before him. Facing the people, he invites them to pray, using these or similar words:

Dear friends,
this water will be used
to remind us of our baptism.
Let us ask God to bless it,
and to keep us faithful
to the Spirit he has given us.

After a brief silence, he joins his hands and continues:

A.

God our Father,
your gift of water
brings life and freshness to the earth;
it washes away our sins
and brings us eternal life.

We ask you now
to bless ✠ this water,
and to give us your protection on this day
which you have made your own.
Renew the living spring of your life within us
and protect us in spirit and body,
that we may be free from sin
and come into your presence
to receive your gift of salvation.
We ask this through Christ our Lord. R̷. **Amen.**

B.   Or:

Lord God almighty,
creator of all life,
of body and soul,
we ask you to bless ✣ this water:
as we use it in faith
forgive our sins
and save us from all illness
and the power of evil.

Lord,
in your mercy
give us living water,
always springing up as a fountain of salvation:
free us, body and soul, from every danger,
and admit us to your presence
in purity of heart.
Grant this through Christ our Lord.

C.   Or (during the Easter season):

Lord God almighty,
hear the prayers of your people:
we celebrate our creation and redemption.
Hear our prayers and bless ✣ this water
which gives fruitfulness to the fields,
and refreshment and cleansing to man.
You chose water to show your goodness
when you led your people to freedom
through the Red Sea
and satisfied their thirst in the desert
with water from the rock.
Water was the symbol used by the prophets
to foretell your new covenant with man.
You made the water of baptism holy
by Christ's baptism in the Jordan:
by it you give us a new birth
and renew us in holiness.
May this water remind us of our baptism,
and let us share the joy

of all who have been baptized at Easter.
We ask this through Christ our Lord.

*Where it is customary, salt may be mixed with the holy
water. The priest blesses the salt, saying:*

Almighty God,
we ask you to bless ✠ this salt
as once you blessed the salt scattered over the water
by the prophet Elisha.
Wherever this salt and water are sprinkled,
drive away the power of evil,
and protect us always
by the presence of your Holy Spirit.
Grant this through Christ our Lord.

Then he pours the salt into the water in silence.

*Taking the sprinkler, the priest sprinkles himself and
his ministers, then the rest of the clergy and people. He
may move through the church for the sprinkling of the
people. Meanwhile, an antiphon or another appropriate
song is sung.*

*When he returns to his place and the song is finished, the
priest faces the people and, with joined hands, says:*

May almighty God cleanse us of our sins,
and through the eucharist we celebrate
make us worthy to sit at his table
in his heavenly kingdom.

The people answer: **Amen.**

When it is prescribed, the Gloria *is then sung or said.*

PENITENTIAL RITE

ALTERNATIVE FORMS FOR C (p. 13)

ii

Priest or other minister:
Lord Jesus, you came to gather the nations
into the peace of God's kingdom:
Lord, have mercy.

People: Lord, have mercy.

Priest or other minister:
You come in word and sacrament to strengthen us in
   holiness:
Christ, have mercy.

People: Christ, have mercy.

Priest or other minister:
You will come in glory with salvation for your people:
   Lord, have mercy.

People: Lord, have mercy.   (→ p. 13)

iii

Priest or other minister:
Lord Jesus, you are mighty God and Prince of peace:
Lord, have mercy.

People: Lord have mercy.

Priest or other minister:
Lord Jesus, you are the Son of God and Son of Mary:
Christ, have mercy.

People: Christ, have mercy.

Priest or other minister:
Lord Jesus, you are Word made flesh and splendor of
   the Father:
Lord, have mercy.

People: Lord, have mercy.   (→ p. 13)

75

iv

Priest or other minister:
Lord Jesus, you came to reconcile us
to one another and to the Father:
Lord, have mercy.

People: **Lord have mercy.**

Priest or other minister:
Lord Jesus, you heal the wounds of sin and division:
Christ, have mercy.

People: **Christ, have mercy.**

Priest or other minister:
Lord Jesus, intercede for us with your Father:
Lord, have mercy.

People: **Lord, have mercy.**　　　　(→ p. 13)

v

Priest or other minister:
You raise the dead to life in the Spirit:
Lord, have mercy.

People: **Lord have mercy.**

Priest or other minister:
You bring pardon and peace to the sinner:
Christ, have mercy.

People: **Christ, have mercy.**

Priest or other minister:
You bring light to those in darkness:
Lord, have mercy.

People: **Lord, have mercy.**　　　　(→ p. 13)

vi

Priest or other minister:
Lord Jesus, you raise us to new life:
Lord, have mercy.

People: **Lord have mercy.**

Priest or other minister:
Lord Jesus, you forgive us our sins:
Christ, have mercy.

People: **Christ, have mercy.**

Priest or other minister:
Lord Jesus, you feed us with your body and blood:
Lord, have mercy.

People: **Lord, have mercy.**   (→ p. 13)

vii

Priest or other minister:
Lord Jesus, you have shown us the way to the Father:
Lord, have mercy.

People: **Lord, have mercy.**

Priest or other minister:
Lord Jesus, you have given us the consolation of the
  truth:
Christ, have mercy.

People: **Christ, have mercy.**

Priest or other minister:
Lord Jesus, you are the Good Shepherd,
leading us into everlasting life:
Lord, have mercy.

People: **Lord, have mercy.**   (→ p. 13)

viii

Priest or other minister:
Lord Jesus, you healed the sick:
Lord, have mercy.

People: **Lord, have mercy.**

Priest or other minister:
Lord Jesus, you forgave sinners:
Christ, have mercy.

People: **Christ, have mercy.**

Priest or other minister:
Lord Jesus, you give us yourself to heal us and bring us
  strength:
Lord, have mercy.

People: **Lord, have mercy.**   (→ p. 13)

PREFACES

ADVENT I (P 1)

The Two Comings of Christ
(From the First Sunday of Advent to December 16)

Father, all-powerful and ever-living God,
we do well always and everywhere to give you thanks
through Jesus Christ our Lord.

When he humbled himself to come among us as a man,
he fulfilled the plan you formed long ago
and opened for us the way to salvation.

Now we watch for the day,
hoping that the salvation promised us will be ours
when Christ our Lord will come again in his glory.

And so, with all the choirs of angels in heaven
we proclaim your glory
and join in their unending hymn of praise: → No. 23, p. 23

ADVENT II (P 2)

Waiting for the Two Comings of Christ
(From December 17 to December 24)

Father, all-powerful and ever-living God,
we do well always and everywhere to give you thanks
through Jesus Christ our Lord.

His future coming was proclaimed by all the prophets.
The virgin mother bore him in her womb
with love beyond all telling.
John the Baptist was his herald
and made him known when at last he came.

In his love Christ has filled us with joy
as we prepare to celebrate his birth,
so that when he comes he may find us watching in prayer,
our hearts filled with wonder and praise.

78

And so, with all the choirs of angels in heaven
we proclaim your glory
and join in their unending hymn of praise: → No. 23, p. 23

CHRISTMAS I (P 3)

Christ the Light

(From Christmas to Saturday before Epiphany)

Father, all-powerful and ever-living God,
we do well always and everywhere to give you thanks
through Jesus Christ our Lord.

In the wonder of the incarnation
your eternal Word has brought to the eyes of faith
a new and radiant vision of your glory.
In him we see our God made visible
and so are caught up in love of the God we cannot see.

And so, with all the choirs of angels in heaven
we proclaim your glory
and join in their unending hymn of praise: → No. 23, p. 23

CHRISTMAS II (P 4)

Christ Restores Unity to All Creation

(From Christmas to Saturday before Epiphany)

Father, all-powerful and ever-living God,
we do well always and everywhere to give you thanks
through Jesus Christ our Lord.

Today you fill our hearts with joy
as we recognize in Christ the revelation of your love.
No eye can see his glory as our God,
yet now he is seen as one like us.

Christ is your Son before all ages,
yet now he is born in time.
He has come to lift up all things to himself,
to restore unity to creation,
and to lead mankind from exile into your heavenly kingdom.
With all the angels of heaven
we sing our joyful hymn of praise: → No. 23, p. 23

CHRISTMAS III (P 5)

Divine and Human Exchange in the
Incarnation of the Word
(From Christmas to Saturday before Epiphany)

Father, all-powerful and ever-living God,
we do well always and everywhere to give you thanks
through Jesus Christ our Lord.

Today in him a new light has dawned upon the world:
God has become one with man,
and man has become one again with God.

Your eternal Word has taken upon himself our human
　　weakness,
giving our mortal nature immortal value.
So marvelous is this oneness between God and man
that in Christ man restores to man the gift of everlasting life.

In our joy we sing to your glory
with all the choirs of angels:　　　　　　→ No. 23, p. 23

LENT I (P 8)

The Spiritual Meaning of Lent

Father, all-powerful and ever-living God,
we do well always and everywhere to give you thanks
through Jesus Christ our Lord.

Each year you give us this joyful season
when we prepare to celebrate the paschal mystery
with mind and heart renewed.
You give us a spirit of loving reverence for you, our Father,
and of willing service to our neighbor.

As we recall the great events that gave us new life in Christ,
you bring the image of your Son to perfection within us.

Now, with angels and archangels,
and the whole company of heaven,
we sing the unending hymn of your praise:　　→ No. 23, p. 23

LENT II (P 9)

The Spirit of Penance

Father, all-powerful and ever-living God,
we do well always and everywhere to give you thanks.

This great season of grace is your gift to your family
to renew us in spirit.
You give us strength to purify our hearts,
to control our desires,
and so to serve you in freedom.
You teach us how to live in this passing world
with our heart set on the world that will never end.

Now, with all the saints and angels,
we praise you for ever: → No. 23, p. 23

EASTER I (P 21)

The Paschal Mystery

(Easter Vigil, Easter Sunday and during the octave and season)

Father, all-powerful and ever-living God,
we do well always and everywhere to give you thanks
through Jesus Christ our Lord.

We praise you with greater joy than ever
on this Easter night (day) (in this Easter Season),
when Christ became our paschal sacrifice.

He is the true Lamb who took away the sins of the world.
By dying he destroyed our death;
by rising he restored our life.

And so, with all the choirs of angels in heaven
we proclaim your glory
and join in their unending hymn of praise: → No. 23, p. 23

EASTER II (P 22)

New Life in Christ

Father, all-powerful and ever-living God,
we do well always and everywhere to give you thanks
through Jesus Christ our Lord.

We praise you with greater joy than ever in this Easter season,
when Christ became our paschal sacrifice.

He has made us children of the light,
rising to new and everlasting life.
He has opened the gates of heaven
to receive his faithful people.

His death is our ransom from death;
his resurrection is our rising to life.

The joy of the resurrection renews the whole world,
while the choirs of heaven sing for ever to your glory:

→ No. 23, p. 23

EASTER III (P 23)

Christe Lives and Intercedes for Us for Ever

Father, all-powerful and ever-living God,
we do well always and everywhere to give you thanks
through Jesus Christ our Lord.

We praise you with greater joy than ever in this Easter season,
when Christ became our paschal sacrifice.

He is still our priest,
our advocate who always pleads our cause.
Christ is the victim who dies no more,
the Lamb, once slain, who lives for ever.

They joy of the resurrection renews the whole world,
while the choirs of heaven sing for ever to your glory:

→ No. 23, p. 23

EASTER IV (P 24)

*The Restoration of the Universe through the
Paschal Mystery*

Father, all-powerful and ever-living God,
we do well always and everywhere to give you thanks
through Jesus Christ our Lord.

We praise you with greater joy than ever in this Easter season,
when Christ became our paschal sacrifice.

In him a new age has dawned,
the long reign of sin is ended,
a broken world has been renewed,
and man is once again made whole.

The joy of the resurrection renews the whole world,
while the choirs of heaven sing for ever to your glory:

→ No. 23, p. 23

EASTER V (P 25)

Christ Is Priest and Victim

Father, all-powerful and ever-living God,
we do well always and everywhere to give you thanks
through Jesus Christ our Lord.

We praise you with greater joy than ever in this Easter season,
when Christ became our paschal sacrifice.

As he offered his body on the cross,
his perfect sacrifice fulfilled all others.
As he gave himself into your hands for our salvation,
he showed himself to be the priest, the altar, and the lamb of sacrifice.
The joy of the resurrection renews the whole world,
while the choirs of heaven sing for ever to your glory:

→ No. 23, p. 23

ASCENSION I (P 26)

The Mystery of the Ascension

(Ascension to the Saturday before Pentecost inclusive)

Father, all-powerful and ever-living God,
we do well always and everywhere to give you thanks.

[Today] the Lord Jesus, the king of glory,
the conqueror of sin and death,
ascended to heaven while the angels sang his praises.

Christ, the mediator between God and man,
judge of the world and Lord of all,
has passed beyond our sight,
not to abandon us but to be our hope.
Christ is the beginning, the head of the Church;
where he has gone, we hope to follow.

The joy of the resurrection and ascension renews the whole world,
while the choirs of heaven sing for ever to your glory:

→ No. 23, p. 23

ASCENSION II (P 27)
The Mystery of the Ascension
(Ascension to the Saturday before Pentecost inclusive)

Father, all-powerful and ever-living God,
we do well always and everywhere to give you thanks
through Jesus Christ our Lord.

In his risen body he plainly showed himself to his disciples
and was taken up to heaven in their sight
to claim for us a share in his divine life.

And so, with all the choirs of angels in heaven
we proclaim your glory
and join in their unending hymn of praise: ➞ No. 23, p. 23

SUNDAYS IN ORDINARY TIME I (P 29)
The Paschal Mystery and the People of God

Father, all-powerful and ever-living God,
we do well always and everywhere to give you thanks
through Jesus Christ our Lord.

Through his cross and resurrection
he freed us from sin and death
and called us to the glory that has made us
a chosen race, a royal priesthood,
a holy nation, a people set apart.

Everywhere we proclaim your mighty works
for you have called us out of darkness
into your own wonderful light.

And so, with all the choirs of angels in heaven
we proclaim your glory
and join in their unending hymn of praise: ➞ No. 23, p. 23

SUNDAYS IN ORDINARY TIME II (P 30)
The Mystery of Salvation

Father, all-powerful and ever-living God,
we do well always and everywhere to give you thanks
through Jesus Christ our Lord.

Out of love for sinful man,
he humbled himself to be born of the Virgin.

By suffering on the cross
he freed us from unending death,
and by rising from the dead
he gave us eternal life.

And so, with all the choirs of angels in heaven
we proclaim your glory
and join in their unending hymn of praise: → No. 23, p. 23

SUNDAYS IN ORDINARY TIME III (P 31)
The Salvation of Man by a Man

Father, all-powerful and ever-living God,
we do well always and everywhere to give you thanks.

We see your infinite power
in your loving plan of salvation.
You came to our rescue by your power as God,
but you wanted us to be saved by one like us.
Man refused your friendship,
but man himself was to restore it
through Jesus Christ our Lord.

Through him the angels of heaven offer their prayer of
adoration
as they rejoice in your presence for ever.
May our voices be one with theirs
in their triumphant hymn of praise: → No. 23, p. 23

SUNDAYS IN ORDINARY TIME IV (P 32)
The History of Salvation

Father, all-powerful and ever-living God,
we do well always and everywhere to give you thanks
through Jesus Christ our Lord.

By his birth we are reborn.
In his suffering we are freed from sin.
By his rising from the dead we rise to everlasting life.
In his return to you in glory
we enter into your heavenly kingdom.

And so, we join the angels and the saints
as they sing their unending hymn of praise: → No. 23, p. 23

SUNDAYS IN ORDINARY TIME V (P 33)
Creation

Father, all-powerful and ever-living God,
we do well always and everywhere to give you thanks.

All things are of your making,
all times and seasons obey your laws,
but you chose to create man in your own image,
setting him over the whole world in all its wonder.
You made man the steward of creation,
to praise you day by day for the marvels of your wisdom
    and power,
through Jesus Christ our Lord.

We praise you, Lord, with all the angels in their song of
joy: → No. 23, p. 23

SUNDAYS IN ORDINARY TIME VI (P 34)
The Pledge of an Eternal Easter

Father, all-powerful and ever-living God,
we do well always and everywhere to give you thanks.

In you we live and move and have our being.
Each day you show us a Father's love;
your Holy Spirit, dwelling within us,
gives us on earth the hope of unending joy.

Your gift of the Spirit,
who raised Jesus from the dead,
is the foretaste and promise
of the paschal feast of heaven.

With thankful praise,
in company with the angels,
we glorify the wonders of your power: → No. 23, p. 23

SUNDAYS IN ORDINARY TIME VII (P 35)
Salvation through the Obedience of Christ

Father, all-powerful and ever-living God,
we do well always and everywhere to give you thanks.

So great was your love
that you gave us your Son as our redeemer.
You sent him as one like ourselves,

though free from sin,
that you might see and love in us
what you see and love in Christ.
Your gifts of grace, lost by disobedience,
are now restored by the obedience of your Son.

We praise you, Lord, with all the angels and saints
in their song of joy: → No. 23, p. 23

SUNDAYS IN ORDINARY TIME VIII (P 36)
The Church United in the Mystery of the Trinity

Father, all-powerful and ever-living God,
we do well always and everywhere to give you thanks.

When your children sinned
and wandered far from your friendship,
you reunited them with yourself
through the blood of your Son
and the power of the Holy Spirit.

You gather them into your Church,
to be one as you, Father, are one
with your Son and the Holy Spirit.
You call them to be your people,
to praise your wisdom in all your works.
You make them the body of Christ
and the dwelling-place of the Holy Spirit.

In our joy we sing to your glory
with all the choirs of angels: → No. 23, p. 23

HOLY EUCHARIST I (P 47)
The Sacrifice and Sacrament of Christ

Father, all-powerful and ever-living God,
we do well always and everywhere to give you thanks
through Jesus Christ our Lord.

He is the true and eternal priest
who established this unending sacrifice.
He offered himself as a victim for our deliverance
and taught us to make this offering in his memory.
As we eat his body which he gave for us,
we grow in strength.
As we drink his blood which he poured out for us,
we are washed clean.

Now, with angels and archangels,
and the whole company of heaven,
we sing the unending hymn of your praise:　　→ No. 23, p. 23

HOLY EUCHARIST II (P 48)
The Effects of the Holy Eucharist

Father, all-powerful and ever-living God,
we do well always and everywhere to give you thanks
through Jesus Christ our Lord.

At the last supper,
as he sat at table with his apostles,
he offered himself to you as the spotless lamb,
the acceptable gift that gives you perfect praise.
Christ has given us this memorial of his passion
to bring us its saving power until the end of time.

In this great sacrament you feed your people
and strengthen them in holiness,
so that the family of mankind
may come to walk in the light of one faith,
in one communion of love.
We come then to this wonderful sacrament
to be fed at your table
and grow into the likeness of the risen Christ.

Earth unites with heaven
to sing the new song of creation
as we adore and praise you for ever:　　→ No. 23, p. 23

CHRISTIAN DEATH I (P 77)
The Hope of Rising in Christ

Father, all-powerful and ever-living God,
we do well always and everywhere to give you thanks
through Jesus Christ our Lord.

In him, who rose from the dead,
our hope of resurrection dawned.
The sadness of death gives way
to the bright promise of immortality.

Lord, for your faithful people life is changed, not ended.
When the body of our earthly dwelling lies in death
we gain an everlasting dwelling place in heaven.

And so, with all the choirs of angels in heaven
we proclaim your glory
and join in their unending hymn of praise: → No. 23, p. 23

CHRISTIAN DEATH II (P 78)
Christ's Death, Our Life

Father, all-powerful and ever-living God,
we do well always and everywhere to give you thanks
through Jesus Christ our Lord.

He chose to die
that he might free all men from dying.
He gave his life
that we might live to you alone for ever.

In our joy we sing to your glory
with all the choirs of angels: → No. 23, p. 23

CHRISTIAN DEATH III (P 79)
Christ, Salvation and Life

Father, all-powerful and ever-living God,
we do well always and everywhere to give you thanks
through Jesus Christ our Lord.

In him the world is saved,
man is reborn,
and the dead rise again to life.

Through Christ the angels of heaven
offer their prayer of adoration
as they rejoice in your presence for ever.
May our voices be one with theirs
in their triumphant hymn of praise: → No. 23, p. 23

CHRISTIAN DEATH IV (P 80)
From Earthly Life to Heaven's Glory

Father, all-powerful and ever-living God,
we do well always and everywhere to give you thanks.

By your power you bring us to birth.
By your providence you rule our lives.
By your command you free us at last from sin
as we return to the dust from which we came.
Through the saving death of your Son
we rise at your word to the glory of the resurrection.

Now we join the angels and the saints
as they sing their unending hymn of praise: → No. 23, p. 23

CHRISTIAN DEATH V (P 81)
Our Resurrection through Christ's Glory

Father, all-powerful and ever-living God,
we do well always and everywhere to give you thanks
through Jesus Christ our Lord.
Death is the just reward for our sins,
yet, when at last we die,
your loving kindness calls us back to life
in company with Christ,
whose victory is our redemption.

Our hearts are joyful,
for we have seen your salvation,
and now with the angels and saints
we praise you for ever: → No. 23, p. 23

PROPER COMMUNICANTES
AND HANC IGITUR
FOR EUCHARISTIC PRAYER I
Communicantes for Christmas

In union with the whole Church
we celebrate that day (night)
when Mary without loss of her virginity
gave this world its savior.
We honor Mary,
the ever-virgin mother of Jesus Christ, our Lord and God,
    etc., p. 25.

Communicantes for the Epiphany

In union with the whole Church
we celebrate that day
when your only Son,
sharing your eternal glory,
showed himself in a human body.
We honor Mary, etc., p. 25.

Communicantes for Easter

In union with the whole Church
we celebrate that day (night)
when Jesus Christ, our Lord,
rose from the dead in his human body.
We honor Mary, etc., p. 25.

Hanc Igitur for Easter

Father, accept this offering
from your whole family
and from those born into the new life
of water and the Holy Spirit,
with all their sins forgiven.
Grant us your peace in this life,
save us from final damnation,
and count us among those you have chosen.
[Through Christ our Lord. Amen.]

→ Canon, p. 25: Bless, etc.

Communicantes for Ascension

In union with the whole Church
we celebrate that day
when your only Son, our Lord,
took his place with you
and raised our frail human nature to glory.
We honor Mary, etc., p. 25

Communicantes for Pentecost

In union with the whole Church
we celebrate the day of Pentecost
when the Holy Spirit appeared to the apostles
in the form of countless tongues.
We honor Mary, etc., p. 25.

SOLEMN BLESSINGS

The following blessings may be used, at the discretion of the priest, at the end of Mass, or after the liturgy of the word, the office, and the celebration of the sacraments.

The deacon gives the invitation, or in his absence the priest himself may also give it: Bow your heads and pray for God's blessing. *Another form of invitation may be used. Then the priest extends his hands over the people while he says or sings the blessings. All respond:* Amen.

I. Celebrations During the Proper of Seasons

1. ADVENT

You believe that the Son of God once came to us;
you look for him to come again.
May his coming bring you the light of his holiness
and free you with his blessing. ℞. **Amen.**

May God make you steadfast in faith,
joyful in hope, and untiring in love
all the days of your life. ℞. **Amen.**

You rejoice that our Redeemer came to live with us as man.
When he comes again in glory,
may he reward you with endless life. ℞. **Amen.**

May almighty God bless you,
the Father, and the Son, ✠ and the Holy Spirit. ℞. **Amen.**

2. CHRISTMAS

When he came to us as man,
the Son of God scattered the darkness of this world,
and filled this holy night (day) with his glory.
May the God of infinite goodness
scatter the darkness of sin
and brighten your hearts with holiness. ℞. **Amen.**

God sent his angels to shepherds
to herald the great joy of our Savior's birth.
May he fill you with joy
and make you heralds of his gospel. ℞. **Amen.**

When the Word became man,
earth was joined to heaven.

May he give you his peace and good will,
and fellowship with all the heavenly host. R̸. **Amen.**

May almighty God bless you,
the Father, and the Son, ✤ and the Holy Spirit. R̸. **Amen.**

3. BEGINNING OF THE NEW YEAR

Every good gift comes from the Father of light.
May he grant you his grace and every blessing,
and keep you safe throughout the coming year. R̸. **Amen.**

May he grant you unwavering faith,
constant hope, and love that endures to the end. R̸. **Amen.**

May he order your days and work in his peace,
hear your every prayer,
and lead you to everlasting life and joy. R̸. **Amen.**

May almighty God bless you,
the Father, and the Son, ✤ and the Holy Spirit. R̸. **Amen.**

4. EPIPHANY

God has called you out of darkness
into his wonderful light.
May you experience his kindness and blessings,
and be strong in faith, in hope, and in love. R̸. **Amen.**

Because you are followers of Christ,
who appeared on this day as a light shining in darkness,
may he make you a light to all your sisters and brothers.
R̸. **Amen.**

The wise men followed the star,
and found Christ who is light from light.
May you too find the Lord
when your pilgrimage is ended. R̸. **Amen.**

May almighty God bless you,
the Father, and the Son, ✤ and the Holy Spirit. R̸. **Amen.**

5. PASSION OF THE LORD

The Father of mercies has given us an example of unselfish
love
in the sufferings of his only Son.

Through your service of God and neighbor
may you receive his countless blessings. R̷. **Amen.**

You believe that by his dying
Christ destroyed death for ever.
May he give you everlasting life. R̷. **Amen.**

He humbled himself for our sakes.
May you follow his example
and share in his resurrection. R̷. **Amen.**

May almighty God bless you,
the Father, and the Son, ✠ and the Holy Spirit. R̷. **Amen.**

6. EASTER VIGIL AND EASTER SUNDAY

May almighty God bless you on this solemn feast of Easter, and may he protect you against all sin. R̷. **Amen.**

Through the resurrection of his Son
God has granted us healing.
May he fulfill his promises,
and bless you with eternal life. R̷. **Amen.**

You have mourned for Christ's sufferings;
now you celebrate the joy of his resurrection.
May you come with joy to the feast which lasts for ever.
   R̷. **Amen.**

May almighty God bless you,
the Father, and the Son, ✠ and the Holy Spirit. R̷. **Amen.**

7. EASTER SEASON

Through the resurrection of his Son
God has redeemed you and made you his children.
May he bless you with joy. R̷. **Amen.**

The Redeemer has given you lasting freedom.
May you inherit his everlasting life. R̷. **Amen.**

By faith you rose with him in baptism.
May your lives be holy,
so that you will be united with him for ever. R̷. **Amen.**

May almighty God bless you,
the Father, and the Son, ✠ and the Holy Spirit. R̷. **Amen.**

8. ASCENSION

May almighty God bless you on this day
when his only Son ascended into heaven
to prepare a place for you. ℟. **Amen.**

After his resurrection, Christ was seen by his disciples.
When he appears as judge
may you be pleasing for ever in his sight. ℟. **Amen.**

You believe that Jesus has taken his seat in majesty
at the right hand of the Father.
May you have the joy of experiencing
that he is also with you to the end of time,
according to his promise. ℟. **Amen.**

May almighty God bless you,
the Father, and the Son, ✚ and the Holy Spirit. ℟. **Amen.**

9. HOLY SPIRIT

(This day) the Father of light
has enlightened the minds of the disciples
by the outpouring of the Holy Spirit.
May he bless you
and give you the gifts of the Spirit for ever. ℟. **Amen.**

May that fire which hovered over the disciples
as tongues of flame
burn out all evil from your hearts
and make them glow with pure light. ℟. **Amen.**

God inspired speech in different tongues
to proclaim one faith.
May he strengthen your faith
and fulfill your hope of seeing him face to face. ℟. **Amen.**

May almighty God bless you,
the Father, and the Son, ✚ and the Holy Spirit. ℟. **Amen.**

10. ORDINARY TIME I

Blessing of Aaron (Num 6:24-26)

May the Lord bless you and keep you. ℟. **Amen.**

May his face shine upon you,
and be gracious to you. ℟. **Amen.**

May he look upon you with kindness,
and give you his peace. ℟. **Amen.**

May almighty God bless you,
the Father, and the Son, ✠ and the Holy Spirit. ℟. **Amen.**

11. ORDINARY TIME II *(Phil 4:7)*
May the peace of God
which is beyond all understanding
keep your hearts and minds
in the knowledge and love of God
and of his Son, our Lord Jesus Christ. ℟. **Amen.**
May almighty God bless you,
the Father, and the Son, ✠ and the Holy Spirit. ℟. **Amen.**

12. ORDINARY TIME III
May almighty God bless you in his mercy,
and make you always aware of his saving wisdom. ℟. **Amen.**
May he strengthen your faith with proofs of his love,
so that you will persevere in good works. ℟. **Amen.**
May he direct your steps to himself,
and show you how to walk in charity and peace. ℟. **Amen.**
May almighty God bless you,
the Father, and the Son, ✠ and the Holy Spirit. ℟. **Amen.**

13. ORDINARY TIME IV
May the God of all consolation
bless you in every way
and grant you peace all the days of your life. ℟. **Amen.**
May he free you from all anxiety
and strengthen your hearts in his love. ℟. **Amen.**
May he enrich you with his gifts of faith, hope, and love,
so that what you do in this life
will bring you to the happiness of everlasting life. ℟. **Amen.**
May almighty God bless you,
the Father, and the Son, ✠ and the Holy Spirit. ℟. **Amen.**

14. ORDINARY TIME V
May almighty God keep you from all harm
and bless you with every good gift. ℟. **Amen.**

May he set his Word in your heart
and fill you with lasting joy. ℟. **Amen.**

May you walk in his ways,
always knowing what is right and good,
until you enter your heavenly inheritance. ℟. **Amen.**

May almighty God bless you,
the Father, and the Son, ✠ and the Holy Spirit. ℟. **Amen.**

II. Celebrations of Saints

15. BLESSED VIRGIN MARY

Born of the Blessed Virgin Mary,
the Son of God redeemed mankind.
May he enrich you with his blessings. ℟. **Amen.**

You received the author of life through Mary.
May you always rejoice in her loving care. ℟. **Amen.**

You have come to rejoice at Mary's feast.
May you be filled with the joys of the Spirit
and the gifts of your eternal home. ℟. **Amen.**

May almighty God bless you,
the Father, and the Son, ✠ and the Holy Spirit. ℟. **Amen.**

16. PETER AND PAUL

The Lord has set you firm within his Church,
which he built upon the rock of Peter's faith.
May he bless you with a faith that never falters. ℟. **Amen.**

The Lord has given you knowlege of the faith
through the labors and preaching of St. Paul.
May his example inspire you to lead others to Christ
by the manner of your life. ℟. **Amen.**

May the keys of Peter, and the words of Paul,
their undying witness and their prayers,
lead you to the joy of that eternal home
which Peter gained by his cross, and Paul by the sword.
    ℟. **Amen.**

May almighty God bless you,
the Father, and the Son, ✠ and the Holy Spirit. ℟. **Amen.**

17. APOSTLES

May God who founded his Church upon the apostles
bless you through the prayers of St. *N.* (and St. *N.*). ℞.
   Amen.

May God inspire you to follow the example of the apostles,
and give witness to the truth before all men. ℞. **Amen.**

The teaching of the apostles has strengthened your faith.
May their prayers lead you
to your true and eternal home. ℞. **Amen.**

May almighty God bless you,
the Father, and the Son, ✠ and the Holy Spirit. ℞. **Amen.**

18. ALL SAINTS

God is the glory and joy of all his saints,
whose memory we celebrate today.
May his blessing be with you always. ℞. **Amen.**

May the prayers of the saints deliver you from present evil.
May their example of holy living
turn your thoughts to service of God and neighbor. ℞. **Amen.**

God's holy Church rejoices that her saints
have reached their heavenly goal,
and are in lasting peace.
May you come to share all the joys of our Father's house.
   ℞. **Amen.**

May almighty God bless you,
the Father, and the Son, ✠ and the Holy Spirit. ℞. **Amen.**

III. Other Blessings

19. DEDICATION OF A CHURCH

The Lord of earth and heaven
has assembled you before him this day
to dedicate this house of prayer
(to recall the dedication of this church).
May he fill you with the blessings of heaven. ℞. **Amen.**

God the Father wills that all his children
scattered throughout the world
become one family in his Son.

May he make you his temple,
the dwelling-place of his Holy Spirit. ℟. **Amen.**

May God free you from every bond of sin,
dwell within you and give you joy.
May you live with him for ever
in the company of all his saints. ℟. **Amen.**

May almighty God bless you,
the Father, and the Son, ✠ and the Holy Spirit. ℟. **Amen.**

20. THE DEAD

In his great love,
the God of all consolation gave man the gift of life.
May he bless you with faith
in the resurrection of his Son,
and with the hope of rising to new life. ℟. **Amen.**

To us who are alive
may he grant forgiveness,
and to all who have died
a place of light and peace. ℟. **Amen.**

As you believe that Jesus rose from the dead,
so may you live with him for ever in joy. ℟. **Amen.**

May almighty God bless you,
the Father, and the Son, ✠ and the Holy Spirit. ℟. **Amen.**

PRAYERS OVER THE PEOPLE

The following prayers may be used, at the discretion of the priest, at the end of the Mass, or after the liturgy of the word, the office, and the celebration of the sacraments.

The deacon gives the invitation, or in his absence the priest himself may also give it: Bow your heads and pray for God's blessing. *Another form of invitation may be used. Then the priest extends his hands over the people while he says or sings the prayer. All respond:* Amen.

After the prayer, the priest always adds:

May almighty God bless you,
the Father, and the Son, ✠ and the Holy Spirit. ℟. **Amen.**

1. Lord,
     have mercy on your people.
     Grant us in this life the good things
     that lead to the everlasting life you prepare for us.
     We ask this through Christ our Lord.

2. Lord,
     grant your people your protection and grace.
     Give them health of mind and body,
     perfect love for one another,
     and make them always faithful to you.
     Grant this through Christ our Lord.

3. Lord,
     may all Christian people both know and cherish
     the heavenly gifts they have received.
     We ask this in the name of Jesus the Lord.

4. Lord,
     bless your people and make them holy
     so that, avoiding evil,
     they may find in you the fulfillment of their longing.
     We ask this through Christ our Lord.

5. Lord,
     bless and strengthen your people.
     May they remain faithful to you
     and always rejoice in your mercy.
     We ask this in the name of Jesus the Lord.

6. Lord,
     you care for your people even when they stray.
     Grant us a complete change of heart,
     so that we may follow you with greater fidelity.
     Grant this through Christ our Lord.

7. Lord,
     send your light upon your family.
     May they continue to enjoy your favor
     and devote themselves to doing good.
     We ask this through Christ our Lord.

8. Lord,
     we rejoice that you are our creator and ruler.

As we call upon your generosity,
renew and keep us in your love.
Grant this through Christ our Lord.

9. Lord,
we pray for your people who believe in you.
May they enjoy the gift of your love,
share it with others,
and spread it everywhere.
We ask this in the name of Jesus the Lord.

10. Lord,
bless your people who hope for your mercy.
Grant that they may receive
the things they ask for at your prompting.
Grant this through Christ our Lord.

11. Lord,
bless us with your heavenly gifts,
and in your mercy make us ready to do your will.
We ask this through Christ our Lord.

12. Lord,
protect your people always,
that they may be free from every evil
and serve you with all their hearts.
We ask this through Christ our Lord.

13. Lord,
help your people to seek you with all their hearts
and to deserve what you promise.
Grant this through Christ our Lord.

14. Father
help your people to rejoice in the mystery of redemp-
    tion
and to win its reward.
We ask this in the name of Jesus the Lord.

15. Lord,
have pity on your people;
help them each day to avoid what displeases you
and grant that they may serve you with joy.
We ask this through Christ our Lord.

16. Lord,
    care for your people and purify them.
    Console them in this life
    and bring them to the life to come.
    We ask this in the name of Jesus the Lord.

17. Father,
    look with love upon your people,
    the love which our Lord Jesus Christ showed us
    when he delivered himself to evil men
    and suffered the agony of the cross,
    for he is Lord for ever.

18. Lord,
    grant that your faithful people
    may continually desire to relive the mystery of the
        eucharist
    and so be reborn to lead a new life.
    We ask this through Christ our Lord.

19. Lord God,
    in your great mercy,
    enrich your people with your grace
    and strengthen them by your blessing
    so that they may praise you always.
    Grant this through Christ our Lord.

20. May God bless you with every good gift from on high.
    May he keep you pure and holy in his sight at all times.
    May he bestow the riches of his grace upon you,
    bring you the good news of salvation,
    and always fill you with love for all men.
    We ask this through Christ our Lord.

21. Lord,
    make us pure in mind and body,
    that we will avoid all evil pleasures
    and always delight in you,
    We ask this in the name of Jesus the Lord.

22. Lord,
    bless your people and fill them with zeal.
    Strengthen them by your love to do your will.
    We ask this through Christ our Lord.

23. Lord,
    come, live in your people
    and strengthen them by your grace.
    Help them to remain close to you in prayer
    and give them a true love for one another.
    Grant this through Christ our Lord.

24. Father,
    look kindly on your children who put their trust in you;
    bless them and keep them from all harm,
    strengthen them against the attacks of the devil.
    May they never offend you
    but seek to love you in all they do.
    We ask this through Christ our Lord.

Feasts of Saints

25. God our Father,
    may all Christian people rejoice in the glory of your
    saints.
    Give us fellowship with them
    and unending joy in your kingdom.
    We ask this in the name of Jesus the Lord.

26. Lord,
    you have given us many friends in heaven.
    Through their prayers we are confident
    that you will watch over us always
    and fill our hearts with your love.
    Grant this through Christ our Lord.

"Holy Mother Church is conscious that she must celebrate the saving work of her divine Spouse by devoutly recalling it on certain days throughout the course of the year. Every week, on the day which she has called the Lord's day, she keeps the memory of the Lord's resurrection, which she also celebrates once in the year, together with his blessed passion, in the most solemn festival of Easter.

"Within the cycle of a year, moreover, she unfolds the whole mystery of Christ, from the incarnation and birth until the ascension, the day of Pentecost, and the expectation of blessed hope and of the coming of the Lord.

"Recalling thus the mysteries of redemption, the Church opens to the faithful the riches of her Lord's powers and merits, so that these are in some way made present for all time, and the faithful are enabled to lay hold upon them and become filled with saving grace" (*Vatican II:* Constitution on the Sacred Liturgy, no. 102).

OUR CHURCH'S YEAR OF PRAYER

Advent

We prepare for the coming of Jesus,
who is here and yet to come

Christmas season

We celebrate the gift of our Father's love:
Jesus is our brother and our Lord

Ordinary Time

With Jesus
we enter into the work of his body, the Church

Lent

In our daily life and prayer
we die with Christ to sin, and live for God

Easter triduum

We celebrate Jesus' dying and rising
and our sharing with him through baptism

Easter season

Sharing in the new life of Christ
we are filled with his Spirit

Ordinary time

Guided by the Spirit of Jesus
we build the kingdom of God by our lives.

"The name of Jesus was given the child."

JANUARY 1

SOLEMNITY OF MARY, MOTHER OF GOD

ENTRANCE ANT. See Is 9, 2. 6; Lk 1, 33   [Wonderful God]

A light will shine on us this day, the Lord is born for us: he shall be called Wonderful God, Prince of peace, Father of the world to come; and his kingship will never end.

OR Sedulius   [Hail, Holy Mother]

Hail, holy Mother! The child to whom you gave birth is the King of heaven and earth for ever.

→ No. 2, p. 10

OPENING PRAYER   [Mary's Prayers]

Let us pray
  [that Mary, the mother of the Lord,
   will help us by her prayers]
God our Father,
may we always profit by the prayers
of the Virgin Mother Mary,
for you bring us life and salvation
through Jesus Christ her Son
who lives and reigns with you and the Holy Spirit,
one God, for ever and ever. R̷. **Amen.** ↓

ALTERNATIVE OPENING PRAYER [Gift of a Mother's Love]

Let us pray
  [in the name of Jesus,
    born of a virgin and Son of God]
Father,
source of light in every age,
the virgin conceived and bore your Son
who is called Wonderful God, Prince of Peace.
May her prayer, the gift of a mother's love,
be your people's joy through all ages.
May her response, born of a humble heart,
draw your Spirit to rest on your people.
Grant this through Christ our Lord. ℟. **Amen.** ↓

READING I Nm 6, 22-27   [The Aaronic Blessing]

God speaks to Moses instructing him to have Aaron and
the Israelites pray that he may answer their prayers with
blessings.

A reading from the book of Numbers

THE Lord said to Moses: "Speak to Aaron and his
sons and tell them: This is how you shall bless the
Israelites. Say to them:
The Lord bless you and keep you!

The Lord let his face shine upon you, and be gracious
  to you!

The Lord look upon you kindly and give you peace!

So shall they invoke my name upon the Israelites and
I will bless them."
The word of the Lord. ℟. **Thanks be to God.** ↓

RESPONSORIAL PSALM Ps 67   [God Bless Us]

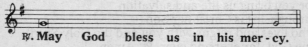

℟. **May God bless us in his mer-cy.**

May God have pity on us and bless us;
  may he let his face shine upon us.

So may your way be known upon earth;
   among all nations, your salvation.

R/. **May God bless us in his mercy.**

May the nations be glad and exult
   because you rule the peoples in equity;
   the nations on the earth you guide.

R/. **May God bless us in his mercy.**

May the peoples praise you, O God;
   may all the peoples praise you!

May God bless us,
   and may all the ends of the earth fear him!

R/. **May God bless us in his mercy.** ↓

READING II Gal 4, 4-7   [Heirs by God's Design]

**God sent Jesus, his Son, born of Mary, to deliver all from
the bondage of sin and slavery of the law. By God's choice
we are heirs of heaven.**

A reading from the letter of Paul to the Galatians

WHEN the designated time had come, God sent
forth his Son born of a woman, born under the
law, to deliver from the law those who were subjected
to it, so that we might receive our status as adopted
sons. The proof that you are sons is the fact that God
has sent forth into our hearts the spirit of his Son
which cries out "Abba!" ("Father!") You are no longer
a slave but a son! And the fact that you are a son
makes you an heir, by God's design.—The word of the
Lord. R/. **Thanks be to God.** ↓

GOSPEL Lk 2, 16-21   [The Name of Jesus]

Alleluia (Heb 1, 1-2)

R/. **Alleluia.** In the past God spoke to our fathers
   through the prophets;
now he speaks to us through his Son. R/. **Alleluia.** ↓

When the shepherds came to Bethlehem, they began to understand the message of the angels. Mary prayed about this great event. Jesus received his name according to the Jewish ritual of circumcision.

℣. The Lord be with you. ℟. **And also with you.**
✝ A reading from the holy gospel according to Luke.
℟. **Glory to you, Lord.**

THE shepherds went in haste to Bethlehem and found Mary and Joseph, and the baby lying in the manger; once they saw, they understood what had been told them concerning this child. All who heard of it were astonished at the report given them by the shepherds.

Mary treasured all these things and reflected on them in her heart. The shepherds returned, glorifying and praising God for all they had heard and seen, in accord with what had been told them.

When the eighth day arrived for his circumcision, the name Jesus was given the child, the name the angel had given him before he was conceived.—The gospel of the Lord. ℟. **Praise to you, Lord Jesus Christ.**   → No. 14, p. 18

PRAYER OVER THE GIFTS   [Salvation Fulfilled]
God our Father,
we celebrate at this season
the beginning of our salvation.
On this feast of Mary, the Mother of God,
we ask that our salvation
will be brought to its fulfillment.
We ask this through Christ our Lord. ℟. **Amen.** ↓

PREFACE (P 56)   [Mary, Virgin and Mother]
℣. The Lord be with you. ℟. **And also with you.**
℣. Lift up your hearts. ℟. **We lift them up to the Lord.**
℣. Let us give thanks to the Lord our God. ℟. **It is right to give him thanks and praise.**

Father, all-powerful and ever-living God,
we do well always and everywhere to give you thanks
(as we celebrate . . . of the Blessed Virgin Mary).
Through the power of the Holy Spirit,
she became the virgin mother of your only Son,
our Lord Jesus Christ,
who is for ever the light of the world.
Through him the choirs of angels
and all the powers of heaven
praise and worship your glory.
May our voices blend with theirs
as we join in their unending hymn: → No. 23, p. 23

*When Eucharistic Prayer I is used, the special Christmas
form of* In union with the whole Church *is said.*

COMMUNION ANT. Heb 13, 18   [Jesus Forever]
**Jesus Christ is the same yesterday, today, and for
ever.** ↓

PRAYER AFTER COMMUNION   [Mother of the Church]
Father,
as we proclaim the Virgin Mary
to be the mother of Christ and the mother of the
    Church,
may our communion with her Son
bring us to salvation.
We ask this through Christ our Lord.
℟. **Amen.**   → No. 32, p. 70

Optional Solemn Blessings, p. 92, and Prayers Over the People, p. 99

"They prostrated themselves and did him homage."

JANUARY 5

EPIPHANY

ENTRANCE ANT. See Mal 3, 1; 1 Chr 29, 12 **[Lord and Ruler]**

The Lord and ruler is coming; kingship is his, and government and power. → No. 2, p. 10

OPENING PRAYER **[Light of Faith]**

Let us pray
  [that we will be guided by the light of faith]
Father,
you revealed your Son to the nations
by the guidance of a star.
Lead us to your glory in heaven
by the light of faith.
We ask this through our Lord Jesus Christ, your Son,
who lives and reigns with you and the Holy Spirit,
one God, for ever and ever. ℟. **Amen.** ↓

ALTERNATIVE OPENING PRAYER **[God's Love Is Near]**

Let us pray
  [grateful for the glory revealed today
    through God made man]
Father of light, unchanging God,
today you reveal to men of faith

112

the resplendent fact of the Word made flesh.
Your light is strong,
your love is near;
draw us beyond the limits which this world imposes,
to the life where your Spirit makes all life complete.
We ask this through Christ our Lord. ℟. **Amen.** ↓

READING I Is 60, 1-6   [Glory of God's Church]

Jerusalem is favored by the Lord. Kings and peoples will come before you. The riches of the earth will be placed at the gates of Jerusalem.

A reading from the book of the prophet Isaiah

RISE up in splendor, Jerusalem! Your light has come,
    the glory of the Lord shines upon you.
See, darkness covers the earth,
    and thick clouds cover the peoples;
But upon you the Lord shines,
    and over you appears his glory.
Nations shall walk by your light,
    and kings by your shining radiance.
Raise your eyes and look about;
    they all gather and come to you:
Your sons come from afar,
    and your daughters in the arms of their nurses.
Then you shall be radiant at what you see,
    your heart shall throb and overflow,
For the riches of the sea shall be emptied out before
        you,
    the wealth of nations shall be brought to you.
Caravans of camels shall fill you,
    dromedaries from Midian and Ephah;
All from Sheba shall come
    bearing gold and frankincense,
    and proclaiming the praises of the Lord.
The word of the Lord. ℟. **Thanks be to God.** ↓

RESPONSORIAL PSALM Ps 72   [The Messiah-King]

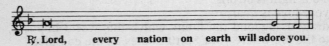

℟. Lord, every nation on earth will adore you.

O God, with your judgment endow the king,
   and with your justice, the king's son;
He shall govern your people with justice
   and your afflicted ones with judgment.

℟. **Lord, every nation on earth will adore you.**

Justice shall flower in his days,
   and profound peace, till the moon be no more.
May he rule from sea to sea,
   and from the River to the ends of the earth.

℟. **Lord, every nation on earth will adore you.**

The kings of Tarshish and the Isles shall offer gifts;
   the kings of Arabia and Seba shall bring tribute.
All kings shall pay him homage,
   all nations shall serve him.

℟. **Lord, every nation on earth will adore you.**

For he shall rescue the poor man when he cries out,
   and the afflicted when he has no one to help him.
He shall have pity for the lowly and the poor;
   the lives of the poor he shall save.

℟. **Lord, every nation on earth will adore you.** ↓

READING II Eph 3, 2-3. 5-6   [Good News for All]

> Paul admits that God has revealed the divine plan of salvation to him. Not only the Jews, but also the whole Gentile world, will share in the Good News.

A reading from the letter of Paul to the Ephesians

I AM sure you have heard of the ministry which God
in his goodness gave me in your regard. God's secret plan, as I have briefly described it, was revealed

to me, unknown to men in former ages but now revealed by the Spirit to the holy apostles and prophets.
It is no less than this: in Christ Jesus the Gentiles are
now co-heirs with the Jews, members of the same
body and sharers of the promise through the preaching of the gospel.—The word of the Lord. ℟. **Thanks
be to God.** ↓

GOSPEL Mt 2, 1-12   [Astrologers with Gifts]
Alleluia (Mk 2, 2)
℟. **Alleluia.** We have seen his star in the east,
and have come to adore the Lord. ℟. **Alleluia.** ↓

> King Herod, being jealous of his earthly crown, was threat-
> ened by the coming of another king. The astrologers from
> the east followed the star to Bethlehem from which a ruler
> was to come.

℣. The Lord be with you. ℟. **And also with you.**
✛ A reading from the holy gospel according to Matthew. ℟. **Glory to you, Lord.**

AFTER Jesus' birth in Bethlehem of Judea during
the reign of King Herod, astrologers from the east
arrived one day in Jerusalem inquiring, "Where is the
newborn king of the Jews? We observed his star at its
rising and have come to pay him homage." At this
news King Herod became greatly disturbed, and with
him all Jerusalem. Summoning all of the chief priests
and scribes of the people, he inquired of them where
the Messiah was to be born. "In Bethlehem of Judea,"
they informed him. "Here is what the prophet has
written:

'And you, Bethlehem, land of Judah,
    are by no means least among the princes of Judah,
since from you shall come a ruler
    who is to shepherd my people Israel.' "

Herod called the astrologers aside and found out from
them the exact time of the star's appearance. Then he
sent them to Bethlehem, after having instructed them:

"Go and get detailed information about the child. When you have discovered something, report your findings to me so that I may go and offer him homage too."

After their audience with the king, they set out. The star which they had observed at its rising went ahead of them until it came to a standstill over the place where the child was. They were overjoyed at seeing the star, and on entering the house, found the child with Mary his mother. They prostrated themselves and did him homage. Then they opened their coffers and presented him with gifts of gold, frankincense and myrrh.

They received a message in a dream not to return to Herod, so they went back to their own country by another route.—The gospel of the Lord. ℟. **Praise to you, Lord Jesus Christ.**   ➜ No. 14, p. 18

PRAYER OVER THE GIFTS   [Offering of Jesus]

Lord,
accept the offerings of your Church,
not gold, frankincense and myrrh,
but the sacrifice and food they symbolize:
Jesus Christ, who is Lord for ever and ever.
℟. **Amen.** ↓

PREFACE (P 6)   [Jesus Revealed to All]

℣. The Lord be with you. ℟. **And also with you.**
℣. Lift up your hearts. ℟. **We lift them up to the Lord.**
℣. Let us give thanks to the Lord our God. ℟. **It is right to give him thanks and praise.**

Father, all-powerful and ever-living God,
we do well always and everywhere to give you
    thanks.
Today you revealed in Christ your eternal plan of salvation
and showed him as the light of all peoples.

Now that his glory has shone among us
you have renewed humanity in his immortal image.
Now, with angels and archangels,
and the whole company of heaven,
we sing the unending hymn of your praise:

→ No. 23, p. 23

*When Eucharistic Prayer I is used, the special Epiphany
form of* In union with the whole Church *is said.*

COMMUNION ANT. See Mt 2, 2   [Adore the Lord]

**We have seen his star in the east, and have come with
gifts to adore the Lord.** ↓

PRAYER AFTER COMMUNION   [Christ in the Eucharist]

Father,
guide us with your light.
Help us to recognize Christ in this eucharist
and welcome him with love,
for he is Lord for ever and ever.
℟. **Amen.**   → No. 32, p. 70

Optional Solemn Blessings, p. 92, and Prayers Over the People, p. 99

"This is my beloved Son. My favor rests on him."

JANUARY 12

BAPTISM OF THE LORD

ENTRANCE ANT. See Mt 3, 16-17 [Beloved Son]

When the Lord had been baptized, the heavens opened, and the Spirit came down like a dove to rest on him. Then the voice of the Father thundered: This is my beloved Son, with him I am well pleased.

→ No. 2, p. 10

OPENING PRAYER [Faithful to Our Baptism]

Let us pray
   [that we will be faithful to our baptism]
Almighty, eternal God,
when the Spirit descended upon Jesus
at his baptism in the Jordan,
you revealed him as your own beloved Son.
Keep us, your children born of water and the Spirit,
faithful to our calling.
We ask this . . . for ever and ever. ℟. **Amen.** ↓

OR [God Became Man]

Father,
your only Son revealed himself to us by becoming
   man.

May we who share his humanity
come to share his divinity,
for he lives and reigns with you and the Holy Spirit,
one God, for ever and ever. ℟. **Amen.** ↓

ALTERNATIVE OPENING PRAYER   [Radiating Christ]

Let us pray
    [as we listen to the voice of God's Spirit]
Father in heaven,
you revealed Christ as your Son
by the voice that spoke over the waters of the Jordan.
May all who share in the sonship of Christ
follow in his path of service to man,
and reflect the glory of his kingdom
even to the ends of the earth,
for he is Lord for ever and ever. ℟. **Amen.** ↓

READING I Is 42, 1-4. 6-7   [Works of the Messiah]

Isaiah prefigures the Messiah who is to establish justice on
the earth. God has formed a pact with his people to open
the eyes of the blind and set prisoners free.

A reading from the book of the prophet Isaiah

HERE is my servant whom I uphold,
my chosen one with whom I am pleased,
Upon whom I have put my spirit;
    he shall bring forth justice to the nations,
Not crying out, not shouting,
    not making his voice heard in the street.
A bruised reed he shall not break,
    and a smoldering wick he shall not quench,
Until he establishes justice on the earth;
    the coastlands will wait for his teaching.
I, the Lord, have called you for the victory of justice,
    I have grasped you by the hand;
I formed you, and set you
    as a covenant of the people,
    a light for the nations,

To open the eyes of the blind,
   to bring out prisoners from confinement,
   and from the dungeon, those who live in darkness.
The word of the Lord. R̞. **Thanks be to God.** ↓

RESPONSORIAL PSALM Ps 29   [Peace for God's People]

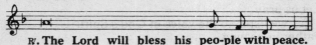

   R̞. **The Lord will bless his peo-ple with peace.**

Give to the Lord, you sons of God,
   give to the Lord glory and praise,
Give to the Lord the glory due his name;
   adore the Lord in holy attire.

R̞. **The Lord will bless his people with peace.**

The voice of the Lord is over the waters,
   the Lord, over vast waters,
The voice of the Lord is mighty;
   the voice of the Lord is majestic.

R̞. **The Lord will bless his people with peace.**

The God of glory thunders,
   and in his temple all say, "Glory!"
The Lord is enthroned above the flood;
   the Lord is enthroned as king forever.

R̞. **The Lord will bless his people with peace.** ↓

READING II Acts 10, 34-38   [Preparing the Way]

   God is all-just. He receives all who are upright. Jesus came
   to proclaim the "good news" to all. John the Baptizer prepared the way for Jesus by doing good.

   A reading from the Acts of the Apostles

PETER addressed Cornelius and the people assembled at his house in these words: "I begin to see
how true it is that God shows no partiality. Rather, the
man of any nation who fears God and acts uprightly is
acceptable to him. This is the message he has sent to

the sons of Israel, 'the good news of peace' proclaimed through Jesus Christ who is Lord of all. I take it you know what has been reported all over Judea about Jesus of Nazareth, beginning in Galilee with the baptism John preached; of the way God anointed him with the Holy Spirit and power. He went about doing good works and healing all who were in the grip of the devil, and God was with him."—The word of the Lord. ℞. **Thanks be to God.** ↓

GOSPEL Mk 1, 7-11   [Beloved Son]
Alleluia (See Mk 9, 6)

℞.   **Alleluia.** The heavens were opened and the
    Father's voice was heard:
this is my beloved Son, hear him. ℞. **Alleluia.** ↓

> The Spirit of God is seen coming upon Christ. The words of
> Isaiah are beginning to be fulfilled.

℣. The Lord be with you. ℞. **And also with you.**
✝ A reading from the holy gospel according to Mark. ℞.
Glory to you, Lord.

THE theme of John's preaching was: "One more powerful than I is to come after me. I am not fit to stoop and untie his sandal straps. I have baptized you in water; he will baptize you in the Holy Spirit."

During that time, Jesus came from Nazareth in Galilee and was baptized in the Jordan by John. Immediately on coming up out of the water he saw the sky rent in two and the Spirit descending on him like a dove. Then a voice came from the heavens: "You are my beloved Son. On you my favor rests."—The gospel of the Lord. ℞. **Praise to you, Lord Jesus Christ.**

→ No. 14, p. 18

PRAYER OVER THE GIFTS   [Christ's Revelation]
Lord,
we celebrate the revelation of Christ your Son
who takes away the sins of the world.

Accept our gifts
and let them become one with his sacrifice,
for he is Lord for ever and ever. ℟. **Amen.** ↓

PREFACE (P 7)   [New Gift of Baptism]

℣. The Lord be with you. ℟. **And also with you.**
℣. Lift up your hearts. ℟. **We lift them up to the Lord.**
℣. Let us give thanks to the Lord our God. ℟. **It is right to give him thanks and praise.**

Father, all-powerful and ever-living God,
we do well always and everywhere to give you
   thanks.
You celebrated your new gift of baptism
by signs and wonders at the Jordan.
Your voice was heard from heaven
to awaken faith in the presence among us
of the Word made man.
Your Spirit was seen as a dove,
revealing Jesus as your servant,
and anointing him with joy as the Christ,
sent to bring to the poor
the good news of salvation.
In our unending joy we echo on earth
the song of the angels in heaven
as they praise your glory for ever: → No. 23, p. 23

COMMUNION ANT. Jn 1, 32, 34   [Witness to God's Son]
This is he of whom John said: I have seen and have given witness that this is the Son of God. ↓

PRAYER AFTER COMMUNION   [Children in Fact]
Lord,
you feed us with bread from heaven.
May we hear your Son with faith
and become your children in name and in fact.
We ask this in the name of Jesus the Lord.
℟. **Amen.**   → No. 32, p. 70

Optional Solemn Blessings, p. 92, and Prayers Over the People, p. 99

"Look! There is the Lamb of God!"

JANUARY 19

2nd SUNDAY IN ORDINARY TIME

ENTRANCE ANT. Ps 66, 4   [Proclaim His Glory]
**May all the earth give you worship and praise, and
break into song to your name, O God, Most High.**

→ No. 2, p. 10

OPENING PRAYER   [Peace in the World]

Let us pray
  [to our Father for the gift of peace]
Father of heaven and earth,
hear our prayers,
and show us the way to peace in the world.
Grant this through our Lord Jesus Christ, your Son,
who lives and reigns with you and the Holy Spirit,
one God, for ever and ever. ℟. **Amen.** ↓

ALTERNATIVE OPENING PRAYER
                              [Reflecting God's Peace]

Let us pray
  [for the gift of peace]
Almighty and ever-present Father,
your watchful care reaches from end to end

and orders all things in such power
that even the tensions and the tragedies of sin
cannot frustrate your loving plans.
Help us to embrace your will,
give us the strength to follow your call,
so that your truth may live in our hearts
and reflect peace to those who believe in your love.
We ask this through Christ our Lord. ℟. **Amen.** ↓

READING I 1 Sm 3, 3-10. 19   [Answering God's Call]

The Lord called Samuel, but he did not recognize him.
Samuel receives advice from Eli, who is already a prophet
for the Lord. Following instructions from Eli, Samuel listens
to the Lord.

A reading from the first book of Samuel

SAMUEL was sleeping in the temple of the Lord
where the ark of God was. The Lord called to
Samuel, who answered, "Here I am." He ran to Eli and
said, "Here I am. You called me." "I did not call you,"
Eli said. "Go back to sleep." So he went back to sleep.
Again the Lord called Samuel, who rose and went to
Eli. "Here I am," he said. "You called me." But he answered, I did not call you, my son. Go back to sleep."
At that time Samuel was not familiar with the Lord,
because the Lord had not revealed anything to him as
yet. The Lord called Samuel again, for the third time.
Getting up and going to Eli, he said, "Here I am. You
called me." Then Eli understood that the Lord was
calling the youth. So he said to Samuel, "Go to sleep,
and if you are called, reply, 'Speak, Lord, for your servant is listening.' " When Samuel went to sleep in his
place, the Lord came and revealed his presence, calling out as before, "Samuel, Samuel!" Samuel answered, "Speak, for your servant is listening."

Samuel grew up, and the Lord was with him, not
permitting any word of his to be without effect.—The
word of the Lord. ℟. **Thanks be to God.** ↓

RESPONSORIAL PSALM Ps 40   [Doing God's Will]

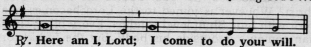

℟. **Here am I, Lord;   I come to do your will.**

I have waited, waited for the Lord,
  and he stooped toward me and heard my cry.
And he put a new song into my mouth,
  a hymn to our God.

℟. **Here am I, Lord;**
  I come to do your will.

Sacrifice or oblation you wished not,
  but ears open to obedience you gave me.
Holocausts or sin-offerings you sought not;
  then said I, "Behold I come."

℟. **Here am I, Lord;**
  I come to do your will.

"In the written scroll it is prescribed for me,
  to do your will, O my God, is my delight,
And your law is within my heart!"

℟. **Here am I, Lord;**
  I come to do your will.

I announced your justice in the vast assembly;
  I did not restrain my lips, as you, O Lord, know.

℟. **Here am I, Lord;**
  I come to do your will. ↓

READING II 1 Cor 6, 13-15. 17-20   [The Spirit in Us]

**The body is made for the Lord. With the price of the Cross,
Jesus redeemed all humanity. The Holy Spirit dwells within
each person.**

A reading from the first letter of Paul
to the Corinthians

THE body is not for immorality; it is for the Lord,
and the Lord is for the body. God, who raised up
the Lord, will raise us also by his power.

Do you not see that your bodies are members of Christ? Whoever is joined to the Lord becomes one spirit with him. Shun lewd conduct. Every other sin a man commits is outside his body, but the fornicator sins against his own body. You must know that your body is a temple of the Holy Spirit, who is within—the Spirit you have received from God. You are not your own. You have been purchased, and at what a price! So glorify God in your body.—The word of the Lord. ℟. **Thanks be to God.** ↓

GOSPEL Jn 1, 35-42   [Encountering Christ]
Alleluia (Jn 1, 41. 17)
℟. **Alleluia.** We have found the Messiah:
Jesus Christ, who brings us truth and grace. ℟. **Alleluia.** ↓

In place of the Alleluia given for each Sunday in Ordinary Time, another may be selected .

It was John the Baptizer's purpose to point out Jesus, the Messiah. Andrew and his companion followed Jesus. Andrew summons Peter. Jesus identifies Peter and gives him a new name.

℣. The Lord be with you. ℟. **And also with you.**
✚ A reading from the holy gospel according to John.
℟. **Glory to you, Lord.**

JOHN was in Bethany across the Jordan with two of his disciples. As he watched Jesus walk by he said, "Look! There is the Lamb of God!" The two disciples heard what he said, and followed Jesus. When Jesus turned around and noticed them following him, he asked them, "What are you looking for?" They said to him, "Rabbi (which means Teacher), where do you stay?" "Come and see," he answered. So they went to see where he was lodged, and stayed with him that day. (It was about four in the afternoon.)

One of the two who had followed him after hearing

John was Simon Peter's brother Andrew. The first thing he did was seek out his brother Simon and tell him, "We have found the Messiah!" (which means the Anointed). He brought him to Jesus, who looked at him and said, "You are Simon, son of John; your name shall be Cephas (which is rendered Peter)."— The gospel of the Lord. R̸. **Praise to you, Lord Jesus Christ.**

→ No. 14, p. 18

PRAYER OVER THE GIFTS   [Work of Salvation]

Father,
may we celebrate the eucharist
with reverence and love,
for when we proclaim the death of the Lord
you continue the work of his redemption,
who is Lord for ever and ever.
R̸. **Amen.**

→ No. 21, p. 22 (Pref. P 29-36)

COMMUNION ANT. Ps 23, 5   [A Feast for Me]

The Lord has prepared a feast for me: given wine in plenty for me to drink. ↓

OR 1 Jn 4, 16   [God's Love]

We know and believe in God's love for us. ↓

PRAYER AFTER COMMUNION   [One in Love]

Lord,
you have nourished us with bread from heaven.
Fill us with your Spirit,
and make us one in peace and love.
We ask this through Christ our Lord.
R̸. **Amen.**

→ No. 32, p. 70

Optional Solemn Blessings, p. 92, and Prayers Over the People, p. 99

"Come after me; I will make you fishers of men."

JANUARY 26

3rd SUNDAY IN ORDINARY TIME

ENTRANCE ANT. Ps 96, 1. 6   [Sing to the Lord]

Sing a new song to the Lord! Sing to the Lord, all the earth. Truth and beauty surround him, he lives in holiness and glory.   → No. 2, p. 10

OPENING PRAYER   [Working for Unity]

Let us pray
  [for unity and peace]
All-powerful and ever-living God,
direct your love that is within us,
that our efforts in the name of your Son
may bring mankind to unity and peace.
We ask this . . . for ever and ever. ℞. **Amen.** ↓

ALTERNATIVE OPENING PRAYER   [Vision of God]

Let us pray
  [pleading that our vision
  may overcome our weakness]
Almighty Father,
the love you offer
always exceeds the furthest expression of our human
  longing,

128

for you are greater than the human heart.
Direct each thought, each effort of our life,
so that the limits of our faults and weaknesses
may not obscure the vision of your glory
or keep us from the peace you have promised.
We ask this through Christ our Lord. ℟. **Amen.** ↓

READING I Jon 3, 1-5. 10   [God's Mercy for All]

The mercy of God is shown to the people of Nineveh. He sends Jonah to Nineveh to preach penance for sin. The king proclaims a universal fast to appease the Lord.

A reading from the book of the prophet Jonah

THE word of the Lord came to Jonah saying: "Set out for the great city of Nineveh, and announce to it the message that I will tell you." So Jonah made ready and went to Nineveh, according to the Lord's bidding. Now Nineveh was an enormously large city; it took three days to go through it. Jonah began his journey through the city, and had gone out but a single day's walk announcing, "Forty days more and Nineveh shall be destroyed," when the people of Nineveh believed God; they proclaimed a fast and all of them, great and small, put on sackcloth.

When God saw by their actions how they turned from their evil way, he repented of the evil that he had threatened to do to them; he did not carry it out.—The word of the Lord. ℟. **Thanks be to God.** ↓

RESPONSORIAL PSALM Ps 25   [God's Ways]

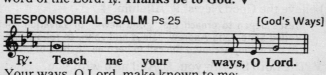

℟. **Teach me your ways, O Lord.**

Your ways, O Lord, make known to me;
    teach me your paths,
Guide me in your truth and teach me,
    for you are God my savior.—℟.

Remember that your compassion, O Lord,
    and your kindness are from of old.

In your kindness remember me,
   because of your goodness, O Lord.—RJ.

Good and upright is the Lord;
   thus he shows sinners the way.
He guides the humble to justice,
   he teaches the humble his way.—RJ. ↓

READING II 1 Cor 7, 29-31   [Shortness of Time]

Paul warns the Corinthians of the shortness of time in this world. All must conduct themselves worthily in the eyes of God and be detached from this world's pleasure.

A reading from the first letter of Paul
to the Corinthians

I TELL you, brothers, the time is short. From now on those with wives should live as though they had none; those who weep should live as though they were not weeping, and those who rejoice as though they were not rejoicing; buyers should conduct themselves as though they owned nothing, and those who make use of the world as though they were not using it, for the world as we know it is passing away.—The word of the Lord. RJ. **Thanks be to God.** ↓

GOSPEL Mk 1, 14-20   [Reform Your Lives]
Alleluia (Mk 1, 15)
RJ. **Alleluia.** The kingdom of God is near:
believe the Good News! RJ. **Alleluia.** ↓

Jesus began to preach the "good news" of salvation. He called Simon and Andrew, James and John, to follow him. At once, they accepted the call to become "fishers of men."

℣. The Lord be with you. RJ. **And also with you.**
✠ A reading from the holy gospel according to Mark.
RJ. **Glory to you, Lord.**

A FTER John's arrest, Jesus appeared in Galilee proclaiming God's good news: "This is the time of fulfillment. The reign of God is at hand! Reform your lives and believe in the good news!"

As he made his way along the Sea of Galilee, he observed Simon and his brother Andrew casting their nets into the sea; they were fishermen. Jesus said to them, "Come after me; I will make you fishers of men." They immediately abandoned their nets and became his followers. Proceeding a little farther along, he caught sight of James, Zebedee's son, and his brother John. They too were in their boat putting their nets in order. He summoned them on the spot. They abandoned their father Zebedee, who was in the boat with the hired men, and went off in his company.— The gospel of the Lord. ℟. **Praise to you, Lord Jesus Christ.**

→ No. 14, p. 18

PRAYER OVER THE GIFTS   [Offerings of Salvation]

Lord,
receive our gifts.
Let our offerings make us holy
and bring us salvation.
Grant this through Christ our Lord.
℟. **Amen.**   → No. 21, p. 22 (Pref. P 29-36)

COMMUNION ANT. Ps 34, 6   [Gladness]

Look up at the Lord with gladness and smile; your face will never be ashamed. ↓

OR Jn 8, 12   [Light of Life]

I am the light of the world, says the Lord; the man who follows me will have the light of life. ↓

PRAYER AFTER COMMUNION   [New Life]

God, all-powerful Father,
may the new life you give us increase our love
and keep us in the joy of your kingdom.
We ask this in the name of Jesus the Lord.
℟. **Amen.**   → No. 32, p. 70

Optional Solemn Blessings, p. 92, and Prayers Over the People, p. 99

"This child is destined to be the downfall and the rise of many in Israel."

FEBRUARY 2

PRESENTATION OF THE LORD
(4th SUNDAY IN ORDINARY TIME)

BLESSING OF CANDLES AND PROCESSION
First Form: Procession

The people gather in a chapel or other suitable place outside the church where the Mass will be celebrated. They carry unlighted candles.

While the candles are being lighted, this canticle or another hymn is sung:

[The Lord's Light]

The Lord will come with mighty power, and give light to the eyes of all who serve him, alleluia.

The priest greets the people as usual, and briefly invites the people to take an active part in this celebration. He may use these or similar words:

[Welcoming Christ]

Forty days ago we celebrated the joyful feast of the birth of our Lord Jesus Christ. Today we recall the holy day on which he was presented in the temple,

fulfilling the law of Moses and at the same time going
to meet his faithful people. Led by the Spirit, Simeon
and Anna came to the temple, recognized Christ as
their Lord, and proclaimed him with joy.

United by the Spirit, may we now go to the house of
God to welcome Christ the Lord. There we shall recognize him in the breaking of bread until he comes
again in glory.

Then the priest joins his hands and blesses the candles:

[Light to the Nations]

Let us pray.
God our Father, source of all light,
today you revealed to Simeon
your Light of revelation to the nations.
Bless ✛ these candles and make them holy.
May we who carry them to praise your glory
walk in the path of goodness
and come to the light that shines for ever.
Grant this through Christ our Lord. ℟. **Amen.** ↓

OR   **[Light of Glory]**

Let us pray.
God our Father, source of eternal light,
fill the hearts of all believers
with the light of faith.
May we who carry these candles in your church
come with joy to the light of glory.
We ask this through Christ our Lord. ℟. **Amen.** ↓

He sprinkles the candles in silence.

*The priest then takes the candle prepared for him, and the
procession begins with the acclamation:*

Let us go in peace to meet the Lord.

*During the procession, the following canticle or another
hymn is sung:*

ANTIPHON   [The Glory of Israel]

**Christ is the light of the nations
and the glory of Israel his people.**

CANTICLE   [God's Salvation]

**Now, Lord, you have kept your word:
let your servant go in peace.**

The Antiphon is repeated: "Christ is the light, etc."

**With my own eyes I have seen the salvation
which you have prepared in the sight of every people.**

The Antiphon is repeated: "Christ is the light, etc."

**A light to reveal you to the nations
and the glory of your people Israel.**

The Antiphon is repeated: "Christ is the light, etc."

*As the procession enters the church, the Entrance Song of the
Mass is sung. When the priest reaches the altar, he venerates
it, and may incense it. Then he goes to the chair (and replaces the cope with the chasuble). After the* Gloria, *he sings
or says the Opening Prayer. The Mass continues as usual.*

Second Form: Solemn Entrance

*The people, carrying unlighted candles, assemble in the
church. The priest, vested in white, is accompanied by his
ministers and by a representative group of the faithful. They
go to a suitable place (either in front of the door or in the
church itself) where most of the congregation can easily take
part.*

*Then the candles are lighted while the following antiphon, or
another hymn is sung.*

[The Lord's Light]

**The Lord will come with mighty power, and give light
to the eyes of all who serve him, alleluia.**

*After the greeting and introduction, he blesses the candles,
as above, and goes in procession to the altar, while all are
singing. The Mass is as described above.*

THE MASS

ENTRANCE ANT. Ps 48, 10-11   [God's Loving Kindness]

Within your temple we ponder your loving kindness, O God. As your praise reaches to the ends of the earth, your right hand is filled with justice.

→ No. 2, p. 10

OPENING PRAYER   [Led into God's Presence]

All-powerful Father,
Christ your Son became man for us
and was presented in the temple.
May he free our hearts from sin
and bring us into your presence.
We ask this through our Lord Jesus Christ, your Son,
who lives and reigns with you and the Holy Spirit,
one God, for ever and ever. ℞. **Amen.** ↓

READING I Mal 3, 1-4   [With Purified Hearts]

Malachi speaks of God's great intervention in sacred history—God's speaking to the patriarch (Gn 16, 7ff), and to Moses (Ex 3, 2), and God's leading the way through the Red Sea (Ex 23, 20). These wondrous ways in which God is manifested will be applied to messianic messengers.

A reading from the book of the prophet Malachi

THE Lord God said:
Lo, I am sending my messenger
  to prepare the way before me;
And suddenly there will come to the temple
  the Lord whom you seek,
And the messenger of the covenant whom you desire.
  Yes, he is coming, says the Lord of hosts.
But who will endure the day of his coming?
  And who can stand when he appears?
For he is like the refiner's fire,
  or like the fuller's lye.
He will sit refining and purifying [silver],

and he will purify the sons of Levi,
Refining them like gold or like silver
   that they may offer due sacrifice to the Lord.
Then the sacrifice of Judah and Jerusalem
   will please the Lord,
   as in the days of old, as in years gone by.
The word of the Lord. ℟. **Thanks be to God.** ↓

RESPONSORIAL PSALM Ps 24   [The King of Glory]

℟. Who is this king of glor-y? It is the Lord!

Lift up, O gates, your lintels;
   reach up, you ancient portals,
   that the king of glory may come in!—℟.

Who is this king of glory?
   The Lord, strong and mighty,
   the Lord, mighty in battle.—℟.

Lift up, O gates, your lintels;
   reach up, you ancient portals,
   that the king of glory may come in!—℟.

Who is this king of glory?
   The Lord of hosts; he is the king of glory.

℟. **Who is this king of glory?**
  It is the Lord! ↓

READING II Heb 2, 14-18   [Christ Our Brother]

In the biblical sense, "flesh" means human nature considered in its weakness. It is contrasted with "spirit" and God.
Because of the connection between sin and death, Christ
overcame the power of death through his priestly work.

A reading from the letter to the Hebrews

NOW, since the children are men of blood and
flesh, Jesus likewise had a full share in these, that
by his death he might rob the devil, the prince of

death, of his power, and free those who through fear
of death had been slaves their whole life long. Surely
he did not come to help angels, but rather the children
of Abraham; therefore he had to become like his
brothers in every way, that he might be a merciful and
faithful high priest before God on their behalf, to examine the sins of the people. Since he was himself
tested through what he suffered, he is able to help
those who are tempted.—The word of the Lord. ℟.
Thanks be to God. ↓

GOSPEL Lk 2, 22-40 or 2, 22-32   [The Lord's Salvation]
Alleluia
℟. **Alleluia.** This is the light of revelation to the nations,
and the glory of your people, Israel. ℟. **Alleluia.** ↓

> Mary is seen here, united with Jesus and Joseph in the
> Temple ceremony. Jesus is formally recognized as a mem-
> ber of God's chosen people through whom world salvation
> was to be achieved.

*[If the "Short Form" is used, the indented text in brackets is
omitted.]*

℣. The Lord be with you. ℟. **And also with you.**
✠ A reading from the holy gospel according to Luke.
℟. **Glory to you, Lord.**

WHEN the day came to purify them according to
the law of Moses, the couple brought Jesus up to
Jerusalem so that he could be presented to the Lord,
for it is written in the law of the Lord, "Every first-
born male shall be consecrated to the Lord." They
came to offer in sacrifice "a pair of turtledoves or two
young pigeons," in accord with the dictate in the law
of the Lord.

There lived in Jerusalem at the time a certain man
named Simeon. He was just and pious, and awaited
the consolation of Israel, and the Holy Spirit was upon

him. It was revealed to him by the Holy Spirit that he would not experience death until he had seen the Anointed of the Lord. He came to the temple now, inspired by the Spirit; and when the parents brought in the child Jesus to perform for him the customary ritual of the law, he took him in his arms and blessed God in these words:

"Now, Master, you can dismiss your servant in peace;
    you have fulfilled your word.
For my eyes have witnessed your saving deed
    displayed for all the peoples to see:
A revealing light to the Gentiles,
    the glory of your people Israel."

[The child's father and mother were marveling at what was being said about him. Simeon blessed them and said to Mary his mother: "This child is destined to be the downfall and the rise of many in Israel, a sign that will be opposed—and you yourself shall be pierced with a sword—so that the thoughts of many hearts may be laid bare."

There was also a certain prophetess, Anna by name, daughter of Phanuel of the tribe of Asher. She had seen many days, having lived seven years with her husband after her marriage and then as a widow until she was eighty-four. She was constantly in the temple, worshiping day and night in fasting and prayer. Coming on the scene at this moment, she gave thanks to God and talked about the child to all who looked forward to the deliverance of Jerusalem.

When the pair had fulfilled all the prescriptions of the law of the Lord, they returned to Galilee and their own town of Nazareth. The child grew in size and strength, filled with wisdom, and the grace of God was upon him.]

The gospel of the Lord. ℟. **Praise to you, Lord Jesus Christ.**   → No. 14, p. 18

PRAYER OVER THE GIFTS   [Lamb without Blemish]

Lord,
accept the gifts your Church offers you with joy,
since in fulfillment of your will
your Son offered himself as a lamb without blemish
for the life of the world.
We ask this through Christ our Lord. ℟. **Amen.** ↓

PREFACE (P 49)   [Manifestation of Christ the Light]

℣. The Lord be with you. ℟. **And also with you.**
℣. Lift up your hearts. ℟. **We lift them up to the Lord.**
℣. Let us give thanks to the Lord our God. ℟. **It is right to give him thanks and praise.**

Father, all-powerful and ever-living God,
we do well always and everywhere to give you thanks
through Jesus Christ our Lord.
Today your Son,
who shares your eternal splendor,
was presented in the temple,
and revealed by the Spirit
as the glory of Israel
and the light of all peoples.
Our hearts are joyful,
for we have seen your salvation,
and now with the angels and saints
we praise you for ever: → No. 23, p. 23

COMMUNION ANT. Lk 2, 30-31   [Sight of Salvation]

With my own eyes I have seen the salvation which you have prepared in the sight of all the nations. ↓

PRAYER AFTER COMMUNION   [Preparing To Meet Christ]

Lord,
you fulfilled the hope of Simeon,

who did not die
until he had been privileged to welcome the Messiah.
May this communion perfect your grace in us
and prepare us to meet Christ
when he comes to bring us into everlasting life,
for he is Lord for ever and ever.
℞. **Amen.**   ➜ No. 32, p. 70

Optional Solemn Blessings, p. 92, and Prayers Over the People, p. 99

"He went over to her . . . , and the fever left her."

FEBRUARY 9

5th SUNDAY IN ORDINARY TIME

ENTRANCE ANT. Ps 95, 6-7   [Adoration]

**Come, let us worship the Lord. Let us bow down in
the presence of our maker, for he is the Lord our God.**
                                                ➜ No. 2, p. 10

OPENING PRAYER   [God's Care]
Let us pray
   [that God will watch over us and protect us]
Father,
watch over your family
and keep us safe in your care,

for all our hope is in you.
Grant this through our Lord Jesus Christ, your Son,
who lives and reigns with you and the Holy Spirit,
one God, for ever and ever. ℟. **Amen.** ↓

ALTERNATIVE OPENING PRAYER   [God's Presence]

Let us pray
   [with reverence in the presence of the living God]
In faith and love we ask you, Father,
to watch over your family gathered here.
In your mercy and loving kindness
no thought of ours is left unguarded,
no tear unheeded, no joy unnoticed.
Through the prayer of Jesus
may the blessings promised to the poor in spirit
lead us to the treasures of your heavenly kingdom.
We ask this in the name of Jesus the Lord. ℟. **Amen.** ↓

READING I Jb 7, 1-4. 6-7   [Life Is Fleeting]

**Job describes our life on earth. The days of our life come to
a swift end.**

A reading from the book of Job

JOB spoke, saying:
   Is not man's life on earth a drudgery?
   Are not his days those of a hireling?
He is a slave who longs for the shade,
   a hireling who waits for his wages.
So I have been assigned months of misery,
   and troubled nights have been told off for me.
If in bed I say, "When shall I arise?"
   then the night drags on;
   I am filled with restlessness until the dawn.
My days are swifter than a weaver's shuttle;
   they come to an end without hope.
Remember that my life is like the wind;
   I shall not see happiness again.
The word of the Lord. ℟. **Thanks be to God.** ↓

RESPONSORIAL PSALM Ps 147   [Healer of Brokenhearted]

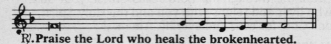

℟. **Praise the Lord who heals the brokenhearted.**

Praise the Lord, for he is good;
 sing praise to our God, for he is gracious;
 it is fitting to praise him.
The Lord rebuilds Jerusalem;
 the dispersed of Israel he gathers.—℟.

He heals the brokenhearted
 and binds up their wounds.
He tells the number of the stars;
 he calls each by name.—℟.

Great is our Lord and mighty in power;
 to his wisdom there is no limit.
The Lord sustains the lowly;
 the wicked he casts to the ground.—℟. ↓

℟. Or: **Alleluia.** ↓

READING II 1 Cor 9, 16-19. 22-23   [All Things to All]

**Paul writes that he must preach the gospel. Although he
has no obligation to any person, he has tried to become
one with his hearers to convince them of the saving message of the gospel.**

A reading from the first letter of Paul
to the Corinthians

PREACHING the gospel is not the subject of a
boast; I am under compulsion and have no choice.
I am ruined if I do not preach it! If I do it willingly, I
have my recompense; if unwillingly, I am nonetheless
entrusted with a charge. And this recompense of
mine? It is simply this, that when preaching I offer the
gospel free of charge and do not make full use of the
authority the gospel gives me.

Although I am not bound to anyone, I made myself the slave of all so as to win over as many as possible. To the weak I became a weak person with a view to winning the weak. I have made myself all things to all men in order to save at least some of them. In fact, I do all that I do for the sake of the gospel in the hope of having a share in its blessings.—The word of the Lord. ℟. **Thanks be to God.** ↓

GOSPEL Mk 1, 29-39   [Jesus the Healer]
Alleluia (Mt 8, 17)
℟. **Alleluia.** He took our sicknesses away,
and carried our diseases for us. ℟. **Alleluia.** ↓

> Jesus visits the home of Simon and Andrew. He cures Simon's mother-in-law. Jesus also expels many demons and then goes off to pray alone. When found by Simon, Jesus goes in the villages to preach the good news.

℣. The Lord be with you. ℟. **And also with you.**
✛ A reading from the holy gospel according to Mark.
℟. **Glory to you, Lord.**

UPON leaving the synagogue, Jesus entered the house of Simon and Andrew with James and John. Simon's mother-in-law lay ill with a fever, and the first thing they did was to tell him about her. He went over to her and grasped her hand and helped her up, and the fever left her. She immediately began to wait on them.

After sunset, as evening drew on, they brought him all who were ill and those possessed by demons. Before long the whole town was gathered outside the door. Those whom he cured, who were variously afflicted, were many, and so were the demons he expelled. But he would not permit the demons to speak, because they knew him. Rising early the next morning, he went off to a lonely place in the desert; there he was absorbed in prayer. Simon and his companions managed to track him down; and when they found him, they told him, "Everybody is looking for you!" He said to them: "Let us move on to the neighboring villages so that I may proclaim the good news there also. That is what I have come to do." So he went into their synagogues preaching the good news and expelling demons throughout the whole of Galilee.—The gospel of the Lord. ℟. **Praise to you, Lord Jesus Christ.**   → No. 14, p. 18

PRAYER OVER THE GIFTS   [Eternal Life]

Lord our God,
may the bread and wine
you give us for our nourishment on earth
become the sacrament of our eternal life.
We ask this through Christ our Lord.
℟. **Amen.**   → No. 21, p. 22 (Pref. P 29-36)

COMMUNION ANT. Ps 107, 8-9   [The Lord's Kindness]

Give praise to the Lord for his kindness, for his wonderful deeds toward men. He has filled the hungry with good things, he has satisfied the thirsty. ↓

OR Mt 5, 5-6   [The Sorrowing]

Happy are the sorrowing; they shall be consoled. Happy those who hunger and thirst for what is right; they shall be satisfied. ↓

PRAYER AFTER COMMUNION   [Salvation and Joy]

God our Father,
you give us a share in the one bread and the one cup
and make us one in Christ.
Help us to bring your salvation and joy
to all the world.
We ask this through Christ our Lord.
℟. **Amen.**   → No. 32, p. 70

Optional Solemn Blessings, p. 92, and Prayers Over the People, p. 99

Jesus was "put to the test . . . by Satan."

FEBRUARY 16

1st SUNDAY OF LENT

ENTRANCE ANT. Ps 91, 15-16   **[Long Life]**
**When he calls to me, I will answer; I will rescue him
and give him honor. Long life and contentment will
be his.**   ➙ No. 2, p. 10 (Omit Gloria)

OPENING PRAYER   **[Christ's Saving Love]**
Let us pray
   [that this Lent will help us reproduce in our lives
   the self-sacrificing love of Christ]
Father,
through our observance of Lent,
help us to understand the meaning
of your Son's death and resurrection,
and teach us to reflect it in our lives.
Grant this . . . for ever and ever. ℟. **Amen.** ↓

ALTERNATIVE OPENING PRAYER   **[Spirit of Repentance]**
Let us pray
   [at the beginning of Lent
   for the spirit of repentance]

Lord our God,
you formed man from the clay of the earth
and breathed into him the spirit of life,
but he turned from your face and sinned.
In this time of repentance
we call out for your mercy.
Bring us back to you
and to the life your Son won for us
by his death on the cross,
for he lives and reigns for ever and ever. ℟. **Amen.** ↓

READING I Gn 9, 8-15 [Sign of Covenant]

God promises Noah that the world will never again be destroyed by a flood. God gives a sign of his covenant—his rainbow among the clouds.

A reading from the book of Genesis

GOD said to Noah and to his sons with him: "See, I am now establishing my covenant with you and your descendants after you and with every living creature that was with you: all the birds, and the various tame and wild animals that were with you and came out of the ark. I will establish my covenant with you, that never again shall all bodily creatures be destroyed by the waters of a flood; there shall not be another flood to devastate the earth." God added: "This is the sign that I am giving for all ages to come, of the covenant between me and you and every living creature with you: I set my bow in the clouds to serve as a sign of the covenant between me and the earth. When I bring clouds over the earth, and the bow appears in the clouds, I will recall the covenant I have made between me and you and all living beings, so that the waters shall never again become a flood to destroy all mortal beings."—The word of the Lord. ℟. **Thanks be to God.** ↓

RESPONSORIAL PSALM Ps 25   [Keeping God's Covenant]

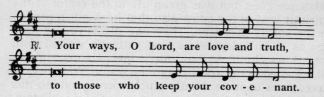

℟. Your ways, O Lord, are love and truth, to those who keep your cov-e-nant.

Your ways, O Lord, make known to me;
    teach me your paths,
Guide me in your truth and teach me,
    for you are God my savior.

℟. **Your ways, O Lord, are love and truth,
    to those who keep your covenant.**

Remember that your compassion, O Lord,
    and your kindness are from of old.
In your kindness remember me,
    because of your goodness, O Lord.

℟. **Your ways, O Lord, are love and truth,
    to those who keep your covenant.**

Good and upright is the Lord;
    thus he shows sinners the way.
He guides the humble to justice,
    he teaches the humble his way.

℟. **Your ways, O Lord, are love and truth,
    to those who keep your covenant.** ↓

READING II 1 Pt 3, 18-22   [Power of the Resurrection]
    **Christ died once for sin. Because of sin, God destroyed the
    earth by water. Now Christians are saved by the water of
    baptism. It becomes the pledge of resurrection.**

A reading from the first letter of Peter

THIS is why Christ died for sins once for all, a just
    man for the sake of the unjust: so that he could

lead you to God. He was put to death insofar as fleshly existence goes, but was given life in the realm of the spirit. It was in the spirit also that he went to preach to the spirits in prison. They had disobeyed as long ago as Noah's day, while God patiently waited until the ark was built. At that time, a few persons, eight in all, escaped in the ark through the water. You are now saved by a baptismal bath which corresponds to this exactly. This baptism is no removal of physical stain, but the pledge to God of an irreproachable conscience through the resurrection of Jesus Christ. He went to heaven and is at God's right hand, with angelic rulers and powers subjected to him.—The word of the Lord.

℟. **Thanks be to God.** ↓

GOSPEL Mk 1, 12-15   [Time of Fulfillment]

Verse before the Gospel (Mt 4, 4)

℟. **Praise to you, Lord Jesus Christ, king of endless glory!**

Man does not live on bread alone,
but on every word that comes from the mouth of God.

℟. **Praise to you, Lord Jesus Christ, king of endless glory!** ↓

> Jesus prayed in the desert for forty days. After John's arrest, Jesus came forth, announcing the time of fulfillment. It is the time to believe and reform.

℣. The Lord be with you. ℟. **And also with you.**

✚ A reading from the holy gospel according to Mark.

℟. **Glory to you, Lord.**

THE Spirit sent Jesus out toward the desert. He stayed in the wasteland forty days, put to the test there by Satan. He was with the wild beasts, and angels waited on him.

After John's arrest, Jesus appeared in Galilee proclaiming God's good news: "This is the time of fulfillment. The reign of God is at hand! Reform your lives

and believe in the good news!"—The gospel of the
Lord. ℟. **Praise to you, Lord Jesus Christ.**

→ No. 14, p. 18

PRAYER OVER THE GIFTS   [Better Lives]

Lord,
make us worthy to bring you these gifts.
May this sacrifice
help to change our lives.
We ask this in the name of Jesus the Lord. ℟. **Amen.** ↓

PREFACE (P 12)   [Christ's Self-Denial]

℣. The Lord be with you. ℟. **And also with you.**
℣. Lift up your hearts. ℟. **We lift them up to the Lord.**
℣. Let us give thanks to the Lord our God. ℟. **It is
right to give him thanks and praise.**

Father, all-powerful and ever-living God,
we do well always and everywhere to give you thanks
through Jesus Christ our Lord.
His fast of forty days
makes this a holy season of self-denial.
By rejecting the devil's temptations
he has taught us
to rid ourselves of the hidden corruption of evil,
and so to share his paschal meal in purity of heart,
until we come to its fulfillment
in the promised land of heaven.
Now we join the angels and the saints
as they sing their unending hymn of praise:

→ No. 23, p. 23

COMMUNION ANT. Mt 4, 4   [Life-Giving Word]

**Man does not live on bread alone, but on every word
that comes from the mouth of God.** ↓

OR Ps 91, 4   [Refuge in God]

**The Lord will overshadow you, and you will find
refuge under his wings.** ↓

PRAYER AFTER COMMUNION   [Words and Bread of Life]

Father,
you increase our faith and hope,
you deepen our love in this communion.
Help us to live by your words
and to seek Christ, our bread of life,
who is Lord for ever and ever.
R̸. **Amen.**   ➜ No. 32, p. 70

Optional Solemn Blessings, p. 92, and Prayers Over the People, p. 99

*"Elijah appeared to them along with Moses;
the two were in conversation with Jesus."*

FEBRUARY 23

2nd SUNDAY OF LENT

ENTRANCE ANT. Ps 25, 6. 3. 22   [God's Mercies]

**Remember your mercies, Lord, your tenderness from
ages past. Do not let our enemies triumph over us; O
God, deliver Israel from all her distress.**

OR Ps 27, 8-9   [God's Face]

**My heart has prompted me to seek your face; I seek it,
Lord; do not hide from me.** ➜ No. 2, p. 10 (Omit Gloria)

OPENING PRAYER   [Our Response]

Let us pray
  [for the grace to respond
  to the Word of God]
God our Father,
help us to hear your Son.
Enlighten us with your word,
that we may find the way to your glory.
We ask this through our Lord Jesus Christ, your Son,
who lives and reigns with you and the Holy Spirit,
one God, for ever and ever. R̸. **Amen.** ↓

ALTERNATIVE OPENING PRAYER   [Gift of Integrity]

Let us pray
  [in this season of Lent
  for the gift of integrity]
Father of light,
in you is found no shadow of change
but only the fullness of life and limitless truth.
Open our hearts to the voice of your Word
and free us from the original darkness that shadows
  our vision.
Restore our sight that we may look upon your Son
who calls us to repentance and a change of heart,
for he lives and reigns with you for ever and ever.
R̸. **Amen.** ↓

READING I Gn 22, 1-2. 9. 10-13. 15-18 [Testing of Abraham]

**Abraham and his son, Isaac, prefigure God, the Father, and
Jesus, his divine Son. God tests Abraham's faith and because of it, God promises abundant blessings on the family
of Abraham and all his descendants.**

A reading from the book of Genesis

GOD put Abraham to the test. He called to him,
"Abraham!" "Ready!" he replied. Then God said:
"Take your son Isaac, your only one, whom you love,
and go to the land of Moriah. There you shall offer

him up as a holocaust on a height that I will point out
to you."

When they came to the place of which God had told
him, Abraham built an altar there and arranged the
wood on it. Then he reached out and took the knife to
slaughter his son. But the Lord's messenger called to
him from heaven, "Abraham, Abraham!" "Yes, Lord,"
he answered. "Do not lay your hand on the boy," said
the messenger. "Do not do the least thing to him. I
know now how devoted you are to God, since you did
not withhold from me your own beloved son." As
Abraham looked about, he spied a ram caught by its
horns in the thicket. So he went and took the ram and
offered it up as a holocaust in place of his son.

Again the Lord's messenger called to Abraham
from heaven and said: "I swear by myself, declares
the Lord, that because you acted as you did in not
withholding from me your beloved son, I will bless
you abundantly and make your descendants as countless as the stars of the sky and the sands of the
seashore; your descendants shall take possession of
the gates of their enemies, and in your descendants all
the nations of the earth shall find blessing—all this because you obeyed my command."—The word of the
Lord. ℟. **Thanks be to God.** ↓

RESPONSORIAL PSALM Ps 116   [Walking with God]

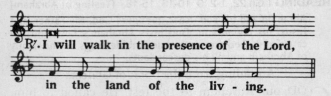

℟. I will walk in the presence of the Lord, in the land of the liv-ing.

I believed, even when I said,
   "I am greatly afflicted."

Precious in the eyes of the Lord
   is the death of his faithful ones.

℟. **I will walk in the presence of the Lord,**
   in the land of the living.

O Lord, I am your servant;
   I am your servant, the son of your handmaid;
   you have loosed my bonds.
To you will I offer sacrifice of thanksgiving,
   and I will call upon the name of the Lord.

℟. **I will walk in the presence of the Lord,**
   in the land of the living.

My vows to the Lord I will pay
   in the presence of all his people,
In the courts of the house of the Lord,
   in your midst, O Jerusalem.

℟. **I will walk in the presence of the Lord,**
   in the land of the living. ↓

READING II Rom 8, 31-34   [God Is for Us]

   God sent his Son into the world to die for us. Who is then
   going to judge God's chosen ones? Is this not the right of
   Jesus, who loves those for whom he gave his life?

   A reading from the letter of Paul to the Romans

IF God is for us, who can be against us? Is it possible
that he who did not spare his own Son but handed
him over for the sake of us all will not grant us all
things besides? Who shall bring a charge against
God's chosen ones? God, who justifies? Who shall
condemn them? Christ Jesus, who died or rather was
raised up, who is at the right hand of God and who intercedes for us?—The word of the Lord. ℟. **Thanks be**
to God. ↓

GOSPEL Mk 9, 2-10   [Jesus Transfigured]
Verse before the Gospel
℟. **Praise and honor to you, Lord Jesus Christ!**

From the shining cloud the Father's voice is heard:
this is my beloved Son; hear him.

℟. **Praise and honor to you, Lord Jesus Christ!**

> Jesus becomes transfigured before Peter, James and John.
> God spoke, "This is my Son, my beloved. Listen to him."
> Jesus asked his disciples to keep this a strict secret until he
> would be raised from the dead.

℣. The Lord be with you. ℟. **And also with you.**

✝ A reading from the holy gospel according to Mark.

℟. **Glory to you, Lord.**

JESUS took Peter, James and John off by themselves with him and led them up a high mountain.
He was transfigured before their eyes and his clothes
became dazzlingly white—whiter than the work of
any bleacher could make them. Elijah appeared to
them along with Moses; the two were in conversation
with Jesus. Then Peter spoke to Jesus: "Rabbi, how
good it is for us to be here. Let us erect three booths
on this site, one for you, one for Moses, and one for
Elijah." He hardly knew what to say, for they were all
overcome with awe. A cloud came, overshadowing
them, and out of the cloud a voice: "This is my Son,
my beloved. Listen to him." Suddenly looking around
they no longer saw anyone with them—only Jesus.

As they were coming down the mountain, he strictly
enjoined them not to tell anyone what they had seen
before the Son of Man had risen from the dead. They
kept this word of his to themselves, though they continued to discuss what "to rise from the dead"
meant.—The gospel of the Lord. ℟. **Praise to you,
Lord Jesus Christ.**   ➔ No. 14, p. 18

PRAYER OVER THE GIFTS   [Holiness]

Lord,
make us holy.
May this eucharist take away our sins

that we may be prepared
to celebrate the resurrection.
We ask this in the name of Jesus the Lord. ℟. **Amen.** ↓

PREFACE (P 13)   [Jesus in Glory]

℣. The Lord be with you. ℟. **And also with you.**
℣. Lift up your hearts. ℟. **We lift them up to the Lord.**
℣. Let us give thanks to the Lord our God. ℟. **It is right to give him thanks and praise.**

Father, all-powerful and ever-living God,
we do well always and everywhere to give you thanks
through Jesus Christ our Lord.
On your holy mountain he revealed himself in glory
in the presence of his disciples.
He had already prepared them for his approaching
   death.
He wanted to teach them through the Law and the
   Prophets
that the promised Christ had first to suffer
and so come to the glory of his resurrection.
In our unending joy we echo on earth
the song of the angels in heaven
as they praise your glory for ever: → No. 23, p. 23

COMMUNION ANT. Mt 17, 5   [Son of God]

This is my Son, my beloved, in whom is all my delight: listen to him. ↓

PRAYER AFTER COMMUNION   [Life To Come]

Lord,
we give thanks for these holy mysteries
which bring to us here on earth
a share in the life to come, through Christ our Lord.
℟. **Amen.**   → No. 32, p. 70

Optional Solemn Blessings, p. 92, and Prayers Over the People, p. 99

"Stop turning my Father's house into a marketplace."

MARCH 2

3rd SUNDAY OF LENT

ENTRANCE ANT. Ps 25, 15-16   [Eyes on God]

My eyes are ever fixed on the Lord, for he releases
my feet from the snare. O look at me and be merciful,
for I am wretched and alone.

OR Ez 36, 23-26   [A New Spirit]

I will prove my holiness through you. I will gather
you from the ends of the earth; I will pour clean water
on you and wash away all your sins. I will give you a
new spirit within you, says the Lord.

→ No. 2, p. 10 (Omit Gloria)

OPENING PRAYER   [Prayer, Fasting, Works]

Let us pray
   [for confidence in the love of God
   and the strength to overcome all our weaknesses]
Father,
you have taught us to overcome our sins
by prayer, fasting and works of mercy.
When we are discouraged by our weakness,
give us confidence in your love.

We ask this through our Lord Jesus Christ, your Son,
who lives and reigns with you and the Holy Spirit,
one God, for ever and ever. ℟. **Amen.** ↓

ALTERNATIVE OPENING PRAYER   [A New Heart]

Let us pray
  [to the Father and ask him
  to form a new heart within us]
God of all compassion, Father of all goodness,
to heal the wounds our sins and selfishness bring
    upon us
you bid us turn to fasting, prayer, and sharing with
    our brothers.
We acknowledge our sinfulness, our guilt is ever be-
    fore us:
when our weakness causes discouragement,
let your compassion fill us with hope
and lead us through a Lent of repentance to the
    beauty of Easter joy.
Grant this through Christ our Lord. ℟. **Amen.** ↓

READING I Ex 20, 1-17 or 20, 1-3. 7-8. 12-17

[Ten Commandments]

**God speaks to his people and gives them a code of life to
follow—the Commandments. The first three describe how
he is to be worshiped and the remaining rules outline how
the people are to respect and live with one another.**

*[If the "Short Form" is used, the indented text in brackets is
omitted.]*

A reading from the book of Exodus

GOD delivered all these commandments: "I, the
Lord, am your God, who brought you out of the
land of Egypt, that place of slavery. You shall not
have other gods besides me.

  [You shall not carve idols for yourselves in the
  shape of anything in the sky above or on the

earth below or in the waters beneath the earth; you shall not bow down before them or worship them. For I, the Lord, your God, am a jealous God, inflicting punishment for their fathers' wickedness on the children of those who hate me, down to the third and fourth generation; but bestowing mercy down to the thousandth generation, on the children of those who love me and keep my commandments.]

"You shall not take the name of the Lord, your God, in vain. For the Lord will not leave unpunished him who takes his name in vain.

"Remember to keep holy the sabbath day.

[Six days you may labor and do all your work, but the seventh day is the sabbath of the Lord, your God. No work may be done then either by you, or your son or daughter, or your male or female slave, or your beast, or by the alien who lives with you. In six days the Lord made the heavens and the earth, the sea and all that is in them; but on the seventh day he rested. That is why the Lord has blessed the sabbath day and made it holy.]

"Honor your father and your mother, that you may have a long life in the land which the Lord, your God, is giving you.

"You shall not kill.

"You shall not commit adultery.

"You shall not steal.

"You shall not bear false witness against your neighbor.

"You shall not covet your neighbor's house. You shall not covet your neighbor's wife, nor his male or female slave, nor his ox or ass, nor anything else that belongs to him."—The word of the Lord. ℟. **Thanks be to God.** ↓

RESPONSORIAL PSALM Ps 19   [Words of Life]

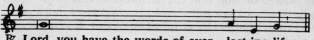

℟. **Lord, you have the words of ever - last-ing life.**

The law of the Lord is perfect,
    refreshing the soul;
The decree of the Lord is trustworthy,
    giving wisdom to the simple.

℟. **Lord, you have the words of everlasting life.**

The precepts of the Lord are right,
    rejoicing the heart;
The command of the Lord is clear,
    enlightening the eye.

℟. **Lord, you have the words of everlasting life.**

The fear of the Lord is pure,
    enduring forever;
The ordinances of the Lord are true,
    all of them just.

℟. **Lord, you have the words of everlasting life.**

They are more precious than gold,
    than a heap of purest gold;
Sweeter also than syrup
    or honey from the comb.

℟. **Lord, you have the words of everlasting life.** ↓

READING II 1 Cor 1, 22-25   [Christ, the Power of God]

Paul admits that the preaching of Christ crucified is regarded as absurd by some. Still, for those who have faith,
Christ is the power and wisdom of God.

A reading from the first letter of Paul
to the Corinthians

JEWS demand "signs" and Greeks look for "wisdom," but we preach Christ crucified, a stumbling
block to Jews, and an absurdity to Gentiles; but to

those who are called, Jews and Greeks alike, Christ is the power of God and the wisdom of God. For God's folly is wiser than men, and his weakness more powerful than men.—The word of the Lord. ℟. **Thanks be to God.** ↓

GOSPEL Jn 2, 13-25   [Prediction of the Resurrection]
Verse before the Gospel (Jn 3, 16)

℟. **Glory and praise to you, Lord Jesus Christ!**

God loved the world so much, he gave us his only Son, that all who believe in him might have eternal life.

℟. **Glory and praise to you, Lord Jesus Christ!** ↓

> Jesus becomes angry when the temple, which is to be a house of prayer, is turned into a place of business. He drives the merchants out.

℣. The Lord be with you. ℟. **And also with you.**
✢ A reading from the holy gospel according to John.
℟. **Glory to you, Lord.**

AS the Jewish Passover was near, Jesus went up to Jerusalem. In the temple precincts he came upon people engaged in selling oxen, sheep and doves, and others seated changing coins. He made a [kind of] whip of cords and drove them all out of the temple area, sheep and oxen alike, and knocked over the money-changers' tables, spilling their coins. He told those who were selling doves: "Get them out of here! Stop turning my Father's house into a marketplace!" His disciples recalled the words of Scripture: "Zeal for your house consumes me."

At this the Jews responded, "What sign can you show us authorizing you to do these things?" "Destroy this temple," was Jesus' answer, "and in three days I will raise it up." They retorted, "This temple took forty-six years to build, and you are going to raise it up in three days!" Actually he was talking about the temple of his body. Only after Jesus had been raised

from the dead did his disciples recall that he had said
this, and come to believe the Scripture and the word
he had spoken.

While he was in Jerusalem during the Passover festival, many believed in his name, for they could see
the signs he was performing. For his part, Jesus would
not trust himself to them because he knew them all.
He needed no one to give him testimony about human
nature. He was well aware of what was in man's
heart.—The gospel of the Lord. ℟. **Praise to you, Lord
Jesus Christ.**   → No. 14, p. 18

Or the Gospel (Jn 4, 5-42) from Year A may be said.

PRAYER OVER THE GIFTS   [Forgiveness]

Lord,
by the grace of this sacrifice
may we who ask forgiveness
be ready to forgive one another.
We ask this through Christ our Lord.
℟. **Amen.**   → No. 21, p. 22 (Pref. P 8-9)

COMMUNION ANT. Ps 84, 4-5   [God's House]

**The sparrow even finds a home, the swallow finds a
nest wherein to place her young, near to your altars,
Lord of hosts, my King, my God! How happy they who
dwell in your house! For ever they are praising you. ↓**

PRAYER AFTER COMMUNION   [Unity and Peace]

Lord,
in sharing this sacrament
may we receive your forgiveness
and be brought together in unity and peace.
We ask this through Christ our Lord.
℟. **Amen.**   → No. 32, p. 70

Optional Solemn Blessings, p. 92, and Prayers Over the People, p. 99

"The light came into the world but men loved darkness rather than the light."

MARCH 9

4th SUNDAY OF LENT

ENTRANCE ANT. See Is 66, 10-11 **[Rejoice]**

Rejoice, Jerusalem! Be glad for her, you who love her; rejoice with her, you who mourned for her, and you will find contentment at her consoling breasts.

→ No. 2, p. 10 (Omit Gloria)

OPENING PRAYER **[Faith and Love]**

Let us pray
  [for a greater faith and love]
Father of peace,
we are joyful in your Word,
your Son Jesus Christ,
who reconciles us to you.
Let us hasten toward Easter
with the eagerness of faith and love.
We ask this through our Lord Jesus Christ, your Son,
who lives and reigns with you and the Holy Spirit,
one God, for ever and ever. ℟. **Amen.** ↓

ALTERNATIVE OPENING PRAYER   [Bringing Peace]

Let us pray

[that by growing in love this lenten season
we may bring the peace of Christ to our world]
God our Father,
your Word, Jesus Christ, spoke peace to a sinful world
and brought mankind the gift of reconciliation
by the suffering and death he endured.
Teach us, the people who bear his name,
to follow the example he gave us:
may our faith, hope, and charity
turn hatred to love, conflict to peace, death to eternal life.
We ask this through Christ our Lord. ℟. **Amen.** ↓

READING I 2 Chr 36, 14-17. 19-23 [Punishment for Infidelity]

**The Israelites were repeatedly unfaithful to God. They ig-
nored the prophets sent to them. God allowed them to fall
to the Chaldeans. Jeremiah had foretold this punishment.**

A reading from the second book of Chronicles

ALL the princes of Judah, the priests and the people added infidelity to infidelity, practicing all the
abominations of the nations and polluting the Lord's
temple which he had consecrated in Jerusalem.

Early and often did the Lord, the God of their fathers, send his messengers to them, for he had compassion on his people and his dwelling place. But they
mocked the messengers of God, despised his warnings,
and scoffed at his prophets, until the anger of the Lord
against his people was so inflamed that there was no
remedy. Then he brought up against them the king of
the Chaldeans, who slew their young men in their own
sanctuary building, sparing neither young man nor
maiden, neither the aged nor the decrepit; he delivered
all of them over into his grip. Finally, their enemies
burnt the house of God, tore down the walls of Jerusalem, set all its palaces afire, and destroyed all its pre-

cious objects. Those who escaped the sword he carried captive to Babylon, where they became his and his son's servants until the kingdom of the Persians came to power. All this was to fulfill the word of the Lord spoken by Jeremiah: "Until the land has retrieved its lost sabbaths, during all the time it lies waste it shall have rest while seventy years are fulfilled."

In the first year of Cyrus, king of Persia, in order to fulfill the word of the Lord spoken by Jeremiah, the Lord inspired King Cyrus of Persia to issue this proclamation throughout his kingdom, both by word of mouth and in writing: "Thus says Cyrus, king of Persia: 'All the kingdoms of the earth the Lord, the God of heaven, has given to me, and he has also charged me to build him a house in Jerusalem, which is in Judah. Whoever, therefore, among you belongs to any part of his people, let him go up, and may his God be with him.' "—The word of the Lord. ℟. **Thanks be to God.** ↓

RESPONSORIAL PSALM Ps 137   [Remembrance of Zion]

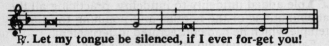

℟. **Let my tongue be silenced, if I ever for-get you!**

By the streams of Babylon
    we sat and wept when we remembered Zion.
On the aspens of that land
    we hung up our harps.

℟. **Let my tongue be silenced, if I ever forget you!**

Though there our captors asked of us
    the lyrics of our songs,
And our despoilers urged us to be joyous:
    "Sing for us the songs of Zion!"

℟. **Let my tongue be silenced, if I ever forget you!**

How could we sing a song of the Lord
    in a foreign land?

If I forget you, Jerusalem,
  may my right hand be forgotten!

℟. **Let my tongue be silenced, if I ever forget you!**

May my tongue cleave to my palate
  if I remember you not,
If I place not Jerusalem
  ahead of my joy.

℟. **Let my tongue be silenced, if I ever forget you!** ↓

READING II Eph 2, 4-10   [God's Gift: Salvation]

God's mercy and love brought Jesus into the world. Salvation is God's gift, it is not the work of human beings. Jesus leads all to perform good works.

A reading from the letter of Paul
to the Ephesians

GOD is rich in mercy; because of his great love for us he brought us to life with Christ when we were dead in sin. By this favor you were saved. Both with and in Christ Jesus he raised us up and gave us a place in the heavens, that in the ages to come he might display the great wealth of his favor, manifested by his kindness to us in Christ Jesus. I repeat, it is owing to his favor that salvation is yours through faith. This is not your own doing, it is God's gift; neither is it a reward for anything you have accomplished, so let no one pride himself on it. We are truly his handiwork, created in Christ Jesus to lead the life of good deeds which God prepared for us in advance.—The word of the Lord. ℟. **Thanks be to God.** ↓

GOSPEL Jn 3, 14-21   [Salvation in Christ]
Verse before the Gospel (Jn 3, 16)

℟. **Glory to you, Word of God, Lord Jesus Christ!**

God loved the world so much, he gave us his only Son, that all who believe in him might have eternal life.

℞. **Glory to you, Word of God, Lord Jesus Christ!** ↓

Jesus is to die on the cross—the proof of God's unlimited love for his people. God sent Jesus that we might believe.Through belief in him human beings will be saved.

℣. The Lord be with you. ℞. **And also with you.**
✝ A reading from the holy gospel according to John.
℞. **Glory to you, Lord.**

JESUS said to Nicodemus:
"Just as Moses lifted up the serpent in the desert,
so must the Son of Man be lifted up,
that all who believe
may have eternal life in him.
Yes, God so loved the world
that he gave his only Son,
that whoever believes in him may not die
but may have eternal life.
God did not send the Son into the world
to condemn the world,
but that the world might be saved through him.
Whoever believes in him avoids condemnation,
but whoever does not believe is already condemned
for not believing in the name of God's only Son.
The judgment in question is this:
the light came into the world,
but men loved darkness rather than light
because their deeds were wicked.
Everyone who practices evil
hates the light;
he does not come near it
for fear his deeds will be exposed.
But he who acts in truth
comes into the light,
to make clear
that his deeds are done in God."
The gospel of the Lord. ℞. **Praise to you, Lord Jesus Christ.**
→ No. 14, p. 18

Or the Gospel (Jn 9, 1-41) from Year A may be said.

PRAYER OVER THE GIFTS   [Increased Reverence]

Lord,
we offer you these gifts
which bring us peace and joy.
Increase our reverence by this eucharist,
and bring salvation to the world.
We ask this through Christ our Lord.
℞. **Amen.**   ➔ No. 21, p. 22 (Pref. P 8-9)

COMMUNION ANT. Ps 122, 3-4   [Praise]

**To Jerusalem, that binds them together in unity, the
tribes of the Lord go up to give him praise.** ↓

PRAYER AFTER COMMUNION   [Light of the Gospel]

Father,
you enlighten all who come into the world.
Fill our hearts with the light of your gospel,
that our thoughts may please you,
and our love be sincere.
Grant this through Christ our Lord.
℞. **Amen.**   ➔ No. 32, p. 70

Optional Solemn Blessings, p. 92, and Prayers Over the People, p. 99

Some bystanders heard a voice from the sky and maintained,
"An angel from heaven was speaking to him."

MARCH 16

5th SUNDAY OF LENT

ENTRANCE ANT. Ps 43, 1-2   [Rescue Me]

**Give me justice, O God, and defend my cause against
the wicked; rescue me from deceitful and unjust men.
You, O God, are my refuge.**

→ No. 2, p. 10 (Omit Gloria)

OPENING PRAYER   [Courage To Follow Christ]

Let us pray
  [for the courage to follow Christ]
Father,
help us to be like Christ your Son,
who loved the world and died for our salvation.
Inspire us by his love,
guide us by his example,
who lives and reigns with you and the Holy Spirit,
one God, for ever and ever. ℟. **Amen.** ↓

ALTERNATIVE OPENING PRAYER

[Transforming the World]

Let us pray
  [for the courage to embrace the world
  in the name of Christ]
Father in heaven,
the love of your Son led him to accept the suffering of
    the cross
that his brothers might glory in new life.
Change our selfishness into self-giving.
Help us to embrace the world you have given us,
that we may transform the darkness of its pain
into the life and joy of Easter.
Grant this through Christ our Lord. ℞. **Amen.** ↓

READING I Jer 31, 31-34   [A New Covenant]

**The Lord promises a new covenant wherein his law will be
written in the hearts of his people. They will recognize God
as their Lord and he will forgive their sins.**

A reading from the book of the prophet Jeremiah

THE days are coming, says the Lord, when I will
    make a new covenant with the house of Israel and
the house of Judah. It will not be like the covenant I
made with their fathers the day I took them by the
hand to lead them forth from the land of Egypt; for
they broke my covenant, and I had to show myself
their master, says the Lord. But this is the covenant
which I will make with the house of Israel after those
days, says the Lord. I will place my law within them,
and write it upon their hearts; I will be their God,
and they shall be my people. No longer will they have
need to teach their friends and kinsmen how to know
the Lord. All, from least to greatest, shall know me,
says the Lord, for I will forgive their evildoing and remember their sin no more.—The word of the Lord. ℞.
Thanks be to God. ↓

RESPONSORIAL PSALM Ps 51   [A Clean Heart]

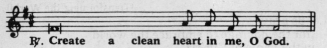

℟. **Create   a   clean   heart in me, O God.**

Have mercy on me, O God, in your goodness;
  in the greatness of your compassion wipe out my of-
    fense.
Thoroughly wash me from my guilt
  and of my sin cleanse me.

℟. **Create a clean heart in me, O God.**

A clean heart create for me, O God,
  and a steadfast spirit renew within me.
Cast me not out from your presence,
  and your holy spirit take not from me.

℟. **Create a clean heart in me, O God.**

Give me back the joy of your salvation,
  and a willing spirit sustain in me.
I will teach transgressors your ways,
  and sinners shall return to you.

℟. **Create a clean heart in me, O God.** ↓

READING II Heb 5, 7-9   [Christ's Obedience]

**We recall how Jesus prayed to his Father. Through obedi-
ence to suffering, Jesus became perfect and is the source of
salvation for all who obey him.**

A reading from the letter to the Hebrews

IN the days when Christ was in the flesh, he offered
prayers and supplications with loud cries and tears
to God, who was able to save him from death, and he
was heard because of his reverence. Son though he
was, he learned obedience from what he suffered; and
when perfected, he became the source of eternal salvation for all who obey him.—The word of the Lord.
℟. **Thanks be to God.** ↓

GOSPEL Jn 12, 20-33   [Christ Draws All]
Verse before the Gospel (Jn 12, 26)

℟. **Praise and honor to you, Lord Jesus Christ!**

If you serve me, follow me, says the Lord;
and where I am, my servant will also be.

℟. **Praise and honor to you, Lord Jesus Christ!**

> Jesus predicts his glorification. It comes by dying like the grain of wheat. Those who love their life inordinately will lose it. The Father from heaven answers Jesus.

℣. The Lord be with you. ℟. **And also with you.**
✤ A reading from the holy gospel according to John.
℟. **Glory to you, Lord.**

AMONG those who had come up to worship at the feast of Passover were some Greeks. They approached Philip, who was from Bethsaida in Galilee, and put this request to him: "Sir, we should like to see Jesus." Philip went to tell Andrew; Philip and Andrew in turn came to inform Jesus. Jesus answered them:

"The hour has come
for the Son of Man to be glorified.
I solemnly assure you,
unless the grain of wheat falls to the earth and dies,
it remains just a grain of wheat.
But if it dies,
it produces much fruit.
The man who loves his life
loses it,
while the man who hates his life in this world
preserves it to life eternal.
If anyone would serve me,
let him follow me;
where I am,
there will my servant be.
Anyone who serves me,
the Father will honor.

My soul is troubled now,
yet what should I say—
Father, save me from this hour?
But it was for this that I came to this hour.
Father, glorify your name!"

Then a voice came from the sky:

"I have glorified it,
and will glorify it again."

When the crowd of bystanders heard the voice, they said it was thunder. Others maintained, "An angel was speaking to him." Jesus answered, "That voice did not come for my sake, but for yours.

"Now has judgment come upon this world,
now will this world's prince be driven out,
and I—once I am lifted up from earth—
will draw all men to myself."

(This statement of his indicated the sort of death he was going to die.)—The gospel of the Lord. ℟. **Praise to you, Lord Jesus Christ.**   ➜ No. 14, p. 18

Or the Gospel (Jn 11, 1-45) from Year A may be said.

PRAYER OVER THE GIFTS   [Take Away Sins]

Almighty God,
may the sacrifice we offer
take away the sins of those
whom you enlighten with the Christian faith.
We ask this in the name of Jesus the Lord.
℟. **Amen.**   ➜ No. 21, p. 22 (Pref. P 8-9)

COMMUNION ANT. Jn 12, 24-25   [Life Through Death]

I tell you solemnly: Unless a grain of wheat falls on the ground and dies, it remains a single grain; but if it dies, it yields a rich harvest. ↓

PRAYER AFTER COMMUNION   [Union with Jesus]

Almighty Father,
by this sacrifice
may we always remain one with your Son, Jesus
    Christ,
whose body and blood we share,
for he is Lord for ever and ever.
℞. **Amen.**   → No. 32, p. 70

Optional Solemn Blessings, p. 92, and Prayers Over the People, p. 99

*"Blessed are you who have come to us
so rich in love and mercy."*

MARCH 23

PASSION SUNDAY
[PALM SUNDAY]

Commemoration of the Lord's Entrance
into Jerusalem

FIRST FORM: THE PROCESSION

At the scheduled time, the congregation assembles in a secondary church or chapel or in some other suitable place distinct from the church to which the procession will move. The faithful carry palm branches.

The following antiphon or any other appropriate song is sung.

ANTIPHON Mt 21, 9   [Hosanna]

**Hosanna to the Son of David,
the King of Israel.
Blessed is he who comes
in the name of the Lord.
Hosanna in the highest.**

The priest then greets the people in the usual way and gives a brief introduction, inviting them to take a full part in the celebration, using these or similar words:

174

Dear friends in Christ, for five weeks of Lent we have been preparing, by works of charity and self-sacrifice, for the celebration of our Lord's paschal mystery. Today we come together to begin this solemn celebration in union with the whole Church throughout the world. Christ entered in triumph into his own city, to complete his work as our Messiah: to suffer, to die, and to rise again. Let us remember with devotion this entry which began his saving work and follow him with a lively faith. United with him in his suffering on the cross, may we share his resurrection and new life.

Afterwards the priest, with hands joined, says one of the following prayers:

PRAYER   [Following Christ]

Let us pray.
Almighty God,
we pray you
bless ✠ these branches
and make them holy.
Today we joyfully acclaim Jesus our Messiah and
    King.
May we reach one day the happiness of the new and
    everlasting Jerusalem
by faithfully following him
who lives and reigns for ever and ever. ℟. **Amen.** ↓

OR   [Christ Our King]

Let us pray.
Lord,
increase the faith of your people
and listen to our prayers.
Today we honor Christ our triumphant King
by carrying these branches.
May we honor you every day
by living always in him,
for he is Lord for ever and ever. ℟. **Amen.** ↓

The priest sprinkles the branches with holy water in silence.

*Then the account of the Lord's entrance is proclaimed from
one of the four gospels. This is done in the usual way or, if
there is no deacon, by the priest.*

GOSPEL Mk 11, 1-10   [Jesus' Triumphal Entry]

In triumphant glory Jesus comes into Jerusalem. The people spread their cloaks on the ground for him, wave olive
branches and sing in his honor.

℣. The Lord be with you. ℟. **And also with you.**

✛ A reading from the holy gospel according to Mark.

℟. **Glory to you, Lord.**

AS the crowd drew near Bethphage and Bethany on
the Mount of Olives, close to Jerusalem, Jesus
sent off two of his disciples with the instruction: "Go
to the village straight ahead of you, and as soon as
you enter it you will find tethered there a colt on
which no one has ridden. Untie it and bring it back. If
anyone says to you, 'Why are you doing that?' say,
'The Master needs it but he will send it back here at
once.' " So they went off, and finding a colt tethered
out on the street near a gate, they untied it. Some of
the bystanders said to them, "What do you mean by
untying that colt?" They answered as Jesus had told
them to, and the men let them take it. They brought
the colt to Jesus and threw their cloaks across its
back, and he sat on it. Many people spread their
cloaks on the road, while others spread reeds which
they had cut in the fields. Those preceding him as well
as those who followed cried out:

"Hosanna!
Blessed be he who comes in the name of the Lord!
Blessed be the reign of our father David to come!
God save him from on high!"

The gospel of the Lord. ℟. **Praise to you, Lord Jesus
Christ.**

OR

GOSPEL Jn 12, 12-16   [Blessed Is Israel's King]

(See commentary in preceding Gospel.)

℣. The Lord be with you. ℟. **And also with you.**

✝ A reading from the holy gospel according to John.
℟. **Glory to you, Lord.**

THE great crowd that had come for the feast heard
that Jesus was to enter Jerusalem, so they got
palm branches and came out to meet him. They kept
shouting:

"Hosanna!
Blessed is he who comes in the name of the Lord!
Blessed is the King of Israel!"

Jesus found a donkey and mounted it, in accord with
Scripture:

"Fear not, O daughter of Zion!
Your king approaches you
on a donkey's colt."

(At first, the disciples did not understand all this, but
after Jesus was glorified they recalled that the people
had done to him precisely what had been written
about him.)—The gospel of the Lord. ℟. **Praise to you,
Lord Jesus Christ.**

After the gospel, a brief homily may be given. Before the pro-
cession begins, the celebrant or other suitable minister may
address the people in these or similar words:

Let us go forth in peace
praising Jesus our Messiah,
as did the crowds who welcomed him to Jerusalem.

The procession to the church where Mass will be celebrated
then begins.

If incense is used, the thurifer goes first with a lighted censer,
followed by the cross-bearer (with the cross suitably deco-
rated) between two ministers with lighted candles, then the
priest with the ministers, and finally the congregation carry-
ing branches.

*During the procession, the choir and people sing the follow-
ing or other appropriate songs:*

ANTIPHON 1   [Hosanna]

**The children of Jerusalem
welcomed Christ the King.
They carried olive branches
and loudly praised the Lord:
Hosanna in the highest.**

*The above antiphon may be repeated between verses of Psalm
24.*

PSALM 24   [The King of Glory]

The Lord's are the earth and its fullness;
  the world and those who dwell in it.
For he founded it upon the seas
  and established it upon the rivers.

Repeat antiphon 1

Who can ascend the mountain of the Lord?
  or who may stand in his holy place?
He whose hands are sinless, whose heart is clean,
  who desires not what is vain,
  nor swears deceitfully to his neighbor.

Repeat antiphon 1

He shall receive a blessing from the Lord,
  a reward from God his savior.
Such is the race that seeks for him,
  that seeks the face of the God of Jacob.

Repeat antiphon 1

Lift up, O gates, your lintels;
  reach up, you ancient portals,
  that the king of glory may come in!
Who is this king of glory?
  The Lord, strong and mighty,
  the Lord, mighty in battle.

Repeat antiphon 1

Lift up, O gates, your lintels;
    reach up, you ancient portals,
        that the king of glory may come in!
Who is this king of glory?
    The Lord of hosts; he is the king of glory.

Repeat antiphon 1

ANTIPHON 2   [Hosanna]

The children of Jerusalem
welcomed Christ the King.
They spread their cloaks before him
and loudly praised the Lord:
Hosanna to the Son of David!
Blessed is he who comes
in the name of the Lord!

The above antiphon may be repeated between the verses of Psalm 47.

Psalm 47   [The Great King]

All you peoples, clap your hands,
    shout to God with cries of gladness.
For the Lord, the Most High, the awesome,
    is the great king over all the earth.

Repeat antiphon 2

He brings peoples under us;
    nations under our feet.
He chooses for us our inheritance,
    the glory of Jacob, whom he loves.

Repeat antiphon 2

God mounts his throne amid shouts of joy;
    the Lord, amid trumpet blasts.
Sing praise to God, sing praise;
    sing praise to our king, sing praise.

Repeat antiphon 2

For king of all the earth is God;
   sing hymns of praise.
God reigns over the nations,
   God sits upon his holy throne.

Repeat antiphon 2

The princes of the peoples are gathered together
   with the people of the God of Abraham.
For God's are the guardians of the earth;
   he is supreme.

Repeat antiphon 2

A hymn in honor of Christ the King, such as All Glory,
Laud and Honor, *is sung during the procession. See p. 614
for text.*

*As the procession enters the church, the following responsory
or another song which refers to the Lord's entrance is sung.*

RESPONSORY   [Hosanna]

℟. The children of Jerusalem
welcomed Christ the King.
They proclaimed the resurrection of life,
and, waving olive branches,
they loudly praised the Lord:
Hosanna in the highest.

℣. When the people heard that Jesus
was entering Jerusalem,
they went to meet him
and, waving olive branches,
they loudly praised the Lord:
Hosanna in the highest.

*When the priest comes to the altar he venerates it and may
also incense it. Then he goes to his chair (removes the cope
and puts on the chasuble) and begins immediately the opening prayer of Mass, which concludes the procession. Mass
then continues in the usual way.*

SECOND FORM: THE SOLEMN ENTRANCE

If the procession cannot be held outside the church, the commemoration of the Lord's entrance may be celebrated before the principal Mass with the solemn entrance, which takes place within the church.

The faithful, holding the branches, assemble either in front of the church door or inside the church. The priest and ministers, with a representative group of the faithful, go to a suitable place in the church outside the sanctuary, so that most of the people will be able to see the rite.

While the priest goes to the appointed place, the antiphon Hosanna *or other suitable song is sung. Then the blessing of branches and proclamation of the gospel about the Lord's entrance into Jerusalem take place, as above. After the gospel the priest, with the ministers and the group of the faithful, moves solemnly through the church to the sanctuary, while the responsory* The children of Jerusalem *or other appropriate song is sung.*

When the priest comes to the altar he venerates it, goes to his chair, and immediately begins the opening prayer of Mass, which then continues in the usual way.

THIRD FORM: THE SIMPLE ENTRANCE

At all other Masses on this Sunday, if the solemn entrance is not held, the Lord's entrance is commemorated with the following simple entrance.

While the priest goes to the altar, the entrance antiphon with its psalm or another song with the same theme is sung.

ENTRANCE ANT.   [Praise the Lord]

Six days before the solemn passover the Lord came to Jerusalem, and children waving palm branches ran out to welcome him. They loudly praised the Lord: Blessed are you who have come to us so rich in love and mercy.

PSALM 24:9-10   [The King of Glory]

Open wide the doors and gates.
Lift high the ancient portals.
The King of glory enters.
Who is this King of glory?
He is God the mighty Lord.
Hosanna in the highest.
Blessed are you who have come to us
so rich in love and mercy.
Hosanna in the highest.

*Where neither the procession nor the solemn entrance can be
celebrated, there should be a bible service on the theme of the
Lord's messianic entrance and passion, either on Saturday
evening or on Sunday at a convenient time.*

MASS

*After the procession or solemn entrance the priest begins the
Mass with the opening prayer.*

OPENING PRAYER   [Union with Christ]

Let us pray
   [for a closer union with Christ
   during this holy season]
Almighty, ever-living God,
you have given the human race Jesus Christ our Savior
as a model of humility.
He fulfilled your will
by becoming man and giving his life on the cross.
Help us to bear witness to you
by following his example of suffering
and make us worthy to share in his resurrection.
We ask this through our Lord Jesus Christ, your Son,
who lives and reigns with you and the Holy Spirit,
one God, for ever and ever. ℟. **Amen.** ↓

ALTERNATIVE OPENING PRAYER

[Guided by Christ's Truth]

Let us pray
[as we accompany our King to Jerusalem]
Almighty Father of our Lord Jesus Christ,
you sent your Son
to be born of woman and to die on a cross,
so that through the obedience of one man,
estrangement might be dissolved for all men.
Guide our minds by his truth
and strengthen our lives by the example of his death,
that we may live in union with you
in the kingdom of your promise.
Grant this through Christ our Lord. ℟. **Amen.** ↓

READING I Is 50, 4-7   [Christ's Suffering]

Isaiah was persecuted and struck by his own people; he
was spit upon and beaten. He proclaims the true faith and
suffers to atone for the sins of his people. Here we see a
foreshadowing of the true servant of God.

A reading from the book of the prophet Isaiah

THE Lord God has given me
a well-trained tongue,
That I might know how to speak to the weary
a word that will rouse them.
Morning after morning
he opens my ear that I may hear;
And I have not rebelled,
have not turned back.
I gave my back to those who beat me,
my cheeks to those who plucked my beard;
My face I did not shield
from buffets and spitting.
The Lord God is my help,
therefore I am not disgraced;
I have set my face like flint,
knowing that I shall not be put to shame.
The word of the Lord. ℟. **Thanks be to God.** ↓

RESPONSORIAL PSALM Ps 22 [Christ's Abandonment]

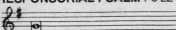

℟. **My God, my God, why have you a-ban-doned me?**

All who see me scoff at me;
  they mock me with parted lips, they wag their
    heads:
"He relied on the Lord; let him deliver him,
  let him rescue him, if he loves him."—℟.

Indeed, many dogs surround me,
  a pack of evildoers closes in upon me;
They have pierced my hands and my feet;
  I can count all my bones.—℟.

They divide my garments among them,
  and for my vesture they cast lots.
But you, O Lord, be not far from me;
  O my help, hasten to aid me.—℟.

I will proclaim your name to my brethren;
  in the midst of the assembly I will praise you:
"You who fear the Lord, praise him;
  all you descendants of Jacob, give glory to him."

℟. **My God, my God, why have you abandoned me?** ↓

READING II Phil 2, 6-11 [Humility]

**Paul urges us to humility by which we are made like to
Christ, our Lord, who, putting off the majesty of his divinity, became man and humbled himself in obedience to the
ignominious death of the cross.**

A reading from the letter of Paul
to the Philippians

YOUR attitude must be Christ's:
  though he was in the form of God
he did not deem equality with God
something to be grasped at.

Rather, he emptied himself
    and took the form of a slave,
    being born in the likeness of men.
He was known to be of human estate,
    and it was thus that he humbled himself,
    obediently accepting even death,
    death on a cross!
Because of this,
    God highly exalted him
    and bestowed on him the name
    above every other name,
So that at Jesus' name
    every knee must bend
    in the heavens, on the earth,
    and under the earth,
    and every tongue proclaim
    to the glory of God the Father:
    JESUS CHRIST IS LORD!
The word of the Lord. ℟. **Thanks be to God.** ↓

GOSPEL Mk 14, 1—15, 47 or 15, 1-39   [Christ's Passion]
Verse before the Gospel

℟. **Praise to you, Lord Jesus Christ, king of endless glory!**

Christ became obedient for us even to death,
dying on the cross.
Therefore God raised him on high
and gave him a name above all other names.

℟. **Praise to you, Lord Jesus Christ, king of endless glory!** ↓

The Passion of our Lord Jesus Christ
according to Mark

Mark recounts the events that led up to the betrayal of
Jesus and his final condemnation—his death on the cross.
At the Last Supper, Jesus institutes the Holy Eucharist.

*When the Short Form is read, the Passion begins at no. 8
below and ends after no. 13, pp. 191-193.*

*The fourteen subheadings introduced into the reading enable
those who so desire to meditate on this text while making the
Stations of the Cross.*

*The Passion may be read by lay readers, with the part of
Christ, if possible, read by a priest. The Narrator is noted by
C (Chronista), the words of Jesus by a ✠ and the words of
others by S (Synagoga), groups in the account by SS. The
words of the narrator enclosed in brackets may be omitted.
The part of the Synagoga marked with SS and printed in
boldface type may be recited by the people.*

1. THE PLOT AGAINST JESUS AND
THE SUPPER AT BETHANY

C. The feasts of Passover and Unleavened Bread
were to be observed in two days' time, and therefore
the chief priests and scribes began to look for a way to
arrest Jesus by some trick and kill him. Yet they
pointed out, **SS. "Not during the festival, or the people may riot."**

C. When Jesus was in Bethany reclining at table in
the house of Simon the leper, a woman entered carrying an alabaster jar of perfume made from expensive
aromatic nard. Breaking the jar, she began to pour the
perfume on his head. Some were saying to themselves
indignantly: **SS. "What is the point of this extrava-
gant waste of perfume? It could have been sold for
over three hundred silver pieces and the money given
to the poor." C.** They were infuriated at her. But Jesus
said: ✠ "Let her alone. Why do you criticize her? She
has done me a kindness. The poor you will always
have with you and you can be generous to them whenever you wish, but you will not always have me. She
has done what she could. By perfuming my body she
is anticipating its preparation for burial. I assure you,
wherever the good news is proclaimed throughout the
world, what she has done will be told in her memory."

2. THE TREASON OF JUDAS

C. Then Judas Iscariot, one of the Twelve, went off to the chief priests to hand Jesus over to them. Hearing what he had to say, they were jubilant and promised to give him money. He for his part kept looking for an opportune way to hand him over.

3. THE LAST SUPPER

On the first day of Unleavened Bread, when it was customary to sacrifice the paschal lamb, his disciples said to him, **SS. "Where do you wish us to go to prepare the Passover supper for you?" C.** He sent two of his disciples with these instructions: ✠ "Go into the city and you will come upon a man carrying a water jar. Follow him. Whatever house he enters, say to the owner, 'The Teacher asks, Where is my guest room where I may eat the Passover with my disciples?' Then he will show you an upstairs room, spacious, furnished, and all in order. That is the place you are to get ready for us." **C.** The disciples went off. When they reached the city they found it just as he had told them, and they prepared the Passover supper.

As it grew dark he arrived with the Twelve. They reclined at table, and in the course of the meal Jesus said, ✠ "I give you my word, one of you is about to betray me, yes, one who is eating with me." **C.** They began to say to him sorrowfully, one by one, **S. "Surely not I!" C.** Jesus said, ✠ "It is one of the Twelve—a man who dips into the dish with me. The Son of Man is going the way the Scripture tells of him. Still, accursed be that man by whom the Son of Man is betrayed. It were better for him had he never been born."

C. During the meal he took bread, blessed and broke it, and gave it to them, saying: ✠ "Take this, this is my body." **C.** He likewise took a cup, gave thanks and passed it to them, and they all drank from it. He said to them: ✠ "This is my blood, the blood of the covenant, to be poured out on behalf of many. I solemnly assure you, I will never again drink of the fruit of the vine until the day when I drink it in the reign of God."

C. After singing songs of praise, they walked out to the Mount of Olives. Jesus then said to them: ✠ "Your faith in me shall be shaken, for Scripture has it,

'I will strike the shepherd
and the sheep will be dispersed.'

But after I am raised up, I will go to Galilee ahead of you." **C.** Peter said to him, **S.** "Even though all are shaken in faith, it will not be that way with me." **C.** Jesus answered, ✠ "I give you my assurance, this very night before the cock crows twice, you will deny me three times." **C.** But Peter kept reasserting vehemently, **S.** "Even if I have to die with you, I will not deny you." **C.** They all said the same.

4. THE PRAYER IN GETHSEMANI

They went then to a place named Gethsemani. He said to his disciples: ✠ "Sit down here while I pray." **C.** At the same time he took along with him Peter, James, and John. Then he began to be filled with fear and distress. He said to them, ✠ "My heart is filled with sorrow to the point of death. Remain here and stay awake." **C.** He advanced a little and fell to the ground, praying that if it were possible this hour might pass him by. He kept saying, ✠ "Abba (O Father), you have the power to do all things. Take this cup away from me. But let it be as you would have it, not as I." **C.** When he returned he found them asleep. He said to Peter, ✠ "Asleep, Simon? You could not stay awake for even an hour? Be on guard and pray that you may not be put to the test. The spirit is willing but nature is weak." **C.** Going back again he began to pray in the same words. Once again he found them asleep on his return. They could not keep their eyes open, nor did they know what to say to him. He returned a third time and said to them, ✠ "Still sleeping? Still taking your ease? It will have to do. The hour is on us. You will see that the Son of Man is to be handed over to the clutches of evil men. Rouse yourselves and come along. See! My betrayer is near."

5. THE ARREST OF JESUS

C. Even while he was still speaking, Judas, one of the Twelve, made his appearance accompanied by a crowd with swords and clubs; these people had been sent by the chief priests, the scribes, and the elders. The betrayer had arranged a signal for them, saying, **S.** "The man I shall embrace is the one; arrest him and lead him away, taking every precaution." **C.** He then went directly over to him and said, embracing him, **S.** "Rabbi!" **C.** At this, they laid hands on him and arrested him. One of the bystanders drew his sword and struck the high priest's slave, cutting off his ear. Addressing himself to them, Jesus said, ✠ "You have come out to arrest me armed with swords and clubs as if against a brigand. I was within your reach daily, teaching in the temple precincts, yet you never arrested me. But now, so that the Scriptures may be fulfilled. . . ." **C.** With that, all deserted him and fled. There was a young man following him who was covered by nothing but a linen cloth. As they seized him he left the cloth behind and ran off naked.

6. JESUS BEFORE CAIAPHAS

Then they led Jesus off to the high priest, and all the chief priests, the elders, and the scribes came together. Peter followed him at a distance right into the high priest's courtyard, where he found a seat with the temple guard and began to warm himself at the fire. The chief priests with the whole Sanhedrin were busy soliciting testimony against Jesus that would lead to his death, but they could not find any. Many spoke against him falsely under oath but their testimony did not agree. Some, for instance, on taking the stand, testified falsely by alleging, **SS. "We heard him declare, 'I will destroy this temple made by human hands,' and 'In three days I will construct another not made by human hands.' "** **C.** Even so, their testimony did not agree.

The high priest rose to his feet before the court and began to interrogate Jesus: **S.** "Have you no answer to what these men testify against you?" **C.** But Jesus remained silent; he made no reply. Once again the high priest interrogated him: **S.** "Are you the Messiah, the Son of the Blessed One?" **C.** Then Jesus answered: ✠ "I am; and you will see the Son of Man seated at the right hand of the Power and coming with the clouds of heaven." **C.** At that the high priest tore his robes and said: **S.** "What further need do we have of witnesses? You have heard the blasphemy. What is your verdict?" **C.** They all concurred in the verdict "guilty," with its sentence of death. Some of them then began to spit on him. They blindfolded him and hit him while the officers manhandled him, saying, **SS. "Play the prophet!"**

7. PETER'S DENIAL

C. While Peter was down in the courtyard, one of the servant girls of the high priest came along. When she noticed Peter warming himself, she looked more closely at him and said, **S.** "You too were with Jesus of Nazareth." **C.** But he denied it: **S.** "I do not know what you are talking about! What are you getting at?" **C.** Then he went out into the gateway. At that moment a cock crowed. The servant girl, keeping an eye on him, started again to tell the bystanders, **S.** "This man is one of them." **C.** Once again he denied it. A little later the bystanders said to Peter once more, **SS. "You are certainly one of them! You are a Galilean, are you not?" C.** He began to curse, and to swear, **S.** "I do not even know the man you are talking about!" **C.** Just then a second cockcrow was heard and Peter recalled the prediction Jesus had made to him, "Before the cock crows twice you will deny me three times." He broke down and began to cry.

[Beginning of Short Form]

8. JESUS BEFORE PILATE

As soon as it was daybreak the chief priests, with the elders and scribes (that is, the whole Sanhedrin), reached a decision. They bound Jesus, led him away, and handed him over to Pilate. Pilate interrogated him: **S.** "Are you the king of the Jews?" **C.** Jesus replied: ✝ "You are the one who is saying it." **C.** The chief priests, meanwhile, brought many accusations against him. Pilate interrogated him again: **S.** "Surely you have some answer? See how many accusations they are leveling against you." **C.** But greatly to Pilate's surprise, Jesus made no further response.

9. BARABBAS

Now on the occasion of a festival he would release for them one prisoner—any man they asked for. There was a prisoner named Barabbas jailed along with the rebels who had committed murder in the uprising. When the crowd came up to press their demand that he honor the custom, Pilate rejoined, **S.** "Do you want me to release the king of the Jews for you?" **C.** He was aware, of course, that it was out of jealousy that the chief priests had handed him over. Meanwhile, the chief priests incited the crowd to have him release Barabbas instead. Pilate again asked them, **S.** "What am I to do with the man you call the king of the

Jews?" **C.** They shouted back, **SS. "Crucify him!"** **C.** Pilate protested, **S.** "Why? What crime has he committed?" **C.** They only shouted the louder, **SS. "Crucify him!"** **C.** So Pilate, who wished to satisfy the crowd, released Barabbas to them, and after he had had Jesus scourged, he handed him over to be crucified.

10. THE CROWNING WITH THORNS

The soldiers now led Jesus away into the hall known as the praetorium; at the same time they assembled the whole cohort. They dressed him in royal purple, then wove a crown of thorns and put it on him, and began to salute him, **SS. "All hail! King of the Jews!"** **C.** Continually striking Jesus on the head with a reed and spitting at him, they genuflected before him and pretended to pay him homage. When they had finished mocking him, they stripped him of the purple, dressed him in his own clothes, and led him out to crucify him.

11. THE CRUCIFIXION

A man named Simon of Cyrene, the father of Alexander and Rufus, was coming in from the fields, and they pressed him into service to carry the cross. When they brought Jesus to the site of Golgotha (which means "Skull Place"), they tried to give him wine drugged with myrrh, but he would not take it. Then they crucified him and divided up his garments by rolling dice for them to see what each should take. It was about nine in the morning when they crucified him. The inscription proclaiming his offense read, "The King of the Jews." With him they crucified two insurgents, one at his right and one at his left.

12. ON CALVARY

People going by kept insulting him, tossing their heads and saying, **SS. "Ha, ha! So you were going to** destroy the temple and rebuild it in three days! Save yourself now by coming down from that cross!" **C.** The chief priests and the scribes also joined in and jeered: **SS. "He saved others but he cannot save himself! Let the 'Messiah,' the 'king of Israel,' come down from that cross here and now so that we can see it and believe in him!" C.** The men who had been crucified with him likewise kept taunting him.

13. THE DEATH OF JESUS

When noon came, darkness fell on the whole countryside and lasted until midafternoon. At that time Jesus cried in a loud voice, ✟ "Eloi, Eloi, lama sabachthani?" **C.** Which means, ✟ "My God, my God, why have you forsaken me?" **C.** A few of the bystanders who heard it remarked, **SS. "Listen! He is calling on Elijah!" C.** Someone ran off, and soaking a sponge in sour wine, stuck it on a reed to try to make him drink. The man said, **S.** "Now let's see whether Elijah comes to take him down." **C.** Then Jesus, uttering a loud cry, breathed his last.

(HERE KNEEL AND PAUSE MOMENTARILY)

At that moment the curtain in the sanctuary was torn in two from top to bottom. The centurion who stood guard over him, on seeing the manner of his death, declared, **S.** "Clearly this man was the Son of God!"

[End of Short Form]

14. THE BURIAL

C. There were also women looking on from a distance. Among them were Mary Magdalene, Mary the mother of James the younger and Joses, and Salome. These women had followed Jesus when he was in Galilee and attended to his needs. There were also many others who had come up with him to Jerusalem.

As it grew dark (it was Preparation Day, that is, the eve of the sabbath), Joseph from Arimathea arrived—a distinguished member of the Sanhedrin. He was another who looked forward to the reign of God. He was bold enough to seek an audience with Pilate, and urgently requested the body of Jesus. Pilate was surprised that Jesus should have died so soon. He summoned the centurion and inquired whether Jesus was already dead. Learning from him that he was dead, Pilate released the corpse to Joseph. Then, having bought a linen shroud, Joseph took him down, wrapped him in the linen, and laid him in a tomb which had been cut out of rock. Finally he rolled a stone across the entrance of the tomb. Meanwhile, Mary Magdalene and Mary the mother of Joses observed where he had been laid.　　→ No. 14, p. 18

PRAYER OVER THE GIFTS　　[Pleasing to God]

Lord,
may the suffering and death of Jesus, your only Son,
make us pleasing to you.
Alone we can do nothing,
but may this perfect sacrifice
win us your mercy and love.
We ask this in the name of Jesus the Lord. ℟. **Amen.** ↓

PREFACE (P 19)　　[Raised to Holiness of Life]

℣. The Lord be with you. ℟. **And also with you.**
℣. Lift up your hearts. ℟. **We lift them up to the Lord.**
℣. Let us give thanks to the Lord our God. ℟. **It is right to give him thanks and praise.**

Father, all-powerful and ever-living God,
we do well always and everywhere to give you thanks
through Jesus Christ our Lord.
Though he was sinless, he suffered willingly for sinners.

Though innocent, he accepted death to save the guilty.
By his dying he has destroyed our sins.
By his rising he has raised us up to holiness of life.
We praise you, Lord, with all the angels
in their song of joy: → No. 23, p. 23

COMMUNION ANT. Mt 26, 42   [God's Will]
**Father, if this cup may not pass, but I must drink it,
then your will be done.** ↓

PRAYER AFTER COMMUNION   [Perseverance]
Lord,
you have satisfied our hunger with this eucharistic
    food.
The death of your Son gives us hope and strengthens
    our faith.
May his resurrection give us perseverance
and lead us to salvation.
We ask this through Christ our Lord.
℟. **Amen.**   → No. 32, p. 70

Optional Solemn Blessings, p. 92, and Prayers Over the People, p. 99

"The Spirit of the Lord has been given to me."

MARCH 27

HOLY THURSDAY
CHRISM MASS

This Mass, which the bishop concelebrates with his presbyterium and at which the oils are blessed, manifests the communion of the priests with their bishop. It is thus desirable that, if possible, all the priests take part in it, together with parish representatives, and receive communion under both kinds. This day also is dedicated to the renewal of priestly ministry.

ENTRANCE ANT. Rv 1, 6   [Kingdom of Priests]

Jesus Christ has made us a kingdom of priests to serve his God and Father: glory and kingship be his for ever and ever. Amen.   → No. 2, p. 10

The Gloria is sung or said.

OPENING PRAYER   [Faithful Witnesses]

Father,
by the power of the Holy Spirit
you anointed your only Son Messiah and Lord of creation;
you have given us a share in his consecration
to priestly service in your Church.

196

Help us to be faithful witnesses in the world
to the salvation Christ won for all mankind.
We ask this . . . for ever and ever. ℟. **Amen.** ↓

READING I Is 61, 1-3. 6. 8-9   [The Lord's Anointed]

Isaiah the prophet, anointed by God to bring the Good
News to the poor, proclaims a message filled with hope. It
is one that replaces mourning with gladness.

A reading from the book of the prophet Isaiah

THE spirit of the Lord God is upon me,
    because the Lord has anointed me;
He has sent me to bring glad tidings to the lowly,
    to heal the brokenhearted,
To proclaim liberty to the captives
    and release to the prisoners,
To announce a year of favor from the Lord
    and a day of vindication by our God,
    to comfort all who mourn;
To place on those who mourn in Zion
    a diadem instead of ashes,
To give them oil of gladness in place of mourning,
    a glorious mantle instead of a listless spirit.
You yourselves shall be named priests of the Lord,
    ministers of our God you shall be called.
I will give them their recompense faithfully,
    a lasting covenant I will make with them.
Their descendants shall be renowned among the nations,
    and their offspring among the peoples;
All who see them shall acknowledge them as a race
    the Lord has blessed.
The word of the Lord. ℟. **Thanks be to God.** ↓

RESPONSORIAL PSALM Ps 89   [God the Savior]

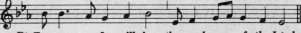

℟. For ev - er I   will sing the good-ness of the Lord.

I have found David, my servant;
  with my holy oil I have anointed him,
That my hand may be always with him,
  and that my arm may make him strong.—R̸.

My faithfulness and my kindness shall be with him,
  and through my name shall his horn be exalted.
"He shall say of me, 'You are my father,
  my God, the rock, my savior.' "—R̸. ↓

READING II Rv 1, 5-8   [The Alpha and the Omega]

> God says, "I am the Alpha and the Omega, the One who is
> and who was and who is to come, the Almighty!" All shall
> see God as he comes amid the clouds.

  A reading from the book of Revelation

[G RACE and peace to you] from Jesus Christ the
    faithful witness, the first-born from the dead
and ruler of the kings of earth. To him who loves us
and freed us from our sins by his own blood, who has
made us a royal nation of priests in the service of his
God and Father—to him be glory and power forever
and ever! Amen.
See, he comes amid the clouds!
  Every eye shall see him,
  even of those who pierced him.
All the peoples of the earth
  shall lament him bitterly.
  So it is to be! Amen!
  The Lord God says, "I am the Alpha and the Omega,
the One who is and who was and who is to come, the
Almighty!"—The word of the Lord. R̸. **Thanks be to
God.** ↓

GOSPEL Lk 4, 16-21   [Christ the Messiah]

Verse before the Gospel (Is 61, 1: cited in Lk 4, 18)

R̸. **Glory to you, Word of God, Lord Jesus Christ!**
The spirit of the Lord is upon me;
he sent me to bring Good News to the poor.

℟. **Glory to you, Word of God, Lord Jesus Christ!**

Jesus reads in the synagogue at Nazareth the words of Isaiah quoted in the first reading. Jesus is the Anointed One. He tells the people that today Isaiah's prophecy is fulfilled.

℣. The Lord be with you. ℟. **And also with you.**

✝ A reading from the holy gospel according to Luke.

℟. **Glory to you, Lord.**

JESUS came to Nazareth where he had been reared, and entering the synagogue on the sabbath as he was in the habit of doing, he stood up to do the reading. When the book of the prophet Isaiah was handed him, he unrolled the scroll and found the passage where it was written:

"The spirit of the Lord is upon me;
    therefore he has anointed me.
He has sent me to bring glad tidings to the poor,
    to proclaim liberty to captives,
Recovery of sight to the blind
    and release to prisoners,
To announce a year of favor from the Lord."

Rolling up the scroll, he gave it back to the assistant and sat down. All in the synagogue had their eyes fixed on him. Then he began by saying to them, "Today this Scripture passage is fulfilled in your hearing."—The gospel of the Lord. ℟. **Praise to you, Lord Jesus Christ.**   → No. 14, p. 18

Renewal of Commitment to Priestly Service

After the homily the bishop speaks to the priests:

My brothers,
today we celebrate the memory of the first eucharist,
at which our Lord Jesus Christ
shared with his apostles and with us
his call to the priestly service of his Church.
Now, in the presence of your bishop and God's holy
    people,

are you ready to renew your own dedication to Christ
as priests of his new covenant?

Priests: I am.

Bishop: At your ordination
you accepted the responsibilities of the priesthood
out of love for the Lord Jesus and his Church.
Are you resolved to unite yourselves more closely to
    Christ
and to try to become more like him
by joyfully sacrificing your own pleasure and ambi-
    tion
to bring his peace and love to your brothers and sis-
    ters?

Priests: I am.

Bishop: Are you resolved
to be faithful ministers of the mysteries of God,
to celebrate the eucharist and the other liturgical ser-
    vices
with sincere devotion?
Are you resolved to imitate Jesus Christ,
the head and shepherd of the Church,
by teaching the Christian faith
without thinking of your own profit,
solely for the well-being of the people
you were sent to serve?

Priests: I am.

Then the bishop addresses the people:

My brothers and sisters,
pray for your priests.
Ask the Lord to bless them with the fullness of his love,
to help them be faithful ministers of Christ the High
    Priest,
so that they will be able to lead you to him,
the fountain of your salvation.

**People: Lord Jesus Christ, hear us and answer our
    prayer.**

Bishop: Pray also for me
that despite my own unworthiness
I may faithfully fulfill the office of apostle
which Jesus Christ, has entrusted to me.
Pray that I may become more like
our High Priest and Good Shepherd,
the teacher and servant of all,
and so be a genuine sign
of Christ's loving presence among you.

**People: Lord Jesus Christ, hear us and answer our
   prayer.**

Bishop: May the Lord in his love
keep you close to him always,
and may he bring all of us,
his priests and people,
to eternal life.
All: **Amen.**

*The Profession of Faith and General Intercessions are omit-
ted.*   → *No. 17, p. 20*

PRAYER OVER THE GIFTS   [New Life]

Lord God,
may the power of this sacrifice
cleanse the old weakness of our human nature.
Give us a newness of life
and bring us to salvation.
Grant this through Christ our Lord. ℟. **Amen.** ↓

PREFACE (P 20)   [Continuation of Christ's Priesthood]

℣. The Lord be with you. ℟. **And also with you.**
℣. Lift up your hearts. ℟. **We lift them up to the Lord.**
℣. Let us give thanks to the Lord our God. ℟. **It is
right to give him thanks and praise.**

Father, all-powerful and ever-living God,
we do well always and everywhere to give you
   thanks.

By your Holy Spirit
you anointed your only Son
High Priest of the new and eternal covenant.
With wisdom and love you have planned
that this one priesthood should continue in the Church.
Christ gives the dignity of a royal priesthood
to the people he has made his own.
From these, with a brother's love,
he chooses men to share his sacred ministry
by the laying on of hands.
He appoints them to renew in his name
the sacrifice of our redemption
as they set before your family his paschal meal.
He calls them to lead your holy people in love,
nourish them by your word,
and strengthen them through the sacraments.
Father, they are to give their lives in your service
and for the salvation of your people
as they strive to grow in the likeness of Christ
and honor you by their courageous witness of faith
    and love.
We praise you Lord, with all the angels and saints
in their song of joy: → No. 23, p. 23

COMMUNION ANT. Ps 89, 2   [The Lord's Faithfulness]

**For ever I will sing the goodness of the Lord; I will
proclaim your faithfulness to all generations.** ↓

PRAYER AFTER COMMUNION   [Renewed in Christ]

Lord God almighty,
you have given us fresh strength
in these sacramental gifts.
Renew in us the image of Christ's goodness.
We ask this in the name of Jesus the Lord.
℟. Amen.   → No. 32, p. 70

Optional Solemn Blessings, p. 92, and Prayers Over the People, p. 99

"Do this in remembrance of me."

MARCH 27

EASTER TRIDUUM

EVENING MASS OF THE LORD'S SUPPER

The Evening Mass of the Lord's Supper commemorates the institution of the Holy Eucharist and the sacrament of Holy Orders. It was at this Mass that Jesus changed bread and wine into his Body and Blood. He then directed his disciples to carry out this same ritual: "Do this in remembrance of me."

Introductory Rites and Liturgy of the Word

ENTRANCE ANT. See Gal 6, 14   [Glory in the Cross]

We should glory in the cross of our Lord Jesus Christ, for he is our salvation, our life and our resurrection; through him we are saved and made free.

→ No. 2, p. 10

During the singing of the Gloria, *the church bells are rung and then remain silent until the Easter Vigil, unless the conference of bishops or the Ordinary decrees otherwise.*

OPENING PRAYER   [Fullness of Love]

God our Father,
we are gathered here to share in the supper
which your only Son left to his Church to reveal his
   love.

203

He gave it to us when he was about to die
and commanded us to celebrate it as the new and eternal sacrifice.
We pray that in this eucharist
we may find the fullness of love and life.
Grant this through our Lord Jesus Christ, your Son,
who lives and reigns with you and the Holy Spirit,
one God, for ever and ever. R). **Amen.** ↓

READING I Ex 12, 1-8. 11-14   [The First Passover]

For the protection of the Jewish people, strict religious and
dietary instructions are given to Moses by God. The law of
the Passover meal requires that the doorposts and lintels of
each house be marked with the blood of the sacrificial ani-
mal so that the Lord can "go through Egypt striking down
every first-born of the land, both man and beast."

A reading from the book of Exodus

THE Lord said to Moses and Aaron in the land of
   Egypt, "This month shall stand at the head of your
calendar; you shall reckon it the first month of the
year. Tell the whole community of Israel: On the tenth
of this month every one of your families must procure
for itself a lamb, one apiece for each household. If a
family is too small for a whole lamb, it shall join the
nearest household in procuring one and shall share in
the lamb in proportion to the number of persons who
partake of it. The lamb must be a year-old male and
without blemish. You may take it from either the
sheep or the goats. You shall keep it until the four-
teenth day of this month, and then, with the whole assembly of Israel present, it shall be slaughtered during
the evening twilight. They shall take some of its blood
and apply it to the two doorposts and the lintel of
every house in which they partake of the lamb. That
same night they shall eat its roasted flesh with unleavened bread and bitter herbs.

"This is how you are to eat it: with your loins girt, sandals on your feet and your staff in hand, you shall eat like those who are in flight. It is the Passover of the Lord. For on this same night I will go through Egypt, striking down every first-born of the land, both man and beast, and executing judgment on all the gods of Egypt—I, the Lord! But the blood will mark the houses where you are. Seeing the blood, I will pass over you; thus, when I strike the land of Egypt, no destructive blow will come upon you.

"This day shall be a memorial feast for you, which all your generations shall celebrate with pilgrimage to the Lord, as a perpetual institution."—The word of the Lord. ℟. **Thanks be to God.** ↓

RESPONSORIAL PSALM Ps 116   [Thanksgiving]

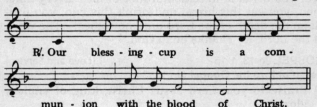

How shall I make a return to the Lord
   for all the good he has done for me?
The cup of salvation I will take up,
   and I will call upon the name of the Lord.—℟.

Precious in the eyes of the Lord
   is the death of his faithful ones.
I am your servant, the son of your handmaid;
   you have loosed my bonds.—℟.

To you will I offer sacrifice of thanksgiving,
   and I will call upon the name of the Lord.
My vows to the Lord I will pay
   in the presence of all his people.—℟. ↓

READING II 1 Cor 11, 23-26   [The Lord's Supper]

Paul recounts the events of the Last Supper which were handed down to him. The changing of bread and wine into the Body and Blood of the Lord proclaimed again his death. It was to be a sacrificial meal.

A reading from the first letter of Paul
to the Corinthians

I RECEIVED from the Lord what I handed on to you, namely, that the Lord Jesus on the night in which he was betrayed took bread, and after he had given thanks, broke it and said, "This is my body, which is for you. Do this in remembrance of me." In the same way, after the supper, he took the cup, saying, "This cup is the new covenant in my blood. Do this, whenever you drink it, in remembrance of me." Every time, then, you eat this bread and drink this cup, you proclaim the death of the Lord until he comes!—The word of the Lord. ℟. **Thanks be to God.** ↓

GOSPEL Jn 13, 1-15   [Love and Service]
Verse before the Gospel (Jn 13, 34)

℟. **Praise to you, Lord Jesus Christ, king of endless glory!**

I give you a new commandment:
Love one another as I have loved you.

℟. **Praise to you, Lord Jesus Christ, king of endless glory!** ↓

Jesus washes the feet of his disciples to prove to them his sincere love and great humility which they should imitate. He teaches them that, although free from sin and not unworthy to receive his most holy body and blood, they should be purified of all evil inclinations.

℣. The Lord be with you. ℟. **And also with you.**

✛ A reading from the holy gospel according to John.

℟. **Glory to you, Lord.**

BEFORE the feast of Passover, Jesus realized that the hour had come for him to pass from this world to the Father. He had loved his own in this world, and would show his love for them to the end. The devil had already induced Judas, son of Simon Iscariot, to hand Jesus over; and so, during the supper, Jesus—fully aware that he had come from God and was going to God, the Father who had handed everything over to him—rose from the meal and took off his cloak. He picked up a towel and tied it around himself. Then he poured water into a basin and began to wash his disciples' feet and dry them with the towel he had around him. Thus he came to Simon Peter, who said to him, "Lord, are you going to wash my feet?" Jesus answered, "You may not realize now what I am doing, but later you will understand." Peter replied, "You shall never wash my feet!" "If I do not wash you," Jesus answered, "you will have no share in my heritage." "Lord," Simon Peter said to him, "then not only my feet, but my hands and head as well." Jesus told him, "The man who has bathed has no need to wash [except for his feet]; he is entirely cleansed, just as you are; though not all." (The reason he said, "Not all are washed clean," was that he knew his betrayer.)

After he had washed their feet, he put his cloak back on and reclined at table once more. He said to them:

"Do you understand what I just did for you?
You address me as 'Teacher' and 'Lord,'
and fittingly enough,
for that is what I am.
But if I washed your feet—
I who am Teacher and Lord—
then you must wash each other's feet.
What I just did was to give you an example:
as I have done, so you must do."

The gospel of the Lord. ℟. **Praise to you, Lord Jesus Christ.** → No. 14, p. 18

The homily should explain the principal mysteries which are commemorated in this Mass: the institution of the eucharist, the institution of the priesthood, and Christ's commandment of brotherly love.

WASHING OF FEET

Depending on pastoral circumstances, the washing of feet follows the homily.

The men who have been chosen are led by the ministers to chairs prepared in a suitable place. Then the priest (removing his chasuble if necessary) goes to each man. With the help of the ministers, he pours water over each one's feet and dries them.

Meanwhile some of the following antiphons or other appropriate songs are sung.

ANTIPHON 1 See Jn 13, 4. 5. 15   [Jesus' Example]

The Lord Jesus,
when he had eaten with his disciples,
poured water into a basin
and began to wash their feet, saying:
This example I leave you.

ANTIPHON 2 Jn 13, 6. 7. 8   [Peter's Understanding]

Lord, do you wash my feet?
Jesus said to him:
If I do not wash your feet,
you can have no part with me.

℣. So he came to Simon Peter,
who said to him:
Lord, do you wash my feet?

℣. Now you do not know what I am doing,
but later you will understand.
Lord, do you wash my feet?

ANTIPHON 3 See Jn 13, 14   [Service]

If I, your Lord and Teacher, have washed your feet,
then surely you must wash one another's feet.

ANTIPHON 4 Jn 13, 35   [Identified by Love]

If there is this love among you,
all will know that you are my disciples.

℣. Jesus said to his disciples:
If there is this love among you,
all will know that you are my disciples.

ANTIPHON 5 Jn 13, 34   [New Commandment]

I give you a new commandment:
love one another as I have loved you, says the Lord.

ANTIPHON 6 1 Cor 13, 13   [Greatest Is Love]

Faith, hope, and love,
let these endure among you;
and the greatest of these is love.

*The general intercessions follow the washing of feet, or, if
this does not take place, they follow the homily. The profession of faith is not said in this Mass.*

The Liturgy of the Eucharist

*At the beginning of the liturgy of the eucharist, there may be
a procession of the faithful with gifts for the poor. During the
procession the following may be sung, or another appropriate
song.*

[Christ's Love]

Ant. ℣. **Where charity and love are found, there is
God.**
℣. **The love of Christ has gathered us together into
one.**
℣. **Let us rejoice and be glad in him.**
℣. **Let us fear and love the living God,**
℣. **and love each other from the depths of our heart.**
Ant. **Where charity and love are found, there is God.**
℣. **Therefore when we are together,**
℣. **let us take heed not to be divided in mind.**
℣. **Let there be an end to bitterness and quarrels, an
end to strife,**

℣. and in our midst be Christ our God.

Ant. **Where charity and love are found, there is God.**

℣. **And, in company with the blessed, may we see**

℣. **your face in glory, Christ our God,**

℣. **pure and unbounded joy**

℣. **for ever and ever.**

Ant. **Where charity and love are found, there is God.**

→ No. 17, p. 20

PRAYER OVER THE GIFTS   [Work of Redemption]

Lord,

make us worthy to celebrate these mysteries.

Each time we offer this memorial sacrifice

the work of our redemption is accomplished.

We ask this in the name of Jesus the Lord.

℟. **Amen.**   → No. 21, p. 22 (Pref. P 47)

When Eucharistic Prayer I is used, the special Holy Thursday forms of In union with the whole Church, Father, accept this offering, *and* The day before he suffered *are said:*

In union with the whole Church

we celebrate that day

when Jesus Christ, our Lord,

was betrayed for us.

We honor Mary,

the ever-virgin mother of Jesus Christ our Lord and
    God.

We honor Joseph, her husband,

the apostles and martyrs

Peter and Paul, Andrew,

(James, John, Thomas,

James, Philip,

Bartholomew, Matthew, Simon and Jude;

we honor Linus, Cletus, Clement, Sixtus,

Cornelius, Cyprian, Lawrence, Chrysogonus,

John and Paul, Cosmas and Damian)

and all the saints.

May their merits and prayers

gain us your constant help and protection.
(Through Christ our Lord. Amen.)

Father, accept this offering
from your whole family
in memory of the day when Jesus Christ, our Lord,
gave the mysteries of his body and blood
for his disciples to celebrate.
Grant us your peace in this life,
save us from final damnation,
and count us among those you have chosen.
(Through Christ our Lord. Amen.)

Bless and approve our offering;
make it acceptable to you,
an offering in spirit and in truth.
Let it become for us
the body and blood of Jesus Christ,
your only Son, our Lord.

The day before he suffered
to save us and all men,
that is, today,
he took bread in his sacred hands
and looking up to heaven,
to you, his almighty Father,
he gave you thanks and praise.
He broke the bread,
gave it to his disciples, and said:

Take this, all of you, and eat it:
this is my body which will be given up for you.

The rest follows the Roman canon, pp. 26-28.

COMMUNION ANT. 1 Cor 11, 24-25 [In Remembrance of Christ]
**This body will be given for you. This is the cup of the
new covenant in my blood; whenever you receive
them, do so in remembrance of me.** ↓

After the distribution of communion, the ciborium with hosts for Good Friday is left on the altar.

A period of silence may be observed after communion, or a psalm or song of praise may be sung.

PRAYER AFTER COMMUNION   [New Life]

Almighty God,
we receive new life
from the supper your Son gave us in this world.
May we find full contentment
in the meal we hope to share
in your eternal kingdom.
We ask this through Christ our Lord. ℟. **Amen.**

The Mass concludes with this prayer.

Transfer of the Holy Eucharist

After the prayer the priest stands before the altar and puts incense in the thurible. Kneeling, he incenses the Blessed Sacrament three times. Then he receives the humeral veil, takes the ciborium, and covers it with the ends of the veil.

The Blessed Sacrament is carried through the church in procession, led by a cross-bearer and accompanied by candles and incense, to the place of reposition prepared in a chapel suitably decorated for the occasion. During the procession the hymn Pange, lingua (exclusive of the last two stanzas) or some other eucharistic song is sung.

PANGE LINGUA   [Adoring the Lord]

Sing my tongue, the Savior's glory,
Of his flesh the mystery sing;
Of his blood all price exceeding,
Shed by our immortal king,
Destined for the world's redemption,
From a noble womb to spring.

Of a pure and spotless Virgin
Born for us on earth below,
He, as man with man conversing,
Stayed the seeds of truth to sow;
Then he closed in solemn order
Wondrously his life of woe.

On the night of that Last Supper,
Seated with his chosen band,
He, the paschal victim eating,
First fulfills the law's command;
Then as food to all his brethren
Gives himself with his own hand.

Word made Flesh, the bread of nature,
By his word to flesh he turns;
Wine into his blood he changes:
What though sense no change discerns,
Only be the heart in earnest,
Faith her lesson quickly learns.

When the procession reaches the place of reposition, the priest sets the ciborium down. Then he puts incense in the thurible and, kneeling, incenses the Blessed Sacrament, while Tantum ergo Sacramentum *is sung. The tabernacle of reposition is then closed.*

Down in adoration falling,
Lo! the sacred host we hail,
Lo! o'er ancient forms departing
Newer rites of grace prevail;
Faith for all defects supplying,
Where the feeble senses fail.

To the everlasting Father,
And the Son who reigns on high
With the Holy Spirit proceeding
Forth from each eternally,
Be salvation, honor, blessing,
Might and endless majesty.
Amen.

After a period of silent adoration, the priest and ministers genuflect and return to the sacristy.

Then the altar is stripped and, if possible, the crosses are removed from the church. It is desirable to cover any crosses which remain in the church.

The faithful should be encouraged to continue adoration before the Blessed Sacrament for a suitable period of time during the night.

———

"[Jesus] bowed his head, and delivered over his spirit."

MARCH 28

GOOD FRIDAY

CELEBRATION OF THE LORD'S PASSION

The liturgy of Good Friday recalls graphically the passion and death of Jesus. The reading of the passion describes the suffering and death of Jesus. Today we show great reverence for the crucifix, the sign of our redemption.

According to the Church's ancient tradition, the sacraments, except for Penance and the Anointing of the Sick, are not celebrated today or tomorrow. The celebration of the Lord's passion takes place in the afternoon, about three o'clock, unless pastoral reasons suggest a later hour.

The priest and deacon, wearing red Mass vestments, go to the altar. There they make a reverence and prostrate themselves, or they may kneel. All pray silently for a while. Then the priest goes to the chair with the ministers. He faces the people and, with hands joined, sings or says one of the following prayers.

PRAYER   [Make Us Holy]

Lord,
by shedding his blood for us,
your Son, Jesus Christ,

214

established the paschal mystery.
In your goodness, make us holy
and watch over us always.
We ask this through Christ our Lord. R̸. **Amen.** ↓

OR   [Likeness of Christ]

Lord,
by the suffering of Christ your Son
you have saved us all from the death
we inherited from sinful Adam.
By the law of nature
we have borne the likeness of his manhood.
May the sanctifying power of grace
help us to put on the likeness of our Lord in heaven,
who lives and reigns for ever and ever. R̸. **Amen.** ↓

PART ONE: LITURGY OF THE WORD

READING I Is 52, 13—53, 12   [Suffering and Glory]

> The suffering Servant shall be raised up and exalted. The
> Servant remains one with all people in sorrow and yet dis-
> tinct from each of them in innocence of life and total ser-
> vice to God. The doctrine of expiatory suffering finds
> supreme expression in these words.

A reading from the book of the prophet Isaiah

S EE, my servant shall prosper,
he shall be raised high and greatly exalted.
Even as many were amazed at him—
    so marred was his look beyond that of man,
    and his appearance beyond that of mortals—
So shall he startle many nations,
    because of him kings shall stand speechless;
For those who have not been told shall see,
    those who have not heard shall ponder it.
Who would believe what we have heard?
    To whom has the arm of the Lord been revealed?
He grew up like a sapling before him,

like a shoot from the parched earth;
There was in him no stately bearing to make us look
   at him,
   nor appearance that would attract us to him.
He was spurned and avoided by men,
   a man of suffering, accustomed to infirmity,
One of those from whom men hide their faces,
   spurned, and we held him in no esteem.
Yet it was our infirmities that he bore,
   our sufferings that he endured,
While we thought of him as stricken,
   as one smitten by God and afflicted.
But he was pierced for our offenses,
   crushed for our sins;
Upon him was the chastisement that makes us whole,
   by his stripes we were healed.
We had all gone astray like sheep,
   each following his own way;
But the Lord laid upon him
   the guilt of us all.
Though he was harshly treated, he submitted
   and opened not his mouth;
Like a lamb led to the slaughter
   or a sheep before the shearers,
   he was silent and opened not his mouth.
Oppressed and condemned, he was taken away,
      and who would have thought any more of his des-
      tiny?
When he was cut off from the land of the living,
   and smitten for the sin of his people,
A grave was assigned him among the wicked
   and a burial place with evildoers,
Though he had done no wrong
   nor spoken any falsehood.
[But the Lord was pleased
   to crush him in infirmity.]
If he gives his life as an offering for sin,

he shall see his descendants in a long life,
and the will of the Lord shall be accomplished
through him.
Because of his affliction
he shall see the light in fullness of days;
Through his suffering, my servant shall justify many,
and their guilt he shall bear.
Therefore I will give him his portion among the great,
and he shall divide the spoils with the mighty,
Because he surrendered himself to death
and was counted among the wicked;
And he shall take away the sins of many,
and win pardon for their offenses.

The word of the Lord. ℟. **Thanks be to God.** ↓

RESPONSORIAL PSALM Ps 31   [Trust in God]

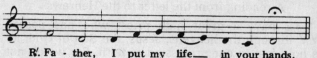

℟. Fa - ther, I put my life__ in your hands.

In you, O Lord, I take refuge;
let me never be put to shame.
In your justice rescue me,
Into your hands I commend my spirit;
you will redeem me, O Lord, O faithful God.

℟. **Father, I put my life in your hands.**

For all my foes I am an object of reproach,
a laughingstock to my neighbors, and a dread to my
friends;
they who see me abroad flee from me.
I am forgotten like the unremembered dead;
I am like a dish that is broken.

℟. **Father, I put my life in your hands.**

But my trust is in you, O Lord;
I say, "You are my God."
In your hands is my destiny; rescue me

from the clutches of my enemies and my persecutors.

R̸. **Father, I put my life in your hands.**

Let your face shine upon your servant;
  save me in your kindness.

Take courage and be stouthearted,
  all you who hope in the Lord.

R̸. **Father, I put my life in your hands.** ↓

READING II Heb 4, 14-16; 5, 7-9   [Access to Christ]

> The theme of the compassionate high priest appears again in this passage. In him the Christian can approach God confidently and without fear. Christ learned obedience from his sufferings whereby he became the source of eternal life for all.

A reading from the letter to the Hebrews

WE have a great high priest who has passed through the heavens, Jesus, the Son of God; let us hold fast to our profession of faith. For we do not have a high priest who is unable to sympathize with our weakness, but one who was tempted in every way that we are, yet never sinned. So let us confidently approach the throne of grace to receive mercy and favor and to find help in time of need.

In the days when he was in the flesh, Christ offered prayers and supplications with loud cries and tears to God, who was able to save him from death, and he was heard because of his reverence. Son though he was, he learned obedience from what he suffered; and when perfected, he became the source of eternal salvation for all who obey him.—The word of the Lord.

R̸. **Thanks be to God.** ↓

GOSPEL Jn 18, 1—19, 42   [Christ's Passion]
Verse before the Gospel (Phil 2, 8-9)

R̸. **Praise and honor to you, Lord Jesus Christ!**

Christ became obedient for us even to death,
dying on the cross.
Therefore God raised him on high
and gave him a name above all other names.
℟. **Praise and honor to you, Lord Jesus Christ!**

Finally the passion is read in the same way as on the preceding Sunday. The narrator is noted by C (Chronista), the words of Jesus by a ✚ and the words of others by S (Synagoga), groups in the account by SS. The words of the narrator enclosed in brackets may be omitted. The parts of the Synagoga marked with SS and printed in boldface type may be recited by the people.

> The beginning scene is Christ's agony in the garden. Our Lord knows what is to happen. The Scriptures recount the betrayal, the trial, the condemnation, and the crucifixion of Jesus.

The Passion of our Lord Jesus Christ according to John

1. JESUS IS ARRESTED

C. Jesus went out with his disciples across the Kidron Valley. There was a garden there, and he and his disciples entered it. The place was familiar to Judas as well (the one who was to hand him over) because Jesus had often met there with his disciples. Judas took the cohort as well as guards supplied by the chief priest and the Pharisees, and came there with lanterns, torches, and weapons. Jesus, aware of all that would happen to him, stepped forward and said to them, ✚ "Who is it you want?" C. [They replied,] SS. **"Jesus the Nazorean."** C. He answered, ✚ "I am he." C. (Now Judas, the one who was to hand him over, was there with them.) As Jesus said to them, "I am he," they retreated slightly and fell to the ground. Jesus put the question to them again, ✚ "Who is it you want?" C. They repeated, SS. **"Jesus the Nazorean."** C. [Jesus said,] ✚ "I have told you, I am he. If

I am the one you want, let these men go." **C.** (This was
to fulfill what he had said, "I have not lost one of those
you gave me.") Then Simon Peter, who had a sword,
drew it and struck the slave of the high priest, sever-
ing his right ear. (The slave's name was Malchus.) At
that Jesus said to Peter, ✝ "Put your sword back in its
sheath. Am I not to drink the cup the Father has given
me?" **C.** Then the soldiers of the cohort, their tribune,
and the Jewish police arrested Jesus and bound him.
They led him first to Annas, the father-in-law of Caiaphas who was high priest that year. (It was Caiaphas who had proposed to the Jews the advantage
of having one man die for the people.)

2. PETER'S FIRST DENIAL

Simon Peter, in company with another disciple,
kept following Jesus closely. This disciple, who was
known to the high priest, stayed with Jesus as far as
the high priest's courtyard, while Peter was left standing at the gate. The disciple known to the high priest
came out and spoke to the woman at the gate, and
then brought Peter in. This servant girl who kept the
gate said to Peter, **S.** "Are you not one of this man's
followers?" **C.** [Peter replied,] "Not I." **C.** Now the
night was cold, and the servants and the guards who
were standing around had made a charcoal fire to
warm themselves by. Peter joined them and stood
there warming himself.

3. THE INQUIRY BEFORE ANNAS

The high priest questioned Jesus, first about his disciples, then about his teaching. Jesus answered by
saying, ✝ "I have spoken publicly to any who would
listen. I always taught in a synagogue or in the temple
area where all the Jews come together. There was
nothing secret about anything I said. Why do you
question me? Question those who heard me when I
spoke. It should be obvious they will know what I

said." **C.** At this reply, one of the guards who was standing nearby gave Jesus a sharp blow on the face. He said, **S.** "Is that the way to answer the high priest?" **C.** Jesus replied, ✝ "If I said anything wrong produce the evidence, but if I spoke the truth why hit me?" **C.** Annas next sent him, bound, to the high priest Caiaphas.

4. THE FURTHER DENIALS

All through this, Simon Peter had been standing there warming himself. They said to him, **SS. "Are you not a disciple of his?" C.** [He denied it and said:] **S.** "I am not!" **C.** One of the high priest's slaves—as it happened, a relative of the man whose ear Peter had severed—insisted, **S.** "But did I not see you with him in the garden?" **C.** Peter denied it again. At that moment a cock began to crow.

5. JESUS BROUGHT BEFORE PILATE

At daybreak they brought Jesus from Caiaphas to the praetorium. They did not enter the praetorium themselves, for they had to avoid ritual impurity if they were to eat the Passover supper. Pilate came out to them and demanded, **S.** "What accusation do you bring against this man?" **C.** They retorted, **SS. "If he were not a criminal we would certainly not have handed him over to you." C.** At this Pilate said, **S.** "Why do you not take him and pass judgment on him according to your law?" **C.** The Jews answered, **SS. "We may not put anyone to death." C.** (This was to fulfill what Jesus had said, indicating the sort of death he had to die.)

6. JESUS QUESTIONED BY PILATE

Pilate went back into the praetorium and summoned Jesus. He asked him, **S.** "Are you the King of the Jews?" **C.** Jesus answered, ✝ "Are you saying this on your own, or have others been telling you about me?" **C.** Pilate retorted, **S.** "I am no Jew! It is your own people and the chief priests who have handed you over to me. What have you done?" **C.** Jesus answered, ✠ "My kingdom does not belong to this world. If my kingdom were of this world, my subjects would be fighting to save me from being handed over to the Jews. As it is, my kingdom is not here." **C.** At this Pilate said to him, **S.** "So, then, you are a king?" **C.** [Jesus replied,] ✠ "It is you who say I am a king. The reason I was born, the reason why I came into the world, is to testify to the truth. Anyone committed to the truth hears my voice." **C.** Pilate said, **S.** "Truth! What does that mean?"

7. BARABBAS CHOSEN OVER JESUS

C. After this remark, Pilate went out again to the Jews and said to them: **S.** "Speaking for myself, I find no case against this man. Recall your custom whereby I release to you someone at Passover time. Do you want me to release to you the king of the Jews?" **C.** They shouted back, **SS. "We want Barabbas, not this one!"** **C.** (Barabbas was an insurrectionist.)

8. JESUS IS SCOURGED

Pilate's next move was to take Jesus and have him scourged. The soldiers then wove a crown of thorns and fixed it on his head, throwing around his shoulders a cloak of royal purple. Repeatedly they came up to him and while slapping his face said. **SS. "All hail, King of the Jews!"**

9. JESUS IS PRESENTED TO THE CROWD

C. Pilate went out a second time and said to the crowd: **S.** "Observe what I do. I am going to bring him out to you to make you realize that I find no case against him." **C.** When Jesus came out wearing the crown of thorns and the purple cloak, Pilate said to them, **S.** "Look at the man!" **C.** As soon as the chief priests and the temple guards saw him they shouted, **SS.** **"Crucify him! Crucify him!"** **C.** Pilate said, **S.** "Take him and crucify him yourselves; I find no case against him." **C.** The Jews responded, **SS.** **"We have our law, and according to that law he must die because he made himself God's Son."** **C.** When Pilate heard this kind of talk, he was more afraid than ever.

10. JESUS AGAIN QUESTIONED BY PILATE

Going back into the praetorium, he said to Jesus, **S.** "Where do you come from?" **C.** Jesus would not give him any answer. Pilate asked him, **S.** "Do you refuse to speak to me? Do you not know that I have the power to release you and the power to crucify you?" **C.** [Jesus answered,] ✝ "You would have no power over me whatever unless it were given you from above. That is why he who handed me over to you is guilty of the greater sin."

11. JESUS SENTENCED TO BE CRUCIFIED

C. After this, Pilate was eager to release him, but the Jews shouted, **SS.** **"If you free this man you are no 'Friend of Caesar.' Anyone who makes himself a king becomes Caesar's rival."** **C.** Pilate heard what they were saying, then brought Jesus outside and took a seat on a judge's bench at the place called the Stone Pavement—Gabbatha in Hebrew. (It was the Preparation Day for Passover, and the hour was about noon.) He said to the Jews, **S.** "Look at your king!" **C.** At this they shouted, **SS.** **"Away with him! Away with him! Crucify him!"** **C.** Pilate exclaimed, **S.** "What! Shall I crucify your king!" **C.** The chief priests replied, **SS.** **"We have no king but Caesar."** **C.** In the end, Pilate handed Jesus over to be crucified.

12. CRUCIFIXION AND DEATH

Jesus was led away, and carrying the cross by himself, went out to what is called the Place of the Skull (in Hebrew, Golgotha). There they crucified him, and two others with him: one on either side, Jesus in the middle. Pilate had an inscription placed on the cross which read, JESUS THE NAZOREAN, THE KING OF THE JEWS. This inscription, in Hebrew, Latin, and Greek, was read by many of the Jews, since the place where Jesus was crucified was near the city. The chief priests of the Jews tried to tell Pilate, **SS. "You should not have written, 'The King of the Jews.' Write instead, 'This man claimed to be King of the Jews.' " C.** Pilate replied, **S.** "What I have written, I have written." **C.** After the soldiers had crucified Jesus they took his garments and divided them four ways, one for each soldier. There was also his tunic, but this tunic was woven in one piece from top to bottom and had no seam. They said to one another, **SS. "We should not tear it. Let us throw dice to see who gets it." C** (The purpose of this was to have the Scripture fulfilled: "They divided my garments among them; for my clothing they cast lots.") And this was what the soldiers did. Near the cross of Jesus there stood his mother, his mother's sister, Mary the wife of Clopas, and Mary Magdalene. Seeing his mother there with the disciple whom he loved, Jesus said to his mother, ✝ "Woman, there is your son." **C.** In turn he said to the disciple, ✝ "There is your mother." **C.** From that hour onward, the disciple took her into his care. After that, Jesus, realizing that everything was now finished, to bring the Scripture to fulfillment said, ✝ "I am thirsty." **C.** There was a jar there full of common wine. They stuck a sponge soaked in this wine on some hyssop and raised it to his lips. When Jesus took the wine, he said, ✝ "Now it is finished." **C.** Then he bowed his head, and delivered over his spirit. *(HERE KNEEL AND PAUSE MOMENTARILY).*

13. THE BLOOD AND WATER

Since it was the Preparation Day the Jews did not want to have the bodies left on the cross during the sabbath, for that sabbath was a solemn feast day. They asked Pilate that the legs be broken and the bodies be taken away. Accordingly, the soldiers came and broke the legs of the men crucified with Jesus, first of one, then of the other. When they came to Jesus and saw that he was already dead, they did not break his legs. One of the soldiers thrust a lance into his side, and immediately blood and water flowed out. (This testimony has been given by an eyewitness, and his testimony is true. He tells what he knows is true, so that you may believe.) These events took place for the fulfillment of Scripture: "Break none of his bones." There is still another Scripture passage which says: "They shall look on him whom they have pierced."

14. BURIAL OF JESUS

Afterward, Joseph of Arimathea, a disciple of Jesus (although a secret one for fear of the Jews), asked Pilate's permission to remove Jesus' body. Pilate granted it, so they came and took the body away. Nicodemus (the man who had first come to Jesus at night) likewise came, bringing a mixture of myrrh and aloes which weighed about a hundred pounds. They took Jesus' body, and in accordance with Jewish burial custom, bound it up in wrappings of cloth with perfumed oils. In the place where he had been crucified there was a garden, and in the garden a new tomb in which no one had been buried. Because of the Jewish Preparation Day they buried Jesus there, for the tomb was close at hand.

After the reading of the passion there may be a brief Homily.

GENERAL INTERCESSIONS

The general intercessions conclude the liturgy of the word. The deacon, standing at the ambo, sings or says the introduction in which each intention is stated. All kneel and pray silently for some period of time, and then the priest, with hands outstretched, standing either at the chair or at the altar, sings or says the prayer. The people may either kneel or stand throughout the entire period of the general intercessions.

I. For the Church

Let us pray, dear friends,
for the holy Church of God throughout the world,
that God the almighty Father
guide it and gather it together
so that we may worship him
in peace and tranquility.

Silent prayer. Then the priest sings or says:

Almighty and eternal God,
you have shown your glory to all nations
in Christ, your Son.
Guide the work of your Church.
Help it to persevere in faith,
proclaim your name,
and bring your salvation to people everywhere.
We ask this through Christ our Lord. ℟. **Amen.** ↓

II. For the Pope

Let us pray
for our Holy Father, Pope N.,
that God who chose him to be bishop
may give him health and strength
to guide and govern God's holy people.

Silent prayer. Then the priest sings or says:

Almighty and eternal God,
you guide all things by your word,
you govern all Christian people.

In your love protect the Pope you have chosen for us.
Under his leadership deepen our faith
and make us better Christians.
We ask this through Christ our Lord. ℟. **Amen.** ↓

III. For the clergy and laity of the Church

Let us pray
for N., our bishop,
for all bishops, priests and deacons,
for all who have a special ministry in the Church
and for all God's people.

Silent prayer. Then the priest sings or says:

Almighty and eternal God,
your Spirit guides the Church
and makes it holy.
Listen to our prayers
and help each of us
in his own vocation
to do your work more faithfully.
We ask this through Christ our Lord. ℟. **Amen.** ↓

IV. For those preparing for baptism

Let us pray
for those [among us] preparing for baptism,
that God in his mercy
make them responsive to his love,
forgive their sins through the waters of new birth,
and give them life in Jesus Christ our Lord.

Silent prayer. Then the priest sings or says:

Almighty and eternal God,
you continually bless your Church with new members.
Increase the faith and understanding
of those [among us] preparing for baptism.
Give them a new birth in these living waters
and make them members of your chosen family.
We ask this through Christ our Lord. ℟. **Amen.** ↓

V. For the unity of Christians

Let us pray
for all our brothers and sisters
who share our faith in Jesus Christ,
that God may gather and keep together in one Church
all those who seek the truth with sincerity.

Silent prayer. Then the priest sings or says:

Almighty and eternal God,
you keep together those you have united.
Look kindly on all who follow Jesus your Son.
We are all consecrated to you by our common baptism.
Make us one in the fullness of faith,
and keep us one in the fellowship of love.
We ask this through Christ our Lord. ℟. **Amen.** ↓

VI. For the Jewish people

Let us pray
for the Jewish people,
the first to hear the word of God,
that they may continue to grow in the love of his name
and in faithfulness to his covenant.

Silent prayer. Then the priest sings or says:

Almighty and eternal God,
long ago you gave your promise to Abraham and his
    posterity.
Listen to your Church as we pray
that the people you first made your own
may arrive at the fullness of redemption.
We ask this through Christ our Lord. ℟. **Amen.** ↓

VII. For those who do not believe in Christ

Let us pray
for those who do not believe in Christ,
that the light of the Holy Spirit
may show them the way to salvation.

Silent prayer. Then the priest sings or says:

Almighty and eternal God,
enable those who do not acknowledge Christ
to find the truth
as they walk before you in sincerity of heart.
Help us to grow in love for one another,
to grasp more fully the mystery of your godhead,
and to become more perfect witnesses of your love
in the sight of men.
We ask this through Christ our Lord. ℟. **Amen.** ↓

VIII. For those who do not believe in God

Let us pray
for those who do not believe in God,
that they may find him
by sincerely following all that is right.

Silent prayer. Then the priest sings or says:

Almighty and eternal God,
you created mankind
so that all might long to find you
and have peace when you are found.
Grant that, in spite of the hurtful things
that stand in their way,
they may all recognize in the lives of Christians
the tokens of your love and mercy,
and gladly acknowledge you
as the one true God and Father of us all.
We ask this through Christ our Lord. ℟. **Amen.** ↓

IX. For all in public office

Let us pray
for those who serve us in public office,
that God may guide their minds and hearts,
so that all men may live in true peace and freedom.

Silent prayer. Then the priest sings or says:

Almighty and eternal God,
you know the longings of men's hearts

and you protect their rights.
In your goodness
watch over those in authority,
so that people everywhere may enjoy
religious freedom, security, and peace.
We ask this through Christ our Lord. ℟. **Amen.** ↓

X. For those in special need

Let us pray, dear friends,
that God the almighty Father
may heal the sick,
comfort the dying,
give safety to travelers,
free those unjustly deprived of liberty,
and rid the world of falsehood,
hunger, and disease.

Silent prayer. Then the priest sings or says:

Almighty, ever-living God,
you give strength to the weary
and new courage to those who have lost heart.
Hear the prayers of all who call on you in any trouble
that they may have the joy of receiving your help in
    their need.
We ask this through Christ our Lord. ℟. **Amen.** ↓

PART TWO: VENERATION OF THE CROSS

*After the general intercessions, the veneration of the cross
takes place. Pastoral demands will determine which of the
two forms is more effective and should be chosen.*

First Form of Showing the Cross

*The veiled cross is carried to the altar, accompanied by two
ministers with lighted candles. Standing at the altar, the
priest takes the cross, uncovers the upper part of it, then ele-
vates it and begins the invitation* This is the wood of the
cross. *He is assisted in the singing by the deacon or, if convenient, by the choir. All respond:* Come, let us worship. *At the
end of the singing all kneel and venerate the cross briefly in
silence; the priest remains standing and holds the cross high.*

Then the priest uncovers the right arm of the cross, lifts it up, and again begins the invitation This is the wood of the cross, *and the rite is repeated as before.*

Finally he uncovers the entire cross, lifts it up, and begins the invitation This is the wood of the cross *a third time, and the rite is repeated as before.*

Accompanied by two ministers with lighted candles, the priest then carries the cross to the entrance of the sanctuary or to another suitable place. There he lays the cross down or hands it to the ministers to hold. Candles are placed on either side of the cross, and the veneration follows as below.

Second Form of Showing the Cross

The priest or deacon, accompanied by the ministers or by another suitable minister, goes to the church door. There he takes the (uncovered) cross, and the ministers take lighted candles. They go in procession through the church to the sanctuary. Near the entrance of the church, in the middle of the church, and at the entrance to the sanctuary, the one carrying the cross stops, lifts it up and sings the invitation This is the wood of the cross. *All respond:* Come, let us worship. *After each response all kneel and venerate the cross briefly in silence as above.*

Then the cross and candles are placed at the entrance to the sanctuary.

INVITATION

℣. This is the wood of the cross, on which hung the Savior of the world.

℟. **Come, let us worship.**

Veneration of the Cross

The priest, clergy, and faithful approach to venerate the cross in a kind of procession. They make a simple genuflection or perform some other appropriate sign of reverence according to local custom, for example, kissing the cross.

During the veneration the antiphon We worship you, Lord, *the reproaches or other suitable songs are sung. All who have venerated the cross return to their places and sit.*

Only one cross should be used for the veneration. If the number of people makes it impossible for everyone to venerate the cross individually, the priest may take the cross, after some of the faithful have venerated it, and stand in the center in front of the altar. In a few words he invites the people to venerate the cross and then holds it up briefly for them to worship in silence.

In the United States, if pastoral reasons suggest that there be individual veneration even though the number of people is very large, a second or third cross may be used.

After the veneration, the cross is carried to its place at the altar, and the lighted candles are placed around the altar or near the cross.

Songs at the Veneration of the Cross

Individual parts are indicated by no. 1 (first choir) and no. 2 (second choir); parts sung by both choirs together are indicated by nos. 1 and 2.

ANTIPHON   [Holy Cross]

1 and 2: Antiphon
We worship you, Lord,
we venerate your cross,
we praise your resurrection.
Through the cross you brought joy to the world.

1: Psalm 67, 2
May God be gracious and bless us;
and let his face shed its light upon us.

1 and 2: Antiphon
We worship you, Lord,
we venerate your cross,
we praise your resurrection.
Through the cross you brought joy to the world.

I

REPROACHES

1 and 2: **My people, what have I done to you?**
   How have I offended you? Answer me!

1: I led you out of Egypt, from slavery to freedom,
   but you led your Savior to the cross.

2: My people, what have I done to you?
   How have I offended you? Answer me!

1: Holy is God!

2: Holy and strong!

1: Holy immortal One,
   have mercy on us!

1 and 2: For forty years I led you safely through the
   desert.
   I fed you with manna from heaven,
   and brought you to a land of plenty;
   but you led your Savior to the cross.

1: Holy is God!

2: Holy and strong!

1: Holy immortal One,
   have mercy on us!

1 and 2: What more could I have done for you?
   I planted you as my fairest vine,
   but you yielded only bitterness:
   when I was thirsty you gave me vinegar to drink,
   and you pierced your Savior with a lance.

1: Holy is God!

2: Holy and strong!

1: Holy immortal One,
   have mercy on us!

II

1: For your sake I scourged your captors and their
   firstborn sons,
   but you brought your scourges down on me.

2: My people, what have I done to you?
   How have I offended you? Answer me!

1: I led you from slavery to freedom
and drowned your captors in the sea,
but you handed me over to your high priests.

2: My people, what have I done to you?
How have I offended you? Answer me!

1: I opened the sea before you,
but you opened my side with a spear.

2: My people, what have I done to you?
How have I offended you? Answer me!

1: I led you on your way in a pillar of cloud,
but you led me to Pilate's court.

2: My people, what have I done to you?
How have I offended you? Answer me!

1: I bore you up with manna in the desert,
but you struck me down and scourged me.

2: My people, what have I done to you?
How have I offended you? Answer me!

1: I gave you saving water from the rock,
but you gave me gall and vinegar to drink.

2: My people, what have I done to you?
How have I offended you? Answer me!

1: For you I struck down the kings of Canaan,
but you struck my head with a reed.

2: My people, what have I done to you?
How have I offended you? Answer me!

1: I gave you a royal scepter,
but you gave me a crown of thorns.

2: My people, what have I done to you?
How have I offended you? Answer me!

1: I raised you to the height of majesty,
but you have raised me high on a cross.

2: My people, what have I done to you?
How have I offended you? Answer me!

HYMN: PANGE LINGUA
[Sing to the Lord]

Sing, my tongue, the Savior's glory;
    tell his triumph far and wide;
Tell aloud the famous story
    of his body crucified;
How upon the cross a victim,
    vanquishing in death, he died.

Eating of the tree forbidden,
    man had sunk in Satan's snare,
When our pitying Creator did
    this second tree prepare;
Destined, many ages later,
    that first evil to repair.

Such the order God appointed
    when for sin he would atone;
To the serpent thus opposing
    schemes yet deeper than his own;
Thence the remedy procuring,
    when the fatal wound had come.

So when now at length the fullness
    of the sacred time drew nigh,
Then the Son, the world's Creator,
    left his Father's throne on high;
From a virgin's womb appearing,
    clothed in our mortality.

All within a lowly manger,
    lo, a tender babe he lies!
See his gentle Virgin Mother
    lull to sleep his infant cries!
While the limbs of God incarnate
    round with swathing bands she ties.

Thus did Christ to perfect manhood
    in our mortal flesh attain:
Then of his free choice he goeth
    to a death of bitter pain;

And as a lamb, upon the altar of the cross,
   for us is slain.

Lo, with gall his thirst he quenches!
   See the thorns upon his brow!
Nails his tender flesh are rending!
   See, his side is opened now!
Whence, to cleanse the whole creation,
   streams of blood and water flow.

Lofty tree, bend down thy branches,
   to embrace thy sacred load;
Oh, relax the native tension
   of that all too rigid wood;
Gently, gently bear the members
   of thy dying King and God.

Tree, which solely wast found worthy
   the world's great Victim to sustain.
Harbor from the raging tempest!
   Ark, that saved the world again!
Tree, with sacred blood anointed
   of the Lamb for sinners slain.

Blessing, honor everlasting,
   to the immortal Deity;
To the Father, Son, and Spirit,
   equal praises ever be;
Glory through the earth and heaven
   to Trinity in Unity. Amen.

PART THREE: HOLY COMMUNION

The altar is covered with a cloth and the corporal and book are placed on it. Then the deacon or, if there is no deacon, the priest brings the ciborium with the Blessed Sacrament from the place of reposition to the altar without any procession, while all stand in silence.

The priest comes from his chair, genuflects, and goes up to the altar. With hands joined, he says aloud:

Let us pray with confidence to the Father
in the words our Savior gave us:

He extends his hands and continues, with all present:

Our Father . . .

With hands extended, the priest continues alone:

Deliver us, Lord, from every evil,
and grant us peace in our day.
In your mercy keep us free from sin
and protect us from all anxiety
as we wait in joyful hope
for the coming of our Savior, Jesus Christ.

The people end the prayer with the acclamation:

**For the kingdom, the power, and the glory are yours,
now and for ever.**

Then the priest says quietly:

Lord Jesus Christ, with faith in your love and mercy
   I eat your body and drink your blood.
Let it not bring me condemnation, but health in mind
   and body.

Taking the host, the priest says aloud:

This is the Lamb of God
who takes away the sins of the world.
Happy are those who are called to his supper.

He adds, once only, with the people:

**Lord, I am not worthy to receive you,
but only say the word and I shall be healed.**

Facing the altar, he reverently consumes the body of Christ.

Then communion is distributed to the faithful. Any appropriate song may be sung during communion.

When the communion has been completed, a suitable minister may take the ciborium to a place prepared outside the church or, if circumstances require, may place it in the tabernacle.

A period of silence may now be observed. The priest then says the following prayer:

Let us pray.   [Serving God]
Almighty and eternal God,
you have restored us to life
by the triumphant death and resurrection of Christ.
Continue this healing work within us.
May we who participate in this mystery
never cease to serve you.
We ask this through Christ our Lord. R̶̸. **Amen.** ↓

*For the dismissal the priest faces the people, extends his
hands toward them, and says the following prayer:*

PRAYER OVER THE PEOPLE   [Salvation Assured]

Lord,
send down your abundant blessing
upon your people who have devoutly recalled the
    death of your Son
in the sure hope of the resurrection.
Grant them pardon; bring them comfort.
May their faith grow stronger
and their eternal salvation be assured.
We ask this through Christ our Lord. R̶̸. **Amen.** ↓

*All depart in silence. The altar is stripped at a convenient
time.*

MARCH 29

HOLY SATURDAY

*On Holy Saturday the Church waits at the Lord's tomb, med-
itating on his suffering and death. The altar is left bare, and
the sacrifice of the Mass is not celebrated. Only after the
solemn vigil during the night, held in anticipation of the resurrection, does the Easter celebration begin, with a spirit of
joy that overflows into the following period of fifty days.*

"He has been raised up; he is not here."

MARCH 29
EASTER VIGIL

In accord with ancient tradition, this night is one of vigil for the Lord (Ex 12, 42). The Gospel of Luke (12, 35ff) is a reminder to the faithful to have their lamps burning, to be like men awaiting their master's return so that when he arrives he will find them wide awake and will seat them at his table. The night vigil is arranged in four parts: (a) a brief service of light; (b) the liturgy of the word, when the Church meditates on all the wonderful things God has done for his people from the beginning; (c) the liturgy of baptism, when new members of the Church are reborn as the day of resurrection approaches; and (d) the liturgy of the eucharist, when the whole Church is called to the table which the Lord has prepared for his people through his death and resurrection.

PART ONE
SOLEMN BEGINNING OF THE VIGIL:
THE SERVICE OF LIGHT
Blessing of the Fire and Lighting the Candle

All the lights in the church are put out.

A large fire is prepared in a suitable place outside the church. When the people have assembled, the priest goes there with the ministers, one of whom carries the Easter candle.

239

If it is not possible to light the fire outside the church, the rite is carried out as below, p. 241.

The priest greets the congregation in the usual manner and briefly instructs them about the vigil in these or similar words:

Dear friends in Christ,   **[Honoring Christ's Memory]**
on this most holy night,
when our Lord Jesus Christ passed from death to life,
the Church invites her children throughout the world
to come together in vigil and prayer.
This is the passover of the Lord:
if we honor the memory of his death and resurrection
by hearing his word and celebrating his mysteries,
then we may be confident
that we shall share his victory over death
and live with him for ever in God.

Then the fire is blessed.

                        [Light of the World]

Let us pray.
Father,
we share in the light of your glory
through your Son, the light of the world.
Make this new fire ✠ holy, and inflame us with new
   hope.
Purify our minds by this Easter celebration
and bring us one day to the feast of eternal light.
We ask this through Christ our Lord. ℟. **Amen.** ↓

The Easter candle is lighted from the new fire.

Preparation of the Candle

Depending on the nature of the congregation, it may seem appropriate to stress the dignity and significance of the Easter candle with other symbolic rites. This may be done as follows:

After the blessing of the new fire, an acolyte or one of the ministers brings the Easter candle to the celebrant, who cuts a cross in the wax with a stylus. Then he traces the Greek let-

ter alpha above the cross, the letter omega below, and the nu-
merals of the current year between the arms of the cross.
Meanwhile he says:

1. Christ yesterday and today *(as he traces the verti-*
   cal arm of the cross),
2. the beginning and the end *(the horizontal arm),*
3. Alpha *(alpha, above the cross),*
4. and Omega *(omega, below the cross);*
5. all time belongs to him *(the first numeral, in the*
   upper left corner of the cross),
6. and all the ages *(the second numeral in*
   the upper right corner);
7. to him be glory and power *(the third*
   numeral in the lower left corner),
8. through every age for ever. Amen.
   (the last numeral in the lower right cor-
   ner).

```
      A
   1  |  9
  ————+————
   9  |
      Ω
```

When the cross and other marks have been made, the priest
may insert five grains of incense in the candle. He does this in
the form of a cross, saying:

1. By his holy
2. and glorious wounds
3. may Christ our Lord
4. guard us
5. and keep us. Amen.

```
      1
  4   2   5
      3
```

The priest lights the candle from the new fire, saying:

May the light of Christ, rising in glory,
dispel the darkness of our hearts and minds.

Any or all of the preceding rites may be used, depending on
local pastoral circumstances. The conferences of bishops may
also determine other rites better adapted to the culture of the
people.

———————————

Where it may be difficult to have a large fire, the blessing of
the fire is adapted to the circumstances. When the people
have assembled in the church as on other occasions, the

priest goes with the ministers (carrying the Easter candle) to the church door. If possible, the people turn to face the priest.

The greeting and brief instruction take place as above, p. 240. Then the fire is blessed and, if desired, the candle is prepared and lighted as above.

Procession

Then the deacon or, if there is no deacon, the priest takes the Easter candle, lifts it high, and sings alone:

Christ our light.

All answer:

Thanks be to God.

The conferences of bishops may determine a richer acclamation.

Then all enter the church, led by the deacon with the Easter candle. If incense is used, the thurifer goes before the deacon.

At the church door the deacon lifts the candle high and sings a second time:

Christ our light.

All answer:

Thanks be to God.

All light their candles from the Easter candle and continue in the procession.

When the deacon arrives before the altar, he faces the people and sings a third time:

Christ our light.

All answer:

Thanks be to God.

Then the lights in the church are put on.

Easter Proclamation (Exsultet)

When he comes to the altar, the priest goes to his chair. The deacon places the Easter candle on a stand in the middle of the sanctuary or near the lectern. If incense is used, the priest puts some in the censer, as at the gospel of Mass. Then the deacon asks the blessing of the priest, who says in a low voice:

The Lord be in your heart and on your lips,
that you may worthily proclaim his Easter praise.
In the name of the Father, and of the Son ✠ and of the
Holy Spirit. ℟. **Amen.** ↓

The book and candle may be incensed. Then the deacon or, if there is no deacon, the priest sings the Easter proclamation at the lectern or pulpit. All stand and hold lighted candles.

If necessary, the Easter proclamation may be sung by one who is not a deacon. In this case the words My dearest friends *up to the end of the introduction are omitted, as is the greeting* The Lord be with you.

The Easter proclamation may be sung either in the long or short form. The conferences of bishops may also adapt the text by inserting acclamations for the people.

Long Form of the Easter Proclamation (Exsultet)

Rejoice, heavenly powers! Sing, choirs of angels!
    Exult, all creation around God's throne!
    Jesus Christ, our King, is risen!
    Sound the trumpet of salvation!

Rejoice, O earth, in shining splendor,
    radiant in the brightness of your King!
    Christ has conquered! Glory fills you!
    Darkness vanishes for ever!

Rejoice, O Mother Church! Exult in glory!
    The risen Savior shines upon you!
    Let this place resound with joy,
    echoing the mighty song of all God's people!

[My dearest friends, standing with me in this holy light,
    join me in asking God for mercy,
    that he may give his unworthy minister
    grace to sing his Easter praises.]

[℣. The Lord be with you. ℟. **And also with you.**]

℣. Lift up your hearts. ℟. **We lift them up to the Lord.**

℣. Let us give thanks to the Lord our God. ℟. **It is right to give him thanks and praise.**

It is truly right
that with full hearts and minds and voices
we should praise the unseen God, the all-powerful
    Father,
and his only Son, our Lord Jesus Christ.
For Christ has ransomed us with his blood,
    and paid for us the price of Adam's sin
    to our eternal Father!
This is our passover feast,
    when Christ, the true Lamb, is slain,
    whose blood consecrates the homes of all believers.
This is the night when first you saved our fathers:
    you freed the people of Israel from their slavery
    and led them dry-shod through the sea.
This is the night when the pillar of fire
    destroyed the darkness of sin!
This is the night when Christians everywhere,
    washed clean of sin
    and freed from all defilement,
    are restored to grace and grow together in holiness.
This is the night when Jesus Christ
    broke the chains of death
    and rose triumphant from the grave.
What good would life have been to us,
    had Christ not come as our Redeemer?
Father, how wonderful your care for us!
    How boundless your merciful love!
    To ransom a slave
    you gave away your Son.
O happy fault, O necessary sin of Adam,
    which gained for us so great a Redeemer!
Most blessed of all nights, chosen by God
    to see Christ rising from the dead!

Of this night scripture says:
"The night will be as clear as day:
it will become my light, my joy."
The power of this holy night
dispels all evil, washes guilt away,
restores lost innocence, brings mourners joy;
it casts out hatred, brings us peace, and humbles
earthly pride.
Night truly blessed when heaven is wedded to earth
and man is reconciled with God!
Therefore, heavenly Father, in the joy of this night,
receive our evening sacrifice of praise,
your Church's solemn offering.
Accept this Easter candle,
a flame divided but undimmed,
a pillar of fire that glows to the honor of God.
Let it mingle with the lights of heaven
and continue bravely burning
to dispel the darkness of this night!
May the Morning Star which never sets find this flame
still burning:
Christ, that Morning Star, who came back from the
dead,
and shed his peaceful light on all mankind,
your Son who lives and reigns for ever and ever.
℟. **Amen.** ↓

Short Form of the Easter Proclamation (Exsultet)

Rejoice, heavenly powers! Sing, choirs of angels!
Exult, all creation around God's throne!
Jesus Christ, our King, is risen!
Sound the trumpet of salvation!

Rejoice, O earth, in shining splendor,
radiant in the brightness of your King!
Christ has conquered! Glory fills you!
Darkness vanishes for ever!

Rejoice, O Mother Church! Exult in glory!
  The risen Savior shines upon you!
  Let this place resound with joy,
  echoing the mighty song of all God's people!

[V. The Lord be with you.
R̶. **And also with you.**]
V̶. Lift up your hearts.
R̶. **We lift them up to the Lord.**
V̶. Let us give thanks to the Lord our God.
R̶. **It is right to give him thanks and praise.**

It is truly right
that with full hearts and minds and voices
we should praise the unseen God, the all-powerful
    Father,
and his only Son, our Lord Jesus Christ.

For Christ has ransomed us with his blood,
  and paid for us the price of Adam's sin
  to our eternal Father!

This is our passover feast,
  when Christ, the true Lamb, is slain,
  whose blood consecrates the homes of all believers.

This is the night when first you saved our fathers:
  you freed the people of Israel from their slavery
  and led them dry-shod through the sea.

This is the night when Christians everywhere,
  washed clean of sin
  and freed from all defilement,
  are restored to grace and grow together in holiness.

This is the night when Jesus Christ
  broke the chains of death
  and rose triumphant from the grave.

Father, how wonderful your care for us!
  How boundless your merciful love!
  To ransom a slave
  you gave away your Son.

O happy fault, O necessary sin of Adam,
  which gained for us so great a Redeemer!

The power of this holy night
  dispels all evil, washes guilt away,
    restores lost innocence, brings mourners joy.

Night truly blessed when heaven is wedded to earth
  and man is reconciled with God!

Therefore, heavenly Father, in the joy of this night,
  receive our evening sacrifice of praise,
    your Church's solemn offering.

Accept this Easter candle.
  May it always dispel the darkness of this night!

May the Morning Star which never sets find this flame
    still burning:
  Christ, that Morning Star, who came back from the
    dead,
  and shed his peaceful light on all mankind,
    your Son who lives and reigns for ever and ever.
℟. **Amen.** ↓

PART TWO

LITURGY OF THE WORD

In this vigil, the mother of all vigils, nine readings are pro-
vided, seven from the Old Testament and two from the New
Testament (the epistle and gospel).

The number of readings from the Old Testament may be re-
duced for pastoral reasons, but it must always be borne in
mind that the reading of the word of God is the fundamental
element of the Easter Vigil. At least three readings from the
Old Testament should be read, although for more serious rea-
sons the number may be reduced to two. The reading of Exo-
dus 14, however, is never to be omitted.

After the Easter proclamation, the candles are put aside and
all sit down. Before the readings begin, the priest speaks to
the people in these or similar words:

Dear friends in Christ,   [Attentive Listening]
we have begun our solemn vigil.
Let us now listen attentively to the word of God,
recalling how he saved his people throughout history
and, in the fullness of time,
sent his own Son to be our Redeemer.
Through this Easter celebration,
may God bring to perfection
the saving work he has begun in us.

The readings follow. A reader goes to the lectern and pro-claims the first reading. Then the cantor leads the psalm and the people respond. All rise and the priest sings or says Let us pray. *When all have prayed silently for a while, he sings or says the prayer.*

Instead of the responsorial psalm a period of silence may be observed. In this case the pause after Let us pray *is omitted.*

READING I Gn 1, 1—2, 2 or 1, 1. 26-31   [God Our Creator]

God created the world and all that is in it. He saw that it was good. This reading from the first book of the Bible shows that God loved all that he made.

[If the "Short Form" is used, the indented text in brackets is omitted.]

The beginning of the book of Genesis

IN the beginning, when God created the heavens and the earth,

[the earth was a formless wasteland, and dark-ness covered the abyss, while a mighty wind swept over the waters.

Then God said, "Let there be light," and there was light. God saw how good the light was. God then sep-arated the light from the darkness. God called the light "day," and the darkness he called "night." Thus evening came, and morning followed—the first day.

Then God said, "Let there be a dome in the middle of the waters, to separate one body of water from the other." And so it happened: God made the dome, and it separated the water above the dome from the water below it. God called the dome "the sky." Evening came, and morning followed—the second day.

Then God said, "Let the water under the sky be gathered into a single basin, so that the dry land may appear." And so it happened: the water under the sky was gathered into its basin, and the dry land appeared. God called the dry land "the earth," and the basin of the water he called "the sea." God saw how good it was. Then God said, "Let the earth bring forth vegetation: every kind of plant that bears seed and every kind of fruit tree on earth that bears fruit with its seed in it." And so it happened: the earth brought forth every kind of plant that bears seed and every kind of fruit tree on earth that bears fruit with its seed in it. God saw how good it was. Evening came, and morning followed—the third day.

Then God said: "Let there be lights in the dome of the sky, to separate day from night. Let them mark the fixed times, the days and the years, and serve as luminaries in the dome of the sky, to shed light upon the earth." And so it happened: God made the two great lights, the greater one to govern the day, and the lesser one to govern the night; and he made the stars. God set them in the dome of the sky, to shed light upon the earth, to govern the day and the night, and to separate the light from the darkness. God saw how good it was. Evening came, and morning followed—the fourth day.

Then God said, "Let the water teem with an abundance of living creatures, and on the earth let birds fly beneath the dome of the sky." And so it happened: God created the great sea monsters and all kinds of swimming creatures with which the water teems, and all kinds of winged birds. God saw how good it was, and God blessed them, saying, "Be fertile, multiply, and fill the water of the seas; and let the birds multiply on the earth." Evening came, and morning followed—the fifth day.

Then God said, "Let the earth bring forth all kinds of living creatures: cattle, creeping things, and wild animals of all kinds." And so it happened: God made all kinds of wild animals, all kinds of cattle, and all kinds of creeping things of the earth. God saw how good it was. Then]

God said: "Let us make man in our image, after our likeness. Let them have dominion over the fish of the sea, the birds of the air, and the cattle, and over all the wild animals and all the creatures that crawl on the ground."

God created man in his image;
    in the divine image he created him;
    male and female he created them.

God blessed them, saying: "Be fertile and multiply; fill the earth and subdue it. Have dominion over the fish of the sea, the birds of the air, and all the living things that move on the earth." God also said: "See, I give you every seed-bearing plant all over the earth and every tree that has seed-bearing fruit on it to be your food; and to all the animals of the land, all the birds of the air, and all the living creatures that crawl on the ground, I give all the green plants for food." And so it happened. God looked at everything he had made, and he found it very good.

[Evening came, and morning followed—the sixth day.

Thus the heavens and the earth and all their array were completed. Since on the seventh day God was finished with the work he had been doing, he rested on the seventh day from all the work he had undertaken.]

The word of the Lord. ℟. **Thanks be to God.** ↓

RESPONSORIAL PSALM Ps 104   [Come, Holy Spirit]

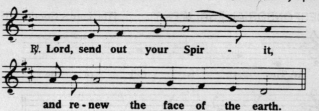

℟. Lord, send out your Spir - it, and re - new the face of the earth.

Bless the Lord, O my soul!
   O Lord, my God, you are great indeed!
You are clothed with majesty and glory,
   robed in light as with a cloak.—℟.

You fixed the earth upon its foundation,
   not to be moved forever;
With the ocean, as with a garment, you covered it;
   above the mountains the waters stood.—℟.

You send forth springs into the watercourses
   that wind among the mountains.
Beside them the birds of heaven dwell;
   from among the branches they send forth their
     song.—℟.

You water the mountains from your palace;
   the earth is replete with the fruit of your works.
You raise grass for the cattle,
   and vegetation for men's use,
Producing bread from the earth.—℟.

How manifold are your works, O Lord!
   In wisdom you have wrought them all—
   the earth is full of your creatures.
Bless the Lord, O my soul! Alleluia.—℟. ↓

OR

RESPONSORIAL PSALM Ps 33   [The Lord's Goodness]

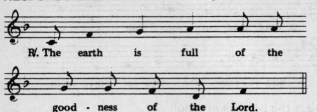

R⟩. The earth is full of the goodness of the Lord.

Upright is the word of the Lord,
   and all his works are trustworthy.
He loves justice and right;
   of the kindness of the Lord the earth is full.

R⟩. **The earth is full of the goodness of the Lord.**

By the word of the Lord the heavens were made;
   by the breath of his mouth all their host.
He gathers the waters of the sea as in a flask;
   in cellars he confines the deep.

R⟩. **The earth is full of the goodness of the Lord.**

Happy the nation whose God is the Lord,
   the people he has chosen for his own inheritance.
From heaven the Lord looks down;
   he sees all mankind.

R⟩. **The earth is full of the goodness of the Lord.**

Our soul waits for the Lord,
   who is our help and our shield.
May your kindness, O Lord, be upon us
   who have put our hope in you.

R⟩. **The earth is full of the goodness of the Lord.** ↓

PRAYER   [New Creation]

Let us pray.
Almighty and eternal God,

you created all things in wonderful beauty and order.
Help us now to perceive
how still more wonderful is the new creation
by which in the fullness of time
you redeemed your people
through the sacrifice of our passover, Jesus Christ,
who lives and reigns for ever and ever. R̰. **Amen.** ↓

OR

PRAYER (on the creation of man)   [Our Redemption]

Let us pray.
Lord God,
the creation of man was a wonderful work,
his redemption still more wonderful.
May we persevere in right reason
against all that entices to sin
and so attain to everlasting joy.
We ask this through Christ our Lord. R̰. **Amen.** ↓

READING II Gn 22, 1-18 or 22, 1-2. 9. 10-13. 15-18 [Obedience]

Abraham is obedient to the will of God. Because God asks him, without hesitation he prepares to sacrifice his son Isaac. In the new order, God sends his Son to redeem man by his death on the cross.

[If the "Short Form" is used, the indented text in brackets is omitted.]

A reading from the book of Genesis

GOD put Abraham to the test. He called to him, "Abraham!" "Ready!" he replied. Then God said: "Take your son Isaac, your only one, whom you love, and go to the land of Moriah. There you shall offer him up as a holocaust on a height that I will point out to you."

[Early the next morning Abraham saddled his donkey, took with him his son Isaac, and two of his servants as well, and with the wood that he had cut

for the holocaust, set out for the place of which God
had told him.

On the third day Abraham got sight of the place
from afar. Then he said to his servants: "Both of you
stay here with the donkey, while the boy and I go
on over yonder. We will worship and then come
back to you." Thereupon Abraham took the wood
for the holocaust and laid it on his son Isaac's shoulders, while he himself carried the fire and the knife.
As the two walked on together, Isaac spoke to his
father Abraham. "Father!" he said. "Yes, son," he
replied. Isaac continued, "Here are the fire and the
wood, but where is the sheep for the holocaust?"
"Son," Abraham answered, "God himself will provide the sheep for the holocaust." Then the two continued going forward.]

When they came to the place of which God had told
him, Abraham built an altar there and arranged the
wood on it.

[Next he tied up his son Isaac, and put him on top
of the wood on the altar.]

Then he reached out and took the knife to slaughter
his son. But the Lord's messenger called to him from
heaven, "Abraham, Abraham!" "Yes, Lord," he answered. "Do not lay your hand on the boy," said the
messenger. "Do not do the least thing to him. I know
now how devoted you are to God, since you did not
withhold from me your own beloved son." As Abraham looked about, he spied a ram caught by its horns
in the thicket. So he went and took the ram and offered it up as a holocaust in place of his son.

[Abraham named the site Yahweh-yireh; hence
people now say, "On the mountain the Lord will see."]

Again the Lord's messenger called to Abraham
from heaven and said: "I swear by myself, declares
the Lord, that because you acted as you did in not
withholding from me your beloved son, I will bless

you abundantly and make your descendants as countless as the stars of the sky and the sands of the
seashore; your descendants shall take possession of
the gates of their enemies, and in your descendants all
the nations of the earth shall find blessing—all this because you obeyed my command."—The word of the
Lord. ℟. **Thanks be to God.** ↓

RESPONSORIAL PSALM Ps 16   [God Our Hope]

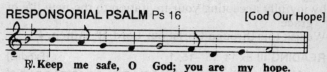

℟. **Keep me safe, O God; you are my hope.**

O Lord, my allotted portion and my cup,
    you it is who hold fast my lot.
I set the Lord ever before me;
    with him at my right I shall not be disturbed.

℟. **Keep me safe, O God;**
    you are my hope.

Therefore my heart is glad and my soul rejoices,
    my body, too, abides in confidence;
Because you will not abandon my soul to the nether
        world,
    nor will you suffer your faithful one to undergo cor-
        ruption.

℟. **Keep me safe, O God;**
    you are my hope.

You will show me the path to life,
    fullness of joys in your presence,
    the delights at your right hand forever.

℟. **Keep me safe, O God;**
    you are my hope. ↓

PRAYER   [Response to God's Call]
Let us pray.
God and Father of all who believe in you,

you promised Abraham that he would become the
  father of all nations,
and through the death and resurrection of Christ
you fulfill that promise:
everywhere throughout the world you increase your
  chosen people.
May we respond to your call
by joyfully accepting your invitation to the new life of
  grace.
We ask this through Christ our Lord. ℟. **Amen.** ↓

READING III Ex 14, 15—15, 1   [Exodus]

> Moses leads the Israelites out of Egypt. He opens a path of
> escape through the Red Sea. God protects his people.
> Through the waters of baptism, men are freed from sin.

A reading from the book of Exodus

THE Lord said to Moses, "Why are you crying out to
me? Tell the Israelites to go forward. And you, lift
up your staff and, with hand outstretched over the
sea, split the sea in two, that the Israelites may pass
through it on dry land. But I will make the Egyptians
so obstinate that they will go in after them. Then I will
receive glory through Pharaoh and all his army, his
chariots and charioteers. The Egyptians shall know
that I am the Lord, when I receive glory through
Pharaoh and his chariots and charioteers."

The angel of God, who had been leading Israel's
camp, now moved and went around behind them. The
column of cloud also, leaving the front, took up its
place behind them, so that it came between the camp
of the Egyptians and that of Israel. But the cloud now
became dark, and thus the night passed without the
rival camps coming any closer together all night long.
Then Moses stretched out his hand over the sea, and
the Lord swept the sea with a strong east wind
throughout the night and so turned it into dry land.

When the water was thus divided, the Israelites marched into the midst of the sea on dry land, with the water like a wall to their right and to their left.

The Egyptians followed in pursuit; all Pharaoh's horses and chariots and charioteers went after them right into the midst of the sea. In the night watch just before dawn the Lord cast through the column of the fiery cloud upon the Egyptian force a glance that threw it into a panic; and he so clogged their chariot wheels that they could hardly drive. With that the Egyptians sounded the retreat before Israel, because the Lord was fighting for them against the Egyptians.

Then the Lord told Moses, "Stretch out your hand over the sea, that the water may flow back upon the Egyptians, upon their chariots and their charioteers." So Moses stretched out his hand over the sea, and at dawn the sea flowed back to its normal depth. The Egyptians were fleeing head on toward the sea, when the Lord hurled them into its midst. As the water flowed back, it covered the chariots and the charioteers of Pharaoh's whole army which had followed the Israelites into the sea. Not a single one of them escaped. But the Israelites had marched on dry land through the midst of the sea, with the water like a wall to their right and to their left. Thus the Lord saved Israel on that day from the power of the Egyptians. When Israel saw the Egyptians lying dead on the seashore and beheld the great power that the Lord had shown against the Egyptians, they feared the Lord and believed in him and in his servant Moses.

Then Moses and the Israelites sang this song to the Lord:

I will sing to the Lord, for he is gloriously triumphant;

horse and chariot he has cast into the sea.

The word of the Lord. ℟. **Thanks be to God.** ↓

RESPONSORIAL PSALM Ex 15   [God the Savior]

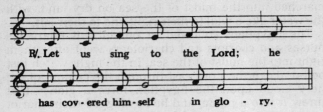

R/. Let us sing to the Lord; he has cov-ered him-self in glo-ry.

I will sing to the Lord, for he is gloriously triumphant;
  horse and chariot he has cast into the sea.
My strength and my courage is the Lord,
  and he has been my savior.
He is my God, I praise him;
  the God of my father, I extol him.

R/. **Let us sing to the Lord;**
  he has covered himself in glory.

The Lord is a warrior,
  Lord is his name!
Pharaoh's chariots and army he hurled into the sea;
  the elite of his officers were submerged into the Red
    Sea.

R/. **Let us sing to the Lord;**
  he has covered himself in glory.

The flood waters covered them,
  they sank into the depths like a stone.
Your right hand, O Lord, magnificent in power,
  your right hand, O Lord, has shattered the enemy.

R/. **Let us sing to the Lord;**
  he has covered himself in glory.

You brought in the people you redeemed
  and planted them on the mountain of your inheri-
    tance.
The place where you made your seat, O Lord,

the sanctuary, O Lord, which your hands established.
The Lord shall reign forever and ever.

℟. **Let us sing to the Lord;**
   he has covered himself in glory. ↓

PRAYER   [Children of Abraham]
Let us pray.
Father,
even today we see the wonders
of the miracles you worked long ago.
You once saved a single nation from slavery,
and now you offer that salvation to all through baptism.
May the peoples of the world become true sons of
   Abraham
and prove worthy of the heritage of Israel.
We ask this through Christ our Lord. ℟. **Amen.** ↓

OR

PRAYER   [New Birth]
Let us pray.
Lord God,
in the new covenant
you shed light on the miracles you worked in ancient
   times:
the Red Sea is a symbol of our baptism,
and the nation you freed from slavery
is a sign of your Christian people.
May every nation
share the faith and privilege of Israel
and come to new birth in the Holy Spirit.
We ask this through Christ our Lord. ℟. **Amen.** ↓

READING IV Is 54, 5-14   [God's Love]

For a time, God hid from his people, but his love for them
is everlasting. He takes pity on them and promises them
prosperity.

A reading from the book of the prophet Isaiah

HE who has become your husband is your Maker;
his name is the Lord of hosts;
Your redeemer is the Holy One of Israel,
    called God of all the earth.
The Lord calls you back,
    like a wife forsaken and grieved in spirit,
A wife married in youth and then cast off,
    says your God.
For a brief moment I abandoned you,
    but with great tenderness I will take you back.
In an outburst of wrath, for a moment
    I hid my face from you;
But with enduring love I take pity on you,
    says the Lord, your redeemer.
This is for me like the days of Noah,
    when I swore that the waters of Noah
    should never again deluge the earth;
So I have sworn not to be angry with you,
    or to rebuke you.
Though the mountains leave their place
    and the hills be shaken,
My love shall never leave you
    nor my covenant of peace be shaken,
    says the Lord, who has mercy on you.
O afflicted one, storm-battered and unconsoled,
    I lay your pavements in carnelians,
    and your foundations in sapphires;
I will make your battlements of rubies,
    your gates of carbuncles,
    and all your walls of precious stones.
All your sons shall be taught by the Lord,
    and great shall be the peace of your children.
In justice shall you be established,
    far from the fear of oppression,
    where destruction cannot come near you.
The word of the Lord. ℟. **Thanks be to God.** ↓

RESPONSORIAL PSALM Ps 30   [God Our Help]

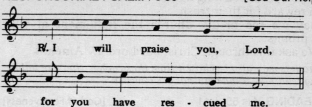

R̸. I will praise you, Lord, for you have res-cued me.

I will extol you, O Lord, for you drew me clear
  and did not let my enemies rejoice over me.
O Lord, you brought me up from the nether world;
  you preserved me from among those going down
    into the pit.

R̸. **I will praise you, Lord,**
  for you have rescued me.

Sing praise to the Lord, you his faithful ones,
  and give thanks to his holy name.
For his anger lasts but a moment;
  a lifetime, his good will.
At nightfall, weeping enters in,
  but with the dawn, rejoicing.

R̸. **I will praise you, Lord,**
  for you have rescued me.

Hear, O Lord, and have pity on me;
  O Lord, be my helper.
You changed my mourning into dancing;
  O Lord, my God, forever will I give you thanks.

R̸. **I will praise you, Lord,**
  for you have rescued me. ↓

PRAYER   [Fulfillment of God's Promise]

Let us pray.
Almighty and eternal God,
glorify your name by increasing your chosen people

as you promised long ago.
In reward for their trust,
may we see in the Church the fulfillment of your
  promise.
We ask this through Christ our Lord. ℟. **Amen.** ↓

*Prayers may also be chosen from those given after the follow-
ing readings, if the readings are omitted.*

READING V Is 55, 1-11   [God of Forgiveness]

> God is a loving Father and he calls his people back. He
> promises an everlasting covenant with them. God is merci-
> ful, generous, and forgiving.

A reading from the book of the prophet Isaiah

T HUS says the Lord:
  All you who are thirsty,
    come to the water!
You who have no money,
    come, receive grain and eat;
Come, without paying and without cost,
    drink wine and milk!
Why spend your money for what is not bread;
    your wages for what fails to satisfy?
Heed me, and you shall eat well,
    you shall delight in rich fare.
Come to me heedfully,
    listen, that you may have life.
I will renew with you the everlasting covenant,
    the benefits assured to David.
As I made him a witness to the peoples,
    a leader and commander of nations,
So shall you summon a nation you knew not,
    and nations that knew you not shall run to you,
Because of the Lord, your God,
    the Holy One of Israel, who has glorified you.
Seek the Lord while he may be found,
    call him while he is near.

Let the scoundrel forsake his way,
 and the wicked man his thoughts;
Let him turn to the Lord for mercy;
 to our God, who is generous in forgiving.
For my thoughts are not your thoughts,
 nor are your ways my ways, says the Lord.
As high as the heavens are above the earth,
 so high are my ways above your ways,
 and my thoughts above your thoughts.
For just as from the heavens
 the rain and snow come down
And do not return there
 till they have watered the earth,
 making it fertile and fruitful,
Giving seed to him who sows
 and bread to him who eats,
So shall my word be
 that goes forth from my mouth;
It shall not return to me void,
 but shall do my will,
 achieving the end for which I sent it.
The word of the Lord. ℟. **Thanks be to God.** ↓

RESPONSORIAL PSALM Is 12 [Make Known God's Deeds]

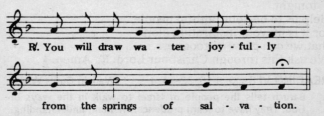

℟. You will draw water joy-ful-ly from the springs of sal-va-tion.

God indeed is my savior;
 I am confident and unafraid.
My strength and my courage is the Lord,
 and he has been my savior.

With joy you will draw water
   at the fountain of salvation.

℟. **You will draw water joyfully from the springs of salvation.**

Give thanks to the Lord, acclaim his name;
   among the nations make known his deeds,
   proclaim how exalted is his name.

℟. **You will draw water joyfully from the springs of salvation.**

Sing praise to the Lord for his glorious achievement;
   let this be known throughout all the earth.
Shout with exultation, O city of Zion,
   for great in your midst
   is the Holy One of Israel!

℟. **You will draw water joyfully from the springs of salvation.** ↓

PRAYER   [Growth in Goodness]
Let us pray.
Almighty, ever-living God,
only hope of the world,
by the preaching of the prophets
you proclaimed the mysteries we are celebrating
   tonight.
Help us to be your faithful people,
for it is by your inspiration alone
that we can grow in goodness.
We ask this through Christ our Lord. ℟. **Amen.** ↓

READING VI Bar 3, 9-15. 32—4, 4   [Walk in God's Ways]
   **Baruch tells the people of Israel to walk in the ways of
   God. They have to learn prudence, wisdom, understanding.
   Then they will have peace forever.**

   A reading from the book of the prophet Baruch

HEAR, O Israel, the commandments of life:
   listen, and know prudence!

How is it, Israel,
    that you are in the land of your foes,
    grown old in a foreign land,
Defiled with the dead,
    accounted with those destined for the nether world?
You have forsaken the fountain of wisdom!
    Had you walked in the way of God,
    you would have dwelt in enduring peace.
Learn where prudence is,
    where strength, where understanding;
That you may know also
    where are length of days, and life,
    where light of the eyes, and peace.
Who has found the place of wisdom,
    who has entered into her treasuries?
He who knows all things knows her;
    he has probed her by his knowledge—
He who established the earth for all time,
    and filled it with four-footed beasts;
He who dismisses the light, and it departs,
    calls it, and it obeys him trembling;
Before whom the stars at their posts
    shine and rejoice;
When he calls them, they answer, "Here we are!"
    shining with joy for their Maker.
Such is our God;
    no other is to be compared to him:
He has traced out all the way of understanding,
    and has given her to Jacob, his servant,
    to Israel, his beloved son.
Since then she has appeared on earth,
    and moved among men.
She is the book of the precepts of God,
    the law that endures forever;
All who cling to her will live,
    but those will die who forsake her.
Turn, O Jacob, and receive her:

walk by her light toward splendor.
Give not your glory to another,
    your privileges to an alien race.
Blessed are we, O Israel;
    for what pleases God is known to us!
The word of the Lord. ℟. **Thanks be to God.** ↓

RESPONSORIAL PSALM Ps 19   [Words of Eternal Life]

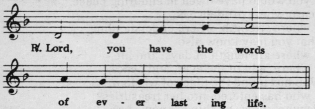

℟. Lord, you have the words of everlasting life.

The law of the Lord is perfect,
    refreshing the soul;
The decree of the Lord is trustworthy,
    giving wisdom to the simple.

℟. **Lord, you have the words of everlasting life.**

The precepts of the Lord are right,
    rejoicing the heart;
The command of the Lord is clear,
    enlightening the eye.

℟. **Lord, you have the words of everlasting life.**

The fear of the Lord is pure,
    enduring forever;
The ordinances of the Lord are true,
    all of them just.

℟. **Lord, you have the words of everlasting life.**

They are more precious than gold,
    than a heap of purest gold;
Sweeter also than syrup
    or honey from the comb.

℟. **Lord, you have the words of everlasting life.** ↓

PRAYER   [Hear Our Prayer]

Let us pray.
Father,
you increase your Church
by continuing to call all people to salvation.
Listen to our prayers
and always watch over those you cleanse in baptism.
We ask this through Christ our Lord. ℟. **Amen.** ↓

READING VII Ez 36, 16-28   [God's People]

Ezekiel, as God's prophet, speaks for God who is to keep
his name holy among his people. All shall know the holiness of God. He will cleanse his people from idol worship
and make them his own again. This promise is again fulfilled in baptism in the restored order of redemption.

A reading from the book of the prophet Ezekiel

THUS the word of the Lord came to me: Son of man,
when the house of Israel lived in their land, they
defiled it by their conduct and deeds. In my sight their
conduct was like the defilement of a menstruous
woman. Therefore I poured out my fury upon them
[because of the blood which they poured out on the
ground, and because they defiled it with idols]. I scattered them among the nations, dispersing them over
foreign lands; according to their conduct and deeds I
judged them. But when they came among the nations
[wherever they came], they served to profane my holy
name, because it was said of them: "These are the people of the Lord, yet they had to leave their land." So I
have relented because of my holy name which the
house of Israel profaned among the nations where
they came. Therefore say to the house of Israel: Thus
says the Lord God: Not for your sakes do I act, house
of Israel, but for the sake of my holy name, which you
profaned among the nations to which you came. I will
prove the holiness of my great name, profaned among

the nations, in whose midst you have profaned it. Thus
the nations shall know that I am the Lord, says the
Lord God, when in their sight I prove my holiness
through you. For I will take you away from among the
nations, gather you from all the foreign lands, and
bring you back to your own land. I will sprinkle clean
water upon you to cleanse you from all your impuri-
ties, and from all your idols I will cleanse you. I will
give you a new heart and place a new spirit within
you, taking from your bodies your stony hearts and
giving you natural hearts. I will put my spirit within
you and make you live by my statutes, careful to observe my decrees. You shall live in the land I gave your
fathers; you shall be my people, and I will be your
God.—The word of the Lord. ℟. Thanks be to God. ↓

RESPONSORIAL PSALM Ps 42   [Longing for God]

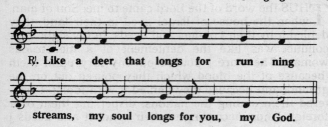

℟. Like a deer that longs for run - ning
streams, my soul longs for you, my God.

Athirst is my soul for God, the living God.
  When shall I go and behold the face of God?

℟. **Like a deer that longs for running streams,**
   my soul longs for you, my God.

I went with the throng
  and led them in procession to the house of God,
Amid loud cries of joy and thanksgiving,
  with the multitude keeping festival.

℟. **Like a deer that longs for running streams,**
   my soul longs for you, my God.

Send forth your light and your fidelity;
  they shall lead me on
And bring me to your holy mountain,
  to your dwelling-place.

℟. **Like a deer that longs for running streams,
  my soul longs for you, my God.**

Then will I go into the altar of God,
  the God of my gladness and joy;
Then will I give you thanks upon the harp,
  O God, my God!

℟. **Like a deer that longs for running streams,
  my soul longs for you, my God. ↓**

OR

*When baptism is celebrated, the responsorial psalm after
Reading V (Is 12, 2-3. 4. 5-6) as above, p. 263 may be used; or
the following:*

RESPONSORIAL PSALM Ps 51   [A Clean Heart]

℟. Cre - ate   a   clean heart   in   me,   O   God.

A clean heart create for me, O God,
  and a steadfast spirit renew within me.
Cast me not out from your presence,
  and your holy spirit take not from me.

℟. **Create a clean heart in me, O God.**

Give me back the joy of your salvation,
  and a willing spirit sustain in me.
I will teach transgressors your ways,
  and sinners shall return to you.

℟. **Create a clean heart in me, O God.**

For you are not pleased with sacrifices;
  should I offer a holocaust, you would not accept it.
My sacrifice, O God, is a contrite spirit;

a heart contrite and humbled, O God, you will not spurn.

R∫. **Create a clean heart in me, O God.** ↓

PRAYER [Lasting Salvation]

Let us pray.
God of unchanging power and light,
look with mercy and favor on your entire Church.
Bring lasting salvation to mankind,
so that the world may see
the fallen lifted up,
the old made new,
and all things brought to perfection,
through him who is their origin,
our Lord Jesus Christ,
who lives and reigns for ever and ever. R∫. **Amen.** ↓

OR

PRAYER [Confirm Our Hope]

Let us pray.
Father,
you teach us in both the Old and the New Testament
to celebrate this passover mystery.
Help us to understand your great love for us.
May the goodness you now show us
confirm our hope in your future mercy.
We ask this through Christ our Lord. R∫. **Amen.** ↓

After the last reading from the Old Testament with its responsory and prayer, the altar candles are lighted, and the priest intones the Gloria, which is taken up by all present. The church bells are rung, according to local custom.

At the end of the hymn, the priest sings or says the opening prayer in the usual way.

OPENING PRAYER [Renewed in Mind and Body]

Let us pray.
Lord God,

you have brightened this night
with the radiance of the risen Christ.
Quicken the spirit of sonship in your Church;
renew us in mind and body
to give you whole-hearted service.
Grant this through our Lord Jesus Christ, your Son,
who lives and reigns with you and the Holy Spirit,
one God, for ever and ever. ℞. **Amen.** ↓

Then a reader proclaims the reading from the Apostle Paul.

EPISTLE Rom 6, 3-11   [Alive in Christ]

By Baptism the Christian is not merely identified with the
dying Christ, who has won a victory over sin, but is introduced into the very act by which Christ died to sin.

A reading from the letter of Paul to the Romans

ARE you not aware that we who were baptized into
Christ Jesus were baptized into his death?
Through baptism into his death we were buried with
him, so that, just as Christ was raised from the dead
by the glory of the Father, we too might live a new
life. If we have been united with him through likeness
to his death, so shall we be through a like resurrection. This we know: our old self was crucified with
him so that the sinful body might be destroyed and we
might be slaves to sin no longer. A man who is dead
has been freed from sin. If we have died with Christ,
we believe that we are also to live with him. We know
that Christ, once raised from the dead, will never die
again; death has no more power over him. His death
was death to sin, once for all; his life is life for God. In
the same way, you must consider yourselves dead to
sin but alive for God in Christ Jesus.—The word of the
Lord. ℞. **Thanks be to God.** ↓

*After the epistle all rise, and the priest solemnly intones the
alleluia, which is repeated by all present.*

RESPONSORIAL PSALM Ps 118   [God's Mercy]

℟. **Al-le-lu-ia. Al - le- lu- ia.   Al - le - lu - ia.**

Give thanks to the Lord, for he is good,
   for his mercy endures forever.
Let the house of Israel say,
   "His mercy endures forever."

℟. **Alleluia. Alleluia. Alleluia.**

The right hand of the Lord has struck with power;
   the right hand of the Lord is exalted.
I shall not die, but live,
   and declare the works of the Lord.

℟. **Alleluia. Alleluia. Alleluia.**

The stone which the builders rejected
   has become the cornerstone.
By the Lord has this been done;
   it is wonderful in our eyes.

℟. **Alleluia. Alleluia. Alleluia.** ↓

Incense may be used at the gospel, but candles are not carried.

GOSPEL Mk 26, 1-8   [The Resurrection]

On Easter morning, Mary Magdalene, Mary the mother of
James, and Salome go to anoint the body of Jesus. An
angel announces to them the amazing news that Jesus of
Nazareth is risen as he had said and is on his way to
Galilee. . . . Alleluia.

℣. The Lord be with you. ℟. **And also with you.**
✛ A reading from the holy gospel according to Mark.
℟. **Glory to you, Lord.**

When the sabbath was over, Mary Magdalene,
   Mary the mother of James, and Salome bought
perfumed oils with which they intended to go and

anoint Jesus. Very early, just after sunrise, on the first day of the week they came to the tomb. They were saying to one another, "Who will roll back the stone for us from the entrance to the tomb?" When they looked, they found that the stone had been rolled back. (It was a huge one.) On entering the tomb they saw a young man sitting at the right, dressed in a white robe. This frightened them thoroughly, but he reassured them: "You need not be amazed! You are looking for Jesus of Nazareth, the one who was crucified. He has been raised up; he is not here. See the place where they laid him. Go now and tell his disciples and Peter, 'He is going ahead of you to Galilee, where you will see him just as he told you.' " They made their way out and fled from the tomb bewildered and trembling; and because of their great fear, they said nothing to anyone.—The gospel of the Lord. ℟. **Praise to you, Lord Jesus Christ.**

PART THREE

LITURGY OF SACRAMENTS OF INITIATION

The following is taken from the Rite of Christian Initiation of Adults.

Celebration of Baptism

PRESENTATION OF THE CANDIDATES

A. When Baptism Is Celebrated Immediately at the Baptismal Font.

The celebrant accompanied by the assisting ministers goes directly to the font. An assisting deacon or other minister calls the candidates for baptism forward and their godparents present them. Then the candidates and the godparents take their place around the font in such a way as not to block the view of the assembly. The invitation to prayer and the Litany of the Saints follow.

B. When Baptism Is Celebrated after a Procession to the Font.

There may be a full procession to the baptismal font. In this case an assisting deacon or other minister calls the candidates for baptism forward and their godparents present them.

The procession is formed in this order: a minister carries the Easter candle at the head of the procession (unless, outside the Easter Vigil, it already rests at the baptismal font), the candidates with their godparents come next, then the celebrant with the assisting ministers. The Litany of the Saints is sung during the procession. When the procession has reached the font, the candidates and their godparents take their place around the font in such a way as not to block the view of the assembly. The invitation to prayer precedes the blessing of the water.

C. When Baptism Is Celebrated in the Sanctuary.

An assisting deacon or other minister calls the candidates for baptism forward and their godparents present them. The candidates and their godparents take their place before the celebrant in the sanctuary in such a way as not to block the view of the assembly. The invitation to prayer and the Litany of the Saints follow.

INVITATION TO PRAYER

The celebrant addresses the following or a similar invitation for the assembly to join in prayer for the candidates for baptism.

Dear friends, let us pray to almighty God for our brothers and sisters, N. and N., who are asking for baptism. He has called them and brought them to this moment; may he grant them light and strength to follow Christ with resolute hearts and to profess the faith of the Church. May he give them the new life of the Holy Spirit, whom we are about to call down on this water.

LITANY OF THE SAINTS

The singing of the Litany of the Saints is led by cantors and may include, at the proper place, names of other saints (for example, the titular of the church, the patron saints of the place or of those to be baptized) or petitions suitable to the occasion.

Lord, have mercy.
Lord, have mercy.

Christ, have mercy.
Christ, have mercy.

Lord, have mercy.
Lord, have mercy.

Holy Mary, Mother of God, **pray for us.**

Saint Michael, **pray for us.**

Holy angels of God, **pray for us.**

Saint John the Baptist, **pray for us.**

Saint Joseph, **pray for us.**

Saint Peter and Saint Paul, **pray for us.**

Saint Andrew, **pray for us.**

Saint John, **pray for us.**

Saint Mary Magdalene, **pray for us.**

Saint Stephen, **pray for us.**

Saint Ignatius, **pray for us.**

Saint Lawrence, **pray for us.**

Saint Perpetua and Saint Felicity, **pray for us.**

Saint Agnes, **pray for us.**

Saint Gregory, **pray for us.**

Saint Augustine, **pray for us.**

Saint Athanasius, **pray for us.**

Saint Basil, **pray for us.**

Saint Martin, **pray for us.**

Saint Benedict, **pray for us.**

Saint Francis and Saint Dominic, **pray for us.**

Saint Francis Xavier, **pray for us.**

Saint John Vianney, **pray for us.**

Saint Catherine, **pray for us.**

Saint Teresa, **pray for us.**

All holy men and women, **pray for us.**

Lord, be merciful, **Lord, save your people.**

From all evil, **Lord, save your people.**

From every sin, **Lord, save your people.**

From everlasting death, **Lord, save your people.**

By your coming as man, **Lord, save your people.**

By your death and rising to new life, **Lord, save your people.**

By your gift of the Holy Spirit, **Lord, save your people.**

Be merciful to us sinners, **Lord, hear our prayer.**

Give new life to these chosen ones by the grace of baptism, **Lord, hear our prayer.**

Jesus, Son of the living God, **Lord, hear our prayer.**

Christ, hear us. **Christ, hear us.**

Lord Jesus, hear our prayer. **Lord Jesus, hear our prayer.**

BLESSING OF THE WATER

Facing the font (or vessel) containing the water, the celebrant sings or says the following:

Father,
you give us grace through sacramental signs,
which tell us the wonders of your unseen power.
In baptism we use your gift of water,
which you have made a rich symbol of the grace
you give us in this sacrament.
At the very dawn of creation
your Spirit breathed on the waters,
making them the wellspring of all holiness.
The waters of the great flood
you made a sign of the waters of baptism,
that make an end of sin
and a new beginning of goodness.
Through the waters of the Red Sea
you led Israel out of slavery,
to be an image of God's holy people,
set free from sin by baptism.
In the waters of the Jordan
your Son was baptized by John
and anointed with the Spirit.

Your Son willed that water and blood should flow
   from his side
as he hung upon the cross.
After his resurrection he told his disciples:
"Go out and teach all nations,
baptizing them in the name of the Father and of the
   Son and of the Holy Spirit."
Father,
look now with love upon your Church,
and unseal for it the fountain of baptism.
By the power of the Spirit
give to this water the grace of your Son,
so that in the sacrament of baptism
all those whom you have created in your likeness may
   be cleansed from sin
and rise to a new birth of innocence
by water and the Holy Spirit.

*Here, if this can be done conveniently, the celebrant before
continuing lowers the Easter candle into the water once or
three times, then holds it there until the acclamation at the
end of the blessing.*

We ask you, Father, with your Son
to send the Holy Spirit upon the waters of this font.
May all who are buried with Christ in the death of
   baptism
rise also with him to newness of life.
We ask this through Christ our Lord.
All: **Amen.**

*The celebrant then raises it and the people sing the following
or another suitable acclamation:*

Springs of water, bless the Lord.
Give him glory and praise for ever.

PROFESSION OF FAITH

*After the blessing of the water, the celebrant continues with
the profession of faith, which includes the renunciation of
sin and the profession itself.*

RENUNCIATION OF SIN

Using one of the following formularies, the celebrant questions all the elect together; or, after being informed of each candidate's name by the godparents, he may use the same formularies to question the candidates individually.

A

Do you reject sin so as to live in the freedom of God's children? **I do.**

Do you reject the glamor of evil, and refuse to be mastered by sin? **I do.**

Do you reject Satan, father of sin and prince of darkness? **I do.**

B

Do you reject Satan, and all his works, and all his empty promises? **I do.**

C

Do you reject Satan? **I do.**
And all his works? **I do.**
And all his empty promises? **I do.**

PROFESSION OF FAITH

Then the celebrant, informed again of each candidate's name by the godparents, questions each candidate individually. Each candidate is baptized immediately after his or her profession of faith.

Celebrant: N., do you believe in God, the Father almighty,
  creator of heaven and earth?
Candidate: **I do.**
Celebrant: Do you believe in Jesus Christ, his only Son, our Lord,
  who was born of the Virgin Mary,
  was crucified, died and was buried,
  rose from the dead,
  and is now seated at the right hand of the Father?

Candidate: **I do.**

Celebrant: Do you believe in the Holy Spirit,
the holy Catholic Church, the communion of saints,
the forgiveness of sins, the resurrection of the body,
and the life everlasting?

Candidate: **I do.**

BAPTISM

The celebrant baptizes each candidate either by immersion or by the pouring of water.

N., I baptize you in the name of the Father, and of the Son, and of the Holy Spirit.

EXPLANATORY RITES

The celebration of baptism continues with the explanatory rites, after which the celebration of confirmation normally follows.

ANOINTING AFTER BAPTISM

If the confirmation of those baptized is separated from their baptism, the celebrant anoints them with chrism immediately after baptism.

The God of power and Father of our Lord Jesus Christ
has freed you from sin
and brought you to new life
through water and the Holy Spirit.

He now anoints you with the chrism of salvation,
so that, united with his people,
you may remain for ever a member of Christ
who is Priest, Prophet, and King.

Newly baptized: **Amen.**

In silence each of the newly baptized is anointed with chrism on the crown of the head.

CLOTHING WITH A BAPTISMAL GARMENT

The garment used in this rite may be white or of a color that conforms to local custom. If circumstances suggest, this rite may be omitted.

N. and N., you have become a new creation
and have clothed yourselves in Christ.
Receive this baptismal garment
and bring it unstained to the judgment seat of our
   Lord Jesus Christ,
so that you may have everlasting life.

Newly baptized: **Amen.**

PRESENTATION OF A LIGHTED CANDLE

The celebrant takes the Easter candle in his hands or touches it, saying:

Godparents, please come forward to give to the newly baptized the light of Christ.

A godparent of each of the newly baptized goes to the celebrant, lights a candle from the Easter candle, then presents it to the newly baptized.

You have been enlightened by Christ.
Walk always as children of the light
and keep the flame of faith alive in your hearts.
When the Lord comes, may you go out to meet him
with all the saints in the heavenly kingdom.

Newly baptized: **Amen.**

Renewal of Baptismal Promises

After the celebration of baptism, the celebrant addresses the community, in order to invite those present to the renewal of their baptismal promises; the candidates for reception into full communion join the rest of the community in this renunciation of sin and profession of faith. All stand and hold lighted candles. The celebrant may use the following or similar words.

Dear friends, through the paschal mystery we have been buried with Christ in baptism, so that we may rise with him to newness of life. Now that we have completed our Lenten observance, let us renew the promises we made in baptism when we rejected Satan and his works, and promised to serve God faithfully in his holy Catholic Church.

RENEWAL OF BAPTISMAL PROMISES

RENUNCIATION OF SIN

A

Celebrant: Do you reject sin so as to live in the freedom of God's children?

All: **I do.**

Celebrant: Do you reject the glamor of evil,
and refuse to be mastered by sin?

All: **I do.**

Celebrant: Do you reject Satan, father of sin and prince of darkness?

All: **I do.**

B

Celebrant: Do you reject Satan?

All: **I do.**

Celebrant: And all his works?

All: **I do.**

Celebrant: And all his empty promises?

All: **I do.**

PROFESSION OF FAITH

Then the celebrant continues:

Celebrant: Do you believe in God, the Father almighty, creator of heaven and earth?

All: **I do.**

Celebrant: Do you believe in Jesus Christ, his only Son, our Lord,
who was born of the Virgin Mary,
was crucified, died and was buried,

rose from the dead,
and is now seated at the right hand of the Father?
All: **I do.**
Celebrant: Do you believe in the Holy Spirit,
the holy Catholic Church, the communion of saints,
the forgiveness of sins, the resurrection of the body,
and the life everlasting?
All: **I do.**

SPRINKLING WITH BAPTISMAL WATER

The celebrant sprinkles all the people with the blessed baptismal water, while all sing the following song or any other that is baptismal in character.

Antiphon See Ez 47:1-2, 9

I saw water flowing
from the right side of the temple, alleluia.
It brought God's life and his salvation,
and the people sang in joyful praise:
alleluia, alleluia.

The celebrant then concludes with the following prayer.

God, the all-powerful Father of our Lord Jesus Christ,
has given us a new birth by water and the Holy Spirit
and forgiven all our sins.
May he also keep us faithful to our Lord Jesus Christ
for ever and ever.
All: **Amen.**

Celebration of Reception

INVITATION

If baptism has been celebrated at the font, the celebrant, the assisting ministers, and the newly baptized with their godparents proceed to the sanctuary. As they do so the assembly may sing a suitable song.

Then in the following or similar words the celebrant invites the candidates for reception, along with their sponsors, to come into the sanctuary and before the community to make a profession of faith.

N. and N., of your own free will you have asked to be received into the full communion of the Catholic Church. You have made your decision after careful thought under the guidance of the Holy Spirit. I now invite you to come forward with your sponsors and in the presence of this community to profess the Catholic faith. In this faith you will be one with us for the first time at the eucharistic table of the Lord Jesus, the sign of the Church's unity.

PROFESSION BY THE CANDIDATES

When the candidates for reception and their sponsors have taken their places in the sanctuary, the celebrant asks the candidates to make the following profession of faith. The candidates say:

I believe and profess all that the holy Catholic Church believes, teaches, and proclaims to be revealed by God.

ACT OF RECEPTION

Then the candidates with their sponsors go individually to the celebrant, who says to each candidate (laying his right hand on the head of any candidate who is not to receive confirmation):

N., the Lord receives you into the Catholic Church.
His loving kindness has led you here,
so that in the unity of the Holy Spirit
you may have full communion with us
in the faith that you have professed in the presence of his family.

Celebration of Confirmation

INVITATION

The newly baptized with their godparents and, if they have not received the sacrament of confirmation, the newly received with their sponsors, stand before the celebrant. He first speaks briefly to the newly baptized and the newly received in these or similar words.

My dear candidates for confirmation, by your baptism you have been born again in Christ and you have become members of Christ and of his priestly people. Now you are to share in the outpouring of the Holy Spirit among us, the Spirit sent by the Lord upon his apostles at Pentecost and given by them and their successors to the baptized.

The promised strength of the Holy Spirit, which you are to receive, will make you more like Christ and help you to be witnesses to his suffering, death, and resurrection. It will strengthen you to be active members of the Church and to build up the Body of Christ in faith and love.

My dear friends, let us pray to God our Father, that he will pour out the Holy Spirit on these candidates for confirmation to strengthen them with his gifts and anoint them to be more like Christ, the Son of God.

All pray briefly in silence.

LAYING ON OF HANDS

The celebrant holds his hands outstretched over the entire group of those to be confirmed and says the following prayer.

All-powerful God, Father of our Lord Jesus Christ,
by water and the Holy Spirit
you freed your sons and daughters from sin
and gave them new life.
Send your Holy Spirit upon them
to be their helper and guide.
Give them the spirit of wisdom and understanding,
the spirit of right judgment and courage,
the spirit of knowledge and reverence.
Fill them with the spirit of wonder and awe in your
  presence.

We ask this through Christ our Lord.
℟. **Amen.**

ANOINTING WITH CHRISM

*Either or both godparents and sponsors place the right hand
on the shoulder of the candidate; and a godparent or a spon-
sor of the candidate gives the candidate's name to the minister of the sacrament. During the conferral of the sacrament
an appropriate song may be sung.*

*The minister of the sacrament dips his right thumb in the
chrism and makes the sign of the cross on the forehead of the
one to be confirmed as he says:*

N., be sealed with the Gift of the Holy Spirit.
Newly confirmed: **Amen.**
Minister: Peace be with you.
Newly confirmed: **And also with you.**

*After all have received the sacrament, the newly confirmed as
well as the godparents and sponsors are led to their places in
the assembly.*

PART FOUR

LITURGY OF THE EUCHARIST

*The priest goes to the altar and begins the liturgy of the eu-
charist in the usual way.*

*It is fitting that the bread and wine be brought forward by
the newly baptized.*

PRAYER OVER THE GIFTS　　　[God's Saving Work]

Lord,
accept the prayers and offerings of your people.
With your help
may this Easter mystery of our redemption
bring to perfection the saving work you have begun in
　　us.
We ask this through Christ our Lord. ℟. **Amen.** ↓

Preface of Easter I (P 21: on this Easter day), p. 81

When Eucharistic Prayer I is used, the special Easter forms of In union *with the whole Church, and* Father, accept this offering *are said.*

COMMUNION ANT. 1 Cor 5, 7-8   [Sincerity and Truth]

Christ has become our paschal sacrifice; let us feast with the unleavened bread of sincerity and truth, alleluia. ↓

PRAYER AFTER COMMUNION   [Peace and Love]

Lord,
you have nourished us with your Easter sacraments.
Fill us with your Spirit,
and make us one in peace and love.
We ask this through Christ our Lord. R̸. **Amen.**

The deacon (or the priest) sings or says the dismissal as follows:

Go in the peace of Christ, alleluia, alleluia.

OR

The Mass is ended, go in peace, alleluia, alleluia.

OR

Go in peace to love and serve the Lord, alleluia, alleluia.

R̸. **Thanks be to God, alleluia, alleluia.**

"I have risen: I am with you once more."

MARCH 30

EASTER SUNDAY

ENTRANCE ANT. Ps 139, 18. 5-6   [Christ's Resurrection]

I have risen: I am with you once more; you placed your hand on me to keep me safe. How great is the depth of your wisdom, alleluia!

OR Lk 24, 34; see Rv 1, 6   [King and Lord]

The Lord has indeed risen, alleluia. Glory and kingship be his for ever and ever.   → No. 2, p. 10

OPENING PRAYER   [Renewal]

Let us pray
   [that the risen Christ will raise us up
   and renew our lives]
God our Father,
by raising Christ your Son
you conquered the power of death
and opened for us the way to eternal life.
Let our celebration today
raise us up and renew our lives
by the Spirit that is within us.
Grant this . . . for ever and ever. ℟. **Amen.** ↓

ALTERNATIVE OPENING PRAYER   [God's Life]

Let us pray
  [on this Easter morning for the life
  that never again shall see darkness]
God our Father, creator of all,
today is the day of Easter joy.
This is the morning on which the Lord appeared to
    men
who had begun to lose hope
and opened their eyes to what the scriptures foretold:
that first he must die, and then he would rise
and ascend into his Father's glorious presence.
May the risen Lord
breathe on our minds and open our eyes
that we may know him in the breaking of bread,
and follow him in his risen life.
Grant this through Christ our Lord. ℟. Amen. ↓

READING I Acts 10, 34. 37-43   [Salvation in Christ]

**In his sermon Peter sums up the "good news," the Gospel.
Salvation comes through Christ, the beloved Son of the
Father, the anointed of the Holy Spirit.**

A reading from the Acts of the Apostles

PETER addressed the people in these words: "I take
it you know what has been reported all over Judea
about Jesus of Nazareth, beginning in Galilee with the
baptism John preached; of the way God anointed him
with the Holy Spirit and power. He went about doing
good works and healing all who were in the grip of
the devil, and God was with him. We are witnesses to
all that he did in the land of the Jews and in Jerusalem. They killed him finally, 'hanging him on a tree,'
only to have God raise him up on the third day and
grant that he be seen, not by all, but only by such witnesses as had been chosen beforehand by God—by us
who ate and drank with him after he rose from the

dead. He commissioned us to preach to the people and to bear witness that he is the one set apart by God as judge of the living and the dead. To him all the prophets testify, saying that everyone who believes in him has forgiveness of sins through his name."—The word of the Lord. ℟. **Thanks be to God.** ↓

RESPONSORIAL PSALM Ps 118   [The Day of the Lord]

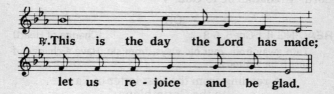

℟. This is the day the Lord has made; let us re-joice and be glad.

Give thanks to the Lord, for he is good,
    for his mercy endures forever.
Let the house of Israel say,
    "His mercy endures forever."—℟.

The right hand of the Lord has struck with power;
    the right hand of the Lord is exalted.
I shall not die, but live,
    and declare the works of the Lord.—℟.

The stone which the builders rejected
    has become the cornerstone.
By the Lord has this been done;
    it is wonderful in our eyes.—℟. ↓

℟. Or: **Alleluia.** ↓

One of the following texts may be chosen as Reading II.

READING II Col 3, 1-4   [Seek Heavenly Things]
    Look to the glory of Christ in which we share because our lives are hidden in him (through baptism) and we are destined to share in the glory.

A reading from the letter of Paul to the Colossians

SINCE you have been raised up in company with Christ, set your heart on what pertains to higher realms where Christ is seated at God's right hand. Be intent on things above rather than on things of earth. After all, you have died! Your life is hidden now with Christ in God. When Christ our life appears, then you shall appear with him in glory.—The word of the Lord. ℟. **Thanks be to God.** ↓

OR

READING II 1 Cor 5, 6-8   [Change of Heart]

Turn away from your old ways, from sin. Have a change of heart; be virtuous.

A reading from the first letter of Paul
to the Corinthians

DO you not know that a little yeast has its effect all through the dough? Get rid of the old yeast to make of yourselves fresh dough, unleavened loaves, as it were; Christ our Passover has been sacrificed. Let us celebrate the feast not with the old yeast, that of corruption and wickedness, but with the unleavened bread of sincerity and truth.—The word of the Lord. ℟. **Thanks be to God.** ↓

One of the following texts may be chosen for the Sequence.

SEQUENCE (Prose text)   [Hymn to the Victor]

To the Paschal Victim let Christians offer a sacrifice of praise.

The Lamb redeemed the sheep. Christ, sinless, reconciled sinners to the Father.

Death and life were locked together in a unique struggle. Life's captain died; now he reigns, never more to die.

Tell us, Mary, "What did you see on the way?"

"I saw the tomb of the now living Christ. I saw the glory of Christ, now risen.

"I saw angels who gave witness; the cloths too which once had covered head and limbs.

"Christ my hope has arisen. He will go before his own into Galilee."

We know that Christ has indeed risen from the dead. Do you, conqueror and king, have mercy on us. Amen. Alleluia. ↓

OR (Poetic text)   [Hymn to the Victor]

Christians, to the Paschal Victim
　　Offer your thankful praises!
A Lamb the sheep redeems: Christ,
　　Who only is sinless,
　　Reconciles sinners to the Father.
Death and life have contended in that combat stupen-
　　dous:
　　The Prince of life, who died, reigns immortal.

Speak, Mary, declaring
　　What you saw, wayfaring.
"The tomb of Christ, who is living,
　　The glory of Jesus' resurrection;
Bright angels attesting,
　　The shroud and napkin resting.
Yes, Christ my hope is arisen:
　　To Galilee he goes before you."
Christ indeed from death is risen, our new life obtain-
　　ing.
　　Have mercy, victor King, ever reigning!
　　Amen. Alleluia. ↓

(For Morning Mass)

GOSPEL Jn 20, 1-9   [Renewed Faith]
Alleluia (1 Cor 5, 7-8)
℟. **Alleluia.** Christ has become our paschal sacrifice; let us feast with joy in the Lord. ℟. **Alleluia.** ↓

Let us discover the empty tomb and ponder this mystery, and like Christ's first followers be strengthened in our faith.

℣. The Lord be with you. ℟.. **And also with you.**

✛ A reading from the holy gospel according to John. ℟. **Glory to you, Lord.**

EARLY in the morning on the first day of the week, while it was still dark, Mary Magdalene came to the tomb. She saw that the stone had been moved away, so she ran off to Simon Peter and the other disciple (the one Jesus loved) and told them, "The Lord has been taken from the tomb! We don't know where they have put him!" At that, Peter and the other disciple started out on their way toward the tomb. They were running side by side, but then the other disciple outran Peter and reached the tomb first. He did not enter but bent down to peer in, and saw the wrappings lying on the ground. Presently, Simon Peter came along behind him and entered the tomb. He observed the wrappings on the ground and saw the piece of cloth which had covered the head not lying with the wrappings, but rolled up in a place by itself. Then the disciple who had arrived first at the tomb went in. He saw and believed. (Remember, as yet they did not understand the Scripture that Jesus had to rise from the dead.)—The gospel of the Lord. ℟. **Praise to you, Lord Jesus Christ.**

→ No. 14, p. 18

OR

GOSPEL Mk 16, 1-8　　　　　　　　**[The Resurrection]**
Alleluia (1 Cor 5, 7-8)
℟. **Alleluia.** Christ has become our paschal sacrifice; let us feast with joy in the Lord. ℟. **Alleluia.**
See p. 272.

(For an Afternoon or Evening Mass)

GOSPEL Lk 24, 13-35   [The Messiah's Need To Suffer]
Alleluia (1 Cor 5, 7-8)

℟. **Alleluia.** Christ has become our paschal sacrifice;
let us feast with joy in the Lord. ℟. **Alleluia.** ↓

> Let us accept the testimony of these two witnesses that our
> hearts may burn with the fire of faith.

℣. The Lord be with you. ℟. **And also with you.**
✛ A reading from the holy gospel according to Luke.
℟. **Glory to you, Lord.**

TWO disciples of Jesus that same day (the first day
of the sabbath) were making their way to a village
named Emmaus seven miles distant from Jerusalem,
discussing as they went all that had happened. In the
course of their lively exchange, Jesus approached and
began to walk along with them. However, they were
restrained from recognizing him. He said to them,
"What are you discussing as you go your way?" They
halted in distress, and one of them, Cleopas by name,
asked him, "Are you the only resident of Jerusalem
who does not know the things that went on there
these past few days?" He said to them, "What things?"
They said: "All those that had to do with Jesus of
Nazareth, a prophet powerful in word and deed in the
eyes of God and all the people; how our chief priests
and leaders delivered him up to be condemned to
death, and crucified him. We were hoping that he was
the one who would set Israel free. Besides all this,
today, the third day since these things happened,
some women of our group have just brought us some
astonishing news. They were at the tomb before dawn
and failed to find his body, but returned with the tale
that they had seen a vision of angels who declared he
was alive. Some of our number went to the tomb and
found it to be just as the women said; but him they did
not see."

Then he said to them, "What little sense you have! How slow you are to believe all that the prophets have announced! Did not the Messiah have to undergo all this so as to enter into his glory?" Beginning, then, with Moses and all the prophets, he interpreted for them every passage of Scripture which referred to him. By now they were near the village to which they were going, and he acted as if he were going farther. But they pressed him: "Stay with us. It is nearly evening—the day is practically over." So he went in to stay with them.

When he had seated himself with them to eat, he took bread, pronounced the blessing, then broke the bread and began to distribute it to them. With that their eyes were opened and they recognized him; whereupon he vanished from their sight. They said to one another, "Were not our hearts burning inside us as he talked to us on the road and explained the Scriptures to us?" They got up immediately and returned to Jerusalem, where they found the Eleven and the rest of the company assembled. They were greeted with, "The Lord has been raised! It is true! He has appeared to Simon." Then they recounted what had happened on the road and how they had come to know him in the breaking of bread.—The gospel of the Lord. ℟. **Praise to you, Lord Jesus Christ.**   ➔ No. 14, p. 18

Renewal of Baptismal Promises, p. 280 (omit Creed).

PRAYER OVER THE GIFTS   [Renewing Sacrifice]

Lord,
with Easter joy we offer you the sacrifice
by which your Church is reborn and nourished
through Christ our Lord. ℟. **Amen.**

➔ No. 21, p. 22 (Pref. P 21: on this Easter Day)

When Eucharistic Prayer I is used, the special Easter forms of In union with the whole Church *and* Father, accept this offering *are said.*

COMMUNION ANT. 1 Cor 5, 7-8   [Sincerity and Truth]
Christ has become our paschal sacrifice; let us feast
with the unleavened bread of sincerity and truth, alleluia. ↓

PRAYER AFTER COMMUNION   [Glory of Resurrection]
Father of love,
watch over your Church
and bring us to the glory of the resurrection
promised by this Easter sacrament.
We ask this in the name of Jesus the Lord.
℟. **Amen.**   → No. 32, p. 70

Optional Solemn Blessings, p. 92, and Prayers Over the People, p. 99

"Thomas said in response, 'My Lord and my God!' "

APRIL 6

2nd SUNDAY OF EASTER

ENTRANCE ANT. 1 Pt 2, 2   [Thirst for Spiritual Milk]
Like newborn children you should thirst for milk, on
which your spirit can grow to strength, alleluia.

OR 4 Ezr 2, 36-37   [Give Thanks]
**Rejoice to the full in the glory that is yours, and give
thanks to God who called you to his kingdom, alleluia.**   ➔ No. 2, p. 10

OPENING PRAYER   [Renewed Gift of Life]

Let us pray
   [for a deeper awareness of our Christian baptism]
God of mercy,
you wash away our sins in water,
you give us new birth in the Spirit,
and redeem us in the blood of Christ.
As we celebrate Christ's resurrection
increase our awareness of these blessings,
and renew your gift of life within us.
We ask this through our Lord Jesus Christ, your Son,
who lives and reigns with you and the Holy Spirit,
one God, for ever and ever. ℟. **Amen.** ↓

ALTERNATIVE OPENING PRAYER
                              [Growth as God's People]
Let us pray
   [as Christians thirsting for the risen life]
Heavenly Father and God of mercy,
we no longer look for Jesus among the dead,
for he is alive and has become the Lord of life.
From the waters of death you raise us with him
and renew your gift of life within us.
Increase in our minds and hearts
the risen life we share with Christ
and help us to grow as your people
toward the fullness of eternal life with you.
We ask this through Christ our Lord. ℟. **Amen.** ↓

READING I Acts 4, 32-35   [True Christian Fellowship]
The faithful lived a common life, sharing all their goods.
The apostles worked many miracles. They prayed together
and broke bread. Daily their numbers increased.

A reading from the Acts of the Apostles

THE community of believers were of one heart and one mind. None of them ever claimed anything as his own; rather everything was held in common. With power the apostles bore witness to the resurrection of the Lord Jesus, and great respect was paid to them all; nor was there anyone needy among them, for all who owned property or houses sold them and donated the proceeds. They used to lay them at the feet of the apostles to be distributed to everyone according to his need.—The word of the Lord. R̃. **Thanks be to God.** ↓

RESPONSORIAL PSALM Ps 118   [The Lord's Goodness]

R̃. **Give thanks to the Lord for he is good, his love is everlasting.**

Let the house of Israel say,
    "His mercy endures forever."
Let the house of Aaron say,
    "His mercy endures forever."
Let those who fear the Lord say,
    "His mercy endures forever."

R̃. **Give thanks to the Lord for he is good, his love is everlasting.**

I was hard pressed and was falling
    but the Lord helped me.
My strength and my courage is the Lord
    and he has been my savior.
The joyful shout of victory
    in the tents of the just:

R̃. **Give thanks to the Lord for he is good, his love is everlasting.**

The stone which the builders rejected
   has become the cornerstone.
By the Lord has this been done;
   it is wonderful in our eyes.
This is the day the Lord has made;
   let us be glad and rejoice in it.

℞. **Give thanks to the Lord for he is good,**
   his love is everlasting. ↓

℞. Or: **Alleluia.** ↓

READING II 1 Jn 5, 1-6   [The Power of Faith]

   A believing faith comes from God. The proof of loving God
   comes from observing his commandments. The Spirit, the
   Spirit of truth, will testify to this.

   A reading from the first letter of John

EVERYONE who believes that Jesus is the Christ
   has been begotten by God.
Now, everyone who loves the father
   loves the child he has begotten.
We can be sure that we love God's children
   when we love God
   and do what he has commanded.
The love of God consists in this:
   that we keep his commandments—
   and his commandments are not burdensome.
Everyone begotten of God conquers the world,
   and the power that has conquered the world
   is this faith of ours.
Who, then, is conqueror of the world?
   The one who believes that Jesus is the Son of God.
Jesus Christ it is who came through water and blood—
   not in water only,
   but in water and in blood.
It is the Spirit who testifies to this,
   and the Spirit is truth.
The word of the Lord. ℞. **Thanks be to God.** ↓

GOSPEL Jn 20, 19-31   [Living Faith]
Alleluia (Jn 20, 29)

℟. **Alleluia.** You believe in me, Thomas, because you
    have seen me;
happy those who have not seen me, but still believe!
    ℟. **Alleluia.** ↓

Jesus appears to the disciples, coming through locked
doors. He shows them his hands and side. He greets them
in peace and gives them the power to forgive sin. A week
later Jesus appears again and speaks directly to Thomas
who now professes his belief.

℣. The Lord be with you. ℟. **And also with you.**
✝ A reading from the holy gospel according to John.
℟. **Glory to you, Lord.**

O N the evening of that first day of the week, even
    though the disciples had locked the doors of the
place where they were for fear of the Jews, Jesus
came and stood before them. "Peace be with you," he
said. When he had said this, he showed them his
hands and his side. At the sight of the Lord the disciples rejoiced. "Peace be with you," he said again.
    "As the Father has sent me,
    so I send you."
Then he breathed on them and said:
    "Receive the Holy Spirit.
    If you forgive men's sins,
    they are forgiven them;
    if you hold them bound,
    they are held bound."
    It happened that one of the Twelve, Thomas (the
name means "Twin"), was absent when Jesus came.
The other disciples kept telling him: "We have seen
the Lord!" His answer was, "I'll never believe it without probing the nail-prints in his hands, without
putting my finger in the nail-marks and my hand into
his side."

A week later, the disciples were once more in the room, and this time Thomas was with them. Despite the locked doors, Jesus came and stood before them. "Peace be with you," he said; then, to Thomas: "Take your finger and examine my hands. Put your hand into my side. Do not persist in your unbelief, but believe!" Thomas said in response, "My Lord and my God!" Jesus then said to him:

"You became a believer because you saw me.

Blest are they who have not seen and have believed."

Jesus performed many other signs as well—signs not recorded here—in the presence of his disciples. But these have been recorded to help you believe that Jesus is the Messiah, the Son of God, so that through this faith you may have life in his name.—The gospel of the Lord. ℟. **Praise to you, Lord Jesus Christ.**

→ No. 14, p. 18

PRAYER OVER THE GIFTS   [Offerings Leading to Bliss]

Lord,
through faith and baptism
we have become a new creation.
Accept the offerings of your people
(and of those born again in baptism)
and bring us to eternal happiness.
Grant this through Christ our Lord.
℟. **Amen.**   → No. 21, p. 22 (Pref. P 21)

When Eucharistic Prayer I is used, the special Easter forms of In union with the whole Church *and* Father, accept this offering *are said.*

COMMUNION ANT. See Jn 20, 27   [Believe]

Jesus spoke to Thomas: Put your hand here, and see the place of the nails. Doubt no longer, but believe, alleluia. ↓

PRAYER AFTER COMMUNION   [Devout Reception]

Almighty God,
may the Easter sacraments we have received
live for ever in our minds and hearts.
We ask this through Christ our Lord.
℟. **Amen.**   → No. 32, p. 70

Optional Solemn Blessings, p. 92, and Prayers Over the People, p. 99

*"It is likewise written that the Messiah must suffer
and rise from the dead . . . ."*

APRIL 13

3rd SUNDAY OF EASTER

ENTRANCE ANT. Ps 33, 5-6   [Praise the Lord]

**Let all the earth cry out to God with joy; praise the
glory of his name; proclaim his glorious praise, alleluia.**   → No. 2, p. 10

OPENING PRAYER   [Hope of Resurrection]

Let us pray
    [that Christ will give us
    a share in the glory of his unending life]
God our Father,
may we look forward with hope to our resurrection,

for you have made us your sons and daughters,
and restored the joy of our youth.
We ask this through our Lord Jesus Christ, your Son,
who lives and reigns with you and the Holy Spirit,
one God, for ever and ever. ℟. **Amen.** ↓

ALTERNATIVE OPENING PRAYER   [Eternal Light]

Let us pray
   [in confident peace and Easter hope]
Father in heaven, author of all truth,
a people once in darkness has listened to your Word
and followed your Son as he rose from the tomb.
Hear the prayer of this newborn people
and strengthen your Church to answer your call.
May we rise and come forth into the light of day
to stand in your presence until eternity dawns.
We ask this through Christ our Lord. ℟. **Amen.** ↓

READING I Acts 3, 13-15. 17-19   [Culpable Ignorance]

Peter teaches how God glorified his Son, but the people
were guilty of crucifying Jesus. They acted out of ignorance, however. Now they are to reform and ask God for
forgiveness.

A reading from the Acts of the Apostles

PETER said to the people: "The 'God of Abraham, of
Isaac, and of Jacob, the God of our fathers,' has
glorified his Servant Jesus, whom you handed over
and disowned in Pilate's presence when Pilate was
ready to release him. You disowned the Holy and Just
One and preferred instead to be granted the release of
a murderer. You put to death the Author of life. But
God raised him from the dead, and we are his witnesses.

"Yet I know, my brothers, that you acted out of ignorance, just as your leaders did. God has brought to
fulfillment by this means what he announced long ago
through all the prophets: that his Messiah would suf-

fer. Therefore, reform your lives! Turn to God, that
your sins may be wiped away."—The word of the
Lord. ℟. **Thanks be to God.** ↓

RESPONSORIAL PSALM Ps 4   [Divine Security]

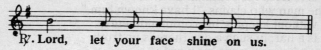

℟. **Lord, let your face shine on us.**

When I call, answer me, O my just God,
  you who relieve me when I am in distress;
  have pity on me, and hear my prayer!

℟. **Lord, let your face shine on us.**

Know that the Lord does wonders for his faithful one;
  the Lord will hear me when I call upon him.

℟. **Lord, let your face shine on us.**

O Lord, let the light of your countenance shine upon us!
  You put gladness into our heart.

℟. **Lord, let your face shine on us.**

As soon as I lie down, I fall peacefully asleep,
  for you alone, O Lord,
  bring security to my dwelling.

℟. **Lord, let your face shine on us.** ↓

℟. Or: **Alleluia.** ↓

READING II 1 Jn 2, 1-5   [Fruitful Knowledge]

If anyone should sin, Jesus is an offering for sin—for the
sins of the whole world. Anyone who claims to know Jesus
but disobeys the commandments is a liar.

A reading from the first letter of John

MY little ones,
  I am writing this to keep you from sin.
But if any one should sin,
  we have, in the presence of the Father,
Jesus Christ, an intercessor who is just.

He is an offering for our sins,
and not for our sins only,
but for those of the whole world.
The way we can be sure of our knowledge of him
is to keep his commandments.
The man who claims, "I have known him,"
without keeping his commandments,
is a liar; in such a one there is no truth.
But whoever keeps his word
truly has the love of God made perfect in him.
The word of the Lord. ℟. **Thanks be to God.** ↓

GOSPEL Lk 24, 35-48 [Understanding the Scriptures]
Alleluia (See Lk 24, 32)
℟. **Alleluia.** Lord Jesus, make your word plain to us,
make our hearts burn with love when you speak. ℟.
 Alleluia. ↓

> Again Jesus appears in the midst of the disciples. He
> proves he is not a ghost. He eats with them and reassures
> them that all that happened was to fulfill the words of the
> Scriptures.

℣. The Lord be with you. ℟. **And also with you.**
✤ A reading from the holy gospel according to Luke.
℟. **Glory to you, Lord.**

THE disciples recounted what had happened on the
road to Emmaus and how they had come to know
Jesus in the breaking of bread.

While they were still speaking about all this, he
himself stood in their midst [and said to them, "Peace
to you"]. In their panic and fright they thought they
were seeing a ghost. He said to them, "Why are you
disturbed? Why do such ideas cross your mind? Look
at my hands and my feet; it is really I. Touch me, and
see that a ghost does not have flesh and bones as I
do." [As he said this he showed them his hands and
feet.] They were still incredulous for sheer joy and

wonder, so he said to them, "Have you anything here to eat?" They gave him a piece of cooked fish, which he took and ate in their presence. Then he said to them, "Recall those words I spoke to you when I was still with you: everything written about me in the law of Moses and the prophets and psalms had to be fulfilled." Then he opened their minds to the understanding of the Scriptures.

He said to them: "Thus it is likewise written that the Messiah must suffer and rise from the dead on the third day. In his name, penance for the remission of sins is to be preached to all the nations, beginning at Jerusalem. You are witnesses of this."—The gospel of the Lord. ℟. **Praise to you, Lord Jesus Christ.**

→ No. 14, p. 18

PRAYER OVER THE GIFTS   [Perfect Joy]

Lord,
receive these gifts from your Church.
May the great joy you give us
come to perfection in heaven.
Grant this through Christ our Lord.
℟. **Amen.**   → No. 21, p. 22 (Pref. P 21-25)

COMMUNION ANT. Lk 24, 46-47   [Penance]

Christ had to suffer and to rise from the dead on the third day. In his name penance for the remission of sins is to be preached to all nations, alleluia. ↓

PRAYER AFTER COMMUNION   [The Lord's Kindness]

Lord,
look on your people with kindness
and by these Easter mysteries
bring us to the glory of the resurrection.
We ask this in the name of Jesus the Lord.
℟. **Amen.**   → No. 32, p. 70

Optional Solemn Blessings, p. 92, and Prayers Over the People, p. 99

"I am the good shepherd. . . ."

APRIL 20

4th SUNDAY OF EASTER

ENTRANCE ANT. Ps 33, 5-6   [God the Creator]
The earth is full of the goodness of the Lord; by the word of the Lord the heavens were made, alleluia.

→ No. 2, p. 10

OPENING PRAYER   [Strengthened in Christ]

Let us pray
   [that Christ our shepherd
   will lead us through the difficulties of this life]
Almighty and ever-living God,
give us new strength
from the courage of Christ our shepherd,
and lead us to join the saints in heaven,
where he lives and reigns with you and the Holy Spirit,
one God for ever and ever. ℟. **Amen.** ↓

ALTERNATIVE OPENING PRAYER   [God Our Helper]

Let us pray
   [to God our helper in time of distress]
God and Father of our Lord Jesus Christ,

306

though your people walk in the valley of darkness,
no evil should they fear;
for they follow in faith the call of the shepherd
whom you have sent for their hope and strength.
Attune our minds to the sound of his voice,
lead our steps in the path he has shown,
that we may know the strength of his outstretched arm
and enjoy the light of your presence for ever.
We ask this through Christ our Lord. ℟. **Amen.** ↓

READING I Acts 4, 8-12   [Salvation in Jesus]

Peter explains the cure of the cripple. It was a miracle performed in the name of Jesus, whom the people had rejected and crucified. There is no salvation except in Jesus.

A reading from the Acts of the Apostles

PETER, filled with the Holy Spirit, spoke up: "Leaders of the people! Elders! If we must answer today
for a good deed done to a cripple and explain how he
was restored to health, then you and all the people of
Israel must realize that it was done in the name of
Jesus Christ the Nazorean whom you crucified and
whom God raised from the dead. In the power of that
name this man stands before you perfectly sound. This
Jesus is 'the stone rejected by you the builders which
has become the cornerstone.' There is no salvation in
anyone else, for there is no other name in the whole
world given to men by which we are to be saved."—
The word of the Lord. ℟. **Thanks be to God.** ↓

RESPONSORIAL PSALM Ps 118   [Refuge in God]

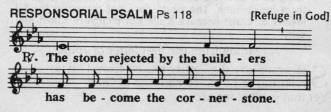

℟. **The stone rejected by the build - ers
has be - come the cor - ner - stone.**

Give thanks to the Lord, for he is good,
  for his mercy endures forever.
It is better to take refuge in the Lord
  than to trust in man.
It is better to take refuge in the Lord
  than to trust in princes.

℟. **The stone rejected by the builders has become the cornerstone.**

I will give thanks to you, for you have answered me
  and have been my savior.
The stone which the builders rejected
  has become the cornerstone.
By the Lord has this been done;
  it is wonderful in our eyes.

℟. **The stone rejected by the builders has become the cornerstone.**

Blessed is he who comes in the name of the Lord;
  we bless you from the house of the Lord.
I will give thanks to you, for you have answered me
  and have been my savior.
Give thanks to the Lord, for he is good;
  for his kindness endures forever.

℟. **The stone rejected by the builders has become the cornerstone.** ↓

℟. Or: **Alleluia.** ↓

READING II 1 Jn 3, 1-2   [Children of God]

The Father shows his love for human beings by calling them his children. The world does not recognize the followers of Christ because it did not recognize Christ himself.

A reading from the first letter of John

SEE what love the Father has bestowed on us
in letting us be called children of God!
Yet that is what we are.

The reason the world does not recognize us
is that it never recognized the Son.
Dearly beloved,
   we are God's children now;
   what we shall later be has not yet come to light.
We know that when it comes to light
   we shall be like him,
   for we shall see him as he is.
The word of the Lord. ℟. **Thanks be to God.** ↓

GOSPEL Jn 10, 11-18   [The Good Shepherd]
Alleluia (Jn 10, 14)
℟. **Alleluia.** I am the good shepherd, says the Lord;
I know my sheep, and mine know me. ℟. **Alleluia.** ↓

> **Jesus compares himself to "the good Shepherd." A shepherd cares for his sheep, lives and dies for them if necessary. There is to be one flock and one shepherd.**

℣. The Lord be with you. ℟. **And also with you.**
✝ A reading from the holy gospel according to John.
℟. **Glory to you, Lord.**

JESUS said:
   "I am the good shepherd;
      the good shepherd lays down his life for the
         sheep.
      The hired hand, who is no shepherd
      nor owner of the sheep,
      catches sight of the wolf coming
      and runs away, leaving the sheep
      to be snatched and scattered by the wolf.
      That is because he works for pay;
      he has no concern for the sheep.

   "I am the good shepherd.
      I know my sheep
      and my sheep know me
      in the same way that the Father knows me
      and I know the Father;

for these sheep I will give my life.
I have other sheep
that do not belong to this fold.
I must lead them, too,
and they shall hear my voice.
There shall be one flock then, one shepherd.
The Father loves me for this:
that I lay down my life
to take it up again.
No one takes it from me;
I lay it down freely.
I have power to lay it down,
and I have power to take it away again.
This command I received from my Father."

The gospel of the Lord. ℟. **Praise to you, Lord Jesus Christ.**　　　→ No. 14, p. 18

PRAYER OVER THE GIFTS　　　[Eternal Joy]

Lord,
restore us by these Easter mysteries.
May the continuing work of our redeemer
bring us eternal joy.
We ask this through Christ our Lord.
℟. **Amen.**　　　→ No. 21, p. 22 (Pref. P 21-25)

COMMUNION ANT.　　　[The Risen Shepherd]

The Good Shepherd is risen! He who laid down his life for his sheep, who died for his flock, he is risen, alleluia. ↓

PRAYER AFTER COMMUNION　　　[Eternal Shepherd]

Father, eternal shepherd,
watch over the flock redeemed by the blood of Christ
and lead us to the promised land.
Grant this through Christ our Lord.
℟. **Amen.**　　　→ No. 32, p. 70

Optional Solemn Blessings, p. 92, and Prayers Over the People, p. 99

"I am the true vine and my Father is the vinegrower."

APRIL 27

5th SUNDAY OF EASTER

ENTRANCE ANT. Ps 98, 1. 2   [Marvelous Deeds]

Sing to the Lord a new song, for he has done marvelous deeds; he has revealed to the nations his saving power, alleluia.   → No. 2, p. 10

OPENING PRAYER   [True Freedom]

Let us pray
   [that we may enjoy true freedom]
God our Father,
look upon us with love.
You redeem us and make us your children in Christ.
Give us true freedom
and bring us to the inheritance you promised.
We ask this . . . for ever and ever. ℟. **Amen.** ↓

ALTERNATIVE OPENING PRAYER   [God's Praise]

Let us pray
   [in the freedom of the sons of God]
Father of our Lord Jesus Christ,
you have revealed to the nations your saving power

311

and filled all ages with the words of a new song.
Hear the echo of this hymn.
Give us voice to sing your praise
throughout this season of joy.
We ask this through Christ our Lord. ℟. **Amen.** ↓

READING I Acts 9, 26-31   [Paul's Conversion]

Because of Paul's earlier reputation, the Christians were fearful of him. He was then accepted and began to spread the message of the gospel.

A reading from the Acts of the Apostles

WHEN Saul arrived back in Jerusalem he tried to join the disciples there; but it turned out that they were all afraid of him. They even refused to believe that he was a disciple. Then Barnabas took him in charge and introduced him to the apostles. He explained to them how on his journey Saul had seen the Lord, who had conversed with him, and how Saul had been speaking out fearlessly in the name of Jesus at Damascus. Saul stayed on with them, moving freely about Jerusalem and expressing himself quite openly in the name of the Lord. He even addressed the Greek-speaking Jews and debated with them. They for their part responded by trying to kill him. When the brothers learned of this, some of them took him down to Caesarea and sent him off to Tarsus.

Meanwhile throughout all Judea, Galilee and Samaria the church was at peace. It was being built up and was making steady progress in the fear of the Lord; at the same time it enjoyed the increased consolation of the Holy Spirit.—The word of the Lord. ℟. **Thanks be to God.** ↓

RESPONSORIAL PSALM Ps 22   [Praise God]

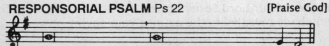

℟. **I will praise you, Lord, in the assembly of your people.**

I will fulfill my vows before those who fear the Lord.
  The lowly shall eat their fill;
They who seek the Lord shall praise him:
  "May your hearts be ever merry!"

℟. **I will praise you, Lord, in the assembly of your people.**

All the ends of the earth
  shall remember and turn to the Lord;
All the families of the nations
  shall bow down before him.
To him alone shall bow down
  all who sleep in the earth;
Before him shall bend
  all who go down into the dust.

℟. **I will praise you, Lord, in the assembly of your people.**

And to him my soul shall live;
  my descendants shall serve him.
Let the coming generation be told of the Lord
  that they may proclaim to a people yet to be born
  the justice he has shown.

℟. **I will praise you, Lord, in the assembly of your people.** ↓

℟. Or: **Alleluia.** ↓

READING II 1 Jn 3, 18-24   [Love in Action]

  Christians are to love in deed and in truth. A clear conscience is proof of God's favor. To keep the commandments is to please God.

A reading from the first letter of John

L ITTLE children,
  let us love in deed and in truth
  and not merely talk about it.
This is our way of knowing we are committed to the
  truth

and are at peace before him
no matter what our consciences may charge us with;
for God is greater than our hearts
and all is known to him.

Beloved,
if our consciences have nothing to charge us with,
we can be sure that God is with us
and that we will receive at his hands
whatever we ask.

Why? Because we are keeping his commandments
and doing what is pleasing in his sight.

His commandment is this:
we are to believe in the name of his Son, Jesus Christ,
and are to love one another as he commanded us.

Those who keep his commandments remain in him
and he in them.

And this is how we know that he remains in us:
from the Spirit that he gave us.

The word of the Lord. ℟. **Thanks be to God.** ↓

GOSPEL Jn 15, 1-8   [Vine and the Branches]
Alleluia (Jn 15, 4. 5)

℟. **Alleluia.** Live in me and let me live in you, says the
Lord;

my branches bear much fruit. ℟. **Alleluia.** ↓

Jesus compared himself to the vine and the branches.
Whoever is united to Jesus will do good and be rewarded.
But anyone who does not live in Jesus will wither like a
cut-off vine.

℣. The Lord be with you. ℟. **And also with you.**
✝ A reading from the holy gospel according to John.
℟. **Glory to you, Lord.**

JESUS said to his disciples:
"I am the true vine
and my Father is the vinegrower.
He prunes away

every barren branch,
but the fruitful ones
he trims clean
to increase their yield.
You are clean already,
thanks to the word I have spoken to you.
Live on in me, as I do in you.
No more than a branch can bear fruit of itself
apart from the vine,
can you bear fruit
apart from me.
I am the vine, you are the branches.
He who lives in me and I in him,
will produce abundantly,
for apart from me you can do nothing.
A man who does not live in me
is like a withered, rejected branch,
picked up to be thrown in the fire and burnt.
If you live in me,
and my words stay part of you,
you may ask what you will—
it will be done for you.
My Father has been glorified
in your bearing much fruit
and becoming my disciples."

The gospel of the Lord. ℟. **Praise to you, Lord Jesus Christ.**
→ No. 14, p. 18

PRAYER OVER THE GIFTS   [Guided by God's Truth]

Lord God,
by this holy exchange of gifts
you share with us your divine life.
Grant that everything we do
may be directed by the knowledge of your truth.
We ask this in the name of Jesus the Lord.
℟. **Amen.**
→ No. 21, p. 22 (Pref. P 21-25)

COMMUNION ANT. Jn 15, 5   [Union with Christ]

I am the vine and you are the branches, says the
Lord; he who lives in me, and I in him, will bear much
fruit, alleluia. ↓

PRAYER AFTER COMMUNION   [New Life]

Merciful Father,
may these mysteries give us new purpose
and bring us to a new life in you.
Grant this through Christ our Lord.
℟. **Amen.**   → No. 32, p. 70

Optional Solemn Blessings, p. 92, and Prayers Over the People, p. 99

"The command I give you is this, that you love
one another."

MAY 4

6th SUNDAY OF EASTER

ENTRANCE ANT. Is 48, 20   [Spiritual Freedom]

Speak out with a voice of joy; let it be heard to the
ends of the earth: The Lord has set his people free, alleluia.   → No. 2, p. 10

OPENING PRAYER   [Operative Faith]

Let us pray
   [that we may practice in our lives
   the faith we profess]
Ever-living God,
help us to celebrate our joy
in the resurrection of the Lord
and to express in our lives
the love we celebrate.
Grant this through our Lord Jesus Christ, your Son,
who lives and reigns with you and the Holy Spirit,
one God, for ever and ever. ℟. **Amen.** ↓

ALTERNATIVE OPENING PRAYER   [Resurrection]

Let us pray
   [in silence, reflecting on the joy of Easter]
God our Father, maker of all,
the crown of your creation was the Son of Man,
born of a woman, but without beginning;
he suffered for us but lives for ever.
May our mortal lives be crowned with the ultimate joy
of rising with him,
who is Lord for ever and ever. ℟. **Amen.** ↓

READING I Acts 10, 25-26. 34-35. 44-48   [God Loves All]

Peter visits Cornelius and his family. God will favor anyone who acts uprightly, Jews, and Gentiles alike. He gave orders that all who believe should be baptized.

A reading from the Acts of the Apostles

PETER entered the house of Cornelius who met him, dropped to his knees before Peter and bowed low. Peter said as he helped him to his feet, "Get up! I am only a man myself."

Peter proceeded to address [the relatives and friends of Cornelius] in these words: "I begin to see how true it is that God shows no partiality. Rather, the

Peter had not finished these words when the Holy Spirit descended upon all who were listening to Peter's message. The circumcised believers who had accompanied Peter were surprised that the gift of the Holy Spirit should have been poured out on the Gentiles also, whom they could hear speaking in tongues and glorifying God. Peter put the question at that point: "What can stop these people who have received the Holy Spirit, even as we have, from being baptized with water?" So he gave orders that they be baptized in the name of Jesus Christ. After this was done, they asked him to stay with them for a few days.—The word of the Lord. ℟. **Thanks be to God.** ↓

RESPONSORIAL PSALM Ps 98   [Revelation to the Nations]

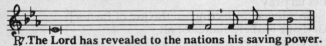

℟.**The Lord has revealed to the nations his saving power.**

Sing to the Lord a new song,
   for he has done wondrous deeds;
His right hand has won victory for him,
   his holy arm.—℟.

The Lord has made his salvation known:
   in the sight of the nations he has revealed his justice.
He has remembered his kindness and his faithfulness
   toward the house of Israel.—℟.

All the ends of the earth have seen
   the salvation by our God.
Sing joyfully to the Lord, all you lands;
   break into song; sing praise.—℟. ↓

℟. Or: **Alleluia.** ↓

READING II 1 Jn 4, 7-10   [God Is Love]

Christians should love one another as God himself is love. A person without love does not know God. Love is that God has sent his Son as an offering for sin.

A reading from the first letter of John

BELOVED,
let us love one another
  because love is of God;
  everyone who loves is begotten of God
  and has knowledge of God.
The man without love has known nothing of God,
  for God is love.
God's love was revealed in our midst in this way:
  he sent his only Son to the world
  that we might have life through him.
Love, then, consists in this:
  not that we have loved God,
  but that he has loved us
  and has sent his Son as an offering for our sins.
The word of the Lord. ℟. **Thanks be to God.** ↓

GOSPEL Jn 15, 9-17   [Love One Another]
Alleluia (Jn 14, 23)
℟. **Alleluia.** If anyone loves me, he will hold to my
  words,
and my Father will love him, and we will come to him.
  ℟. **Alleluia.** ↓

Jesus admonishes his disciples to continue the love he has
shown to them. The keeping of the commandments will
prove this. "You are to love one another. . . . It was I who
chose you."

℣. The Lord be with you. ℟. **And also with you.**
✚ A reading from the holy gospel according to John.
℟. **Glory to you, Lord.**

JESUS said to his disciples:
  "As the Father has loved me,
  so I have loved you.
  Live on in my love.
  You will live in my love
  if you keep my commandments,
  even as I have kept my Father's commandments,

and live in his love.
All this I tell you
that my joy may be yours
and your joy may be complete.
This is my commandment:
love one another
as I have loved you.
There is no greater love than this:
to lay down one's life for one's friends.
You are my friends
if you do what I command you.
I no longer speak of you as slaves,
for a slave does not know what his master is about.
Instead, I call you friends
since I have made known to you all that I heard
   from my Father.
It was not you who chose me,
it was I who chose you
to go forth and bear fruit.
Your fruit must endure,
so that all you ask the Father in my name
he will give you.
The command I give you is this,
that you love one another."

The gospel of the Lord. R̸. **Praise to you, Lord Jesus Christ.**   → No. 14, p. 18

PRAYER OVER THE GIFTS   [Forgiveness]

Lord,
accept our prayers and offerings.
Make us worthy of your sacraments of love
by granting us your forgiveness.
We ask this in the name of Jesus the Lord.

R̸. **Amen.**   → No. 21, p. 22 (Pref. P 21-25)

COMMUNION ANT. Jn 14, 15-16   [Role of the Spirit]

If you love me, keep my commandments, says the Lord. The Father will send you the Holy Spirit, to be with you for ever, alleluia. ↓

PRAYER AFTER COMMUNION   [Eucharistic Strength]

Almighty and ever-living Lord,
you restored us to life
by raising Christ from death.
Strengthen us by this Easter sacrament;
may we feel its saving power in our daily life.
We ask this through Christ our Lord.
℟. **Amen.**

➜ No. 32, p. 70

Optional Solemn Blessings, p. 92, and Prayers Over the People, p. 99

*"Go into the whole world and proclaim the good news
to all creation."*

*In the states of Alaska, California, Hawaii, Idaho, Montana,
Nevada, Oregon, Utah, and Washington, the following Mass
of the Ascension is celebrated on May 11, in place of the Mass
of the 7th Sunday of Easter that appears on p. 326.*

MAY 8

ASCENSION

ENTRANCE ANT. Acts 1, 11   [The Lord Will Return]

**Men of Galilee, why do you stand looking in the sky?
The Lord will return, just as you have seen him ascend, alleluia.**

➜ No. 2, p. 10

OPENING PRAYER   [Joy in the Ascension]

Let us pray
   [that the risen Christ
   will lead us to eternal life]
God our Father,
make us joyful in the ascension of your Son Jesus Christ.
May we follow him into the new creation,
for his ascension is our glory and our hope.
We ask this . . . for ever and ever. ℟. **Amen.** ↓

ALTERNATIVE OPENING PRAYER   [Hope in Christ]

Let us pray
   [on this day of Ascension
   as we watch and wait for Jesus' return]
Father in heaven,
our minds were prepared for the coming of your kingdom
when you took Christ beyond our sight
so that we might seek him in his glory.
May we follow where he has led
and find our hope in his glory,
for he is Lord for ever. ℟. **Amen.** ↓

READING I Acts 1, 1-11   [Christ's Ascension]

**Luke recounts the life, suffering and death of Jesus and
what Jesus did the forty days after his resurrection. Jesus
promises the Holy Spirit to the apostles. Jesus then as-
cends into heaven while they watch.**

The beginning of the Acts of the Apostles

IN my first account, Theophilus, I dealt with all that
Jesus did and taught until the day he was taken up
to heaven, having first instructed the apostles he had
chosen through the Holy Spirit. In the time after his
suffering he showed them in many convincing ways
that he was alive, appearing to them over the course

of forty days and speaking to them about the reign of
God. On one occasion when he met with them, he told
them not to leave Jerusalem: "Wait, rather, for the fulfillment of my Father's promise, of which you have
heard me speak. John baptized with water, but within
a few days you will be baptized with the Holy Spirit."

While they were with him they asked, "Lord, are you
going to restore the rule to Israel now?" His answer
was: "The exact time it is not yours to know. The
Father has reserved that to himself. You will receive
power when the Holy Spirit comes down on you; then
you are to be my witnesses in Jerusalem, throughout
Judea and Samaria, yes, even to the ends of the earth."
No sooner had he said this than he was lifted up before
their eyes in a cloud which took him from their sight.

They were still gazing up into the heavens when
two men dressed in white stood beside them. "Men of
Galilee," they said, "why do you stand here looking up
at the skies? This Jesus who has been taken from you
will return, just as you saw him go up into the heavens."—The word of the Lord. ℟. **Thanks be to God.** ↓

RESPONSORIAL PSALM Ps 47   [Praise to the Lord]

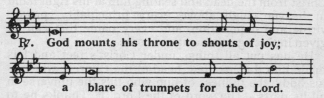

℟. **God mounts his throne to shouts of joy;**
a **blare of trumpets for the Lord.**

All you peoples, clap your hands,
   shout to God with cries of gladness.
For the Lord, the Most High, the awesome,
   is the great king over all the earth.—℟.

God mounts his throne amid shouts of joy;
   the Lord, amid trumpet blasts.

Sing praise to God, sing praise;
 sing praise to our king, sing praise.—℟.

For king of all the earth is God;
 sing hymns of praise.
God reigns over the nations,
 God sits upon his holy throne.—℟. ↓
℟. Or: **Alleluia.** ↓

READING II Eph 1, 17-23   [Glorification of Jesus]
 **Paul speaks of Jesus as the Father of glory who is ready to
 hear our prayers, to grant wisdom and knowledge.**

A reading from the letter of Paul
to the Ephesians

MAY the God of our Lord Jesus Christ, the Father
of glory, grant you a spirit of wisdom and insight
to know him clearly. May he enlighten your innermost
vision that you may know the great hope to which he
has called you, the wealth of his glorious heritage to
be distributed among the members of the church, and
the immeasurable scope of his power in us who believe. It is like the strength he showed in raising
Christ from the dead and seating him at his right hand
in heaven, high above every principality, power,
virtue and domination, and every name that can be
given in this age or the age to come.

 He has put all things under Christ's feet and has
made him thus exalted, head of the Church, which is
his body: the fullness of him who fills the universe in
all its parts.—The word of the Lord. ℟. **Thanks be to
God.** ↓

GOSPEL Mk 16, 15-20   [Preaching the Good News]
Alleluia (Mt 28, 19. 20)
℟. **Alleluia.** Go and teach all people my gospel.
I am with you always, until the end of the world. ℟.
 Alleluia. ↓

Jesus makes his disciples apostles to preach the good news. He promises them special signs for protection on earth and then finally Jesus is taken up into heaven.

℣. The Lord be with you. ℟. **And also with you.**
✣ The conclusion of the holy gospel according to Mark. ℟. **Glory to you, Lord.**

[J ESUS appeared to the Eleven and] said to them: "Go into the whole world and proclaim the good news to all creation. The man who believes in it and accepts baptism will be saved; the man who refuses to believe in it will be condemned. Signs like these will accompany those who have professed their faith: they will use my name to expel demons, they will speak entirely new languages, they will be able to handle serpents, they will be able to drink deadly poison without harm, and the sick upon whom they lay their hands will recover." Then, after speaking to them, the Lord Jesus was taken up into heaven and took his seat at God's right hand. The Eleven went forth and preached everywhere. The Lord continued to work with them throughout and confirm the message through the signs which accompanied them.—The gospel of the Lord. ℟. **Praise to you, Lord Jesus Christ.**   → No. 14, p. 18

PRAYER OVER THE GIFTS   [Rise to Heavenly Joy]

Lord,
receive our offering
as we celebrate the ascension of Christ your Son.
May his gifts help us rise with him
to the joys of heaven,
where he lives and reigns for ever and ever.
℟. **Amen.**   → No. 21, p. 22 (Pref. P 26-27)

When Eucharistic Prayer I is used, the special Ascension form of In union with the whole Church *is said.*

COMMUNION ANT. Mt 28, 20   [Christ's Presence]

I, the Lord, am with you always, until the end of the world, alleluia. ↓

PRAYER AFTER COMMUNION   [Following Christ]

Father,
in this eucharist
we touch the divine life you give to the world.
Help us to follow Christ with love
to eternal life where he is Lord for ever and ever.
℟. **Amen.**   → No. 32, p. 70

Optional Solemn Blessings, p. 92, and Prayers Over the People, p. 99

*"O Father most holy, protect them with your name
which you have given me."*

*In the following states of Alaska, California, Hawaii, Idaho,
Montana, Nevada, Oregon, Utah, and Washington, the Mass
of the Ascension that appears on p. 321 is celebrated today in
place of the following Mass on the 7th Sunday of Easter.*

MAY 11

7th SUNDAY OF EASTER

ENTRANCE ANT. Ps 27, 7-9   [Seek the Lord]

**Lord, hear my voice when I call to you. My heart has
prompted me to seek your face; I seek it, Lord; do not
hide from me, alleluia.**   → No. 2, p. 10

OPENING PRAYER   [Recognizing Christ among Us]

Let us pray
   [that we may recognize
   the presence of Christ in our midst]
Father,
help us keep in mind that Christ our Savior
lives with you in glory
and promised to remain with us until the end of time.
We ask this through our Lord Jesus Christ, your Son,
who lives and reigns with you and the Holy Spirit,
one God, for ever and ever. R/. **Amen.** ↓

ALTERNATIVE OPENING PRAYER

[Effects of Christ's Presence]

Let us pray
   [to our Father
   who has raised us to life in Christ]
Eternal Father,
reaching from end to end of the universe,
and ordering all things with your mighty arm:
for you, time is the unfolding of truth that already is,
the unveiling of beauty that is yet to be.
Your Son has saved us in history
by rising from the dead,
so that transcending time he might free us from death.
May his presence among us
lead to the vision of unlimited truth
and unfold the beauty of your love.
We ask this in the name of Jesus the Lord. R/. **Amen.** ↓

READING I Acts 1, 15-17. 20-26   [Choice of Matthias]

Peter discusses the question of Judas and his replacement.
Two were nominated and all prayed. Then they drew lots
and the choice fell to Matthias.

A reading from the Acts of the Apostles

IN those days Peter stood up in the midst of the brothers—there must have been a hundred and twenty gathered together. "Brothers," he said, "the saying in Scripture uttered long ago by the Holy Spirit through the mouth of David was destined to be fulfilled in Judas, the one that guided those who arrested Jesus. He was one of our number and he had been given a share in this ministry of ours. It is written in the Book of Psalms,

'May another take his office.'

"It is entirely fitting, therefore, that one of those who was of our company while the Lord Jesus moved among us, from the baptism of John until the day he was taken up from us, should be named as witness with us to his resurrection." At that they nominated two, Joseph (called Barsabbas, also known as Justus) and Matthias. Then they prayed: "O Lord, you read the hearts of men. Make known to us which of these two you choose for this apostolic ministry, replacing Judas, who deserted the cause and went the way he was destined to go." They then drew lots between the two men. The choice fell to Matthias, who was added to the eleven apostles.—The word of the Lord. ℟. **Thanks be to God.** ↓

RESPONSORIAL PSALM Ps 103   [Bless the Lord]

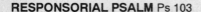

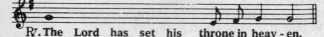

℟. **The Lord has set his throne in heav - en.**

Bless the Lord, O my soul;
   and all my being, bless his holy name.
Bless the Lord, O my soul,
   and forget not all his benefits.—℟.

For as the heavens are high above the earth,
   so surpassing is his kindness toward those who fear
    him.

As far as the east is from the west,
    so far has he put our transgressions from us.—R̕.

The Lord has established his throne in heaven,
    and his kingdom rules over all.
Bless the Lord, all you his angels,
    you mighty in strength, who do his bidding.—R̕. ↓
R̕. Or: **Alleluia.** ↓

READING II 1 Jn 4, 11-16   [God Dwells in Us]

**Christians must have love for one another since the God of
love dwells in them. When Jesus is acknowledged, God
dwells in that person. God is love.**

A reading from the first letter of John

B ELOVED,
    if God has loved us so,
    we must have the same love for one another.
No one has ever seen God.
Yet if we love one another
    God dwells in us,
    and his love is brought to perfection in us.
The way we know we remain in him
    and he in us
    is that he has given us of his Spirit.
We have seen for ourselves, and can testify,
    that the Father has sent the Son as savior of the world.
When anyone acknowledges that Jesus is the Son of
    God,
    God dwells in him
    and he in God.
We have come to know and to believe
    in the love God has for us.
God is love,
    and he who abides in love
    abides in God,
    and God in him.
The word of the Lord. R̕. **Thanks be to God.** ↓

GOSPEL Jn 17, 11-19   [Jesus' Prayer for Us]
Alleluia (Jn 14, 18)

R̦. **Alleluia.** The Lord said: I will not leave you orphans.
I will come back to you, and your hearts will rejoice.
    R̦. **Alleluia.** ↓

> Jesus prays for his followers. They have been looked after
> and have heard the gospel message from Jesus. He prays
> that his Father will continue to look after them and guard
> them from the evil one.

V̦. The Lord be with you. R̦. **And also with you.**
✛ A reading from the holy gospel according to John.
R̦. **Glory to you, Lord.**

JESUS looked up to heaven and prayed:
    "O Father most holy,
        protect them with your name which you have
            given me,
        [that they may be one, even as we are one].
    As long as I was with them,
    I guarded them with your name which you gave
        me.
    I kept careful watch,
    and not one of them was lost,
    none but him whom was destined to be lost—
    in fulfillment of Scripture.
    Now, however, I come to you;
    I say all this while I am still in the world
    that they may share my joy completely.
    I gave them your word,
    and the world has hated them for it;
    they do not belong to the world,
    [any more than I belong to the world.]
    I do not ask you to take them out of the world,
    but to guard them from the evil one.
    They are not of the world,
    any more than I am of the world.
    Consecrate them by means of truth—

'Your word is truth.'
As you have sent me into the world,
so I have sent them into the world;
I consecrate myself for their sakes now,
that they may be consecrated in truth."

The gospel of the Lord. ℟. **Praise to you, Lord Jesus Christ.**   → No. 14, p. 18

PRAYER OVER THE GIFTS   [Gifts of Love]

Lord,
accept the prayers and gifts
we offer in faith and love.
May this eucharist
bring us to your glory.
Grant this through Christ our Lord.
℟. **Amen.**   → No. 21, p. 22 (Pref. P 21-25 or P 26-27)

COMMUNION ANT. Jn 17, 22   [Christian Unity]

This is the prayer of Jesus: that his believers may become one as he is one with the Father, alleluia. ↓

PRAYER AFTER COMMUNION   [Glory of Christ's Body]

God our Savior,
hear us,
and through this holy mystery give us hope
that the glory you have given Christ
will be given to the Church, his body,
for he is Lord for ever and ever.
℟. **Amen.**   → No. 32, p. 70

Optional Solemn Blessings, p. 92, and Prayers Over the People, p. 99

"All were filled with the Holy Spirit."

MAY 18

PENTECOST

VIGIL MASS

ENTRANCE ANT. See Rom 5, 5; 8, 11 **[Love-Imparting Spirit]**
**The love of God has been poured into our hearts by
his Spirit living in us, alleluia.**   → No. 2, p. 10

OPENING PRAYER   **[Spirit of Peace]**
Let us pray
  [that the Holy Spirit
  may bring peace and unity to all mankind]
Almighty and ever-living God,
you fulfilled the Easter promise
by sending us your Holy Spirit.
May that Spirit unite the races and nations on earth
to proclaim your glory.
Grant this through our Lord Jesus Christ, your Son,
who lives and reigns with you and the Holy Spirit,
one God, for ever and ever. ℟. **Amen.** ↓

OR   **[New Birth in the Spirit]**
God our Father,
you have given us new birth.

Strengthen us with your Holy Spirit
and fill us with your light.
Grant this through our Lord Jesus Christ, your Son,
who lives and reigns with you and the Holy Spirit,
one God, for ever and ever. R̶⁄. **Amen.** ↓

ALTERNATIVE OPENING PRAYER   [Eliminate Division]

Let us pray
    [that the flame of the Spirit will descend upon us]
Father in heaven,
fifty days have celebrated the fullness
of the mystery of your revealed love.
See your people gathered in prayer,
open to receive the Spirit's flame.
May it come to rest in our hearts
and disperse the divisions of word and tongue.
With one voice and one song
may we praise your name in joy and thanksgiving.
Grant this through Christ our Lord. R̶⁄. **Amen.** ↓

READING I Gn 11, 1-9   [Dangers of Human Pride]

**People all speaking the same language presumed to build a
super tower, Babel. God realized that in their pride nothing
would stop their future presumptions. Hence, he scattered
them and confused their speech.**

A reading from the book of Genesis

A T that time the whole world spoke the same language, using the same words. While men were mi-
grating in the east, they came upon a valley in the
land of Shinar and settled there. They said to one another, "Come, let us mold bricks and harden them
with fire." They used bricks for stone, and bitumen for
mortar. Then they said, "Come, let us build ourselves
a city and a tower with its top in the sky, and so make
a name for ourselves; otherwise we shall be scattered
all over the earth."

The Lord came down to see the city and the tower
that the men had built. Then the Lord said: "If now,

while they are one people, all speaking the same language, they have started to do this, nothing will later stop them from doing whatever they presume to do. Let us then go down and there confuse their language, so that one will not understand what another says." Thus the Lord scattered them from there all over the earth, and they stopped building the city. That is why it was called Babel, because there the Lord confused the speech of all the world. It was from that place that he scattered them all over the earth.—The word of the Lord. ℟. **Thanks be to God.** ↓

OR

READING I Ex 19, 3-8. 16-20   [The Lord on Mount Sinai]

God spoke to Moses of how he protected the Israelites, showing his love for them. They promised to do God's will. Amid peals of thunder, God summoned Moses to Mt. Sinai.

A reading from the book of Exodus

MOSES went up the mountain to God. Then the Lord called to him and said, "Thus shall you say to the house of Jacob; tell the Israelites: You have seen for yourselves how I treated the Egyptians and how I bore you up on eagle wings and brought you here to myself. Therefore, if you hearken to my voice and keep my covenant, you shall be my special possession, dearer to me than all other people, though all the earth is mine. You shall be to me a kingdom of priests, a holy nation. That is what you must tell the Israelites." So Moses went and summoned the elders of the people. When he set before them all that the Lord had ordered him to tell them, the people all answered together, "Everything the Lord has said, we will do."

On the morning of the third day there were peals of thunder and lightning, and a heavy cloud over the mountain, and a very loud trumpet blast, so that all the people in the camp trembled. But Moses led the people out of the camp to meet God, and they stationed themselves at the foot of the mountain. Mount Sinai was all wrapped in smoke, for the Lord came down upon it in fire. The smoke rose from it as though from a furnace, and the whole mountain trembled violently. The trumpet blast grew louder and louder, while Moses was speaking and God answering him with thunder.

When the Lord came down to the top of Mount Sinai, he summoned Moses to the top of the mountain.—The word of the Lord. ℟. **Thanks be to God.** ↓

OR

READING I Ez 37, 1-14   [Life-Giving Spirit]

Ezekiel speaks of the dry bones in the desert as a figure of the Israelites. It is the Spirit of God that will give them flesh and life.

A reading from the book of the prophet Ezekiel

THE hand of the Lord came upon me, and he led me out in the spirit of the Lord and set me in the center of the plain, which was now filled with bones. He made me walk among them in every direction so that I saw how many they were on the surface of the plain. How dry they were! He asked me: Son of man, can these bones come to life? "Lord God," I answered, "you alone know that." Then he said to me: Prophesy over these bones, and say to them: Dry bones, hear the word of the Lord! Thus says the Lord God to these bones: See! I will bring spirit into you, that you may come to life. I will put sinews upon you, make flesh grow over you, cover you with skin, and put spirit in you so that you may come to life and know that I am the Lord. I prophesied as I had been told, and even as I was prophesying I heard a noise; it was a rattling as the bones came together, bone joining bone. I saw the sinews and the flesh come upon them, and the skin cover them, but there was no spirit in them. Then he said to me: Prophesy to the spirit, prophesy, son of man, and say to the spirit: Thus says the Lord God: From the four winds come, O spirit, and breathe into these slain that they may come to life. I prophesied as he told me, and the spirit came into them; they came alive and stood upright, a vast army. Then he said to me: Son of man, these bones are the whole house of Israel. They have been saying, "Our bones are dried up, our hope is lost, and we are cut off." Therefore, prophesy and say to them: Thus says the Lord God: O my people, I will open your graves and have you rise from them, and bring you back to the land of Israel. Then you shall know that I am the Lord, when I open your graves and have you rise from them, O my people! I will put my spirit in you that you may live, and I will settle you upon your land; thus you shall know that I am the Lord. I have promised, and I will do it, says the Lord.—The word of the Lord. ℟. **Thanks be to God.** ↓

OR

READING I Jl 3, 1-5   [Signs of the Spirit]

Joel brings the Lord's message to his people. He will pour out his Spirit. Signs of God's wonders will be present—prophecy, dreams, blood, fire, smoke, darkened sun—but everyone will be saved who calls on the Lord.

A reading from the book of the prophet Joel

THUS says the Lord:
I will pour out
   my spirit upon all mankind.
Your sons and daughters shall prophesy,
   your old men shall dream dreams,
   your young men shall see visions;
Even upon the servants and the handmaids,
   in those days, I will pour out my spirit.

And I will work wonders in the heavens and on the
   earth,
   blood, fire, and columns of smoke;
The sun will be turned to darkness,
   and the moon to blood,
At the coming of the Day of the Lord,
   the great and terrible day.
Then everyone shall be rescued
   who calls on the name of the Lord;
For on Mount Zion there shall be a remnant,
   as the Lord has said,
And in Jerusalem survivors
   whom the Lord shall call.
The word of the Lord. ℟. **Thanks be to God.** ↓

RESPONSORIAL PSALM Ps 104   [Send Out Your Spirit]

℟. Lord, send out your Spir - it, and re-new the face of the earth.

Bless the Lord, O my soul!
   O Lord, my God, you are great indeed!
You are clothed with majesty and glory,
   robed in light as with a cloak.—℟.

How manifold are your works, O Lord!
   In wisdom you have wrought them all—
   the earth is full of your creatures;
   bless the Lord, O my soul! Alleluia.

℟. **Lord, send out your Spirit,**
   and renew the face of the earth.

Creatures all look to you
   to give them food in due time.
When you give it to them, they gather it;
   when you open your hand, they are filled with good
      things.

℟. **Lord, send out your Spirit,**
   and renew the face of the earth.

If you take away their breath, they perish
   and return to their dust.
When you send forth your spirit, they are created,
   and you renew the face of the earth.

℟. **Lord, send out your Spirit,**
   and renew the face of the earth. ↓

℟. Or: **Alleluia.** ↓

READING II Rom 8, 22-27   [The Spirit Our Helper]

We hope in the Spirit, patiently awaiting redemption. The
Spirit helps our weakness. He prays for us, searches our
hearts, and intercedes for us.

A reading from the letter of Paul to the Romans

WE know that all creation groans and is in agony
even until now. Not only that, but we ourselves,
although we have the Spirit as first fruits, groan in-
wardly while we await the redemption of our bodies.
In hope we were saved. But hope is not hope if its object is seen; how is it possible for one to hope for what
he sees? And hoping for what we cannot see means
awaiting it with patient endurance.

The Spirit too helps us in our weakness, for we do
not know how to pray as we ought; but the Spirit himself makes intercession for us with groanings which
cannot be expressed in speech. He who searches
hearts knows what the Spirit means, for the Spirit intercedes for the saints as God himself wills.—The
word of the Lord. ℟. **Thanks be to God.** ↓

GOSPEL Jn 7, 37-39   [Prediction of the Spirit]
Alleluia

℟. **Alleluia.** Come, Holy Spirit, fill the hearts of your
   faithful;
and kindle in them the fire of your love. ℟. **Alleluia.** ↓

Jesus calls to himself those who are thirsting for the waters of life. Jesus knew that he would send the Holy Spirit to those who believed in him.

℣. The Lord be with you. ℟. **And also with you.**

✠ A reading from the holy gospel according to John.
℟. **Glory to you, Lord**.

O N the last and greatest day of the festival, Jesus stood up and cried out:
"If anyone thirst, let him come to me;
Let him drink who believes in me.
Scripture has it:
'From within him rivers of living water shall flow.' "

(Here he was referring to the Spirit, whom those that came to believe in him were to receive. There was, of course, no Spirit as yet, since Jesus had not yet been glorified.)—The gospel of the Lord. ℟. **Praise to you, Lord Jesus Christ.**   → No. 14, p. 18

PRAYER OVER THE GIFTS   [Manifestation of Salvation]

Lord,
send your Spirit on these gifts
and through them help the Church you love
to show your salvation to all the world.
We ask this in the name of Jesus the Lord.
℟. **Amen.**   → Pref. (P 28), p. 345

When Eucharistic Prayer I is used, the special Pentecost form of In union with the whole Church *is said.*

COMMUNION ANT. Jn 7, 37   [Thirst for the Spirit]

On the last day of the festival, Jesus stood up and cried aloud: If anyone is thirsty, let him come to me and drink, alleluia. ↓

PRAYER AFTER COMMUNION   [Eucharistic Love]

Lord,
through this eucharist,

send the Holy Spirit of Pentecost into our hearts
to keep us always in your love.
We ask this through Christ our Lord.
R̸. **Amen.**   ➜ No. 32, p. 70

Optional Solemn Blessings, p. 92, and Prayers Over the People, p. 99

MASS DURING THE DAY

ENTRANCE ANT. Wis 1, 7   [The Spirit in the World]

**The Spirit of the Lord fills the whole world. It holds
all things together and knows every word spoken by
man, alleluia.**

OR See Rom 5, 5; 8, 11   [God's Love for Us]

**The love of God has been poured into our hearts by
his Spirit living in us, alleluia.**   ➜ No. 2, p. 10

OPENING PRAYER   [Work of the Spirit]

Let us pray
  [that the Spirit will work through our lives
  to bring Christ to the world]
God our Father,
let the Spirit you sent on your Church
to begin the teaching of the gospel
continue to work in the world
through the hearts of all who believe.
We ask this through our Lord Jesus Christ, your Son,
who lives and reigns with you and the Holy Spirit,
one God, for ever and ever. R̸. **Amen.** ↓

ALTERNATIVE OPENING PRAYER   [Power of the Spirit]

Let us pray
  [in the Spirit who dwells within us]
Father of light, from whom every good gift comes,
send your Spirit into our lives

with the power of a mighty wind,
and by the flame of your wisdom
open the horizons of our minds.
Loosen our tongues to sing your praise
in words beyond the power of speech,
for without your Spirit
man could never raise his voice in words of peace
or announce the truth that Jesus is Lord,
who lives and reigns with you and the Holy Spirit,
one God, for ever and ever. ℟. **Amen.** ↓

READING I Acts 2, 1-11   [Coming of the Spirit]

On this day the Holy Spirit in fiery tongues descended
upon the apostles and the Mother of Jesus. Today the law
of grace and purification from sin was announced. Three
thousand were baptized.

A reading from the Acts of the Apostles

WHEN the day of Pentecost came it found the
brethren gathered in one place. Suddenly from
up in the sky there came a noise like a strong, driving
wind which was heard all through the house where
they were seated. Tongues as of fire appeared which
parted and came to rest on each of them. All were
filled with the Holy Spirit. They began to express
themselves in foreign tongues and make bold proclamation as the Spirit prompted them.

Staying in Jerusalem at the time were devout Jews
of every nation under heaven. These heard the sound,
and assembled in a large crowd. They were much confused because each one heard these men speaking his
own language. The whole occurrence astonished
them. They asked in utter amazement, "Are not all of
these men who are speaking Galileans? How is it that
each of us hears them in his native tongue? We are
Parthians, Medes, and Elamites. We live in Mesopota-
mia, Judea and Cappadocia, Pontus, the province of

Asia, Phrygia and Pamphylia, Egypt, and the regions
of Libya around Cyrene. There are even visitors from
Rome—all Jews, or those who have come over to Ju-
daism; Cretans and Arabs too. Yet each of us hears
them speaking in his own tongue about the marvels
God has accomplished."—The word of the Lord. ℞.
Thanks be to God. ↓

RESPONSORIAL PSALM Ps 104   [Renewal by the Spirit]

℞. Lord, send out your Spir - it,   and re-new the face of the earth.

Bless the Lord, O my soul!
  O Lord, my God, you are great indeed!
How manifold are your works, O Lord!
  the earth is full of your creatures.

℞. **Lord, send out your Spirit,**
  and renew the face of the earth.

If you take away their breath, they perish
  and return to their dust.
When you send forth your spirit, they are created,
  and you renew the face of the earth.

℞. **Lord, send out your Spirit,**
  and renew the face of the earth.

May the glory of the Lord endure forever,
  may the Lord be glad in his works!
Pleasing to him be my theme;
  I will be glad in the Lord.

℞. **Lord, send out your Spirit,**
  and renew the face of the earth. ↓

℞. Or: **Alleluia.** ↓

READING II 1 Cor 12, 3-7. 12-13   [Grace of the Spirit]

No one can confess the divinity and sovereignty of Jesus
unless inspired by the Holy Spirit. Different gifts and ministries are given but all for the one body with Jesus.

A reading from the first letter of Paul
to the Corinthians

NO one can say: "Jesus is Lord," except in the Holy
Spirit.

There are different gifts but the same Spirit; there
are different ministries but the same Lord; there are
different works but the same God who accomplishes
all of them in everyone. To each person the manifesta-
tion of the Spirit is given for the common good.

The body is one and has many members, but all the
members, many though they are, are one body; and so
it is with Christ. It was in one Spirit that all of us,
whether Jew or Greek, slave or free, were baptized
into one body. All of us have been given to drink of
the one Spirit.—The word of the Lord. ℟. **Thanks be to
God.** ↓

SEQUENCE (Prose text)   [Come, Holy Spirit]

**Come, Holy Spirit, and from heaven direct on man
the rays of your light. Come, Father of the poor;
come, giver of God's gifts; come, light of men's hearts.**

**Kindly Paraclete, in your gracious visits to man's
soul you bring relief and consolation. If it is weary
with toil, you bring it ease; in the heat of temptation,
your grace cools it; if sorrowful, your words console it.**

**Light most blessed, shine on the hearts of your
faithful—even into their darkest corners; for without
your aid man can do nothing good, and everything is
sinful.**

**Wash clean the sinful soul, rain down your grace
on the parched soul and heal the injured soul. Soften
the hard heart, cherish and warm the ice-cold heart,
and give direction to the wayward.**

**Give your seven holy gifts to your faithful, for their
trust is in you. Give them reward for their virtuous**

acts; give them a death that ensures salvation; give them unending bliss. Amen. Alleluia. ↓

OR (Poetic text)   [Come, Holy Spirit]

Come, Holy Spirit, come! * And from your celestial home * shed a ray of light divine! * Come, Father of the poor! * Come, source of all our store! * Come, within our bosoms shine! * You, of comforters the best; * you, the soul's most welcome guest; * sweet refreshment here below; * in our labor, rest most sweet; * grateful coolness in the heat; * solace in the midst of woe. * O most blessed Light divine, * shine within these hearts of yours, * and our inmost being fill! * Where you are not, man has naught, * nothing good in deed or thought, * nothing free from taint of ill. * Heal our wounds, our strength renew; * on our dryness pour your dew; * wash the stains of guilt away: * bend the stubborn heart and will; * melt the frozen, warm the chill; * guide the steps that go astray. * On the faithful, who adore * and confess you, evermore * in your sev'nfold gift descend; * give them virtue's sure reward; * give them your salvation, Lord; * give them joys that never end. Amen. Alleluia. ↓

GOSPEL Jn 20, 19-23   [Christ Imparts the Spirit]
Alleluia
R̶. **Alleluia.** Come, Holy Spirit, fill the hearts of your faithful;
and kindle in them the fire of your love. R̶. **Alleluia.** ↓

Jesus breathes on the disciples to indicate the conferring of the Holy Spirit. Here we see the origin of power over sin, the Sacrament of Penance. This shows the power of the Holy Spirit in the hearts of human beings.

V̶. The Lord be with you. R̶. **And also with you.**
✟ A reading from the holy gospel according to John.
R̶. **Glory to you, Lord.**

ON the evening of that first day of the week, even though the disciples had locked the doors of the place where they were for fear of the Jews, Jesus came and stood before them. "Peace be with you," he said. When he had said this, he showed them his hands and his side. At the sight of the Lord the disciples rejoiced. "Peace be with you," he said again.

"As the Father has sent me,
so I send you."

Then he breathed on them and said:

"Receive the Holy Spirit.
If you forgive men's sins,
they are forgiven them;
if you hold them bound,
they are held bound."

The gospel of the Lord. ℞. **Praise to you, Lord Jesus Christ.**   → No. 14, p. 18

PRAYER OVER THE GIFTS   [Spirit of Jesus]

Lord,
may the Spirit you promised
lead us into all truth
and reveal to us the full meaning of this sacrifice.
Grant this through Christ our Lord. ℞. **Amen.** ↓

PREFACE (P 28)   [Coming of the Spirit]

℣. The Lord be with you. ℞. **And also with you.**
℣. Lift up your hearts. ℞. **We lift them up to the Lord.**
℣. Let us give thanks to the Lord our God. ℞. **It is right to give him thanks and praise.**

Father, all-powerful and ever-living God,
we do well always and everywhere to give you thanks.
Today you sent the Holy Spirit
on those marked out to be your children
by sharing the life of your only Son,

and so you brought the paschal mystery to its completion.
Today we celebrate the great beginning of your Church
when the Holy Spirit made known to all peoples the
one true God,
and created from the many languages of man
one voice to profess one faith.
The joy of the resurrection renews the whole world,
while the choirs of heaven sing for ever to your glory:
→ No. 23, p. 23

*When Eucharistic Prayer I is used, the special Pentecost
form of* In union with the whole Church *is said.*

COMMUNION ANT. Acts 2, 4. 11   [Filled with the Spirit]

**They were all filled with the Holy Spirit, and they
spoke of the great things God had done, alleluia.** ↓

PRAYER AFTER COMMUNION   [Vigor of the Spirit]
Father,
may the food we receive in the eucharist
help our eternal redemption.
Keep within us the vigor of your Spirit
and protect the gifts you have given to your Church.
We ask this in the name of Jesus the Lord.
℟. **Amen.**   → No. 32, p. 70

*The Blessing, p. 70 is given as usual. (At the end of the Dis-
missal the people answer: "Thanks be to God, alleluia, alleluia.")*

Optional Solemn Blessings, p. 92, and Prayers Over the People, p. 99

"Blessed be God the Father and his only begotten Son and the Holy Spirit."

MAY 25

TRINITY SUNDAY

ENTRANCE ANT. [Blessed Trinity]

Blessed be God the Father and his only-begotten Son and the Holy Spirit: for he has shown that he loves us.
→ No. 2, p. 10

OPENING PRAYER [Witnessing to the Trinity]

Let us pray
  [to the one God, Father, Son and Spirit,
  that our lives may bear witness to our faith]
Father,
you sent your Word to bring us truth
and your Spirit to make us holy.
Through them we come to know the mystery of your
  life.
Help us to worship you, one God in three Persons,
by proclaiming and living our faith in you.
Grant this through our Lord Jesus Christ, your Son,
who lives and reigns with you and the Holy Spirit,
one God, for ever and ever. ℟. **Amen.** ↓

ALTERNATIVE OPENING PRAYER [Praise to Triune God]

Let us pray
  [to our God who is Father, Son, and Holy Spirit]

God, we praise you:
Father all-powerful, Christ Lord and Savior, Spirit of
　　love.
You reveal yourself in the depths of our being,
drawing us to share in your life and your love.
One God, three Persons,
be near to the people formed in your image,
close to the world your love brings to life.
We ask you this, Father, Son, and Holy Spirit,
one God, true and living, for ever and ever. ℟. **Amen.** ↓

READING I Dt 4, 32-34. 39-40　　　　　　　[The One God]

**Moses asks the people to reflect on what has happened
and whether or not God was their sole Creator and protector. For this reason his laws and commandments must be
obeyed.**

A reading from the book of Deuteronomy

MOSES said to the people: "Ask now of the days of
old, before your time, ever since God created
man upon the earth; ask from one end of the sky to
the other: Did anything so great ever happen before?
Was it ever heard of? Did a people ever hear the voice
of God speaking from the midst of fire, as you did, and
live? Or did any god venture to go and take a nation
for himself from the midst of another nation, by test-
ings, by signs and wonders, by war, with his strong
hand and outstretched arm, and by great terrors, all of
which the Lord, your God, did for you in Egypt before
your very eyes? This is why you must now know, and
fix in your heart, that the Lord is God in the heavens
above and on earth below, and that there is no other.
You must keep his statutes and commandments which
I enjoin on you today, that you and your children after
you may prosper, and that you may have long life on
the land which the Lord, your God, is giving you forever."—The word of the Lord. ℟. **Thanks be to God.** ↓

RESPONSORIAL PSALM Ps 33   [God's People Hope in Him]

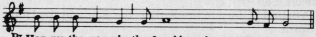

℟. Hap-py the peo-ple the Lord has chosen to be his own.

Upright is the word of the Lord,
   and all his works are trustworthy.
He loves justice and right;
   of the kindness of the Lord the earth is full.—℟.

By the word of the Lord the heavens were made;
   by the breath of his mouth all their host.
For he spoke, and it was made;
   he commanded, and it stood forth.—℟.

See, the eyes of the Lord are upon those who fear him,
   upon those who hope for his kindness,
To deliver them from death
   and preserve them in spite of famine.—℟.

Our soul waits for the Lord,
   who is our help and our shield.
May your kindness, O Lord, be upon us
   who have put our hope in you.—℟. ↓

READING II Rom 8, 14-17   [Children of God]

> The Spirit of God makes Christians adopted children of
> God. They become at the same time heirs of God with
> Christ—to suffer with him and also be glorified.

A reading from the letter of Paul to the Romans

ALL who are led by the Spirit of God are sons of
God. You did not receive a spirit of slavery leading you back into fear, but a spirit of adoption through
which we cry out, "Abba!" (that is, "Father"). The
Spirit himself gives witness with our spirit that we are
children of God. But if we are children, we are heirs as
well: heirs of God, heirs with Christ, if only we suffer
with him so as to be glorified with him.—The word of
the Lord. ℟. **Thanks be to God.** ↓

GOSPEL Mt 28, 16-20   [Disciples of the Trinity]
Alleluia (See Rv 1, 8)

℟. **Alleluia.** Glory to the Father, the Son and the Holy
   Spirit:
to God who is, who was, and who is to come. ℟. **Alleluia.** ↓

> At Jesus' request the eleven assembled and fell down in
> homage. Jesus gives them the all pervading command to
> preach and baptize all human beings. He also promises to
> be with them to the end of time.

℣. The Lord be with you. ℟. **And also with you.**
✚ The conclusion of the holy gospel according to
Matthew. ℟. **Glory to you, Lord.**

T HE eleven disciples made their way to Galilee, to
   the mountain to which Jesus had summoned them.
At the sight of him, those who had entertained doubts
fell down in homage. Jesus came forward and addressed them in these words:

> "Full authority has been given to me
> both in heaven and on earth;
> go therefore, and make disciples of all the na-
>   tions.
> Baptize them in the name
>   'of the Father,
>   and of the Son,
>   and of the Holy Spirit.'
> Teach them to carry out everything I have com-
>   manded you.
> And know that I am with you always, until the
>   end of the world!"

The gospel of the Lord. ℟. **Praise to you, Lord Jesus
Christ.**   → No. 14, p. 18

PRAYER OVER THE GIFTS   [Perfect Offering]

Lord our God,
make these gifts holy,

and through them
make us a perfect offering to you.
We ask this in the name of Jesus the Lord. ℟. **Amen.** ↓

PREFACE (P 43)   **[Mystery of the One Godhead]**

Father, all-powerful and ever-living God,
we do well always and everywhere to give you
    thanks.
We joyfully proclaim our faith
in the mystery of your Godhead.
You have revealed your glory
as the glory also of your Son
and of the Holy Spirit:
three Persons equal in majesty,
undivided in splendor,
yet one Lord, one God,
ever to be adored in your everlasting glory.
And so, with all the choirs of angels in heaven
we proclaim your glory
and join in their unending hymn of praise:

→ No. 23, p. 23

COMMUNION ANT. Gal 4, 6   **[Abba, Father]**

**You are the sons of God, so God has given you the
Spirit of his Son to form your hearts and make you
cry out: Abba, Father.** ↓

PRAYER AFTER COMMUNION   **[Eternal God]**

Lord God,
we worship you, a Trinity of Persons, one eternal God.
May our faith and the sacrament we receive
bring us health of mind and body.
We ask this through Christ our Lord.
℟. **Amen.**   → No. 32, p. 70

Optional Solemn Blessings, p. 92, and Prayers Over the People, p. 99

"This is my body . . . ."

JUNE 1

THE BODY AND BLOOD OF CHRIST
(CORPUS CHRISTI)

ENTRANCE ANT. Ps 81, 17   [Finest Wheat and Honey]

The Lord fed his people with the finest wheat and honey; their hunger was satisfied. → No. 2, p. 10

OPENING PRAYER   [Memorial of Christ]

Let us pray
  [to the Lord who gives himself in the eucharist,
    that this sacrament may bring us salvation and
     peace]
Lord Jesus Christ,
you gave us the eucharist
as the memorial of your suffering and death.
May our worship of this sacrament of your body and
  blood
help us to experience the salvation you won for us
and the peace of the kingdom
where you live with the Father and the Holy Spirit,
one God, for ever and ever. ℞. **Amen.** ↓

ALTERNATIVE OPENING PRAYER   [Eucharistic Love]

Let us pray
   [for the willingness to make present in our world
   the love of Christ shown to us in the eucharist]
Lord Jesus Christ,
we worship you living among us
in the sacrament of your body and blood.
May we offer to our Father in heaven
a solemn pledge of undivided love.
May we offer to our brothers and sisters
a life poured out in loving service of that kingdom
where you live with the Father and the Holy Spirit,
one God, for ever and ever. ℟. **Amen.** ↓

READING I Ex 24, 3-8   [Blood of the Covenant]
**The Israelites promised to observe all the prescriptions of
the Lord as related by Moses. To seal this promise Moses
offered a sacrifice to the Lord and sprinkled the people
with the blood offering.**

A reading from the book of Exodus

WHEN Moses came to the people and related all
the words and ordinances of the Lord, they all
answered with one voice, "We will do everything that
the Lord has told us." Moses then wrote down all the
words of the Lord and, rising early the next day, he
erected at the foot of the mountain an altar and twelve
pillars for the twelve tribes of Israel. Then, having
sent certain young men of the Israelites to offer holocausts and sacrifice young bulls as peace offerings to
the Lord, Moses took half of the blood and put it in
large bowls; the other half he splashed on the altar.
Taking the book of the covenant, he read it aloud to
the people, who answered, "All that the Lord has said,
we will heed and do." Then he took the blood and
sprinkled it on the people, saying, "This is the blood of
the covenant which the Lord has made with you in accordance with all these words of his."—The word of
the Lord. ℟. **Thanks be to God.** ↓

RESPONSORIAL PSALM Ps 116   [The Cup of Salvation]

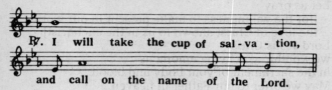

℞. I will take the cup of sal-va-tion,

and call on the name of the Lord.

How shall I make a return to the Lord
    for all the good he has done for me?
The cup of salvation I will take up,
    and I will call upon the name of the Lord.—℞.

Precious in the eyes of the Lord
    is the death of his faithful ones.
I am your servant, the son of your handmaid;
    you have loosed my bonds.—℞.

To you will I offer sacrifice of thanksgiving,
    and I will call upon the name of the Lord.
My vows to the Lord I will pay
    in the presence of all his people.—℞. ↓
℞. Or: Alleluia. ↓

READING II Heb 9, 11-15   [Jesus the High Priest]

Jesus came as high priest, not offering the blood of animals but his own blood, to achieve eternal redemption.
Jesus is mediator of the new covenant.

A reading from the letter to the Hebrews

WHEN Christ came as high priest of the good
things which have come to be, he entered once
for all into the sanctuary, passing through the greater
and more perfect tabernacle not made by hands, that
is, not belonging to this creation. He entered not with
the blood of goats and calves but with his own blood,
and achieved eternal redemption. For if the blood of
goats and bulls and the sprinkling of a heifer's ashes

can sanctify those who are defiled so that their flesh is cleansed, how much more will the blood of Christ, who through the eternal spirit offered himself up unblemished to God, cleanse our consciences from dead works to worship the living God?

This is why he is mediator of a new covenant: since his death has taken place for deliverance from transgressions committed under the first covenant, those who are called may receive the promised eternal inheritance.—The word of the Lord. ℟. **Thanks be to God.** ↓

The sequence is optional before the Alleluia verse.

SEQUENCE (Prose text)   [Praise of the Eucharist]

Zion, praise your Savior. Praise your leader and shepherd in hymns and canticles. Praise him as much as you can, for he is beyond all praising and you will never be able to praise him as he merits.

But today a theme worthy of particular praise is put before us—the living and life-giving bread that, without any doubt, was given to the Twelve at table during the holy supper.

Therefore let our praise be full and resounding and our soul's rejoicing full of delight and beauty, for this is the festival day to commemorate the first institution of this table.

At this table of the new King, the new law's new Pasch puts an end to the old Pasch. The new displaces the old, reality the shadow and light the darkness. Christ wanted what he did at the supper to be repeated in his memory.

And so we, in accordance with his holy directions, consecrate bread and wine to be salvation's Victim. Christ's followers know by faith that bread is changed into his flesh and wine into his blood.

Man cannot understand this, cannot perceive it; but a lively faith affirms that the change, which is outside

the natural course of things, takes place. Under the different species, which are now signs only and not their own reality, there lie hid wonderful realities. His body is our food, his blood our drink.

And yet Christ remains entire under each species. The communicant receives the complete Christ—uncut, unbroken and undivided. Whether one receive or a thousand, the one receives as much as the thousand. Nor is Christ diminished by being received.

The good and the wicked alike receive him, but with the unlike destiny of life or death. To the wicked it is death, but life to the good. See how different is the result, though each receives the same.

Last of all, if the sacrament is broken, have no doubt. Remember there is as much in a fragment as in an unbroken host. There is no division of the reality, but only a breaking of the sign; nor does the breaking diminish the condition or size of the One hidden under the sign.

Behold, the bread of angels is become the pilgrim's food; truly it is bread for the sons, and is not to be cast to dogs. It was prefigured in type when Isaac was brought as an offering, when a lamb was appointed for the Pasch and when manna was given to the Jews of old.

Jesus, good shepherd and true bread, have mercy on us; feed us and guard us. Grant that we find happiness in the land of the living. You know all things, can do all things, and feed us here on earth. Make us your guests in heaven, co-heirs with you and companions of heaven's citizens. Amen. Alleluia. ↓

OR (Poetic text) [Praise of the Eucharist]

Laud, O Zion, your salvation, * laud with hymns of exultation, * Christ, your king and shepherd true: * Bring him all the praise you know, * he is more than

you bestow, * never can you reach his due. * Special
theme for glad thanksgiving * is the quick'ning and
the living * bread today before you set: * From his
hands of old partaken, * as we know, by faith un-
shaken, * where the Twelve at supper met. * Full and
clear ring out your chanting, * joy nor sweetest grace
be wanting, * from your heart let praises burst: * For
today the feast is holden, * when the institution olden
* of that supper was rehearsed.

Here the new law's new oblation, * by the new
king's revelation, * ends the form of ancient rite: *
Now the new the old effaces, * truth away the shadow
chases, * light dispels the gloom of night. * What he
did at supper seated, * Christ ordained to be repeated,
* his memorial ne'er to cease: * And his rule for guidance taking, * bread and wine we hallow, making *
thus our sacrifice of peace. * This the truth each
Christian learns, * bread into his flesh he turns, * to
his precious blood the wine: * Sight has fail'd, nor
thought conceives, * but a dauntless faith believes, *
resting on a pow'r divine.

Here beneath these signs are hidden * priceless
things to sense forbidden; * signs, not things are all
we see: * Blood is poured and flesh is broken, * yet in
either wondrous token * Christ entire we know to be.
* Whoso of this food partakes, * does not rend the
Lord nor breaks; * Christ is whole to all that taste: *
Thousands are, as one, receivers, * one, as thousands
of believers, * eats of him who cannot waste. * Bad
and good the feast are sharing, * of what divers
dooms preparing, * endless death, or endless life. *
Life to these, to those damnation, * see how like participation * is with unlike issues rife.

When the sacrament is broken, * doubt not, but believe 'tis spoken, * that each sever'd outward token *
doth the very whole contain. * Nought the precious gift
divides, * breaking but the sign betides * Jesus still the

same abides, * still unbroken does remain. * Lo! the angel's food is given * to the pilgrim who has striven; * see the children's bread from heaven, * which on dogs may not be spent. * Truth the ancient types fulfilling, * Isaac bound, a victim willing, * paschal lamb, its life blood spilling, * manna to the fathers sent. * Very bread, good shepherd, tend us, * Jesu, of your love befriend us, * you refresh us, you defend us, * your eternal goodness send us * in the land of life to see. * You who all things can and know, * who on earth such food bestow, * grant us with your saints, though lowest, * where the heav'nly feast you show, * fellow heirs and guests to be. Amen. Alleluia. ↓

GOSPEL Mk 14, 12-16, 22-26   [The First Eucharist]

Alleluia (Jn 6, 51-52)

℞. **Alleluia.** I am the living bread from heaven, says the Lord;

if anyone eats this bread he will live for ever. ℞. **Alleluia.** ↓

> Jesus gave instructions for the Passover supper. At this meal he took bread and wine and changed it into his Body and Blood and gave this Eucharist to his disciples. They all ate and drank at Jesus' request.

℣. The Lord be with you. ℞. **And also with you.**

✛ A reading from the holy gospel according to Mark.

℞. **Glory to you, Lord.**

ON the first day of Unleavened Bread, when it was customary to sacrifice the paschal lamb, the disciples said to Jesus, "Where do you wish us to go to prepare the Passover supper for you?" He sent two of his disciples with these instructions: "Go into the city and you will come upon a man carrying a water jar. Follow him. Whatever house he enters, say to the owner, 'The Teacher asks, Where is my guest room where I may eat the Passover with my disciples?' Then he will show you an upstairs room, spacious, furnished, and all in order. That is the place you are to get ready for us." The disciples went off. When they reached the city they found it just as he had told them, and they prepared the Passover supper.

During the meal he took bread, blessed and broke it, and gave it to them. "Take this," he said, "this is my body." He likewise took a cup, gave thanks and passed it to them, and they all drank from it. He said to them: "This is my blood, the blood of the covenant, to be poured out on behalf of many. I solemnly assure you, I will never again drink of the fruit of the vine until the day when I drink it new in the reign of God."

After singing songs of praise they walked out to the Mount of Olives.—The gospel of the Lord. ℟. **Praise to you, Lord Jesus Christ.**   → No. 14, p. 18

PRAYER OVER THE GIFTS   [Unity and Peace]

Lord,
may the bread and cup we offer
bring your Church the unity and peace they signify.
We ask this in the name of Jesus the Lord.
℟. **Amen.**   → No. 21, p. 22 (Pref. P 47-48)

COMMUNION ANT. Jn 6, 57   [Eucharistic Life]

Whoever eats my flesh and drinks my blood will live in me and I in him, says the Lord. ↓

PRAYER AFTER COMMUNION   [Divine Life]

Lord Jesus Christ,
you give us your body and blood in the eucharist
as a sign that even now we share your life.
May we come to possess it completely in the kingdom
where you live for ever and ever.
℟. **Amen.**   → No. 32, p. 70

Optional Solemn Blessings, p. 92, and Prayers Over the People, p. 99

"Whoever does the will of God is brother and sister and mother to me."

JUNE 8

10th SUNDAY IN ORDINARY TIME

ENTRANCE ANT. Ps 27, 1-2 [My Salvation]

The Lord is my light and my salvation. Who shall frighten me? The Lord is the defender of my life. Who shall make me tremble? → No. 2, p. 10

OPENING PRAYER [Guided by the Spirit]

Let us pray
[for the guidance of the Holy Spirit]
God of wisdom and love,
source of all good,
send your Spirit to teach us your truth
and guide our actions in your way of peace.
We ask this through our Lord Jesus Christ, your Son,
who lives and reigns with you and the Holy Spirit,
one God, for ever and ever. ℟. **Amen:** ↓

ALTERNATIVE OPENING PRAYER [Freedom in Christ]

Let us pray
[to our Father
who calls us to freedom in Jesus his Son]

360

Father in heaven,
words cannot measure the boundaries of love
for those born to new life in Christ Jesus.
Raise us beyond the limits this world imposes,
so that we may be free to love as Christ teaches
and find our joy in your glory.
We ask this through Christ our Lord. ℟. **Amen.** ↓

READING I Gn 3, 9-15   [The Garden of Eden]

Our crosses and sufferings stem ultimately from sins of the
human race. Hence, before offering the Eucharist the
Church invites us to acknowledge our sinfulness before
God and our brothers and sisters.

A reading from the book of Genesis

[A FTER Adam had eaten of the tree] the Lord
called him and asked him, "Where are you?" He
answered, "I heard you in the garden; but I was afraid,
because I was naked, so I hid myself." Then he asked,
"Who told you that you were naked? You have eaten,
then, from the tree of which I have forbidden you to
eat!" The man replied, "The woman whom you put
here with me—she gave me fruit from the tree, and so
I ate it." The Lord God then asked the woman, "Why
did you do such a thing?" The woman answered, "The
serpent tricked me into it, so I ate it."
    Then the Lord God said to the serpent:
"Because you have done this, you shall be banned
        from all the animals
        and from all the wild creatures;
On your belly shall you crawl,
        and dirt shall you eat
        all the days of your life.
I will put enmity between you and the woman,
        and between your offspring and hers;
He will strike at your head,
        while you strike at his heel."
The word of the Lord. ℟. **Thanks be to God.** ↓

RESPONSORIAL PSALM Ps 130   **[The Lord's Kindness]**

℟. With the Lord there is mer-cy, and fullness of redemption.

Out of the depths I cry to you, O Lord;
  Lord, hear my voice!
Let your ears be attentive
  to my voice in supplication.

℟. **With the Lord there is mercy,
  and fullness of redemption.**

If you, O Lord, mark iniquities,
  Lord, who can stand?
But with you is forgiveness,
  that you may be revered.

℟. **With the Lord there is mercy,
  and fullness of redemption.**

I trust in the Lord;
  my soul trusts in his word.
More than sentinels wait for the dawn,
  let Israel wait for the Lord.

℟. **With the Lord there is mercy,
  and fullness of redemption.**

For with the Lord is kindness
  and with him is plenteous redemption;
And he will redeem Israel
  from all their iniquities.

℟. **With the Lord there is mercy,
  and fullness of redemption.** ↓

READING II 2 Cor 4, 13—5, 1   **[Eternal Glory]**

  To believe in Jesus means to share in a power of resurrection that saves. Set free from sin and reconciled with God,
  the Christian is a new person who resembles Christ more
  and more.

A reading from the second letter of Paul
to the Corinthians

WE have that spirit of faith of which the Scripture says, "Because I believed, I spoke out." We believe and so we speak, knowing that he who raised up the Lord Jesus will raise us up along with Jesus and place both us and you in his presence. Indeed, everything is ordered to your benefit, so that the grace bestowed in abundance may bring greater glory to God because they who give thanks are many.

We do not lose heart because our inner being is renewed each day, even though our body is being destroyed at the same time. The present burden of our trial is light enough and earns for us an eternal weight of glory beyond all comparison. We do not fix our gaze on what is seen but on what is unseen. What is seen is transitory; what is not seen lasts forever.

Indeed, we know that when the earthly tent in which we dwell is destroyed we have a dwelling provided for us by God, a dwelling in the heavens, not made by hands, but to last forever.—The word of the Lord. ℟. **Thanks be to God.** ↓

GOSPEL Mk 3, 30-35   [Victory in Christ]
Alleluia (Jn 12, 31-32)

℟. **Alleluia.** The prince of this world will now be cast out,
and when I am lifted up from the earth
I will draw all people to myself. ℟. **Alleluia.** ↓

Jesus proclaims the kingdom of God to the crowds. Access to this kingdom is attained by no human privilege. Only those are admitted into it who by their actions give proof of their faith and love.

℣. The Lord be with you. ℟. **And also with you.**
✝ A reading from the holy gospel according to Mark.
℟. **Glory to you, Lord.**

J ESUS came to the house with his disciples and again the crowd assembled, making it impossible for them to get any food whatever. When his family heard of this they came to take charge of him, saying, "He is out of his mind"; while the scribes who arrived from Jerusalem asserted, "He is possessed by Beelzebul," and "He expels demons with the help of the prince of demons." Summoning them, he then began to speak to them by way of examples: "How can Satan expel Satan? If a kingdom is torn by civil strife, that kingdom cannot last. If a household is divided according to loyalties, that household will not survive. Similarly, if Satan has suffered mutiny in his ranks and is torn by dissension, he cannot endure; he is finished. No one can enter a strong man's house and despoil his property unless he has first put him under restraint. Only then can he plunder his house.

"I give you my word, every sin will be forgiven mankind and all the blasphemies men utter, but whoever blasphemes against the Holy Spirit will never be forgiven. He carries the guilt of his sin without end." He spoke thus because they had said, "He is possessed by an unclean spirit."

His mother and his brothers arrived, and as they stood outside they sent word to him to come out. The crowd seated around him told him, "Your mother and your brothers and sisters are outside asking for you." He said in reply, "Who are my mother and my brothers?" And gazing around him at those seated in the circle he continued, "These are my mother and my brothers. Whoever does the will of God is brother and sister and mother to me."—The gospel of the Lord. ℟. **Praise to you, Lord Jesus Christ.**   → No. 14, p. 18

PRAYER OVER THE GIFTS   [Growth in Love]

Lord,
look with love on our service.

IN LOVING MEMORY OF

Gudell Francis Mack

September 25, 1908 - June 12, 1996

Our Father, Who art in heaven hallowed be Thy name. Thy kingdom come, Thy will be done, on earth as it is in heaven. Give us this day our daily bread. And forgive us our trespasses as we forgive those who trespass against us; and lead us not into temptation, but deliver us from evil. Amen.

Accept the gifts we bring
and help us grow in Christian love.
Grant this through Christ our Lord.
℟. Amen.   → No. 21, p. 22 (Pref. P 29-36)

COMMUNION ANT. Ps 18, 3   [God Our Helper]

**I can rely on the Lord; I can always turn to him for
shelter. It was he who gave me my freedom. My God,
you are always there to help me!** ↓

OR 1 Jn 4, 16   [Live in Love]

**God is love, and he who lives in love, lives in God,
and God in him.** ↓

PRAYER AFTER COMMUNION   [Healing Love]

Lord,
may your healing love
turn us from sin
and keep us on the way that leads to you.
We ask this in the name of Jesus the Lord.
℟. Amen.   → No. 32, p. 70

Optional Solemn Blessings, p. 92, and Prayers Over the People, p. 99

"The reign of God . . . is like a mustard seed."

JUNE 15

11th SUNDAY IN ORDINARY TIME

ENTRANCE ANT. Ps 27, 7. 9   **[Hear My Voice]**
Lord, hear my voice when I call to you. You are my help; do not cast me off, do not desert me, my Savior God.
→ No. 2, p. 10

OPENING PRAYER   **[Following Christ]**
Let us pray
   [for the grace to follow Christ more closely]
Almighty God,
our hope and our strength,
without you we falter.
Help us to follow Christ
and to live according to your will.
We ask this through our Lord Jesus Christ, your Son,
who lives and reigns with you and the Holy Spirit,
one God, for ever and ever. ℟. **Amen.** ↓

ALTERNATIVE OPENING PRAYER   **[Constant Strength]**
Let us pray
   [to the Father
   whose love gives us strength to follow his Son]

God our Father,
we rejoice in the faith that draws us together,
aware that selfishness can drive us apart.
Let your encouragement be our constant strength.
Keep us one in the love that has sealed our lives,
help us to live as one family
the gospel we profess.
We ask this through Christ our Lord. ℟. **Amen.** ↓

READING I Ez 17, 22-24   [The Lord's Shoot]

The restoration of Israel will be a kind of resurrection. From the modest beginnings of the Church, the Good News will be spread to all humanity.

A reading from the book of Ezekiel

THUS says the Lord God:
I, too, will take from the crest of the cedar,
   from its topmost branches tear off a tender shoot,
And plant it on a high and lofty mountain;
   on the mountain heights of Israel I will plant it.
It shall put forth branches and bear fruit,
   and become a majestic cedar.
Birds of every kind shall dwell beneath it,
   every winged thing in the shade of its boughs.
And all the trees of the field shall know
   that I, the Lord,
Bring low the high tree,
   lift high the lowly tree,
Wither up the green tree,
   and make the withered tree bloom.
As I, the Lord, have spoken, so will I do.
The word of the Lord. ℟. **Thanks be to God.** ↓

RESPONSORIAL PSALM Ps 92   [Rewards of the Just]

℟. O Lord, it is good to give thanks to you.

It is good to give thanks to the Lord,
  to sing praise to your name, Most High,
To proclaim your kindness at dawn
  and your faithfulness throughout the night.

℟. **O Lord, it is good to give thanks to you.**

The just man shall flourish like the palm tree,
  like a cedar of Lebanon shall he grow.
They that are planted in the house of the Lord
  shall flourish in the courts of our God.

℟. **O Lord, it is good to give thanks to you.**

They shall bear fruit even in old age;
  vigorous and sturdy shall they be,
Declaring how just is the Lord,
  my Rock, in whom there is no wrong.

℟. **O Lord, it is good to give thanks to you.** ↓

READING II 2 Cor 5, 6-10   [Trust in the Lord]

While we wait for the Lord, we should please him in all
things. Then we will be found without reproach when we
appear before him in judgment.

A reading from the second letter of Paul
to the Corinthians

WE continue to be confident. We know that while
we dwell in the body we are away from the
Lord. We walk by faith, not by sight. I repeat, we are
full of confidence, and would much rather be away
from the body and at home with the Lord. This being
so, we make it our aim to please him whether we are
with him or away from him. The lives of all of us are
to be revealed before the tribunal of Christ so that
each one may receive his recompense, good or bad,
according to his life in the body.—The word of the
Lord. ℟. **Thanks be to God.** ↓

GOSPEL Mk 4, 26-34   [The Reign of God]
Alleluia

℟. **Alleluia.** The seed is the word of God, the sower is Christ;

everyone who finds him will live for ever. ℟. **Alleluia.** ↓

> From small beginnings the Church of Christ has arisen for the salvation of all peoples. Through Christ's preaching, God the Father has revealed all that he had to say to us.

℣. The Lord be with you. ℟. **And also with you.**

✛ A reading from the holy gospel according to Mark.

℟. **Glory to you, Lord.**

JESUS said to the crowd: "This is how it is with the reign of God. A man scatters seed on the ground. He goes to bed and gets up day after day. Through it all the seed sprouts and grows without his knowing how it happens. The soil produces of itself first the blade, then the ear, finally the ripe wheat in the ear. When the crop is ready he 'wields the sickle, for the time is ripe for harvest.' "

He went on to say: "What comparison shall we use for the reign of God? What image will help to present it? It is like mustard seed which, when planted in the soil, is the smallest of all the earth's seeds, yet once it is sown, springs up to become the largest of shrubs, with branches big enough for the birds of the sky to build nests in its shade." By means of many such parables he taught them the message in a way they could understand. To them he spoke only by way of parable, while he kept explaining things privately to his disciples.—The gospel of the Lord. ℟. **Praise to you, Lord Jesus Christ.**

→ No. 14, p. 18

PRAYER OVER THE GIFTS   [Health of Mind and Body]

Lord God,
in this bread and wine

you give us food for body and spirit.
May the eucharist renew our strength
and bring us health of mind and body.
We ask this in the name of Jesus the Lord.
℞. Amen.   → No. 21, p. 22 (Pref. P 29-36)

COMMUNION ANT. Ps 27, 4   [Dwelling with the Lord]
**One thing I seek: to dwell in the house of the Lord all
the days of my life.** ↓

OR Jn 17, 11   [One with God]
**Father, keep in your name those you have given me,
that they may be one as we are one, says the Lord.** ↓

PRAYER AFTER COMMUNION   [Church Unity]
Lord,
may this eucharist
accomplish in your Church
the unity and peace it signifies.
Grant this through Christ our Lord.
℞. Amen.   → No. 32, p. 70

Optional Solemn Blessings, p. 92, and Prayers Over the People, p. 99

"Who can this be that the wind and the sea obey him?"

JUNE 22

12th SUNDAY IN ORDINARY TIME

ENTRANCE ANT. Ps 28, 8-9   [Save Us, Lord]

God is the strength of his people. In him, we his chosen live in safety. Save us, Lord, who share in your life, and give us your blessing; be our shepherd for ever. → No. 2, p. 10

OPENING PRAYER   [Growing in God's Love]

Let us pray
   [that we may grow in the love of God]
Father,
guide and protector of your people,
grant us an unfailing respect for your name,
and keep us always in your love.
Grant this through our Lord Jesus Christ, your Son,
who lives and reigns with you and the Holy Spirit,
one God, for ever and ever. ℟. **Amen.** ↓

ALTERNATIVE OPENING PRAYER   [Safe in God's Love]

Let us pray
   [to God whose fatherly love keeps us safe]
God of the universe,
we worship you as Lord.

371

God, ever close to us,
we rejoice to call you Father.
From this world's uncertainty we look to your covenant.
Keep us one in your peace, secure in your love.
We ask this through Christ our Lord. ℟. **Amen.** ↓

READING I Jb 38, 1. 8-11   [Lord of Creation]

> **God recalls for Job that he is the Lord of creation. He has the power to do things which humans cannot explain.**

A reading from the book of Job

THE Lord addressed Job out of the storm and said:
Who shut within doors the sea,
   when it burst forth from the womb;
When I made the clouds its garment
   and thick darkness its swaddling bands?
When I set limits for it
   and fastened the bar of its door,
And said: Thus far shall you come but no farther,
   and here shall your proud waves be stilled!
The word of the Lord. ℟. **Thanks be to God.** ↓

RESPONSORIAL PSALM Ps 107   [God's Wondrous Deeds]

℟. **Give thanks to the Lord, his love is ev-er-last-ing.**

They who sailed the sea in ships,
   trading on the deep waters,
These saw the works of the Lord
   and his wonders in the abyss.

℟. **Give thanks to the Lord,
   his love is everlasting.**

His command raised up a storm wind
   which tossed its waves on high.
They mounted up to heaven; they sank to the depths;
   their hearts melted away in their plight.

℟. **Give thanks to the Lord,**
  his love is everlasting.

They cried to the Lord in their distress;
  from their straits he rescued them.
He hushed the storm to a gentle breeze,
  and the billows of the sea were stilled.

℟. **Give thanks to the Lord,**
  his love is everlasting.

They rejoiced that they were calmed,
  and he brought them to their desired haven.
Let them give thanks to the Lord for his kindness
  and his wondrous deeds to the children of men.

℟. **Give thanks to the Lord,**
  his love is everlasting. ↓

℟. Or: **Alleluia.** ↓

READING II 2 Cor 5, 14-17   [A New Creation]

  **In Christ everyone is a new creation. A new world is al-
  ready born.**

A reading from the second letter of Paul
to the Corinthians

THE love of Christ impels us who have reached the
  conviction that since one died for all, all died. He
died for all so that those who live might live no longer
for themselves, but for him who for their sakes died
and was raised up.

  Because of this we no longer look on anyone in
terms of mere human judgment. If at one time we so
regarded Christ, we no longer know him by this
standard. This means that if anyone is in Christ, he is a
new creation. The old order has passed away; now all
is new!—The word of the Lord. ℟. **Thanks be to God.** ↓

GOSPEL Mk 4, 35-41   [Christ Commands Creation]
Alleluia (Lk 7, 16)
℟. **Alleluia.** A great prophet has appeared among us;
God has visited his people. ℟. **Alleluia.** ↓

Jesus is truly "God-with-us," and we should turn to him in faithful prayer.

℣. The Lord be with you. ℟. **And also with you.**

✛ A reading from the holy gospel according to Mark.
℟. **Glory to you, Lord.**

ONE day as evening drew on Jesus said to his disciples, "Let us cross over to the farther shore." Leaving the crowd, they took him away in the boat in which he was sitting, while the other boats accompanied him. It happened that a bad squall blew up. The waves were breaking over the boat and it began to ship water badly. Jesus was in the stern through it all, sound asleep on a cushion. They finally woke him and said to him, "Teacher, doesn't it matter to you that we are going to drown?" He awoke and rebuked the wind and said to the sea: "Quiet! Be still!" The wind fell off and everything grew calm. Then he said to them, "Why are you so terrified? Why are you lacking in faith?" A great awe overcame them at this. They kept saying to one another, "Who can this be that the wind and the sea obey him?"—The gospel of the Lord. ℟.
Praise to you, Lord Jesus Christ.   → No. 14, p. 18

PRAYER OVER THE GIFTS   [Eager To Serve God]

Lord,
receive our offering,
and may this sacrifice of praise
purify us in mind and heart
and make us always eager to serve you.
We ask this in the name of Jesus the Lord.
℟. **Amen.**   → No. 21, p. 22 (Pref. P 29-36)

COMMUNION ANT Ps 145, 15   [Divine Food]

The eyes of all look to you, O Lord, and you give them food in due season. ↓

OR Jn 10, 11. 15   [The Good Shepherd]

I am the Good Shepherd; I give my life for my sheep, says the Lord. ↓

PRAYER AFTER COMMUNION   [Assure Our Redemption]

Lord,
you give us the body and blood of your Son
to renew your life within us.
In your mercy, assure our redemption
and bring us to the eternal life
we celebrate in this eucharist.
We ask this through Christ our Lord.
R/. **Amen.**   → No. 32, p. 70

Optional Solemn Blessings, p. 92, and Prayers Over the People, p. 99

*"You are 'Rock' and on this rock
I will build my church."*

JUNE 29

STS. PETER AND PAUL, APOSTLES
(13th SUNDAY IN ORDINARY TIME)

ENTRANCE ANT.   [Friends of God]

**These men, conquering all human frailty, shed their
blood and helped the Church to grow. By sharing the
cup of the Lord's suffering, they became the friends
of God.**   → No. 2, p. 10

OPENING PRAYER   [True to the Apostles' Faith]

Let us pray
   [that we will remain true to
   the faith of the apostles]
God our Father,
today you give us the joy
of celebrating the feast of the apostles Peter and Paul.
Through them your Church first received the faith.
Keep us true to their teaching.
Grant this . . . for ever and ever. ℟. **Amen.** ↓

ALTERNATIVE OPENING PRAYER   [United with Apostles]

Let us pray
   [one with Peter and Paul in our faith
   in Christ the Son of the living God]
Praise to you, the God and Father of our Lord Jesus
   Christ,
who in your great mercy
have given us new birth and hope
through the power of Christ's resurrection.
Through the prayers of the apostles Peter and Paul
may we who received this faith through their preaching
share their love in following the Lord
to the unfading inheritance
reserved for us in heaven.
We ask this in the name of Jesus the Lord. ℟. **Amen.** ↓

READING I Acts 12, 1-11   [A Miraculous Escape]

**The apostles are not stopped by accusations and imprison-
ment. They continue their witnessing to the good news of
Jesus Christ. The Lord works with them and through them,
and often saves them from death.**

A reading from the Acts of the Apostles

KING Herod started to harass some of the members
of the church. He beheaded James the brother of
John, and when he saw that this pleased certain of the
Jews, he took Peter into custody too. During the feast

of Unleavened Bread he had him arrested and thrown into prison, with four squads of soldiers to guard him. Herod intended to bring him before the people after the Passover. Peter was thus detained in prison, while the church prayed fervently to God in his behalf. During the night before Herod was to bring him to trial, Peter was sleeping between two soldiers, fastened with double chains, while guards kept watch at the door. Suddenly an angel of the Lord stood nearby and light shone in the cell. He tapped Peter on the side and woke him. "Hurry, get up!" he said. With that, the chains dropped from Peter's wrists. The angel said, "Put on your belt and your sandals!" This he did. Then the angel told him, "Now put on your cloak and follow me."

Peter followed him out, but with no clear realization that this was taking place through the angel's help. The whole thing seemed to him a mirage. They passed the first guard, then the second, and finally came to the iron gate leading out to the city, which opened for them of itself. They emerged and made their way down a narrow alley, when suddenly the angel left him. Peter had recovered his senses by this time, and said, "Now I know for certain that the Lord has sent his angel to rescue me from Herod's clutches and from all that the Jews hoped for."—The word of the Lord. ℟. **Thanks be to God.** ↓

RESPONSORIAL PSALM Ps 34   [The Lord's Protection]

℟. **The angel of the Lord will rescue those who fear him.**

I will bless the Lord at all times;
   his praise shall be ever in my mouth.
Let my soul glory in the Lord;
   the lowly will hear me and be glad.—℟.

Glorify the Lord with me,
  let us together extol his name.
I sought the Lord, and he answered me
  and delivered me from all my fears.

℟. **The angel of the Lord will rescue those who fear
him.**

Look to him that you may be radiant with joy,
  and your faces may not blush with shame.
When the afflicted man called out, the Lord heard,
  and from all his distress he saved him.—℟.

The angel of the Lord encamps
  around those who fear him, and delivers them.
Taste and see how good the Lord is;
  happy the man who takes refuge in him.—℟. ↓

READING II 2 Tm 4, 6-8. 17-18   [A Merited Crown]

**The apostles had to rely totally on God to guide them and
grant faith to those who heard their preaching. Their
human weakness made God's power more obvious.**

A reading from the second letter of Paul to Timothy

I AM already being poured out like a libation. The
time of my dissolution is near. I have fought the
good fight, I have finished the race, I have kept the
faith. From now on a merited crown awaits me; on
that Day the Lord, just judge that he is, will award it
to me—and not only to me but to all who have looked
for his appearing with eager longing. But the Lord
stood by my side and gave me strength, so that
through me the preaching task might be completed
and all the nations might hear the gospel. That is how
I was saved from the lion's jaws. The Lord will continue to rescue me from all attempts to do me harm
and will bring me safe to his heavenly kingdom. To
him be glory forever and ever. Amen.—The word of
the Lord. ℟. **Thanks be to God.** ↓

GOSPEL Mt 16, 13-19   [Peter the Rock]
Alleluia (Mt 16, 18)

℟. **Alleluia.** You are Peter, the rock on which I will build my Church;
the gates of hell will not hold out against it. ℟. **Alleluia.** ↓

> Jesus changes the name of Simon to Peter, which means "rock." He would protect the word of God and would guide the whole Church.

℣. The Lord be with you. ℟. **And also with you.**
✚ A reading from the holy gospel according to Matthew. ℟. **Glory to you, Lord.**

WHEN Jesus came to the neighborhood of Caesarea Philippi, he asked his disciples this question: "Who do people say that the Son of Man is?" They replied, "Some say John the Baptizer, others Elijah, still others Jeremiah or one of the prophets." "And you," he said to them, "who do you say that I am?" "You are the Messiah," Simon Peter answered, "the Son of the living God!" Jesus replied, "Blest are you, Simon son of John! No mere man has revealed this to you, but my heavenly Father. I for my part declare to you, you are 'Rock,' and on this rock I will build my church, and the jaws of death shall not prevail against it. I will entrust to you the keys of the kingdom of heaven. Whatever you declare bound on earth shall be bound in heaven; whatever you declare loosed on earth shall be loosed in heaven."—The gospel of the Lord. ℟. **Praise to you, Lord Jesus Christ.**

→ No. 14, p. 18

PRAYER OVER THE GIFTS   [United with the Apostles]

Lord,
may your apostles join their prayers to our offering

and help us to celebrate this sacrifice in love and
   unity.
We ask this through Christ our Lord. ℟. **Amen.** ↓

PREFACE (P 63)   **[Two Great Apostles]**

℣. The Lord be with you. ℟. **And also with you.**
℣. Lift up your hearts. ℟. **We lift them up to the Lord.**
℣. Let us give thanks to the Lord our God. ℟. **It is
right to give him thanks and praise.**

Father, all-powerful and ever-living God,
we do well always and everywhere to give you
   thanks.
You fill our hearts with joy
as we honor your great apostles:
Peter, our leader in the faith,
and Paul, its fearless preacher.
Peter raised up the Church
from the faithful flock of Israel.
Paul brought your call to the nations,
and became the teacher of the world.
Each in his chosen way gathered into unity
the one family of Christ.
Both shared a martyr's death
and are praised throughout the world.
Now, with the apostles and all the angels and saints,
we praise you for ever: → No. 23, p. 23

COMMUNION ANT. Mt 16, 16. 18   **[Head of the Church]**
**Peter said: You are the Christ, the Son of the living
God. Jesus answered: You are Peter, the rock on
which I will build my Church.** ↓

PRAYER AFTER COMMUNION   **[Renew the Church]**
Lord,
renew the life of your Church
with the power of this sacrament.
May the breaking of bread

and the teaching of the apostles
keep us united in your love.
We ask this in the name of Jesus the Lord.
℞. **Amen.**

→ No. 32, p. 70

Optional Solemn Blessings, p. 92, and Prayers Over the People, p. 99

"No prophet is without honor except in his native place."

JULY 6

14th SUNDAY IN ORDINARY TIME

ENTRANCE ANT. Ps 48, 10-11   [God's Kindness and Justice]

Within your temple, we ponder your loving kindness,
O God. As your name, so also your praise reaches to
the ends of the earth; your right hand is filled with
justice.   → No. 2, p. 10

OPENING PRAYER   [Forgiveness]

Let us pray

   [for forgiveness through the grace of Jesus Christ]
Father,
through the obedience of Jesus,
your servant and your Son,
you raised a fallen world.

Free us from sin
and bring us the joy that lasts for ever.
We ask this through our Lord Jesus Christ, your Son,
who lives and reigns with you and the Holy Spirit,
one God, for ever and ever. ℟. **Amen.** ↓

ALTERNATIVE OPENING PRAYER

[Serving God and Others]

Let us pray
   [for greater willingness
   to serve God and our fellow man]
Father,
in the rising of your Son
death gives birth to new life.
The sufferings he endured restored hope to a fallen
   world.
Let sin never ensnare us
with empty promises of passing joy.
Make us one with you always,
so that our joy may be holy,
and our love may give life.
We ask this through Christ our Lord. ℟. **Amen.** ↓

READING I Ez 2, 2-5   [God's Prophet]

> Ezekiel is selected by God to be a prophet and messenger
> to the Israelites. When resisted, Ezekiel is to say: "Thus
> says the Lord God!" In this way they shall see that he is a
> prophet.

A reading from the book of the prophet Ezekiel

SPIRIT entered into me and set me on my feet, and I
heard the one who was speaking say to me: Son of
man, I am sending you to the Israelites, rebels who
have rebelled against me; they and their fathers have
revolted against me to this very day. Hard of face and
obstinate of heart are they to whom I am sending you.
But you shall say to them: Thus says the Lord God!
And whether they heed or resist—for they are a rebel-

lious house—they shall know that a prophet has been among them.—The word of the Lord. ℟. **Thanks be to God.** ↓

RESPONSORIAL PSALM Ps 123   [Eyes on God]

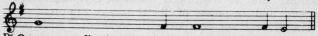

℟. **Our eyes are fixed on the Lord, pleading for his mer-cy.**

To you I lift up my eyes
  who are enthroned in heaven—
As the eyes of servants
  are on the hands of their masters.

℟. **Our eyes are fixed on the Lord,
  pleading for his mercy.**

As the eyes of a maid
  are on the hands of her mistress,
So are our eyes on the Lord, our God,
  till he have pity on us.

℟. **Our eyes are fixed on the Lord,
  pleading for his mercy.**

Have pity on us, O Lord, have pity on us,
  for we are more than sated with contempt;
Our souls are more than sated
  with the mockery of the arrogant,
  with the contempt of the proud.

℟. **Our eyes are fixed on the Lord,
  pleading for his mercy.** ↓

READING II 2 Cor 12, 7-10   [Suffering for Christ]

Paul is given a "thorn in the flesh." He asks God for relief and God replies that his grace is sufficient.

A reading from the second letter of Paul
to the Corinthians

AS to the extraordinary revelations, in order that I
might not become conceited I was given a thorn in

the flesh, an angel of Satan to beat me and keep me from getting proud. Three times I begged the Lord that this might leave me. He said to me, "My grace is enough for you, for in weakness power reaches perfection." And so I willingly boast of my weaknesses instead, that the power of Christ may rest upon me.

Therefore I am content with weakness, with mistreatment, with distress, with persecutions and difficulties for the sake of Christ; for when I am powerless, it is then that I am strong.—The word of the Lord. ℟. **Thanks be to God.** ↓

GOSPEL Mk 6, 1-6   [Spreading the Good News]
Alleluia (Is 61, 1: cited in Lk 4, 18)
℟. **Alleluia.** The spirit of the Lord is upon me; he sent me to bring Good News to the poor. ℟. **Alleluia.** ↓

> Jesus began to teach in his home synagogue. The people, knowing Mary and Joseph, cannot understand the wisdom Jesus shows and Jesus tells them: "No prophet is without honor except in his native place."

℣. The Lord be with you. ℟. **And also with you.**
✠ A reading from the holy gospel according to Mark.
℟. **Glory to you, Lord.**

JESUS went to his own part of the country followed by his disciples. When the sabbath came he began to teach in the synagogue in a way that kept his large audience amazed. They said: "Where did he get all this? What kind of wisdom is he endowed with? How is it such miraculous deeds are accomplished by his hands? Isn't this the carpenter, the son of Mary, a brother of James and Joses, and Judas and Simon? Aren't his sisters our neighbors here?" They found him too much for them. Jesus' response to all this was: "No prophet is without honor except in his native place, among his own kindred, and in his own house."

He could work no miracle there, apart from curing a
few who were sick by laying hands on them, so much
did their lack of faith distress him. He made the
rounds of the neighboring villages instead, and spent
his time teaching.—The gospel of the Lord. ℟. **Praise
to you, Lord Jesus Christ.**   → No. 14, p. 18

PRAYER OVER THE GIFTS   [God's Glory]

Lord,
let this offering to the glory of your name
purify us and bring us closer to eternal life.
We ask this in the name of Jesus the Lord.
℟. **Amen.**   → No. 21, p. 22 (Pref. P 29-36)

COMMUNION ANT. Ps 34, 9   [The Lord's Goodness]

**Taste and see the goodness of the Lord; blessed is he
who hopes in God.** ↓

OR Mt 11, 28   [Refuge in God]

**Come to me, all you that labor and are burdened, and
I will give you rest, says the Lord.** ↓

PRAYER AFTER COMMUNION   [Life and Salvation]

Lord,
may we never fail to praise you
for the fullness of life and salvation
you give us in this eucharist.
We ask this through Christ our Lord.
℟. **Amen.**   → No. 32, p. 70

Optional Solemn Blessings, p. 92, and Prayers Over the People, p. 99

"Jesus summoned the Twelve and began to send them out two by two."

JULY 13

15th SUNDAY IN ORDINARY TIME

ENTRANCE ANT. Ps 17, 15   **[God's Face]**

**In my justice I shall see your face, O Lord; when your
glory appears, my joy will be full.**   → No. 2, p. 10

OPENING PRAYER   **[Rule of Life]**

Let us pray
   [that the gospel may be our rule of life]
God our Father,
your light of truth
guides us to the way of Christ.
May all who follow him
reject what is contrary to the gospel.
We ask this through our Lord Jesus Christ, your Son,
who lives and reigns with you and the Holy Spirit,
one God, for ever and ever. ℟. **Amen.** ↓

ALTERNATIVE OPENING PRAYER   **[Fidelity]**

Let us pray
   [to be faithful to the light we have received,
   to the name we bear]

Father,
let the light of your truth
guide us to your kingdom
through a world filled with lights contrary to your own.
Christian is the name and the gospel we glory in.
May your love make us what you have called us to be.
We ask this through Christ our Lord. ℟. **Amen.** ↓

READING I Am 7, 12-15   [God Makes a Prophet]

Amos writes how he was chosen by God to go out and prophesy to the people of Israel.

A reading from the book of the prophet Amos

AMAZIAH (priest of Bethel) said to Amos, "Off with you, visionary, flee to the land of Judah! There earn your bread by prophesying, but never again prophesy in Bethel; for it is the king's sanctuary and a royal temple." Amos answered Amaziah, "I was no prophet, nor have I belonged to a company of prophets; I was a shepherd and a dresser of sycamores. The Lord took me from following the flock, and said to me, Go, prophesy to my people Israel."—The word of the Lord. ℟. **Thanks be to God.** ↓

RESPONSORIAL PSALM Ps 85   [The Lord's Salvation]

℟. **Lord, let us see your kindness, and grant us your sal-va-tion.**

I will hear what God proclaims;
  the Lord—for he proclaims peace to his people.
Near indeed is his salvation to those who fear him,
  glory dwelling in our land.

℟. **Lord, let us see your kindness,**
  and grant us your salvation.

Kindness and truth shall meet;
  justice and peace shall kiss.

Truth shall spring out of the earth,
   and justice shall look down from heaven.

℟. **Lord, let us see your kindness,**
   and grant us your salvation.

The Lord himself will give his benefits;
   our land shall yield its increase.

Justice shall walk before him,
   and salvation, along the way of his steps.

℟. **Lord, let us see your kindness,**
   and grant us your salvation. ↓

READING II Eph 1, 3-14 or 1, 3-10   [Christ's Headship]

**God chose his followers to be holy, blameless, and filled
with love—to be his adopted children in Jesus. In Jesus and
through the seal of the Holy Spirit, full redemption shall
come to humankind.**

*[If the "Short Form" is used, the indented text in brackets is
omitted.]*

A reading from the letter of Paul to the Ephesians

PRAISED be the God and Father of our Lord Jesus
Christ, who has bestowed on us in Christ every
spiritual blessing in the heavens! God chose us in him
before the world began, to be holy and blameless in
his sight, to be full of love; he likewise predestined us
through Christ Jesus to be his adopted sons—such
was his will and pleasure—that all might praise the divine favor he has bestowed on us in his beloved.

It is in Christ and through his blood that we have
been redeemed and our sins forgiven, so immeasurably
generous is God's favor to us. God has given us the wisdom to understand fully the mystery, the plan he was
pleased to decree in Christ, to be carried out in the fullness of time: namely, to bring all things in the heavens
and on earth into one under Christ's headship.

   [In him we were chosen; for in the decree of
   God, who administers everything according to his

will and counsel, we were predestined to praise his glory by being the first to hope in Christ. In him you too were chosen; when you heard the glad tidings of salvation, the word of truth, and believed in it, you were sealed with the Holy Spirit who had been promised. He is the pledge of our inheritance, the first payment against the full redemption of a people God has made his own to praise his glory.]

The word of the Lord. ℟. **Thanks be to God.** ↓

GOSPEL Mk 6, 7-13 [Spreading the Gospel]
Alleluia (See Eph 1, 17-18)

℟. **Alleluia.** May the Father of our Lord Jesus Christ enlighten the eyes of our hearts
that we may see how great is the hope
to which we are called. ℟. **Alleluia.** ↓

> Jesus sent out the Twelve, instructing them to take only a walking stick and to preach the gospel. If they were refused a listening ear, they should leave the locality. They worked many miracles.

℣. The Lord be with you. ℟. **And also with you.**

✝ A reading from the holy gospel according to Mark.

℟. **Glory to you, Lord.**

JESUS summoned the Twelve and began to send them out two by two, giving them authority over unclean spirits. He instructed them to take nothing on the journey but a walking stick—no food, no traveling bag, not a coin in the purses in their belts. They were, however, to wear sandals. "Do not bring a second tunic," he said, and added: "Whatever house you find yourself in, stay there until you leave the locality. If any place will not receive you or hear you, shake its dust from your feet in testimony against them as you leave." With that they went off, preaching the need of repentance. They expelled many demons, anointed the sick with oil, and worked many cures.—The gospel of the Lord. ℟. **Praise to you, Lord Jesus Christ.**

→ No. 14, p. 18

PRAYER OVER THE GIFTS   [Growth in Faith]

Lord,
accept the gifts of your Church.
May this eucharist
help us grow in holiness and faith.
We ask this in the name of Jesus the Lord.
℟. **Amen.**   → No. 21, p. 22 (Pref. P 29-36)

COMMUNION ANT. Ps 84, 4-5   [The Lord's House]

The sparrow even finds a home, the swallow finds a nest wherein to place her young, near to your altars, Lord of hosts, my King, my God! How happy they who dwell in your house! For ever they are praising you. ↓

OR Jn 6, 57   [Life in Jesus]

Whoever eats my flesh and drinks my blood will live in me and I in him, says the Lord. ↓

PRAYER AFTER COMMUNION   [God's Love]

Lord,
by our sharing in the mystery of this eucharist,
let your saving love grow within us.
Grant this through Christ our Lord.
℟. **Amen.**   → No. 32, p. 70

Optional Solemn Blessings, p. 92, and Prayers Over the People, p. 99

"Jesus and the disciples went off in the boat by themselves."

JULY 20

16th SUNDAY IN ORDINARY TIME

ENTRANCE ANT. Ps 54, 6. 8   [God Our Help]
God himself is my help. The Lord upholds my life. I will offer you a willing sacrifice; I will praise your name, O Lord, for its goodness.   → No. 2, p. 10

OPENING PRAYER   [Faithful Service]
Let us pray
  [to be kept faithful in the service of God]
Lord,
be merciful to your people.
Fill us with your gifts
and make us always eager to serve you
in faith, hope, and love.
Grant this through our Lord Jesus Christ, your Son,
who lives and reigns with you and the Holy Spirit,
one God, for ever and ever. ℟. **Amen.** ↓

ALTERNATIVE OPENING PRAYER   [God's Blessing]
Let us pray
  [that God will continue to bless us
  with his compassion and love]

Father,
let the gift of your life
continue to grow in us,
drawing us from death to faith, hope, and love.
Keep us alive in Christ Jesus.
Keep us watchful in prayer
and true to his teaching
till your glory is revealed in us.
Grant this through Christ our Lord. ℟. **Amen.** ↓

READING I Jer 23, 1-6   [A True Shepherd]

> Woe to those who sow evil. Their evil deeds will be punished. Good shepherds will be appointed. There will come a shoot to David in whose days Judah will be saved.

A reading from the book of the prophet Jeremiah

WOE to the shepherds who mislead and scatter the flock of my pasture, says the Lord. Therefore, thus says the Lord, the God of Israel, against the shepherds who shepherd my people: You have scattered my sheep and driven them away. You have not cared for them, but I will take care to punish your evil deeds. I myself will gather the remnant of my flock from all the lands to which I have driven them and bring them back to their meadow; there they shall increase and multiply. I will appoint shepherds for them who will shepherd them so that they need no longer fear and tremble; and none shall be missing, says the Lord.

Behold, the days are coming, says the Lord,
    when I will raise up a righteous shoot to David;
As king he shall reign and govern wisely,
    he shall do what is just and right in the land.
In his days Judah shall be saved,
    Israel shall dwell in security.
This is the name they give him:
    "The Lord our justice."
The word of the Lord. ℟. **Thanks be to God.** ↓

RESPONSORIAL PSALM Ps 23   [The Lord as Shepherd]

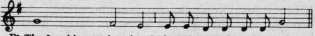

℟. The Lord is my shep-herd; there is noth-ing I shall want.

The Lord is my shepherd; I shall not want.
  In verdant pastures he gives me repose;
Beside restful waters he leads me;
  he refreshes my soul.

℟. **The Lord is my shepherd;**
  there is nothing I shall want.

He guides me in right paths
  for his name's sake.
Even though I walk in the dark valley
  I fear no evil; for you are at my side
With your rod and your staff
  that give me courage.

℟. **The Lord is my shepherd;**
  there is nothing I shall want.

You spread the table before me
  in the sight of my foes;
You anoint my head with oil;
  my cup overflows.

℟. **The Lord is my shepherd;**
  there is nothing I shall want.

Only goodness and kindness follow me
  all the days of my life;
And I shall dwell in the house of the Lord
  for years to come.

℟. **The Lord is my shepherd;**
  there is nothing I shall want. ↓

READING II Eph 2, 13-18   [Access to the Father]

**Paul tells the Ephesians that Christ has brought them to-
gether. Jesus has brought peace and reconciliation through
his cross.**

A reading from the letter of Paul to the Ephesians

IN Christ Jesus you who once were far off have been brought near through the blood of Christ. It is he who is our peace, and who made the two of us one by breaking down the barrier of hostility that kept us apart. In his own flesh he abolished the law with its commands and precepts, to create in himself one new man from us who had been two, and to make peace, reconciling both of us to God in one body through his cross which put that enmity to death. He came and "announced the good news of peace to you who were far off, and to those who were near"; through him we both have access in one Spirit to the Father.—The word of the Lord. ℟. **Thanks be to God.** ↓

GOSPEL Mk 6, 30-34   [Jesus the Shepherd]
Alleluia (Jn 10, 27)
℟. **Alleluia.** My sheep listen to my voice, says the Lord;
I know them, and they follow me. ℟. **Alleluia.** ↓

> Jesus called the apostles aside to rest. Still the people came, so Jesus and the apostles went to a deserted place. Yet the people came.

℣. The Lord be with you. ℟. **And also with you.**
✛ A reading from the holy gospel according to Mark.
℟. **Glory to you, Lord.**

THE apostles returned to Jesus and reported to him all that they had done and what they had taught. He said to them, "Come by yourselves to an out-of-the-way place and rest a little." People were coming and going in great numbers, making it impossible for them to so much as eat. So Jesus and the apostles went off in the boat by themselves to a deserted place. People saw them leaving, and many got to know about it. People from all the towns hastened on foot to the place, arriving ahead of them.

Upon disembarking Jesus saw a vast crowd. He pitied them, for they were like sheep without a shepherd; and he began to teach them at great length.— The gospel of the Lord. ℟. **Praise to you, Lord Jesus Christ.**   → No. 14, p. 18

PRAYER OVER THE GIFTS   [Saving Gifts]

Lord,
bring us closer to salvation
through these gifts which we bring in your honor.
Accept the perfect sacrifice you have given us,
bless it as you blessed the gifts of Abel.
We ask this through Christ our Lord.
℟. **Amen.**   → No. 21, p. 22 (Pref. P 29-36)

COMMUNION ANT. Ps 111, 4-5   [Jesus Provides]

The Lord keeps in our minds the wonderful things he has done. He is compassion and love; he always provides for his faithful. ↓

OR Rv 3, 20   [Jesus Knocks]

I stand at the door and knock, says the Lord. If anyone hears my voice and opens the door, I will come in and sit down to supper with him, and he with me. ↓

PRAYER AFTER COMMUNION   [New Life]

Merciful Father,
may these mysteries
give us new purpose
and bring us to a new life in you.
We ask this in the name of Jesus the Lord.
℟. **Amen.**   → No. 32, p. 70

Optional Solemn Blessings, p. 92, and Prayers Over the People, p. 99

JULY 27

17th SUNDAY IN ORDINARY TIME

ENTRANCE ANT. Ps 68, 6-7. 36   [God Our Strength]

God is in his holy dwelling; he will give a home to the lonely, he gives power and strength to his people.

→ No. 2, p. 10

OPENING PRAYER   [Wise Use of Gifts]

Let us pray
  [that we will make good use of the gifts
    that God has given us]
God our Father and protector,
without you nothing is holy,
nothing has value.
Guide us to everlasting life
by helping us to use wisely
the blessings you have given to the world.
We ask this through our Lord Jesus Christ, your Son,
who lives and reigns with you and the Holy Spirit,
one God, for ever and ever. ℟. **Amen.** ↓

ALTERNATIVE OPENING PRAYER   [God in the World]

Let us pray

[for the faith to recognize God's presence
in our world]

God our Father,
open our eyes to see your hand at work
in the splendor of creation,
in the beauty of human life.
Touched by your hand our world is holy.
Help us to cherish the gifts that surround us,
to share your blessings with our brothers and sisters,
and to experience the joy of life in your presence.
We ask this through Christ our Lord. ℟. **Amen.** ↓

READING I 2 Kgs 4, 42-44   [Miracle of Loaves]

At the command from Elisha, the man of God, the barley
bread was placed before the people, indicating that this
comes from the Lord. Even though the number to be fed
from the twenty loaves was a hundred, some was left over.

A reading from the second book of Kings

A MAN came from Baal-shalishah bringing to Elisha, the man of God, twenty barley loaves made
from the first-fruits, and fresh grain in the ear. "Give it
to the people to eat," Elisha said. But his servant ob-
jected, "How can I set this before a hundred men?"
"Give it to the people to eat," Elisha insisted. "For thus
says the Lord, 'They shall eat and there shall be some
left over.' " And when they had eaten, there was some
left over, as the Lord had said.—The word of the Lord.
℟. **Thanks be to God.** ↓

RESPONSORIAL PSALM Ps 145   [The Bounty of the Lord]

℟. The hand of the Lord feeds us;   he answers all our needs.

Let all your works give you thanks, O Lord,
  and let your faithful ones bless you.
Let them discourse of the glory of your kingdom
  and speak of your might.—℟.

The eyes of all look hopefully to you,
  and you give them their food in due season;
You open your hand
  and satisfy the desire of every living thing.—℟.

The Lord is just in all his ways
  and holy in all his works.
The Lord is near to all who call upon him,
  to all who call upon him in truth.

℟. **The hand of the Lord feeds us;**
  he answers all our needs. ↓

READING II Eph 4, 1-6   [Unity in the Spirit]

A life worthy of the Lord consists of humility, meekness, patience and bearing love for one another.

A reading from the letter of Paul to the Ephesians

I PLEAD with you as a prisoner for the Lord, to live a life worthy of the calling you have received, with perfect humility, meekness, and patience, bearing with one another lovingly. Make every effort to preserve the unity which has the Spirit as its origin and peace as its binding force. There is but one body and one Spirit, just as there is but one hope given all of you by your call. There is one Lord, one faith, one baptism; one God and Father of all, who is over all, and works through all, and is in all.—The word of the Lord. ℟. **Thanks be to God.** ↓

GOSPEL Jn 6, 1-15   [Multiplication of Loaves and Fish]
Alleluia (Lk 7, 16)
℟. **Alleluia.** A great prophet has appeared among us; God has visited his people. ℟. **Alleluia.** ↓

Jesus told the five thousand to sit down. He took the five barley loaves and a couple of dried fish, gave thanks and told the disciples to pass out the food.

℣. The Lord be with you. ℟. **And also with you.**

✚ A reading from the holy gospel according to John.

℟. **Glory to you, Lord.**

JESUS crossed the Sea of Galilee [to the shore] of Tiberias; a vast crowd kept following him because they saw the signs he was performing for the sick. Jesus then went up the mountain and sat down there with his disciples. The Jewish feast of Passover was near; when Jesus looked up and caught sight of a vast crowd coming toward him, he said to Philip, "Where shall we buy bread for these people to eat?" (He knew well what he intended to do but he asked this to test Philip's response.) Philip replied, "Not even with two hundred days' wages could we buy loaves enough to give each of them a mouthful!"

One of Jesus' disciples, Andrew, Simon Peter's brother, remarked to him, "There is a lad here who has five barley loaves and a couple of dried fish, but what good is that for so many?" Jesus said, "Get the people to recline." Even though the men numbered about five thousand, there was plenty of grass for them to find a place on the ground. Jesus then took the loaves of bread, gave thanks, and passed them around to those reclining there; he did the same with the dried fish, as much as they wanted. When they had had enough, he told his disciples, "Gather up the crusts that are left over so that nothing will go to waste." At this, they gathered twelve baskets full of pieces left over by those who had been fed with the five barley loaves.

When the people saw the sign he had performed they began to say, "This is undoubtedly the Prophet who is to come into the world." At that, Jesus realized that they would come and carry him off to make him king, so he fled back to the mountain alone.—The gospel of the Lord. ℟. **Praise to you, Lord Jesus Christ.**   → No. 14, p. 18

PRAYER OVER THE GIFTS   [Sanctifying Mysteries]

Lord,
receive these offerings
chosen from your many gifts.
May these mysteries make us holy
and lead us to eternal joy.
Grant this through Christ our Lord.
℟. **Amen.**   → No. 21, p. 22 (Pref. P 29-36)

COMMUNION ANT. Ps 103, 2   [Bless the Lord]

O bless the Lord, my soul, and remember all his kindness. ↓

OR Mt 5, 7-8   [Happy the Pure of Heart]

Happy are those who show mercy; mercy shall be theirs. Happy are the pure of heart, for they shall see God. ↓

PRAYER AFTER COMMUNION   [Memorial of Christ]

Lord,
we receive the sacrament
which celebrates the memory
of the death and resurrection of Christ your Son.
May this gift bring us closer to our eternal salvation.
We ask this through Christ our Lord.
℟. **Amen.**   → No. 32, p. 70

Optional Solemn Blessings, p. 92, and Prayers Over the People, p. 99

"God's bread comes down from heaven and gives life to the world."

AUGUST 3

18th SUNDAY IN ORDINARY TIME

ENTRANCE ANT. Ps 70, 2. 6   [God's Help]

God, come to my help. Lord, quickly give me assistance. You are the one who helps me and sets me free: Lord, do not be long in coming. → No. 2, p. 10

OPENING PRAYER   [God's Forgiveness]

Let us pray
   [for the gift of God's forgiveness and love]
Father of everlasting goodness,
our origin and guide,
be close to us
and hear the prayers of all who praise you.
Forgive our sins and restore us to life.
Keep us safe in your love.
Grant this through our Lord Jesus Christ, your Son,
who lives and reigns with you and the Holy Spirit,
one God, for ever and ever. ℟. **Amen.** ↓

ALTERNATIVE OPENING PRAYER   [God's Kindness]

Let us pray
   [to the Father whose kindness never fails]

God our Father,
gifts without measure flow from your goodness
to bring us your peace.
Our life is your gift.
Guide our life's journey,
for only your love makes us whole.
Keep us strong in your love.
We ask this through Christ our Lord. ℟. **Amen.** ↓

READING I Ex 16, 2-4. 12-15   [Manna from Heaven]

The Isrealites begin to grumble, and the Lord promises to rain down bread from heaven and give them quail to eat at twilight. In this they will know that the Lord is God.

A reading from the book of Exodus

THE whole Israelite community grumbled against Moses and Aaron. The Israelites said to them, "Would that we had died at the Lord's hand in the land of Egypt, as we sat by our fleshpots and ate our fill of bread! But you had to lead us into this desert to make the whole community die of famine!"

Then the Lord said to Moses, "I will now rain down bread from heaven for you. Each day the people are to go out and gather their daily portion; thus will I test them, to see whether they follow my instructions or not.

"I have heard the grumbling of the Israelites. Tell them: In the evening twilight you shall eat flesh, and in the morning you shall have your fill of bread, so that you may know that I, the Lord, am your God."

In the evening quail came up and covered the camp. In the morning a dew lay all about the camp, and when the dew evaporated, there on the surface of the desert were fine flakes like hoarfrost on the ground. On seeing it, the Israelites asked one another, "What is this?" for they did not know what it was. But Moses told them, "This is the bread which the Lord has given you to eat."—The word of the Lord. ℟. **Thanks be to God.** ↓

RESPONSORIAL PSALM Ps 78   [Heavenly Bread]

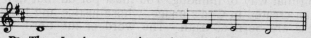

℞. The Lord gave them bread from heav-en.

What we have heard and know,
   and what our fathers have declared to us,
We will declare to the generation to come
   the glorious deeds of the Lord and his strength
   and the wonders that he wrought.

℞. **The Lord gave them bread from heaven.**

He commanded the skies above
   and the doors of heaven he opened;
He rained manna upon them for food
   and gave them heavenly bread.

℞. **The Lord gave them bread from heaven.**

The bread of the mighty was eaten by men;
   even a surfeit of provisions he sent them.
And he brought them to his holy land,
   to the mountain his right hand had won.

℞. **The Lord gave them bread from heaven.** ↓

READING II Eph 4, 17. 20-24   [A New Self]

Paul tells the Ephesians that they must abandon their old
pagan ways and acquire a fresh, spiritual way of living—to
become new people created in God's image.

A reading from the letter of Paul
to the Ephesians

I DECLARE and solemnly attest in the Lord that you
must no longer live as the pagans do—their minds
empty. That is not what you learned when you
learned Christ! I am supposing, of course, that he has
been preached and taught to you in accord with the
truth that is in Jesus: namely, that you must lay aside
your former way of life and the old self which deterio-

rates through illusion and desire, and acquire a fresh, spiritual way of thinking. You must put on that new man created in God's image, whose justice and holiness are born of truth.—The word of the Lord. ℟. **Thanks be to God.** ↓

GOSPEL Jn 6, 24-35   [Christ, True Bread from Heaven]
Alleluia (Mt 4, 4)
℟. **Alleluia.** Man does not live on bread alone,
but on every word that comes from the mouth of God.
℟. **Alleluia.** ↓

After feeding the multitude, Jesus and his disciples went across the lake. The people found them, and Jesus cautioned them that they were looking only for signs and food but the work of God demands faith in the One he sent.

℣. The Lord be with you. ℟. **And also with you.**
✝ A reading from the holy gospel according to John.
℟. **Glory to you, Lord.**

WHEN the crowd saw that neither Jesus nor his disciples were at the place where Jesus had eaten the bread, they too embarked in the boats and went to Capernaum looking for Jesus.
    When they found him on the other side of the lake, they said to him, "Rabbi, when did you come here?" Jesus answered them:
        "I assure you,
        you are not looking for me because you have seen signs
        but because you have eaten your fill of the loaves.
        You should not be working for perishable food
        but for food that remains unto life eternal,
        food which the Son of Man will give you;
        it is on him that God the Father has set his seal."
At this they said to him, "What must we do to perform the works of God?" Jesus replied:
        "This is is the work of God:
        have faith in the One he sent."

"So that we can put faith in you," they asked him, "what sign are you going to perform for us to see? What is the 'work' you do? Our ancestors had manna to eat in the desert; according to Scripture, 'He gave them bread from the heavens to eat.' " Jesus said to them:

> "I solemnly assure you,
> it was not Moses who gave you bread from the heavens;
> it is my Father who gives you the real heavenly bread.
> God's bread comes down from heaven
> and gives life to the world."

"Sir, give us this bread always," they besought him.
> Jesus explained to them:
> > "I myself am the bread of life.
> > No one who comes to me shall ever be hungry,
> > no one who believes in me shall thirst again."

The gospel of the Lord. ℟. **Praise to you, Lord Jesus Christ.**

→ No. 14, p. 18

PRAYER OVER THE GIFTS   [Spiritual Sacrifice]

Merciful Lord,
make holy these gifts,
and let our spiritual sacrifice
make us an everlasting gift to you.
We ask this in the name of Jesus the Lord.
℟. **Amen.**

→ No. 21, p. 22 (Pref. P 29-36)

COMMUNION ANT. Wis 16, 20   [Bread from Heaven]

You gave us bread from heaven, Lord: a sweet-tasting bread that was very good to eat. ↓

OR Jn 6, 35   [Bread of Life]

The Lord says: I am the bread of life. A man who comes to me will not go away hungry, and no one who believes in me will thirst. ↓

PRAYER AFTER COMMUNION   [Strength of New Life]

Lord,
you give us the strength of new life
by the gift of the eucharist.
Protect us with your love
and prepare us for eternal redemption.
We ask this through Christ our Lord.
℟. **Amen.**   → No. 32, p. 70

Optional Solemn Blessings, p. 92, and Prayers Over the People, p. 99

"I am the bread of life."

AUGUST 10

19th SUNDAY IN ORDINARY TIME

ENTRANCE ANT. Ps 74, 20. 19. 22. 23   [Rise Up, O God]
**Lord, be true to your covenant, forget not the life of
your poor ones for ever. Rise up, O God, and defend
your cause; do not ignore the shouts of your enemies.**
→ No. 2, p. 10

OPENING PRAYER   [Growth in God's Love]

Let us pray
[in the Spirit
that we may grow in the love of God]

Almighty and ever-living God,
your Spirit made us your children,
confident to call you Father.
Increase your Spirit within us
and bring us to our promised inheritance.
Grant this through our Lord Jesus Christ, your Son,
who lives and reigns with you and the Holy Spirit,
one God, for ever and ever. ℟. **Amen.** ↓

ALTERNATIVE OPENING PRAYER   [Witnesses for Christ]

Let us pray
   [that through us
   others may find the way to life in Christ]
Father,
we come, reborn in the Spirit,
to celebrate our sonship in the Lord Jesus Christ.
Touch our hearts,
help them grow toward the life you have promised.
Touch our lives,
make them signs of your love for all men.
Grant this through Christ our Lord. ℟. **Amen.** ↓

READING I 1 Kgs 19, 4-8   [Supernatural Food]

Elijah, being discouraged, prayed for death. Twice an angel came to him and supplied him with food. Strengthened by food and the word of God, Elijah got up and continued his journey to the mountain of God, Horeb.

A reading from the first book of Kings

ELIJAH went a day's journey into the desert, until he came to a broom tree and sat beneath it. He prayed for death: "This is enough, O Lord! Take my life, for I am no better than my fathers." He lay down and fell asleep under the broom tree, but then an angel touched him and ordered him to get up and eat. He looked and there at his head was a hearth cake and a jug of water. After he ate and drank, he lay down again, but the angel of the Lord came back a second time, touched him, and ordered, "Get up and eat, else the journey will be too long for you!" He got up, ate and drank; then strengthened by that food, he walked forty days and forty nights to the mountain of God, Horeb.—The word of the Lord. ℞. **Thanks be to God.** ↓

RESPONSORIAL PSALM Ps 34　　　　　[Refuge in God]

℞.**Taste and see　the　goodness of the　Lord.**

I will bless the Lord at all times;
　　his praise shall be ever in my mouth.
Let my soul glory in the Lord;
　　the lowly will hear me and be glad.

℞. **Taste and see the goodness of the Lord.**

Glorify the Lord with me,
　　let us together extol his name.
I sought the Lord, and he answered me
　　and delivered me from all my fears.

℞. **Taste and see the goodness of the Lord.**

Look to him that you may be radiant with joy,
　　and your faces may not blush with shame.
When the afflicted man called out, the Lord heard,
　　and from all his distress he saved him.

℞. **Taste and see the goodness of the Lord.**

The angel of the Lord encamps
　　around those who fear him, and delivers them.
Taste and see how good the Lord is;
　　happy the man who takes refuge in him.

℞. **Taste and see the goodness of the Lord.** ↓

READING II Eph 4, 30—5, 2　　　[Imitating God's Goodness]

　　Paul directs the Ephesians to be kind, compassionate, and forgiving. They are to imitate God as his children and follow the way of love as Christ loved.

A reading from the letter of Paul to the Ephesians

DO nothing to sadden the Holy Spirit with whom you were sealed against the day of redemption. Get rid of all bitterness, all passion and anger, harsh words, slander, and malice of every kind. In place of these, be kind to one another, compassionate, and mutually forgiving, just as God has forgiven you in Christ.

Be imitators of God as his dear children. Follow the way of love, even as Christ loved you. He gave himself for us as an offering to God, a gift of pleasing fragrance.—The word of the Lord. R̸. **Thanks be to God.** ↓

GOSPEL Jn 6, 41-51   [Jesus, Living Bread]
Alleluia (Jn 6, 51-52)
R̸. **Alleluia.** I am the living bread from heaven, says the Lord;
if anyone eats this bread he will live for ever. R̸. **Alleluia.** ↓

The Jews question Jesus' origin, and Jesus tells them that no one can come to him unless drawn by the Father. Those who believe will have eternal life.

V̸. The Lord be with you. R̸. **And also with you.**
✝ A reading from the holy gospel according to John.
R̸. **Glory to you, Lord.**

THE Jews started to murmur in protest because Jesus claimed, "I am the bread that came down from heaven." They kept saying: "Is this not Jesus, the son of Joseph? Do we not know his father and mother? How can he claim to have come down from heaven?"

"Stop your murmuring," Jesus told them.
"No one can come to me
unless the Father who sent me draws him;
I will raise him up on the last day.
It is written in the prophets:
'They shall all be taught by God.'

Everyone who has heard the Father
and learned from him
comes to me.
Not that anyone has seen the Father—
only the one who is from God
has seen the Father.
Let me firmly assure you,
he who believes has eternal life.
I am the bread of life.
Your ancestors ate manna in the desert, but they
    died.
This is the bread that comes down from heaven,
for a man to eat and never die.
I myself am the living bread
come down from heaven.
If anyone eats this bread
he shall live forever;
the bread I will give
is my flesh, for the life of the world."

The gospel of the Lord. ℟. **Praise to you, Lord Jesus
Christ.**   → No. 14, p. 18

PRAYER OVER THE GIFTS   [Sacrament of Salvation]

God of power,
giver of the gifts we bring,
accept the offering of your Church
and make it the sacrament of our salvation.
We ask this through Christ our Lord.
℟. **Amen.**   → No. 21, p. 22 (Pref. P 29-36)

COMMUNION ANT. Ps 148, 12-14   [Praise the Lord]

**Praise the Lord, Jerusalem; he feeds you with the
finest wheat.** ↓

OR Jn 6, 52   [The Flesh of Jesus]

**The bread I shall give is my flesh for the life of the
world, says the Lord.** ↓

PRAYER AFTER COMMUNION   [Faithful to God's Truth]
Lord,
may the eucharist you give us
bring us to salvation
and keep us faithful to the light of your truth.
We ask this in the name of Jesus the Lord.
℟. **Amen.**   → No. 32, p. 70

Optional Solemn Blessings, p. 92, and Prayers Over the People, p. 99

"Alleluia. Mary is taken up to heaven."

AUGUST 15

ASSUMPTION

VIGIL MASS

ENTRANCE ANT.   [Mary in Glory]
**All honor to you, Mary! Today you were raised above
the choirs of angels to lasting glory with Christ.**

→ No. 2, p. 10

OPENING PRAYER   [Mary's Help]
Let us pray
    [that the Virgin Mary will help us
    with her prayers]

Almighty God,
you gave a humble virgin
the privilege of being the mother of your Son,
and crowned her with the glory of heaven.
May the prayers of the Virgin Mary
bring us to the salvation of Christ
and raise us up to eternal life.
We ask this through our Lord Jesus Christ, your Son,
who lives and reigns with you and the Holy Spirit,
one God, for ever and ever. ℟. **Amen.** ↓

ALTERNATIVE OPENING PRAYER   [Praying with Mary]

Let us pray
  [with Mary to the Father,
  in whose presence she now dwells]
Almighty Father of our Lord Jesus Christ,
you have revealed the beauty of your power
by exalting the lowly virgin of Nazareth
and making her the mother of our Savior.
May the prayers of this woman clothed with the sun
bring Jesus to the waiting world
and fill the void of incompletion
with the presence of her child,
who lives and reigns with you and the Holy Spirit,
one God, for ever and ever. ℟. **Amen.** ↓

READING I 1 Chr 15, 3-4. 15. 16; 16, 1-2 [Procession of Glory]

Under David's direction the Israelites brought the ark of the Lord to the tent prepared for it. They showed great respect for it. They offered holocausts and peace offerings. This becomes a figure of Mary who bore the Son of God.

A reading from the first book of Chronicles

D AVID assembled all Israel in Jerusalem to bring
the ark of the Lord to the place which he had prepared for it. David also called together the sons of Aaron and the Levites.

The Levites bore the ark of God on their shoulders with poles, as Moses had ordained according to the word of the Lord.

David commanded the chiefs of the Levites to appoint their brethren as chanters, to play on musical instruments, harps, lyres, and cymbals, to make a loud sound of rejoicing.

They brought in the ark of God and set it within the tent which David had pitched for it. Then they offered up holocausts and peace offerings to God. When David had finished offering up the holocausts and peace offerings, he blessed the people in the name of the Lord.—The word of the Lord. ℟. **Thanks be to God.** ↓

RESPONSORIAL PSALM Ps 132   [Mary, Ark of God]

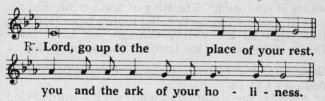

℟. **Lord, go up to the place of your rest, you and the ark of your ho - li - ness.**

Behold, we heard of it in Ephrathah;
   we found it in the fields of Jaar.
Let us enter into his dwelling,
   let us worship at his footstool.—℟.

May your priests be clothed with justice;
   let your faithful ones shout merrily for joy.
For the sake of David your servant,
   reject not the plea of your anointed.

℟. **Lord, go up to the place of your rest, you and the ark of your holiness.**

For the Lord has chosen Zion;
   he prefers her for his dwelling.

"Zion is my resting place forever;
  in her will I dwell, for I prefer her."

℞. **Lord, go up to the place of your rest,
  you and the ark of your holiness.** ↓

READING II 1 Cor 15, 54-57   [Victory Over Death]

Paul reminds the Corinthians that in life after death there is
victory. Through his love for us, God has given victory over
sin and death in Jesus, his Son.

A reading from the first letter of Paul
to the Corinthians

WHEN the corruptible frame takes on incorruptibility and the mortal immortality, then will the
saying of Scripture be fulfilled: "Death is swallowed up
in victory." "O death, where is your victory? O death,
where is your sting?" The sting of death is sin, and sin
gets its power from the law. But thanks be to God who
has given us the victory through our Lord Jesus
Christ.—The word of the Lord. ℞. **Thanks be to God.** ↓

GOSPEL Lk 11, 27-28   [Keeping God's Word]
Alleluia (Lk 11, 28)
℞. **Alleluia.** Blessed are they who hear the word of God
and keep it. ℞. **Alleluia.** ↓

Mary's relationship as the mother of Jesus is unique in all of
history. But Jesus reminds us that those who keep his word
are most pleasing to God. In this Mary has set an example.

℣. The Lord be with you. ℞. **And also with you.**
✝ A reading from the holy gospel according to Luke.
℞. **Glory to you, Lord.**

WHILE Jesus was speaking to the crowd, a woman
called out, "Blest is the womb that bore you and
the breasts that nursed you!" "Rather," he replied,
"blest are they who hear the word of God and keep
it."—The gospel of the Lord. ℞. **Praise to you, Lord
Jesus Christ.**   → No. 14, p. 18

PRAYER OVER THE GIFTS   [Sacrifice of Praise]

Lord,
receive this sacrifice of praise and peace
in honor of the assumption of the Mother of God.
May our offering bring us pardon
and make our lives a thanksgiving to you.
We ask this in the name of Jesus the Lord. ℟. **Amen.** ↓

PREFACE (P 59)   [Assumption—Sign of Hope]

℣. The Lord be with you. ℟. **And also with you.**
℣. Lift up your hearts. ℟. **We lift them up to the Lord.**
℣. Let us give thanks to the Lord our God. ℟. **It is right to give him thanks and praise.**

Father, all-powerful and ever-living God,
we do well always and everywhere to give you thanks
through Jesus Christ our Lord.
Today the virgin Mother of God was taken up into
    heaven
to be the beginning and the pattern of the Church in
    its perfection,
and a sign of hope and comfort for your people on
    their pilgrim way.
You would not allow decay to touch her body,
for she had given birth to your Son, the Lord of all life,
in the glory of the incarnation.
In our joy we sing to your glory
with all the choirs of angels: → No. 23, p. 23

COMMUNION ANT. See Lk 11, 27   [Mary Carried Christ]
**Blessed is the womb of the Virgin Mary; she carried
the Son of the eternal Father.** ↓

PRAYER AFTER COMMUNION   [Rejoice]

God of mercy,
we rejoice because Mary, the mother of our Lord,
was taken into the glory of heaven.
May the holy food we receive at this table

free us from evil.
We ask this through Christ our Lord.
R̶. **Amen.**   → No. 32, p. 70

Optional Solemn Blessings, p. 92, and Prayers Over the People, p. 99

MASS DURING THE DAY

ENTRANCE ANT. Rv 12, 1   [Mary's Glory]
A great sign appeared in heaven: a woman clothed with the sun, the moon beneath her feet, and a crown of twelve stars on her head.

OR   [Joy in Heaven]
Let us rejoice in the Lord and celebrate this feast in honor of the Virgin Mary, at whose assumption the angels rejoice, giving praise to the Son of God.
                                → No. 2, p. 10

OPENING PRAYER   [Sharing Mary's Glory]

Let us pray
   [that we will join Mary, the mother of the Lord,
   in the glory of heaven]
All-powerful and ever-living God,
you raised the sinless Virgin Mary,
mother of your Son,
body and soul to the glory of heaven.
May we see heaven as our final goal
and come to share her glory.
We ask this through our Lord Jesus Christ, your Son,
who lives and reigns with you and the Holy Spirit,
one God, for ever and ever. R̶. **Amen.** ↓

ALTERNATIVE OPENING PRAYER   [Following Mary]

Let us pray
   [that with the help of Mary's prayers
   we too may reach our heavenly home]

Father in heaven,
all creation rightly gives you praise,
for all life and all holiness come from you.
In the plan of your wisdom
she who bore the Christ in her womb
was raised body and soul in glory to be with him in
    heaven.
May we follow her example in reflecting your holiness
and join in her hymn of endless life and praise.
We ask this through Christ our Lord. ℟. **Amen.** ↓

READING I Rv 11, 19; 12, 1-6. 10   [Mary, the Ark]

The appearance of the Ark in this time of retribution indicates that God is now accessible—no longer hidden, but
present in the midst of his people. Filled with hatred, the
devil spares no pains to destroy Christ and his Church. The
dragon seeks to destroy the celestial woman and her Son.
Its hatred is futile.

A reading from the book of Revelation

GOD'S temple in heaven opened and in the temple
could be seen the ark of his covenant.

A great sign appeared in the sky, a woman clothed
with the sun, with the moon under her feet, and on her
head a crown of twelve stars. Because she was with
child, she wailed aloud in pain as she labored to give
birth. Then another sign appeared in the sky: it was a
huge dragon, flaming red, with seven heads and ten
horns; on his head were seven diadems. His tail swept
a third of the stars from the sky and hurled them
down to the earth. Then the dragon stood before the
woman about to give birth, ready to devour her child
when it should be born. She gave birth to a son—a
boy who is destined to shepherd all the nations with
an iron rod. Her child was snatched up to God and to
his throne. The woman herself fled into the desert,
where a special place had been prepared for her by
God.

Then I heard a loud voice in heaven say:
"Now have salvation and power come,
   the reign of our God and the authority of his
      Anointed One."
The word of the Lord. ℟. **Thanks be to God.** ↓

RESPONSORIAL PSALM Ps 45   [Mary the Queen]

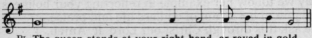

℟. The queen stands at your right hand, ar-rayed in gold.

The queen takes her place at your right hand in gold
   of Ophir.

℟. **The queen stands at your right hand, arrayed in
   gold.**

Hear, O daughter, and see; turn your ear,
   forget your people and your father's house.—℟.

So shall the king desire your beauty;
   for he is your lord.—℟.

They are borne in with gladness and joy;
   they enter the palace of the king.

℟. **The queen stands at your right hand, arrayed in
   gold.** ↓

READING II 1 Cor 15, 20-26   [Christ the King]

The offering of the first fruits was the symbol of the dedication of the entire harvest to God. So the Resurrection of
Christ involves the resurrection of all who are in him. Since
his glorious Resurrection, Christ reigns in glory; he is the
Lord.

A reading from the first letter of Paul
to the Corinthians

CHRIST has been raised from the dead, the first
fruits of those who have fallen asleep. Death came

through a man; hence the resurrection of the dead comes through a man also. Just as in Adam all die, so in Christ all will come to life again, but each one in proper order: Christ the first fruits and then, at his coming, all those who belong to him. After that will come the end, when, after having destroyed every sovereignty, authority, and power, he will hand over the kingdom to God the Father. Christ must reign until God has put all enemies under his feet.—The word of the Lord. ℟. **Thanks be to God.** ↓

GOSPEL Lk 1, 39-56   [Blessed among Women]
Alleluia

℟.. **Alleluia.** Mary is taken up to heaven,
    and the angels of God shout for joy. ℟.. **Alleluia.** ↓

> Mary visits her kinswoman, Elizabeth. Mary's song of thanksgiving, often called the "Magnificat," has been put together from many Old Testament phrases.

℣. The Lord be with you. ℟.. **And also with you.**
✟ A reading from the holy gospel according to Luke.
℟. **Glory to you, Lord.**

MARY set out, proceeding in haste into the hill country to a town of Judah, where she entered Zechariah's house and greeted Elizabeth. When Elizabeth heard Mary's greeting, the baby stirred in her womb. Elizabeth was filled with the Holy Spirit and cried out in a loud voice: "Blessed are you among women and blessed is the fruit of your womb. But who am I that the mother of my Lord should come to me? The moment your greeting sounded in my ears, the baby stirred in my womb for joy. Blessed is she who trusted that the Lord's words to her would be fulfilled."

Then Mary said:

"My being proclaims the greatness of the Lord,
    my spirit finds joy in God my savior,
For he has looked upon his servant in her lowliness;
    all ages to come shall call me blessed.
God who is mighty has done great things for me,
    holy is his name;
His mercy is from age to age
    on those who fear him

"He has shown might with his arm;
    he has confused the proud in their inmost thoughts.
He has deposed the mighty from their thrones
    and raised the lowly to high places.
The hungry he has given every good thing,
    while the rich he has sent empty away.
He has upheld Israel his servant,
    ever mindful of his mercy,
Even as he promised our fathers,
    promised Abraham and his descendants forever."
Mary remained with Elizabeth about three months
and then returned home.—The gospel of the Lord. ℟.
Praise to you, Lord Jesus Christ.   → No. 14, p. 18

PRAYER OVER THE GIFTS   [Living in God's Love]

Lord,
receive this offering of our service.
You raised the Virgin Mary to the glory of heaven.
By her prayers, help us to seek you
and to live in your love.
Grant this through Christ our Lord.
℟. **Amen.**   → Pref. (P 59), p. 415

COMMUNION ANT. Lk 1, 48-49   [Mary Aided by Grace]

**All generations will call me blessed, for the Almighty
has done great things for me.** ↓

PRAYER AFTER COMMUNION   [Mary's Intercession]

Lord,
may we who receive this sacrament of salvation

be led to the glory of heaven
by the prayers of the Virgin Mary.
We ask this in the name of Jesus the Lord.
R/. **Amen.**   → No. 32, p. 70

Optional Solemn Blessings, p. 92, and Prayers Over the People, p. 99

"The bread I will give is my flesh, for the life of the world."

AUGUST 17

20th SUNDAY IN ORDINARY TIME

ENTRANCE ANT. Ps 84, 10-11   [God Our Strength]
**God, our protector, keep us in mind; always give
strength to your people. For if we can be with you
even one day, it is better than a thousand without
you.**   → No. 2, p. 10

OPENING PRAYER   [Joy beyond Imagining]
Let us pray
  [that the love of God
  may raise us beyond what we see
  to the unseen glory of his kingdom]
God our Father,
may we love you in all things and above all things

and reach the joy you have prepared for us
beyond all our imagining.
We ask this through our Lord Jesus Christ, your Son,
who lives and reigns with you and the Holy Spirit,
one God, for ever and ever. ℟. **Amen.** ↓

ALTERNATIVE OPENING PRAYER   [Avoiding Prejudice]

Let us pray
   [with humility and persistence]
Almighty God, ever-loving Father,
your care extends beyond the boundaries of race and
      nation
to the hearts of all who live.
May the walls, which prejudice raises between us,
crumble beneath the shadow of your outstretched
      arm.
We ask this through Christ our Lord. ℟. **Amen.** ↓

READING I Prv 9, 1-6   [Divine Food and Drink]

**Proverbs directing attention to young men who were to
take their places in the royal court speak of food and drink.
A diet of wisdom, however, will lead to prudent living, religious wisdom, long vision and moderation.**

A reading from the book of Proverbs

WISDOM has built her house,
   she has set up her seven columns;
She has dressed her meat, mixed her wine,
   yes, she has spread her table.
She has sent out her maidens; she calls
   from the heights out over the city:
"Let whoever is simple turn in here;
   to him who lacks understanding, I say,
Come, eat of my food,
   and drink of the wine I have mixed!
Forsake foolishness that you may live;
   advance in the way of understanding."
The word of the Lord. ℟. **Thanks be to God.** ↓

RESPONSORIAL PSALM Ps 34 [Taste the Lord's Goodness]

℟. **Taste and see** **the goodness** **of the Lord.**

I will bless the Lord at all times;
  his praise shall be ever in my mouth.
Let my soul glory in the Lord;
  the lowly will hear me and be glad.

℟. **Taste and see the goodness of the Lord.**

Fear the Lord, you his holy ones,
  for nought is lacking to those who fear him.
The great grow poor and hungry;
  but those who seek the Lord want for no good thing.

℟. **Taste and see the goodness of the Lord.**

Come, children, hear me;
  I will teach you the fear of the Lord.
Which of you desires life,
  and takes delight in prosperous days?

℟. **Taste and see the goodness of the Lord.**

Keep your tongue from evil
  and your lips from speaking guile;
Turn from evil, and do good;
  seek peace, and follow after it.

℟. **Taste and see the goodness of the Lord.** ↓

READING II Eph 5, 15-20   [Discern God's Will]

Christians should be careful to live according to the will of the Lord. They should avoid carefree living and give praise and worship to God in the name of Jesus.

A reading from the letter of Paul to the Ephesians

KEEP careful watch over your conduct. Do not act like fools, but like thoughtful men. Make the most of the present opportunity, for these are evil days. Do not continue in ignorance, but try to discern the will of the Lord. Avoid getting drunk on wine that leads to debauchery. Be filled with the Spirit, addressing one another in psalms and hymns and inspired songs. Sing praise to the Lord with all your hearts. Give thanks to God the Father always and for everything in the name of our Lord Jesus Christ.—The word of the Lord. ℟. **Thanks be to God.** ↓

GOSPEL Jn 6, 51-58   [Need for Communion]
Alleluia (Jn 6, 57)
℟. **Alleluia.** Whoever eats my flesh and drinks my blood
will live in me and I in him, says the Lord. ℟. **Alleluia.** ↓

> Jesus proclaims that he is the living bread from heaven. Whoever eats of it shall live forever. When the Jews quarreled about this teaching, Jesus repeated it without any qualification.

℣. The Lord be with you. ℟. **And also with you.**
✢ A reading from the holy gospel according to John.
℟. **Glory to you, Lord.**

JESUS said to the crowds:
"I myself am the living bread
   come down from heaven.
   If anyone eats this bread
   he shall live forever;
   the bread I will give
   is my flesh, for the life of the world."

At this the Jews quarreled among themselves, saying, "How can he give us his flesh to eat?" Thereupon Jesus said to them:

   "Let me solemnly assure you,
   if you do not eat the flesh of the Son of Man
   and drink his blood,
   you have no life in you.
   He who feeds on my flesh
   and drinks my blood

has life eternal,
and I will raise him up on the last day.
For my flesh is real food
and my blood real drink.
The man who feeds on my flesh
and drinks my blood
remains in me, and I in him.
Just as the Father who has life sent me
and I have life because of the Father,
so the man who feeds on me
will have life because of me.
This is the bread that came down from heaven.
Unlike your ancestors who ate and died nonetheless,
the man who feeds on this bread shall live forever."

The gospel of the Lord. ℟. **Praise to you, Lord Jesus Christ.**   → No. 14, p. 18

PRAYER OVER THE GIFTS   [Holy Exchange]

Lord,
accept our sacrifice
as a holy exchange of gifts.
By offering what you have given us
may we receive the gift of yourself.
We ask this in the name of Jesus the Lord.
℟. **Amen.**   → No. 21, p. 22 (Pref. P 29-36)

COMMUNION ANT. Ps 130, 7   [Fullness of Redemption]

With the Lord there is mercy, and fullness of redemption. ↓

OR Jn 6, 51-52   [Eternal Life]

I am the living bread from heaven, says the Lord; if anyone eats this bread he will live for ever. ↓

PRAYER AFTER COMMUNION   [One with Christ]

God of mercy,
by this sacrament you make us one with Christ.

By becoming more like him on earth,
may we come to share his glory in heaven,
where he lives and reigns for ever and ever.
℟. **Amen.**   → No. 32, p. 70

Optional Solemn Blessings, p. 92, and Prayers Over the People, p. 99

*"No one can come to me unless it is granted him
by the Father."*

AUGUST 24

21st SUNDAY IN ORDINARY TIME

ENTRANCE ANT. Ps 86, 1-3   [Save Us]

**Listen, Lord, and answer me. Save your servant who
trusts in you. I call to you all day long; have mercy on
me, O Lord.**   → No. 2, p. 10

OPENING PRAYER   [One in Mind and Heart]

Let us pray
  [that God will make us one in mind and heart]
Father,
help us to seek the values
that will bring us lasting joy in this changing world.
In our desire for what you promise
make us one in mind and heart.

Grant this through our Lord Jesus Christ, your Son,
who lives and reigns with you and the Holy Spirit,
one God, for ever and ever. ℟. **Amen.** ↓

ALTERNATIVE OPENING PRAYER   [Minds on God]

Let us pray
  [with minds fixed on eternal truth]
Lord our God,
all truth is from you,
and you alone bring oneness of heart.
Give your people the joy
of hearing your word in every sound
and of longing for your presence more than for life itself.
May all the attractions of a changing world
serve only to bring us
the peace of your kingdom which this world does not
  give.
Grant this through Christ our Lord. ℟. **Amen.** ↓

READING I Jos 24, 1-2. 15-17. 18   [Serving the Lord]

**Joshua admonished the Israelites to decide their allegiance
to God. They answered that they would serve the God of
their fathers who delivered them from slavery and protected them.**

A reading from the book of Joshua

JOSHUA gathered together all the tribes of Israel at
Shechem, summoning their elders, their leaders,
their judges and their officers. When they stood in
ranks before God, Joshua addressed all the people: "If
it does not please you to serve the Lord, decide today
whom you will serve, the gods your fathers served beyond the River or the gods of the Amorites in whose
country you are dwelling. As for me and my household, we will serve the Lord."

But the people answered, "Far be it from us to forsake the Lord for the service of other gods. For it was

the Lord, our God, who brought us and our fathers up out of the land of Egypt, out of a state of slavery. He performed those great miracles before our very eyes and protected us along our entire journey and among all the peoples through whom we passed. Therefore we also will serve the Lord, for he is our God."—The word of the Lord. ℟. **Thanks be to God.** ↓

RESPONSORIAL PSALM Ps 34   [Refuge in God]

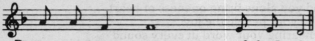

℟. **Taste and see   the goodness   of the Lord.**

I will bless the Lord at all times;
   his praise shall be ever in my mouth.
Let my soul glory in the Lord;
   the lowly will hear me and be glad.

℟. **Taste and see the goodness of the Lord.**

The Lord has eyes for the just,
   and ears for their cry.
The Lord confronts the evildoers,
   to destroy remembrance of them from the earth.

℟. **Taste and see the goodness of the Lord.**

When the just cry out, the Lord hears them,
   and from all their distress he rescues them.
The Lord is close to the brokenhearted;
   and those who are crushed in spirit he saves.

℟. **Taste and see the goodness of the Lord.**

Many are the troubles of the just man,
   but out of them all the Lord delivers him;
He watches over all his bones;
   not one of them shall be broken.

℟. **Taste and see the goodness of the Lord.**

Vice slays the wicked,
   and the enemies of the just pay for their guilt.

But the Lord redeems the lives of his servants;
   no one incurs guilt who takes refuge in him.

℟. **Taste and see the goodness of the Lord.** ↓

READING II Eph 5, 21-32   [Sacrament of Marriage]

Paul gives specific directives to wives and husbands.
Wives are to be submissive to their husbands as the
Church submits to Christ. Husbands must love their wives
as their own bodies. They are to be ever faithful to each
other.

A reading from the letter of Paul to the Ephesians

DEFER to one another out of reverence for Christ.
Wives should be submissive to their husbands as
if to the Lord because the husband is head of his wife
just as Christ is head of his body, the church, as well
as its savior. As the church submits to Christ, so wives
should submit to their husbands in everything.

Husbands, love your wives, as Christ loved the
church. He gave himself up for her to make her holy,
purifying her in the bath of water by the power of the
word, to present to himself a glorious church, holy
and immaculate, without stain or wrinkle or anything
of that sort. Husbands should love their wives as they
do their own bodies. He who loves his wife loves himself. Observe that no one ever hates his own flesh; no,
he nourishes it and takes care of it as Christ cares for
the church—for we are members of his body.

"For this reason a man shall leave his father and
      mother,
   and shall cling to his wife,
   and the two shall be made into one."

This is a great foreshadowing; I mean that it refers to
Christ and the church.—The word of the Lord. ℟.
Thanks be to God. ↓

GOSPEL Jn 6, 60-69   [Words of Life]
Alleluia (Jn 6, 64. 69)

R⁄. **Alleluia.** Your words, Lord, are spirit and life,
you have the words of everlasting life. R⁄. **Alleluia.** ↓

> Jesus emphasizes that to believe in him demands faith—a
> gift from his Father. Many left Jesus, but his Twelve turned
> and said, "Lord, to whom shall we go? You alone have the
> words of eternal life."

V⁄. The Lord be with you. R⁄.. **And also with you.**
✠ A reading from the holy gospel according to John.
R⁄. **Glory to you, Lord.**

MANY of the disciples of Jesus remarked, "This
sort of talk is hard to endure! How can anyone
take it seriously?" Jesus was fully aware that his disciples were murmuring in protest at what he had said.
"Does it shake your faith?" he asked them.

> "What, then, if you were to see the Son of Man
> ascend to where he was before. . . ?
> It is the spirit that gives life;
> the flesh is useless.
> The words I spoke to you
> are spirit and life.
> Yet among you there are some who do not be-
> lieve."

(Jesus knew from the start, of course, the ones who refused to believe, and the one who would hand him
over.) He went on to say:

> "This is why I have told you
> that no one can come to me
> unless it is granted him by the Father."

From this time on, many of his disciples broke away
and would not remain in his company any longer.
Jesus then said to the Twelve, "Do you want to leave
me too?" Simon Peter answered him, "Lord, to whom
shall we go? You have the words of eternal life. We

have come to believe; we are convinced that you are God's holy one."—The gospel of the Lord. ℟. **Praise to you, Lord Jesus Christ.**   → No. 14, p. 18

PRAYER OVER THE GIFTS   [Peace and Unity]

Merciful God,
the perfect sacrifice of Jesus Christ
made us your people.
In your love,
grant peace and unity to your Church.
We ask this through Christ our Lord.
℟. **Amen.**   → No. 21, p. 22 (Pref. P 29-36)

COMMUNION ANT. Ps 104, 13-15   [Sacred Bread and Wine]

Lord, the earth is filled with your gift from heaven; man grows bread from earth, and wine to cheer his heart. ↓

OR Jn 6, 55   [Eternal Life]

The Lord says: The man who eats my flesh and drinks my blood will live for ever; I shall raise him to life on the last day. ↓

PRAYER AFTER COMMUNION   [Pleasing God]

Lord,
may this eucharist increase within us
the healing power of your love.
May it guide and direct our efforts
to please you in all things.
We ask this in the name of Jesus the Lord.
℟. **Amen.**   → No. 32, p. 70

Optional Solemn Blessings, p. 92, and Prayers Over the People, p. 99

*"Nothing that enters a man from outside
can make him impure."*

AUGUST 31

22nd SUNDAY IN ORDINARY TIME

ENTRANCE ANT. Ps 86, 3. 5   **[Call Upon God]**
I call to you all day long, have mercy on me, O Lord.
You are good and forgiving, full of love for all who
call to you.   → No. 2, p. 10

OPENING PRAYER   **[Increasing Our Spiritual Gifts]**
Let us pray
  [that God will increase our faith
  and bring to perfection the gifts he has given us]
Almighty God,
every good thing comes from you.
Fill our hearts with love for you,
increase our faith,
and by your constant care
protect the good you have given us.
We ask this . . . for ever and ever. ℟. **Amen.** ↓

ALTERNATIVE OPENING PRAYER **[Desire To Please God]**
Let us pray
  [to God who forgives all who call upon him]

Lord God of power and might,
nothing is good which is against your will,
and all is of value which comes from your hand.
Place in our hearts a desire to please you
and fill our minds with insight into love,
so that every thought may grow in wisdom
and all our efforts may be filled with your peace.
We ask this through Christ our Lord. ℟. **Amen.** ↓

READING I Dt 4, 1-2. 6-8   [Observing God's Law]

Moses warns the people that they are not to add or subtract from the statutes and decrees of the Lord. God is looking after them directly.

A reading from the book of Deuteronomy

MOSES told the people: "Now, Israel, hear the statutes and decrees which I am teaching you to observe, that you may live, and may enter in and take possession of the land which the Lord, the God of your fathers, is giving you. In your observance of the commandments of the Lord, your God, which I enjoin upon you, you shall not add to what I command you nor subtract from it. Observe them carefully, for thus will you give evidence of your wisdom and intelligence to the nations, who will hear of all these statutes and say, 'This great nation is truly a wise and intelligent people.' For what great nation is there that has gods so close to it as the Lord, our God, is to us whenever we call upon him? Or what great nation has statutes and decrees that are as just as this whole law which I am setting before you today?"—The word of the Lord. ℟. **Thanks be to God.** ↓

RESPONSORIAL PSALM Ps 15   [Practicing Justice]

℟. He who does jus-tice will live in the presence of the Lord.

He who walks blamelessly and does justice;
  who thinks the truth in his heart
  and slanders not with his tongue.

℞. **He who does justice will live in the presence of the Lord.**

Who harms not his fellow-man,
  nor takes up a reproach against his neighbor;
By whom the reprobate is despised,
  while he honors those who fear the Lord.

℞. **He who does justice will live in the presence of the Lord.**

Who lends not his money at usury
  and accepts no bribe against the innocent.
He who does these things
  shall never be disturbed.

℞. **He who does justice will live in the presence of the Lord.** ↓

READING II Jas 1, 17-18. 21-22. 27   [Act on God's Word]

Everything worthwhile comes from God. Christians should welcome God's word, listen and act upon it.

A reading from the letter of James

EVERY worthwhile gift, every genuine benefit comes from above, descending from the Father of the heavenly luminaries, who cannot change and who is never shadowed over. He wills to bring us to birth with a word spoken in truth so that we may be a kind of first-fruits of his creatures.

Humbly welcome the word that has taken root in you, with its power to save you. Act on this word. If all you do is listen to it, you are deceiving yourselves.

Looking after orphans and widows in their distress and keeping oneself unspotted by the world make for pure worship without stain before our God and Father.—The word of the Lord. ℞. **Thanks be to God.** ↓

GOSPEL Mk 7, 1-8. 14-15. 21-23   [Sin Comes from the Heart]
Alleluia (Jas 1, 18)

℟. **Alleluia.** The Father gave us birth by his message of truth,

that we might be as the first fruits of his creation. ℟.
    Alleluia. ↓

> Jesus condemned lip service. It is wicked thoughts from the heart that really make a person impure.

℣. The Lord be with you. ℟. **And also with you.**

✛ A reading from the holy gospel according to Mark.
℟. **Glory to you, Lord.**

THE Pharisees and some of the experts in the law who had come from Jerusalem gathered around Jesus. They had observed a few of his disciples eating meals without having purified—that is to say, washed— their hands. The Pharisees, and in fact all Jews, cling to the custom of their ancestors and never eat without scrupulously washing their hands. Moreover, they never eat anything from the market without first sprinkling it. There are many other traditions they observe— for example, the washing of cups and jugs and kettles. So the Pharisees and the scribes questioned him: "Why do your disciples not follow the tradition of our ancestors, but instead take food without purifying their hands?" He said to them: "How accurately Isaiah prophesied about you hypocrites when he wrote,

'This people pays me lip service
    but their heart is far from me.
Empty is the reverence they do me
because they teach as dogmas mere human precepts.'

You disregard God's commandment and cling to what is human tradition."

He summoned the crowd again and said to them: "Hear me, all of you, and try to understand. Nothing that enters a man from outside can make him impure; that which comes out of him, and only that, constitutes impurity. Let everyone heed what he hears!

"Wicked designs come from the deep recesses of the heart: acts of fornication, theft, murder, adulterous conduct, greed, maliciousness, deceit, sensuality, envy, blasphemy, arrogance, an obtuse spirit. All these evils come from within and render a man impure."—The gospel of the Lord. ℟. **Praise to you, Lord Jesus Christ.**

→ No. 14, p. 18

PRAYER OVER THE GIFTS   [Promise of Salvation]

Lord,
may this holy offering
bring us your blessing
and accomplish within us
its promise of salvation.
Grant this through Christ our Lord.
℟. **Amen.**   → No. 21, p. 22 (Pref. P 29-36)

COMMUNION ANT. Ps 31, 20   [God's Kindness]

O Lord, how great is the depth of the kindness which you have shown to those who love you. ↓

OR Mt 5, 9-10   [Happy the Peacemakers]

Happy are the peacemakers; they shall be called sons of God. Happy are they who suffer persecution for justice' sake; the kingdom of heaven is theirs. ↓

PRAYER AFTER COMMUNION   [Serving God in Others]

Lord,
you renew us at your table with the bread of life.
May this food strengthen us in love
and help us to serve you in each other.
We ask this in the name of Jesus the Lord.
℟. **Amen.**   → No. 32, p. 70

Optional Solemn Blessings, p. 92, and Prayers Over the People, p. 99

"Ephphatha!" (that is, "Be opened!")

SEPTEMBER 7

23rd SUNDAY IN ORDINARY TIME

ENTRANCE ANT. Ps 119, 137. 124   **[Plea for Mercy]**

Lord, you are just, and the judgments you make are right. Show mercy when you judge me, your servant.
→ No. 2, p. 10

OPENING PRAYER   **[Christian Freedom]**

Let us pray
  [that we may realize the freedom God has given us
  in making us his sons and daughters]
God our Father,
you redeem us
and make us your children in Christ.
Look upon us,
give us true freedom
and bring us to the inheritance you promised.
Grant this through our Lord Jesus Christ, your Son,
who lives and reigns with you and the Holy Spirit,
one God, for ever and ever. ℟. **Amen.** ↓

ALTERNATIVE OPENING PRAYER   **[Appreciation of Life]**

Let us pray
  [to our just and merciful God]

437

Lord our God,
in you justice and mercy meet.
With unparalleled love you have saved us from death
and drawn us into the circle of your life.
Open our eyes to the wonders this life sets before us,
that we may serve you free from fear
and address you as God our Father.
We ask this through Christ our Lord. ℞. **Amen.** ↓

READING I Is 35, 4-7   [The Messiah's Coming]

Isaiah speaks of the Messiah's coming. At that time God will
come to save his people and bring many blessings to them.

A reading from the book of the prophet Isaiah

SAY to those whose hearts are frightened:
Be strong, fear not!
Here is your God,
    he comes with vindication;
With divine recompense
    he comes to save you.
Then will the eyes of the blind be opened,
    the ears of the deaf be cleared;
Then will the lame leap like a stag,
    then the tongue of the dumb will sing.
Streams will burst forth in the desert,
    and rivers in the steppe.
The burning sands will become pools,
    and the thirsting ground, springs of water.
The word of the Lord. ℞. **Thanks be to God.** ↓

RESPONSORIAL PSALM Ps 146 [The Lord's Saving Deeds]

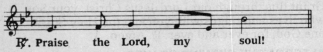

℞. **Praise   the Lord,   my   soul!**

The God of Jacob keeps faith forever,
    secures justice for the oppressed,
    gives food to the hungry.
The Lord sets captives free.

℟. **Praise the Lord, my soul!**

The Lord gives sight to the blind;
    the Lord raises up those that were bowed down.
The Lord loves the just;
    the Lord protects strangers.

℟. **Praise the Lord, my soul!**

The fatherless and the widow the Lord sustains,
    but the way of the wicked he thwarts.
The Lord shall reign forever;
    your God, O Zion, through all generations. Alleluia.

℟. **Praise the Lord, my soul!** ↓

℟. **Or: Alleluia.** ↓

READING II Jas 2, 1-5   [No Favoritism with God]

James warns the Christians about showing favoritism to
the rich. No one is in a position to judge. God chose those
who were poor according to worldly standards to become
rich in faith.

A reading from the letter of James

MY brothers, your faith in our Lord Jesus Christ
glorified must not allow of favoritism. Suppose
there should come into your assembly a man fashion-
ably dressed, with gold rings on his fingers, and at the
same time a poor man dressed in shabby clothes. Suppose further you were to take notice of the well-
dressed man and say, "Sit right here, please"; whereas
you were to say to the poor man, "You can stand!" or
"Sit over there by my footrest." Have you not in a case
like this discriminated in your hearts? Have you not
set yourselves up as judges who hand down corrupt
decisions?

Listen, dear brothers. Did not God choose those
who are poor in the eyes of the world to be rich in
faith and heirs of the kingdom he promised to those
who love him?—The word of the Lord. ℟. **Thanks be
to God.** ↓

GOSPEL Mk 7, 31-37   [Cure of a Deaf-Mute]
Alleluia (Mt 4, 23)

℟. **Alleluia.** Jesus preached the Good News of the
  Kingdom
and healed all who were sick. ℟. **Alleluia.** ↓

> The people brought to Jesus a deaf and dumb man to be
> cured. Taking him aside, Jesus cured him, asking him to
> keep this a secret. But the man proclaimed the cure all the
> more. The people were amazed at this power.

℣. The Lord be with you. ℟. **And also with you.**
✟ A reading from the holy gospel according to Mark.
℟. **Glory to you, Lord.**

JESUS left Tyrian territory and returned by way of
Sidon to the Sea of Galilee, into the district of the
Ten Cities. Some people brought him a deaf man who
had a speech impediment and begged him to lay his
hand on him. Jesus took him off by himself away from
the crowd. He put his fingers into the man's ears and,
spitting, touched his tongue; then he looked up to
heaven and emitted a groan. He said to him, "Ephphatha!" (that is, "Be opened!") At once the man's ears
were opened; he was freed from the impediment, and
began to speak plainly. Then he enjoined them strictly
not to tell anyone; but the more he ordered them not
to, the more they proclaimed it. Their amazement
went beyond all bounds: "He has done everything
well! He makes the deaf hear and the mute speak!"—
The gospel of the Lord. ℟. **Praise to you, Lord Jesus
Christ.**   → No. 14, p. 18

PRAYER OVER THE GIFTS   [True Worship]

God of peace and love,
may our offering bring you true worship
and make us one with you.
Grant this through Christ our Lord.
℟. **Amen.**   → No. 21, p. 22 (Pref. P 29-36)

COMMUNION ANT. Ps 42, 2-3   [Longing for God]

Like a deer that longs for running streams, my soul longs for you, my God. My soul is thirsting for the living God. ↓

OR Jn 8, 12   [The Light of Life]

I am the light of the world, says the Lord; the man who follows me will have the light of life. ↓

PRAYER AFTER COMMUNION   [Word and Sacrament]

Lord,
your word and your sacrament
give us food and life.
May this gift of your Son
lead us to share his life for ever.
We ask this through Christ our Lord.
℟. **Amen.**

→ No. 32, p. 70

Optional Solemn Blessings, p. 92, and Prayers Over the People, p. 99

"God so loved the world that he gave his only Son."

SEPTEMBER 14

TRIUMPH OF THE CROSS
(24th SUNDAY IN ORDINARY TIME)

ENTRANCE ANT. See Gal 6, 14   [Glory in the Cross]

**We should glory in the cross of our Lord Jesus Christ,
for he is our salvation, our life and our resurrection;
through him we are saved and made free.** → No. 2, p. 10

OPENING PRAYER   [Gift of Redemption]

Let us pray
   [that the death of Christ on the cross
   will bring us to the glory of the resurrection]
God our Father,
in obedience to you
your only Son accepted death on the cross
for the salvation of mankind.
We acknowledge the mystery of the cross on earth.
May we receive the gift of redemption in heaven.
We ask this through our Lord Jesus Christ, your Son,
who lives and reigns with you and the Holy Spirit,
one God, for ever and ever. ℟. **Amen.** ↓

READING I Nm 21, 4-9   [The Bronze Serpent]

The bronze serpent raised on high is a healing force for all the afflicted who look upon it.

A reading from the book of Numbers

WITH their patience worn out by the journey, the people complained against God and Moses, "Why have you brought us up from Egypt to die in this desert, where there is no food or water? We are disgusted with this wretched food!"

In punishment the Lord sent among the people saraph serpents, which bit the people so that many of them died. Then the people came to Moses and said, "We have sinned in complaining against the Lord and you. Pray the Lord to take the serpents from us." So Moses prayed for the people, and the Lord said to Moses, "Make a saraph and mount it on a pole, and if anyone who has been bitten looks at it, he will recover." Moses accordingly made a bronze serpent and mounted it on a pole, and whenever anyone who had been bitten by a serpent looked at the bronze serpent, he recovered.—The word of the Lord. ℟. **Thanks be to God.** ↓

RESPONSORIAL PSALM Ps 78   [Remember God's Works]

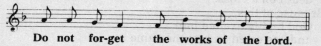

Do not for-get   the works of   the Lord.

Hearken, my people, to my teaching;
  incline your ears to the words of my mouth.
I will open my mouth in a parable,
  I will utter mysteries from of old.—℟.

While he slew them they sought him
  and inquired after God again,
Remembering that God was their rock
  and the Most High God, their redeemer.—℟.

But they flattered him with their mouths
  and lied to him with their tongues,
Though their hearts were not steadfast toward him,
  nor were they faithful to his covenant.—R℣.

Yet he, being merciful, forgave their sin
  and destroyed them not;
Often he turned back his anger
  and let none of his wrath be roused.—R℣. ↓

READING II Phil 2, 6-11   [Christ Humbled Himself]

**Jesus' death on the cross began his rise to exaltation: Jesus
Christ is Lord!**

A reading from the letter of Paul to the Philippians

CHRIST Jesus, though he was in the form of God,
  did not deem equality with God
  something to be grasped at.
Rather, he emptied himself
  and took the form of a slave,
  being born in the likeness of men.
He was known to be of human estate
  and it was thus that he humbled himself,
  obediently accepting even death,
  death on a cross!
Because of this,
  God highly exalted him
  and bestowed on him the name
  above every other name,
So that at Jesus' name
  every knee must bend
  in the heavens, on the earth,
  and under the earth,
  and every tongue proclaim
  to the glory of God the Father:
  JESUS CHRIST IS LORD!
The word of the Lord. R℣. **Thanks be to God.** ↓

GOSPEL Jn 3, 13-17   [Lifted Up on the Cross]
Alleluia

℟. **Alleluia.** We adore you, O Christ, and we praise you, because by your cross you have redeemed the world.
   ℟. **Alleluia.** ↓

> Moses' lifting up the serpent in the desert had the salutary effect of healing. The lifting up of the Son of Man on the cross had the saving effect of redemption.

℣. The Lord be with you. ℟. **And also with you.**
✝ A reading from the holy gospel according to John.
℟. **Glory to you, Lord.**

JESUS said to Nicodemus:
   "No one has gone up to heaven
      except the One who came down from there—
      the Son of Man [who is in heaven].
   Just as Moses lifted up the serpent in the desert,
   so must the Son of Man be lifted up,
      that all who believe
      may have eternal life in him.
   Yes, God so loved the world
      that he gave his only Son,
      that whoever believes in him may not die
      but may have eternal life.
   God did not send the Son into the world
      to condemn the world,
      but that the world might be saved through him."
The gospel of the Lord. ℟. **Praise to you, Lord Jesus Christ.**
                                              → No. 14, p. 18

PRAYER OVER THE GIFTS   [Forgiveness]

Lord,
may this sacrifice once offered on the cross
to take away the sins of the world
now free us from our sins.
We ask this through Christ our Lord.
℟. **Amen.** ↓

PREFACE (P 46)   [Saved through the Cross]

℣. The Lord be with you. ℟. **And also with you.**
℣. Lift up your hearts. ℟. **We lift them up to the Lord.**
℣. Let us give thanks to the Lord our God. ℟. **It is right to give him thanks and praise.**

Father, all-powerful and ever-living God,
we do well always and everywhere to give you
    thanks.
You decreed that man should be saved through the
    wood of the cross.
The tree of man's defeat became his tree of victory;
where life was lost, there life has been restored
through Christ our Lord.
Through him the choirs of angels
and all the powers of heaven
praise and worship your glory.
May our voices blend with theirs
as we join in their unending hymn: → No. 23, p. 23

COMMUNION ANT. Jn 12, 32   [Union with Christ]

**When I am lifted up from the earth, I will draw all
men to myself, says the Lord.** ↓

PRAYER AFTER COMMUNION   [Holy Bread of Life]

Lord Jesus Christ,
you are the holy bread of life.
Bring to the glory of the resurrection
the people you have redeemed by the wood of the
    cross.
We ask this through Christ our Lord.
℟. **Amen.**   → No. 32, p. 70

Optional Solemn Blessings, p. 92, and Prayers Over the People, p. 99

"Whoever welcomes a child such as this for my sake welcomes me."

SEPTEMBER 21

25th SUNDAY IN ORDINARY TIME

ENTRANCE ANT. [Savior of All]

I am the Savior of all people, says the Lord. Whatever their troubles, I will answer their cry, and I will always be their Lord. → No. 2, p. 10

OPENING PRAYER [Growth in Love]

Let us pray
   [that we will grow in the love of God
   and of one another]
Father,
guide us, as you guide creation
according to your law of love.
May we love one another
and come to perfection
in the eternal life prepared for us.
Grant this through our Lord Jesus Christ, your Son,
who lives and reigns with you and the Holy Spirit,
one God, for ever and ever. ℟. **Amen.** ↓

ALTERNATIVE OPENING PRAYER   [Mutual Love]

Let us pray
   [to the Lord who is a God of love to all peoples]
Father in heaven,
the perfection of justice is found in your love
and all mankind is in need of your law.
Help us to find this love in each other
that justice may be attained
through obedience to your law.
We ask this through Christ our Lord. ℟. **Amen.** ↓

READING I Wis 2, 12. 17-20   [The Just Are Persecuted]

The wicked detest the just one because the person of God
disturbs their conscience. They are anxious to do away
with the good, saying that God will care for them if they
are really his.

A reading from the book of Wisdom

[THE wicked say:]
   Let us beset the just one, because he is obnoxious
      to us;
   he sets himself against our doings,
Reproaches us for transgressions of the law
   and charges us with violations of our training.
Let us see whether his words be true;
   let us find out what will happen to him.
For if the just one be the son of God, he will defend
      him
   and deliver him from the hand of his foes.
With revilement and torture let us put him to the test
   that we may have proof of his gentleness
   and try his patience.
Let us condemn him to a shameful death;
   for according to his own words, God will take care
      of him.
The word of the Lord. ℟. **Thanks be to God.** ↓

RESPONSORIAL PSALM Ps 54   [God Our Helper]

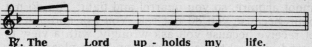

R̷. **The   Lord   up - holds   my   life.**

O God, by your name save me,
  and by your might defend my cause.
O God, hear my prayer;
  hearken to the words of my mouth.

R̷. **The Lord upholds my life.**

For haughty men have risen up against me,
  and fierce men seek my life;
  they set not God before their eyes.

R̷. **The Lord upholds my life.**

Behold, God is my helper;
  the Lord sustains my life.
Freely will I offer you sacrifice;
  I will praise your name, O Lord, for its goodness.

R̷. **The Lord upholds my life.** ↓

READING II Jas 3, 16—4, 3   [Avoiding Conflicts]

**Wisdom begets innocence. It is peace-loving, kind, docile,
impartial, and sincere. The inner cravings of human beings
lead to murder, envy and squandering.**

A reading from the letter of James

WHERE there are jealousy and strife, there also
are inconstancy and all kinds of vile behavior.
Wisdom from above, by contrast, is first of all innocent. It is also peaceable, lenient, docile, rich in sym-
pathy and the kindly deeds that are its fruit, impartial
and sincere. The harvest of justice is sown in peace
for those who cultivate peace.

Where do the conflicts and disputes among you
originate? Is it not your inner cravings that make war
within your members? What you desire you do not ob-

tain, and so you resort to murder. You envy and you cannot acquire, so you quarrel and fight. You do not obtain because you do not ask. You ask and you do not receive because you ask wrongly, with a view to squandering what you receive on your pleasures.— The word of the Lord. ℟. **Thanks be to God.** ↓

GOSPEL Mk 9, 30-37   [Service of Others]
Alleluia (2 Thes 2, 14)
℟. **Alleluia.** God has called us with the Gospel,
the people won for him by Jesus Christ our Lord. ℟.
   Alleluia. ↓

> Jesus tells his trusted disciples of his forthcoming sufferings, death and resurrection. Then he tells the Twelve about humility. To rank first, one must remain the last and be the servant of all.

℣. The Lord be with you. ℟. **And also with you.**
✝ A reading from the holy gospel according to Mark.
℟. **Glory to you, Lord.**

JESUS and his disciples came down the mountain and began to go through Galilee, but he did not want anyone to know about it. He was teaching his disciples in this vein: "The Son of Man is going to be delivered into the hands of men who will put him to death; three days after his death he will arise." Though they failed to understand his words, they were afraid to question him.

They returned to Capernaum and Jesus, once inside the house, began to ask them, "What were you discussing on the way home?" At this they fell silent, for on the way they had been arguing about who was the most important. So he sat down and called the Twelve around him and said, "If anyone wishes to rank first, he must remain the last one of all and the servant of all." Then he took a little child, stood him in their midst, and putting his arms around him, said to them,

"Whoever welcomes a child such as this for my sake welcomes me. And whoever welcomes me welcomes, not me, but him who sent me."—The gospel of the Lord. ℟. **Praise to you, Lord Jesus Christ.**

→ No. 14, p. 18

PRAYER OVER THE GIFTS   [Gifts Become Eucharist]
Lord,
may these gifts which we now offer
to show our belief and our love
be pleasing to you.
May they become for us
the eucharist of Jesus Christ your Son,
who is Lord for ever and ever.
℟. **Amen.**   → No. 21, p. 22 (Pref. P 29-36)

COMMUNION ANT. Ps 119, 4-5 [Keeping God's Commands]
You have laid down your precepts to be faithfully kept. May my footsteps be firm in keeping your commands. ↓

OR Jn 10, 14   [The Good Shepherd]
I am the Good Shepherd, says the Lord; I know my sheep, and mine know me. ↓

PRAYER AFTER COMMUNION   [The Eucharist in Action]
Lord,
help us with your kindness.
Make us strong through the eucharist.
May we put into action
the saving mystery we celebrate.
We ask this in the name of Jesus the Lord.
℟. **Amen.**   → No. 32, p. 70

Optional Solemn Blessings, p. 92, and Prayers Over the People, p. 99

"Anyone who is not against us is with us."

SEPTEMBER 28

26th SUNDAY IN ORDINARY TIME

ENTRANCE ANT. Dn 3, 31. 29. 30. 43. 42   [God's Kindness]

O Lord, you had just cause to judge men as you did: because we sinned against you and disobeyed your will. But now show us your greatness of heart, and treat us with your unbounded kindness. ➙ No. 2, p. 10

OPENING PRAYER   [God's Forgiveness]

Let us pray
  [for God's forgiveness
  and for the happiness it brings]
Father,
you show your almighty power
in your mercy and forgiveness.
Continue to fill us with your gifts of love.
Help us to hurry toward the eternal life you promise
and come to share in the joys of your kingdom.
Grant this through our Lord Jesus Christ, your Son,
who lives and reigns with you and the Holy Spirit,
one God, for ever and ever. ℟. **Amen.** ↓

ALTERNATIVE OPENING PRAYER   [Radiating Christ]

Let us pray
    [for the peace of the kingdom
    which we have been promised]
Father of our Lord Jesus Christ,
in your unbounded mercy
you have revealed the beauty of your power
through your constant forgiveness of our sins.
May the power of this love be in our hearts
to bring your pardon and your kingdom to all we meet.
We ask this through Christ our Lord. ℟. **Amen.** ↓

READING I Nm 11, 25-29   [Prophets Chosen by God]

The Lord empowered seventy elders with the gift of prophecy. Eldad and Medad were absent but they also received the gift. Some elders complained but Moses replied that it would be even more wonderful if all the people were prophets.

A reading from the book of Numbers

THE Lord came down in the cloud and spoke to Moses. Taking some of the spirit that was on him, he bestowed it on the seventy elders; and as the spirit came to rest on them, they prophesied.

Now two men, one named Eldad and the other Medad, were not in the gathering but had been left in the camp. They too had been on the list, but had not gone out to the tent; yet the spirit came to rest on them also, and they prophesied in the camp. So, when a young man quickly told Moses, "Eldad and Medad are prophesying in the camp," Joshua, son of Nun, who from his youth had been Moses' aide, said, "Moses, my lord, stop them." But Moses answered him, "Are you jealous for my sake? Would that all the people of the Lord were prophets! Would that the Lord might bestow his spirit on them all!"—The word of the Lord. ℟. **Thanks be to God.** ↓

RESPONSORIAL PSALM Ps 19   [God's Law]

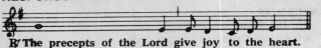

℟ **The precepts of the Lord give joy to the heart.**

The law of the Lord is perfect,
   refreshing the soul;
The decree of the Lord is trustworthy,
   giving wisdom to the simple.

℟. **The precepts of the Lord give joy to the heart.**

The fear of the Lord is pure,
   enduring forever;
The ordinances of the Lord are true,
   all of them just.

℟. **The precepts of the Lord give joy to the heart.**

Though your servant is careful of them,
   very diligent in keeping them,
Yet who can detect failings?
   Cleanse me from my unknown faults!

℟. **The precepts of the Lord give joy to the heart.**

From wanton sin especially, restrain your servant;
   let it not rule over me.
Then shall I be blameless and innocent
   of serious sin.

℟. **The precepts of the Lord give joy to the heart.** ↓

READING II Jas 5, 1-6   [Injustice of the Rich]

> James deplores the injustice committed by the rich. He
> speaks of their pending miseries, their wanton luxury,
> wages withheld from workers. All these will stand as wit-
> ness for greed.

A reading from the letter of James

YOU rich, weep and wail over your impending miseries. Your wealth has rotted, your fine wardrobe
has grown moth-eaten, your gold and silver have cor-

roded, and their corrosion shall be a testimony against you; it will devour your flesh like a fire. See what you have stored up for yourselves against the last days. Here, crying aloud, are the wages you withheld from the farmhands who harvested your fields. The shouts of the harvesters have reached the ears of the Lord of hosts. You lived in wanton luxury on the earth; you fattened yourselves for the day of slaughter. You condemned, even killed, the just man; he does not resist you.—The word of the Lord. ℟. **Thanks be to God.** ↓

GOSPEL Mk 9, 38-43. 45. 47-48   [Everyone Can Proclaim Christ]
Alleluia (Jn 17, 17)

℟. **Alleluia.** Your word, O Lord, is truth;
make us holy in the truth. ℟. **Alleluia.** ↓

> Jesus reminds his followers that nothing done in his name will go unrewarded. But anyone who deceives a simple believer will be severely punished.

℣. The Lord be with you. ℟. **And also with you.**
✝ A reading from the holy gospel according to Mark.
℟. **Glory to you, Lord.**

JOHN said to Jesus, "Teacher, we saw a man using your name to expel demons and we tried to stop him because he is not of our company." Jesus said in reply: "Do not try to stop him. No man who performs a miracle using my name can at once speak ill of me. Anyone who is not against us is with us. Any man who gives you a drink of water because you belong to Christ will not, I assure you, go without his reward. But it would be better if anyone who leads astray one of these simple believers were to be plunged in the sea with a great millstone fastened around his neck.

"If your hand is your difficulty, cut it off! Better for you to enter life maimed than to keep both hands and enter Gehenna, with its unquenchable fire. If your foot is your undoing, cut it off! Better for you to enter life crippled than to be thrown into Gehenna with both feet. If your eye is your downfall, tear it out! Better for you to enter the kingdom of God with one eye than to be thrown with both eyes into Gehenna, where 'the worm dies not and the fire is never extinguished.' "— The gospel of the Lord. ℟. **Praise to you, Lord Jesus Christ.**   → No. 14, p. 18

PRAYER OVER THE GIFTS   [Offering as a Blessing]

God of mercy,
accept our offering
and make it a source of blessing for us.
We ask this in the name of Jesus the Lord.
℟. **Amen.**   → No. 21, p. 22 (Pref. P 29-36)

COMMUNION ANT. Ps 119, 49-50   [Words of Hope]

O Lord, remember the words you spoke to me, your servant, which made me live in hope and consoled me when I was downcast. ↓

OR 1 Jn 3, 16   [Offering of Self]

This is how we know what love is: Christ gave up his life for us; and we too must give up our lives for our brothers. ↓

PRAYER AFTER COMMUNION   [Union with Christ]

Lord,
may this eucharist
in which we proclaim the death of Christ
bring us salvation
and make us one with him in glory,
for he is Lord for ever and ever.
℟. **Amen.**   → No. 32, p. 70

Optional Solemn Blessings, p. 92, and Prayers Over the People, p. 99

"A man shall leave his father and mother and the two shall become as one."

OCTOBER 5

27th SUNDAY IN ORDINARY TIME

ENTRANCE ANT. Est 13, 9. 10-11   **[Lord of All]**
O Lord, you have given everything its place in the world, and no one can make it otherwise. For it is your creation, the heavens and the earth and the stars: you are the Lord of all.   ➔ No. 2, p. 10

OPENING PRAYER   **[Peace and Salvation]**
Let us pray
  [that God will forgive our failings
  and bring us peace]
Father,
your love for us
surpasses all our hopes and desires.
Forgive our failings,
keep us in your peace
and lead us in the way of salvation.
We ask this through our Lord Jesus Christ, your Son,
who lives and reigns with you and the Holy Spirit,
one God, for ever and ever. ℟. **Amen.** ↓

ALTERNATIVE OPENING PRAYER   [Christian Courage]

Let us pray
  [before the face of God,
  in trusting faith]
Almighty and eternal God,
Father of the world to come,
your goodness is beyond what our spirit can touch
and your strength is more than the mind can bear.
Lead us to seek beyond our reach
and give us the courage to stand before your truth.
We ask this through Christ our Lord. ℟. **Amen.** ↓

READING I Gn 2, 18-24   [Man's Companion]

> God, knowing that man needs companionship, created ani-
> mals and birds and finally placed Adam in a deep sleep and
> took one of his ribs, forming a woman.

A reading from the book of Genesis

THE Lord said: "It is not good for the man to be
  alone. I will make a suitable partner for him." So
the Lord God formed out of the ground various wild
animals and various birds of the air, and he brought
them to the man to see what he would call them;
whatever the man called each of them would be its
name. The man gave names to all the cattle, all the
birds of the air, and all the wild animals; but none
proved to be the suitable partner for the man.

So the Lord God cast a deep sleep on the man, and
while he was asleep, he took out one of his ribs and
closed up its place with flesh. The Lord God then built
up into a woman the rib that he had taken from the
man. When he brought her to the man, the man said:
"This one, at last, is bone of my bones
  and flesh of my flesh;
This one shall be called 'woman,'
  for out of 'her man' this one has been taken."
That is why a man leaves his father and mother and

clings to his wife, and the two of them become one
body.—The word of the Lord. ℟. **Thanks be to God.** ↓

RESPONSORIAL PSALM Ps 128   [Fear of the Lord]

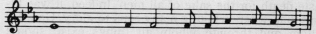

℟. **May the Lord bless us   all the days of our lives.**

Happy are you who fear the Lord,
   who walk in his ways!
For you shall eat the fruit of your handiwork;
   happy shall you be, and favored.

℟. **May the Lord bless us
   all the days of our lives.**

Your wife shall be like a fruitful vine
   in the recesses of your home;
Your children like olive plants
   around your table.

℟. **May the Lord bless us
   all the days of our lives.**

Behold, thus is the man blessed
   who fears the Lord.
The Lord bless you from Zion:
   may you see the prosperity of Jerusalem
   all the days of your life.

℟. **May the Lord bless us
   all the days of our lives.**

May you see your children's children.
   Peace be upon Israel!

℟. **May the Lord bless us
   all the days of our lives.**

READING II Heb 2, 9-11   [Christ Our Brother]

To suffer, Jesus took a human body. In this way God made
our leader perfect through suffering, bringing salvation. All
who are consecrated have thereby a common Father and
become brothers and sisters.

A reading from the letter to the Hebrews

JESUS was made for a little while lower than the angels, that through God's gracious will he might taste death for the sake of all men. Indeed, it was fitting that, when bringing many sons to glory, God, for whom and through whom all things exist, should make their leader in the work of salvation perfect through suffering. He who consecrates and those who are consecrated have one and the same Father. Therefore, he is not ashamed to call them brothers.—The word of the Lord. ℟. **Thanks be to God.** ↓

GOSPEL Mk 10, 2-16 or 10, 2-12   [Unity of Marriage]
Alleluia (1 Jn 4, 12)
℟. **Alleluia.** If we love one another,
God will live in us in perfect love. ℟. **Alleluia.** ↓

> The Pharisees, knowing the permission of Moses about divorce, test Jesus, but he recalls the reason for the command and reminds them of God's intention for the unity of marriage. Divorce followed by remarriage is adultery. (Jesus then speaks about his love for little children and their innocence.)

[If the "Short Form" is used, the indented text in brackets is omitted.]

℣. The Lord be with you. ℟. **And also with you.**
✠ A reading from the holy gospel according to Mark.
℟. **Glory to you, Lord.**

SOME Pharisees came up and as a test began to ask Jesus whether it was permissible for a husband to divorce his wife. In reply he said, "What command did Moses give you?" They answered, "Moses permitted divorce and the writing of a decree of divorce." But Jesus told them: "He wrote that commandment for you because of your stubbornness. At the beginning of creation God made them male and female; for this reason a man shall leave his father and mother and the two shall become as one. They are no longer two but one flesh. Therefore let no man separate what God has joined." Back in the house again, the disciples began to question him about this. He told them, "Whoever divorces his wife and marries another commits adultery against her; and the woman who divorces her husband and marries another commits adultery."

[People were bringing their little children to him to have him touch them, but the disciples were scolding them for this. Jesus became indignant when he noticed it and said to them: "Let the children come to me and do not hinder them. It is to just such as these that the kingdom of God belongs. I assure you that whoever does not accept the kingdom of God like a little child shall not enter into it." Then he embraced them and blessed them, placing his hands on them.]

The gospel of the Lord. ℟. **Praise to you, Lord Jesus Christ.**
→ No. 14, p. 18

PRAYER OVER THE GIFTS   [Fullness of Redemption]

Father,
receive these gifts
which our Lord Jesus Christ
has asked us to offer in his memory.
May our obedient service
bring us to the fullness of your redemption.
We ask this in the name of Jesus the Lord.
℟. **Amen.**   → No. 21, p. 22 (Pref. P 29-36)

COMMUNION ANT. Lam 3, 25   [Hope in the Lord]

The Lord is good to those who hope in him, to those who are searching for his love. ↓

OR See 1 Cor 10, 17   [One Bread, One Body]

Because there is one bread, we, though many, are one body, for we all share in the one loaf and in the one cup. ↓

PRAYER AFTER COMMUNION   [Eucharistic Life]

Almighty God,
let the eucharist we share
fill us with your life.
May the love of Christ
which we celebrate here
touch our lives and lead us to you.
We ask this in the name of Jesus the Lord.
℟. **Amen.**   → No. 32, p. 70

Optional Solemn Blessings, p. 92, and Prayers Over the People, p. 99

"Sell what you have and give to the poor . . . after that come and follow me."

OCTOBER 12

28th SUNDAY IN ORDINARY TIME

ENTRANCE ANT. Ps 130, 3-4   [A Forgiving God]

If you, O Lord, laid bare our guilt, who could endure it? But you are forgiving, God of Israel. → No. 2, p. 10

OPENING PRAYER   [Love in Action]

Let us pray
   [that God will help us to love one another]

Lord,
our help and guide,
make your love the foundation of our lives.
May our love for you express itself
in our eagerness to do good for others.
Grant this through our Lord Jesus Christ, your Son,
who lives and reigns with you and the Holy Spirit,
one God, for ever and ever. ℟. **Amen.** ↓

ALTERNATIVE OPENING PRAYER   [Sincerity]

Let us pray
   [in quiet for the grace of sincerity]
Father in heaven,
the hand of your loving kindness
powerfully yet gently guides all the moments of our day.
Go before us in our pilgrimage of life,
anticipate our needs and prevent our falling.
Send your Spirit to unite us in faith,
that sharing in your service,
we may rejoice in your presence.
We ask this through Christ our Lord. ℟. **Amen.** ↓

READING I Wis 7, 7-11   [Riches of Wisdom]

**To what can Wisdom be compared in value? She is above
all desires because in her all good things are found—
countless riches.**

A reading from the book of Wisdom

I PRAYED, and prudence was given me;
I pleaded, and the spirit of Wisdom came to me.
I preferred her to scepter and throne,
And deemed riches nothing in comparison with her,
   nor did I liken any priceless gem to her;
Because all gold, in view of her, is a little sand,
   and before her, silver is to be accounted mire.
Beyond health and comeliness I loved her,
And I chose to have her rather than the light,
   because the splendor of her never yields to sleep.

Yet all good things together came to me in her company,
and countless riches at her hands.
The word of the Lord. ℟. **Thanks be to God.** ↓

RESPONSORIAL PSALM Ps 90 [Filled with God's Love]

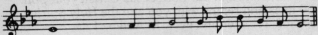

℟. **Fill us with your love, O Lord, and we will sing for joy!**

Teach us to number our days aright,
that we may gain wisdom of heart.
Return, O Lord! How long?
Have pity on your servants!—℟.

Fill us at daybreak with your kindness,
that we may shout for joy and gladness all our days.
Make us glad, for the days when you afflicted us,
for the years when we saw evil.

℟. **Fill us with your love, O Lord,
and we will sing for joy!**

Let your work be seen by your servants
and your glory by their children;
And may the gracious care of the Lord our God be ours;
prosper the work of our hands for us!
[Prosper the work of our hands!]

℟. **Fill us with your love, O Lord,
and we will sing for joy!** ↓

READING II Heb 4, 12-13 [God's Living Word]

God's word is penetrating and sharp. Nothing is hidden from God, and all must render an account to him.

A reading from the letter to the Hebrews

GOD'S word is living and effective, sharper than
any two-edged sword. It penetrates and divides

soul and spirit, joints and marrow; it judges the reflections and thoughts of the heart. Nothing is concealed from him; all lies bare and exposed to the eyes of him to whom we must render an account.—The word of the Lord. ℟. **Thanks be to God.** ↓

GOSPEL Mk 10, 17-30 or 10, 17-27   [All for God]
Alleluia (Mt 5, 3)
℟. **Alleluia.** Happy the poor in spirit;
the kingdom of heaven is theirs! ℟. **Alleluia.** ↓

> A rich man asks Jesus what he must do to be saved. Jesus answers—keep the commandments. The man says that he does. One thing more, then, Jesus lovingly continues—sell what you have and give to the poor. The man left. Jesus added how hard it is for a rich person to get to heaven.

[If the "Short Form" is used, the indented text in brackets is omitted.]

℣. The Lord be with you. ℟. **And also with you.**
✛ A reading from the holy gospel according to Mark.
℟. **Glory to you, Lord.**

AS Jesus was setting out on a journey a man came running up, knelt down before him and asked, "Good Teacher, what must I do to share in everlasting life?" Jesus answered, "Why do you call me good? No one is good but God alone. You know the commandments:

'You shall not kill;
You shall not commit adultery;
You shall not steal;
You shall not bear false witness;
You shall not defraud;
Honor your father and your mother.' "
He replied, "Teacher, I have observed all these since my childhood." Then Jesus looked at him with love

and told him, "There is one thing more you must do.
Go and sell what you have and give to the poor; you
will then have treasure in heaven. After that come and
follow me." At these words the man's face fell. He
went away sad, for he had many possessions. Jesus
looked around and said to his disciples, "How hard it
is for the rich to enter the kingdom of God!" The disciples could only marvel at his words. So Jesus repeated
what he had said: "My sons, how hard it is to enter the
kingdom of God! It is easier for a camel to pass
through a needle's eye than for a rich man to enter the
kingdom of God."

They were completely overwhelmed at this, and exclaimed to one another, "Then who can be saved?"
Jesus fixed his gaze on them and said, "For man it is
impossible but not for God. With God all things are
possible."

   [Peter was moved to say to him, "We have put
   aside everything to follow you!" Jesus answered:
   "I give you my word, there is no one who has
   given up home, brothers or sisters, mother or
   father, children or property, for me and for the
   gospel who will not receive in this present age a
   hundred times as many homes, brothers and sisters, mothers, children, and property—and persecution besides—and in the age to come, everlasting life."]

The gospel of the Lord. ℟. **Praise to you, Lord Jesus
Christ.**   → No. 14, p. 18

PRAYER OVER THE GIFTS   [Faith and Love]

Lord,
accept the prayers and gifts
we offer in faith and love.
May this eucharist bring us to your glory.
We ask this in the name of Jesus the Lord.
℟. **Amen.**   → No. 21, p. 22 (Pref. P 29-36)

COMMUNION ANT. Ps 34, 11   [God's Providence]

The rich suffer want and go hungry, but nothing shall
be lacking to those who fear the Lord. ↓

OR 1 Jn 3, 2   [Vision of God]

When the Lord is revealed we shall be like him, for
we shall see him as he is. ↓

PRAYER AFTER COMMUNION   [Christ's Life]

Almighty Father,
may the body and blood of your Son
give us a share in his life,
for he is Lord for ever and ever.
℞. **Amen.**   → No. 32, p. 70

Optional Solemn Blessings, p. 92, and Prayers Over the People, p. 99

"Sitting at my right or my left is not mine to give."

OCTOBER 19

29th SUNDAY IN ORDINARY TIME

ENTRANCE ANT. Ps 17, 6. 8   [Refuge in God]

I call upon you, God, for you will answer me; bend
your ear and hear my prayer. Guard me as the pupil
of your eye; hide me in the shade of your wings.

→ No. 2, p. 10

OPENING PRAYER   [Faithful Service]

Let us pray
  [for the gift of simplicity and joy
  in our service of God and man]
Almighty and ever-living God,
our source of power and inspiration,
give us strength and joy
in serving you as followers of Christ,
who lives and reigns with you and the Holy Spirit,
one God, for ever and ever. ℟. **Amen.** ↓

ALTERNATIVE OPENING PRAYER   [Spiritual Sight]

Let us pray
  [to the Lord who bends close to hear our prayer]
Lord our God, Father of all,
you guard us under the shadow of your wings
and search into the depths of our hearts.
Remove the blindness that cannot know you
and relieve the fear that would hide us from your sight.
We ask this through Christ our Lord. ℟. **Amen.** ↓

READING I Is 53, 10-11   [The Servant of Yahweh]

**The suffering servant speaks of his life as a sin offering
that his people may prosper enjoying a long life. Through
his suffering he will bear the guilt of many.**

A reading from the book of the prophet Isaiah

[B UT the Lord was pleased
to crush him in infirmity.]
If he gives his life as an offering for sin,
  he shall see his descendants in a long life,
    and the will of the Lord shall be accomplished
    through him.
Because of his affliction
  he shall see the light in fullness of days;
Through his suffering, my servant shall justify many,
  and their guilt he shall bear.
The word of the Lord. ℟. **Thanks be to God.** ↓

RESPONSORIAL PSALM Ps 33   [Trust in God]

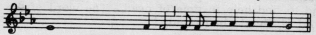

℟. **Lord, let your mercy be on us, as we place our trust in you.**

Upright is the word of the Lord,
  and all his works are trustworthy.
He loves justice and right;
  of the kindness of the Lord the earth is full.

℟. **Lord, let your mercy be on us,
  as we place our trust in you.**

See, the eyes of the Lord are upon those who fear him,
  upon those who hope for his kindness,
To deliver them from death
  and preserve them in spite of famine.

℟. **Lord, let your mercy be on us,
  as we place our trust in you.**

Our soul waits for the Lord,
  who is our help and our shield.
May your kindness, O Lord, be upon us,
  who have put our hope in you.

℟. **Lord, let your mercy be on us,
  as we place our trust in you.** ↓

READING II Heb 4, 14-16   [Jesus Our High Priest]

Jesus Christ, the Son of God, is the high priest who shares
all our weaknesses, except sin. His mercy comes to all who
seek it.

A reading from the letter to the Hebrews

WE have a great high priest who has passed
  through the heavens, Jesus, the Son of God; let
us hold fast to our profession of faith. For we do not
have a high priest who is unable to sympathize with
our weakness, but one who was tempted in every way
that we are, yet never sinned. So let us confidently ap-

proach the throne of grace to receive mercy and favor and to find help in time of need.—The word of the Lord. ℟. **Thanks be to God.** ↓

GOSPEL Mk 10, 35-45 or 10, 42-45   [Greatness in Serving]
Alleluia (Mk 10, 45)

℟. **Alleluia.** The Son of Man has come to serve and to give his life for the redemption of many. ℟. **Alleluia.** ↓

James and John request a special honor in the kingdom of heaven. Jesus reminds them and the other ten that anyone who aspires to greatness must be prepard to serve first.

[If the "Short Form" is used, the indented text in brackets is omitted.]

℣. The Lord be with you. ℟. **And also with you.**
✛ A reading from the holy gospel according to Mark.
℟. **Glory to you, Lord.**

[ZEBEDEE'S sons, James and John, approached Jesus. "Teacher," they said, "we want you to grant our request." "What is it?" he asked. They replied, "See to it that we sit, one at your right and the other at your left, when you come into your glory." Jesus told them, "You do not know what you are asking. Can you drink the cup I shall drink or be baptized in the same bath of pain as I?" "We can," they told him. Jesus said in response, "From the cup I drink of you shall drink; the bath I am immersed in you shall share. But sitting at my right or my left is not mine to give; that is for those for whom it has been reserved." The other ten, on hearing this, became indignant at James and John.]

Jesus called them together and said to them: "You know how among the Gentiles those who seem to exercise authority lord it over them; their great ones make their importance felt. It cannot be like that with you. Anyone among you who aspires to greatness must serve the rest; whoever wants to rank first among you must serve the needs of all. The Son of Man has not come to be served but to serve—to give his life in ransom for the many."—The gospel of the Lord. ℟. **Praise to you, Lord Jesus Christ.**

→ No. 14, p. 18

PRAYER OVER THE GIFTS   [Lives of Service]

Lord God,
may the gifts we offer
bring us your love and forgiveness
and give us freedom to serve you with our lives.
We ask this in the name of Jesus the Lord.
℟. **Amen.**   → No. 21, p. 22 (Pref. P 29-36)

COMMUNION ANT. Ps 33, 18-19   [Divine Protection]

See how the eyes of the Lord are on those who fear him, on those who hope in his love, that he may rescue them from death and feed them in time of famine. ↓

OR Mk 10, 45   [Christ Our Ransom]

The Son of Man came to give his life as a ransom for many. ↓

PRAYER AFTER COMMUNION   [Fidelity]

Lord,
may this eucharist help us to remain faithful.
May it teach us the way to eternal life.
Grant this through Christ our Lord.
℟. **Amen.**   → No. 32, p. 70

Optional Solemn Blessings, p. 92, and Prayers Over the People, p. 99

"Jesus, Son of David, have pity on me!"

OCTOBER 26

30th SUNDAY IN ORDINARY TIME

ENTRANCE ANT. Ps 105, 3-4   **[Seek the Lord]**

Let hearts rejoice who search for the Lord. Seek the Lord and his strength, seek always the face of the Lord.   → No. 2, p. 10

OPENING PRAYER   **[Doing God's Will]**

Let us pray
   [for the strength to do God's will]
Almighty and ever-living God,
strengthen our faith, hope, and love.
May we do with loving hearts
what you ask of us
and come to share the life you promise.
We ask this . . . for ever and ever. ℟. **Amen.** ↓

ALTERNATIVE OPENING PRAYER   **[Faith and Love]**

Let us pray
   [in humble hope for salvation]
Praised be you, God and Father of our Lord Jesus Christ.
There is no power for good
which does not come from your covenant,

and no promise to hope in
that your love has not offered.
Strengthen our faith to accept your covenant
and give us the love to carry out your command.
We ask this through Christ our Lord. ℟. **Amen.** ↓

READING I Jer 31, 7-9   [God's Deliverance]

Jeremiah's hymn opens with joy for God has bestowed salvation on his people. He has delivered his people and will guide and bless them so none will go astray.

A reading from the book of the prophet Jeremiah

THUS says the Lord:
    Shout with joy for Jacob,
    exult at the head of the nations;
    proclaim your praise and say:
The Lord has delivered his people,
    the remnant of Israel.
Behold, I will bring them back
    from the land of the north;
I will gather them from the ends of the world
    with the blind and the lame in their midst,
The mothers and those with child;
    they shall return as an immense throng.
They departed in tears,
    but I will console them and guide them;
I will lead them to brooks of water,
    on a level road, so that none shall stumble.
For I am a father to Israel,
    Ephraim is my first-born.
The word of the Lord. ℟. **Thanks be to God.** ↓

RESPONSORIAL PSALM Ps 126   [God's Mighty Works]

℟. The Lord has done great things for us; we are filled with joy.

When the Lord brought back the captives of Zion
    we were like men dreaming.

Then our mouth was filled with laughter,
and our tongue with rejoicing.—R).

Then they said among the nations,
"The Lord has done great things for them."
The Lord has done great things for us;
we are glad indeed.—R).

Restore our fortunes, O Lord,
like the torrents in the southern desert.
Those that sow in tears
shall reap rejoicing.—R).

Although they go forth weeping,
carrying the seed to be sown,
They shall come back rejoicing,
carrying their sheaves.—R). ↓

READING II Heb 5, 1-6   [Christ the Mediator]

Every high priest is designated by God. He is selected from among the people to be their mediator with God. No one takes this honor by himself.

A reading from the letter to the Hebrews

EVERY high priest is taken from among men and made their representative before God, to offer gifts and sacrifices for sins. He is able to deal patiently with erring sinners, for he is himself beset by weakness and so must make sin offerings for himself as well as for the people. One does not take this honor on his own initiative, but only when called by God as Aaron was. Even Christ did not glorify himself with the office of high priest; he received it from the One who said to him,

"You are my son;
today I have begotten you";
just as he says in another place,
"You are a priest forever,
according to the order of Melchizedek."
The word of the Lord. R). **Thanks be to God.** ↓

GOSPEL Mk 10, 46-52   [Healing of a Blind Man]
Alleluia (2 Tm 1, 10)

℟. **Alleluia.**   Our Savior Jesus Christ has done away
   with death,
and brought us life through his gospel. ℟. **Alleluia.** ↓

> Bartimaeus, a blind man, hearing Jesus called out loudly,
> "Jesus, Son of David, have pity on me!" Jesus summoned
> him and, seeing his faith, cured him. Bartimaeus followed
> Jesus.

℣. The Lord be with you. ℟. **And also with you.**
✝ A reading from the holy gospel according to Mark.
℟. **Glory to you, Lord.**

AS Jesus was leaving Jericho with his disciples and
a sizable crowd, there was a blind beggar Barti-
maeus ("son of Timaeus") sitting by the roadside. On
hearing that it was Jesus of Nazareth, he began to call
out, "Jesus, Son of David, have pity on me!" Many
people were scolding him to make him keep quiet, but
he shouted all the louder, "Son of David, have pity on
me!" Then Jesus stopped and said, "Call him over." So
they called the blind man over, telling him as they did
so, "You have nothing whatever to fear from him! Get
up! He is calling you!" He threw aside his cloak,
jumped up and came to Jesus. Jesus asked him, "What
do you want me to do for you?" "Rabboni," the blind
man said, "I want to see." Jesus said in reply, "Be on
your way. Your faith has healed you." Immediately he
received his sight and started to follow him up the
road.—The gospel of the Lord. ℟. **Praise to you, Lord
Jesus Christ.**

→ No. 14, p. 18

PRAYER OVER THE GIFTS   [Glorifying God]

Lord God of power and might,
receive the gifts we offer
and let our service give you glory.
Grant this through Christ our Lord.
℟. **Amen.**   → No. 21, p. 22 (Pref. P 29-36)

COMMUNION ANT. Ps 20, 6   [Victory of God]

We will rejoice at the victory of God and make our boast in his great name. ↓

OR Eph 5, 2   [Christ's Offering for Us]

Christ loved us and gave himself up for us as a fragrant offering to God. ↓

PRAYER AFTER COMMUNION   [Effective Communion]

Lord,
bring to perfection within us
the communion we share in this sacrament.
May our celebration have an effect in our lives.
We ask this in the name of Jesus the Lord.
℟. **Amen.**   → No. 32, p. 70

Optional Solemn Blessings, p. 92, and Prayers Over the People, p. 99

"Blest are the single-hearted, for they shall see God."

NOVEMBER 1

ALL SAINTS

ENTRANCE ANT.   [Honoring All the Saints]

Let us all rejoice in the Lord and keep a festival in honor of all the saints. Let us join with the angels in joyful praise to the Son of God.   → No. 2, p. 10

OPENING PRAYER   [Forgiveness and Love]

Let us pray
  [that the prayers of all the saints
  will bring us forgiveness for our sins]
Father, all-powerful and ever-living God,
today we rejoice in the holy men and women
of every time and place.
May their prayers bring us your forgiveness and love.
We ask this . . . for ever and ever. ℟. **Amen.** ↓

ALTERNATIVE OPENING PRAYER   [Sharing Saints' Peace]

Let us pray
[as we rejoice and keep festival
in honor of all the saints]
God our Father,
source of all holiness
the work of your hands is manifest in your saints,
the beauty of your truth is reflected in their faith.
May we who aspire to have part in their joy
be filled with the Spirit that blessed their lives,
so that having shared their faith on earth
we may also know their peace in your kingdom.
Grant this through Christ our Lord. ℟. **Amen.** ↓

READING I Rv 7, 2-4. 9-14   [A Huge Crowd of Saints]

**The elect give thanks to God and the Lamb who saved
them. The whole court of heaven joins the acclamation of
the saints.**

A reading from the book of Revelation

I, JOHN, saw another angel come from the east holding the seal of the living God. He cried out at the
top of his voice to the four angels who were given
power to ravage the land and the sea, "Do no harm to
the land or the sea or the trees until we imprint this
seal on the foreheads of the servants of our God." I
heard the number of those who were so marked—one

hundred and forty-four thousand from every tribe of Israel.

After this I saw before me a huge crowd which no one could count from every nation, race, people, and tongue. They stood before the throne and the Lamb, dressed in long white robes and holding palm branches in their hands. They cried out in a loud voice, "Salvation is from our God, who is seated on the throne, and from the Lamb!" All the angels who were standing around the throne and the elders and the four living creatures fell down before the throne to worship God. They said: "Amen! Praise and glory, wisdom, thanksgiving, and honor, power and might to our God forever and ever. Amen!"

Then one of the elders asked me, "Who do you think these are, all dressed in white? And where have they come from?" I said to him, "Sir, you should know better than I." He then told me, "These are the ones who have survived the great period of trial; they have washed their robes and made them white in the blood of the Lamb."—The word of the Lord. ℟. **Thanks be to God.** ↓

RESPONSORIAL PSALM Ps 24   [Longing To See God]

℟. **Lord, this is the peo-ple that longs to see your face.**

The Lord's are the earth and its fullness
    the world and those who dwell in it.
For he founded it upon the seas
    and established it upon the rivers.

℟. **Lord, this is the people that longs to see your face.**

Who can ascend the mountain of the Lord?
    or who may stand in his holy place?
He whose hands are sinless, whose heart is clean,
    who desires not what is vain.

℟. **Lord, this is the people that longs to see your face.**

He shall receive a blessing from the Lord,
  a reward from God his Savior.
Such is the race that seeks for him,
  that seeks the face of the God of Jacob.

℟. **Lord, this is the people that longs to see your
  face.** ↓

READING II 1 Jn 3, 1-3   [We Shall See God]

God's gift of love has been the gift of His only Son as Savior of the world. It is this gift that has made it possible for
us to be called the children of God.

A reading from the first letter of John

SEE what love the Father has bestowed on us
  in letting us be called children of God!
Yet that in fact is what we are.
The reason the world does not recognize us
is that it never recognized the Son.
Dearly beloved
we are God's children now;
what we shall later be has not yet come to light.
We know that when it comes to light
we shall be like him
for we shall see him as he is.
Everyone who has this hope based on him
keeps himself pure, as he is pure.
The word of the Lord. ℟. **Thanks be to God.** ↓

GOSPEL Mt 5, 1-12   [The Beatitudes]
Alleluia (Mt 11, 28)
℟. **Alleluia.** Come to me, all you that labor and are
  burdened,
and I will give you rest, says the Lord. ℟. **Alleluia.** ↓

Jesus is meant to be the new Moses proclaiming the new
revelation on a new Mt. Sinai. This is the proclamation of

the reign, or the "Good News." Blessings are pronounced on those who do not share the values of the world.

℣. The Lord be with you. ℟. **And also with you.**

✠ A reading from the holy gospel according to Matthew. ℟. **Glory to you, Lord.**

WHEN Jesus saw the crowds he went up the mountainside. After he had sat down his disciples gathered around him, and he began to teach them:

"How blest are the poor in spirit: the reign of God is theirs.

Blest too are the sorrowing; they shall be consoled.

[Blest are the lowly, they shall inherit the land.]

Blest are they who hunger and thirst for holiness; they shall have their fill.

Blest are they who show mercy; mercy shall be theirs.

Blest are the single-hearted, for they shall see God.

Blest too the peacemakers; they shall be called sons of God.

Blest are those persecuted for holiness' sake; the reign of God is theirs.

Blest are you when they insult you and persecute you and utter every kind of slander against you because of me.

Be glad and rejoice, for your reward in heaven is great."

The gospel of the Lord. ℟. **Praise to you, Lord Jesus Christ.**   → No. 14, p. 18

PRAYER OVER THE GIFTS   [The Saints' Concern for Us]

Lord,
receive our gifts in honor of the holy men and women who live with you in glory.
May we always be aware
of their concern to help and save us.
We ask this in the name of Jesus the Lord. ℟. **Amen.** ↓

PREFACE (P 71)   [Saints Give Us Help and Encouragement]

℣. The Lord be with you. ℟. **And also with you.**
℣. Lift up your hearts. ℟. **We lift them up to the Lord.**
℣. Let us give thanks to the Lord our God. ℟. **It is right to give him thanks and praise.**

Father, all-powerful and ever-living God,
we do well always and everywhere to give you thanks.
Today we keep the festival of your holy city,
the heavenly Jerusalem, our mother.
Around your throne
the saints, our brothers and sisters,
sing your praise for ever.
Their glory fills us with joy,
and their communion with us in your Church
gives us inspiration and strength,
as we hasten on our pilgrimage of faith,
eager to meet them.
With their great company and all the angels
we praise your glory
as we cry out with one voice: → No. 23, p. 23

COMMUNION ANT. Mt 5, 8-10   [The Saints: Children of God]
**Happy are the pure of heart for they shall see God.
Happy the peacemakers; they shall be called sons of
God. Happy are they who suffer persecution for jus-
tice' sake; the kingdom of heaven is theirs.** ↓

PRAYER AFTER COMMUNION   [Reflectors of God's Glory]
Father, holy one,
we praise your glory reflected in the saints.
May we who share at this table
be filled with your love
and prepared for the joy of your kingdom,
where Jesus is Lord for ever and ever.
℟. **Amen.**   → No. 32, p. 70

Optional Solemn Blessings, p. 92, and Prayers Over the People, p. 99

"Give them eternal rest, O Lord . . . ."

NOVEMBER 2

ALL SOULS

(31st SUNDAY IN ORDINARY TIME)

1

ENTRANCE ANT. 1 Thes 4, 14; 1 Cor 15, 22   [Life in Christ]

Just as Jesus died and rose again, so will the Father bring with him those who have died in Jesus. Just as in Adam all men die, so in Christ all will be made alive. → No. 2, p. 10

OPENING PRAYER [For All the Departed]

Let us pray
  [for all our departed brothers and sisters]
Merciful Father,
hear our prayers and console us.
As we renew our faith in your Son,
whom you raised from the dead,
strengthen our hope that all our departed brothers
   and sisters
will share in his resurrection,
who lives and reigns with you and the Holy Spirit,
one God, for ever and ever. ℞. **Amen.** ↓

The readings found in Masses 2 and 3 may also be used.

READING I Jb 19, 1. 23-27   [I Shall See God]

This is one of the clearest texts of the Old Testament about God's future vindication of the just. It is not as clear as later New Testament texts, but it does emphatically proclaim existence after death and our vision of God.

A reading from the book of Job

JOB answered and said:
   Oh, would that my words were written down!
Would that they were inscribed in a record:
That with an iron chisel and with lead
   they were cut in the rock forever!
But as for me, I know that my Vindicator lives,
   and that he will at last stand forth upon the dust;
Whom I myself shall see:
   my own eyes, not another's, shall behold him,
And from my flesh I shall see God;
   my inmost being is consumed with longing.
The word of the Lord. ℟. **Thanks be to God.** ↓

RESPONSORIAL PSALM Ps 23   [Fearing No Evil]

℟. The Lord is my shep-herd; there is noth-ing I shall want.

The Lord is my shepherd; I shall not want.
   In verdant pastures he gives me repose;
Beside restful waters he leads me;
   he refreshes my soul.—℟.

He guides me in right paths
   for his name's sake.
Even though I walk in the dark valley
   I fear no evil; for you are at my side
With your rod and your staff
   that give me courage.—℟.

You spread the table before me
in the sight of my foes;
You anoint my head with oil;
my cup overflows.—R⫯.

Only goodness and kindness follow me
all the days of my life;
And I shall dwell in the house of the Lord
for years to come.—R⫯. ↓

R⫯. Or: **Though I walk in the valley of darkness,
I fear no evil, for you are with me.** ↓

READING II 1 Cor 15, 51-57　　[O Death, Where Is Your Victory?]

St. Paul tells us that our risen body will be a body so
changed by the power of God as to be immortal. Christ
died for sin which is the cause of our death; he rose from
the dead to be the cause of our resurrection.

A reading from the first letter of Paul
to the Corinthians

I AM going to tell you a mystery. Not all of us shall
fall asleep, but all of us are to be changed—in an instant, in the twinkling of an eye, at the sound of the
last trumpet. The trumpet will sound and the dead will
be raised incorruptible, and we shall be changed. This
corruptible body must be clothed with incorruptibility,
this mortal body with immortality. When the corruptible frame takes on incorruptibility and the mortal immortality, then will the saying of Scripture be fulfilled:
"Death is swallowed up in victory." "O death, where is
your victory? O death, where is your sting?" The sting
of death is sin, and sin gets its power from the law.
But thanks be to God who has given us the victory
through our Lord Jesus Christ.—The word of the
Lord. R⫯. **Thanks be to God.** ↓

GOSPEL Jn 6, 37-40　　　　[Eternal Life for Believers]
Alleluia (Mt 25, 34)

R̶. **Alleluia.** Come, you whom my Father has blessed,
   says the Lord;
inherit the kingdom prepared for you since the foundation of the world. R̶. **Alleluia.** ↓

> Jesus here indicates that God wills to save all people.
> Everyone who approaches the Son and believes in him will
> be raised up on the last day to the glory of eternal life.

V̶. The Lord be with you. R̶. **And also with you.**
✝ A reading from the holy gospel according to John.
R̶. **Glory to you, Lord.**

JESUS said to the crowd:
   "All that the Father gives me shall come to me;
no one who comes will I ever reject,
because it is not to do my own will
that I have come down from heaven,
but to do the will of him who sent me.
It is the will of him who sent me
that I should lose nothing of what he has given me;
rather, that I should raise it up on the last day.
Indeed, this is the will of my Father,
that everyone who looks upon the Son
and believes in him
shall have eternal life.
Him I will raise up on the last day."
The gospel of the Lord. R̶. **Praise to you, Lord Jesus
Christ.**   → No. 14, p. 18

PRAYER OVER THE GIFTS   [United in Christ's Love]
Lord,
we are united in this sacrament
by the love of Jesus Christ.
Accept these gifts
and receive our brothers and sisters
into the glory of your Son,
who is Lord for ever and ever.
R̶. **Amen.**   → No. 21, p. 22 (Pref. P 77-81)

COMMUNION ANT. Jn 11, 25-26 [The Resurrection and the Life]

I am the resurrection and the life, says the Lord. If anyone believes in me, even though he dies, he will live. Anyone who lives and believes in me will not die. ↓

PRAYER AFTER COMMUNION   [Christ's Peace]

Lord God,
may the death and resurrection of Christ
which we celebrate in this eucharist
bring the departed faithful to the peace of your eternal
    home.
We ask this in the name of Jesus the Lord.
℞. Amen.   → No. 32, p. 70

Optional Solemn Blessings, p. 92, and Prayers Over the People, p. 99

ALL SOULS
2

ENTRANCE ANT. See 4 Ezr 2, 34-35   [Eternal Rest]

Give them eternal rest, O Lord, and may your light
shine on them for ever.   → No. 2, p. 10

OPENING PRAYER   [For All the Departed]

Let us pray
    [for all our departed brothers and sisters]
Lord God,
you are the glory of believers
and the life of the just.
Your Son redeemed us
by dying and rising to life again.
Since our departed brothers and sisters believed in the
    mystery of our resurrection,
let them share the joys and blessings of the life to come.
We ask this . . . for ever and ever. ℞. **Amen.** ↓

The readings found in Masses 1 and 3 may also be used.

READING I Wis 3, 1-9 or 3, 1-6. 9   [In God's Care]

In contrast to the illusions of worldly wisdom, the "hope" of those who have known and believed in God is "full of immortality." After being tried by God they will reap their reward.

(SHORT FORM)

A reading from the book of Wisdom

THE souls of the just are in the hand of God,
    and no torment shall touch them.
They seemed, in the view of the foolish, to be dead;
    and their passing away was thought an affliction
    and their going forth from us, utter destruction.
But they are in peace.
For if before men, indeed, they be punished,
    yet is their hope full of immortality;
Chastised a little, they shall be greatly blessed,
    because God tried them
    and found them worthy of himself.
As gold in the furnace, he proved them,
    and as sacrificial offerings he took them to himself.
Because grace and mercy are with his holy ones,
    and his care is with his elect.
The word of the Lord. ℟. **Thanks be to God.** ↓

RESPONSORIAL PSALM Pss 115; 116   [In the Land of Living]

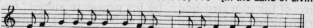

℟. I will walk in the pres-ence of the Lord, in the land of the liv-ing.

They have mouths but speak not;
    they have eyes but see not;
They have ears but hear not;
    they have noses but smell not.

℟. **I will walk in the presence of the Lord,
    in the land of the living.**

I believed, even when I said,
  "I am greatly afflicted";
I said in my alarm,
  "No man is dependable."

℟. **I will walk in the presence of the Lord,**
  in the land of the living.

Precious in the eyes of the Lord
  is the death of his faithful ones.
O Lord, I am your servant;
  you have loosed my bonds.

℟. **I will walk in the presence of the Lord,**
  in the land of the living. ↓

℟. Or: **Alleluia.** ↓

READING II Phil 3, 20-21   **[Citizenship in Heaven]**

> **While toiling for the building up of this earth, Christians know that their ultimate citizenship is in heaven. Salvation does not lie in the body but in Christ, who at his second coming will transform the body of all his faithful to be like his glorious body.**

A reading from the letter of Paul
to the Philippians

W̲E have our citizenship in heaven; it is from there
  that we eagerly await the coming of our Savior,
the Lord Jesus Christ. He will give a new form to this
lowly body of ours and remake it according to the pattern of his glorified body, by his power to subject everything to himself.—The word of the Lord. ℟. **Thanks
be to God.** ↓

GOSPEL Jn 11, 17-27 or 11, 21-27   **[Rising with Christ]**
Alleluia (Jn 11, 25. 26)
℟. **Alleluia.** I am the resurrection and the life, said the
  Lord:
he who believes in me will not die for ever. ℟. **Al-
leluia.** ↓

Amid the human continuous quest for immortality, there is only one who can impart it to us: Jesus, "the resurrection and the life." And this immortality will be coupled with a joy without end.

℣. The Lord be with you. ℟. **And also with you.**

✝ A reading from the holy gospel according to John.
℟. **Glory to you, Lord.**

(SHORT FORM)

MARTHA said to Jesus, "Lord, if you had been here, my brother would never have died. Even now, I am sure that God will give you whatever you ask of him." "Your brother will rise again," Jesus assured her. "I know he will rise again," Martha replied, "in the resurrection on the last day." Jesus told her:
  "I am the resurrection and the life:
  whoever believes in me,
  though he should die, will come to life;
  and whoever is alive and believes in me
  will never die.
"Do you believe this?" "Yes, Lord," she replied. "I have come to believe that you are the Messiah, the Son of God: he who is to come into the world."—The gospel of the Lord. ℟. **Praise to you, Lord Jesus Christ.**

→ No. 14, p. 18

PRAYER OVER THE GIFTS   [Pardon and Peace]

All-powerful Father,
may this sacrifice wash away
the sins of our departed brothers and sisters in the
  blood of Christ.
You cleansed them in the waters of baptism.
In your loving mercy grant them pardon and peace.
We ask this in the name of Jesus the Lord.
℟. **Amen.**

→ No. 21, p. 22 (Pref. P 77-81)

COMMUNION ANT. See 4 Ezr 2, 35. 34   [Eternal Light]

May eternal light shine on them, O Lord, with all your saints for ever, for you are rich in mercy. Give them eternal rest, O Lord, and may perpetual light shine on them for ever, for you are rich in mercy. ↓

PRAYER AFTER COMMUNION   [For All the Departed]

Lord,
in this sacrament you give us your crucified and risen
  Son.
Bring to the glory of the resurrection our departed
  brothers and sisters
who have been purified by this holy mystery.
Grant this through Christ our Lord.
℟. **Amen.**   → No. 32, p. 70

Optional Solemn Blessings, p. 92, and Prayers Over the People, p. 99

ALL SOULS
3

ENTRANCE ANT. Rom 8, 11   [New Life through the Spirit]

God, who raised Jesus from the dead, will give new life to our own mortal bodies through his Spirit living in us.   → No. 2, p. 10

OPENING PRAYER   [For All the Departed]

Let us pray
  [for all our departed brothers and sisters]
God, our creator and redeemer,
by your power Christ conquered death
and returned to you in glory.
May all your people who have gone before us in faith
share his victory
and enjoy the vision of your glory for ever.
We ask this through our Lord Jesus Christ, your Son,
who lives and reigns with you and the Holy Spirit,
one God, for ever and ever. ℟. **Amen.** ↓

The readings found in Masses 1 and 2 may also be used.

READING I 2 Mc 12, 43-46   [Value of Prayer for the Dead]

This is the earliest statement of the doctrine that prayers and sacrifices for the dead are beneficial. It is a holy and pious thought to think of the dead.

A reading from the second book of Maccabees

JUDAS [the ruler of Israel] then took up a collection among all his soldiers, amounting to two thousand silver drachmas, which he sent to Jerusalem to provide for an expiatory sacrifice. In doing this he acted in a very excellent and noble way, inasmuch as he had the resurrection of the dead in view; for if he were not expecting the fallen to rise again, it would have been useless and foolish to pray for them in death. But if he did this with a view to the splendid reward that awaits those who had gone to rest in godliness, it was a holy and pious thought. Thus he made atonement for the dead that they might be freed from this sin.—The word of the Lord. ℟. **Thanks be to God.** ↓

RESPONSORIAL PSALM Ps 130   [Hope in the Lord]

℟.   **Out of   the depths, I   cry   to   you, Lord.**

I trust in the Lord;
    my soul trusts in his word.
My soul waits for the Lord
    more than sentinels wait for the dawn.
More than sentinels wait for the dawn,
    let Israel hope in the Lord.

℟. **Out of the depths, I cry to you, Lord.**

For with the Lord is kindness
    and with him is plenteous redemption;
And he will redeem Israel
    from all their iniquities.

℟. **Out of the depths, I cry to you, Lord.** ↓

℟. Or: **I hope in the Lord.**
I trust in his word. ↓

READING II Rv 14, 13   [Happy Those Who Die in the Lord]

In addition to faith in Jesus there is also need of good
works. These will accompany the doers after death to their
advantage. Happy are the dead who die thus in the Lord.

A reading from the book of Revelation

I, JOHN, heard a voice from heaven say to me:
"Write this down: Happy now are the dead who die
in the Lord!" The Spirit added, "Yes, they shall find
rest from their labors, for their good works accompany them."—The word of the Lord. ℟. **Thanks be to
God.** ↓

GOSPEL Jn 14, 1-6   [A Place for Us]
Alleluia (Phil 3, 20)
℟. **Alleluia.** Our true home is in heaven,
and Jesus Christ whose return we long for
will come from heaven to save us. ℟. **Alleluia.** ↓

Jesus is our way, truth and life who has preceded us to our
Father's heavenly house in order to prepare a place also for
us. If we trust in him we will safely reach our home at our
journey's end.

℣. The Lord be with you. ℟. **And also with you.**
✝ A reading from the holy gospel according to John.
℟. **Glory to you, Lord.**

JESUS said to his disciples:
"Do not let your hearts be troubled.
Have faith in God
and faith in me.
In my Father's house there are many dwelling
    places;
otherwise, how could I have told you
that I was going to prepare a place for you?

I am indeed going to prepare a place for you,
and then I shall come back to take you with me,
that where I am you also may be.
You know the way that leads where I go."

"Lord," said Thomas, "we do not know where you
are going. How can we know the way?" Jesus told him:
"I am the way, and the truth, and the life;
no one comes to the Father but through me."

The gospel of the Lord. ℟. **Praise to you, Lord Jesus
Christ.**
→ No. 14, p. 18

PRAYER OVER THE GIFTS   [Eternal Life]

Lord,
in your kindness accept these gifts for our departed
    brothers and sisters
and for all who sleep in Christ.
May his perfect sacrifice
free them from the power of death
and give them eternal life.
We ask this in the name of Jesus the Lord.
℟. **Amen.**
→ No. 21, p. 22 (Pref. P 77-81)

COMMUNION ANT. Phil 3, 20-21   [Copies of Christ's Body]

**We are waiting for our Savior, the Lord Jesus Christ;
he will transfigure our lowly bodies into copies of his
own glorious body.** ↓

PRAYER AFTER COMMUNION   [Peace and Forgiveness]

Lord,
may our sacrifice bring peace and forgiveness
to our brothers and sisters who have died.
Bring the new life given to them in baptism
to the fullness of eternal joy.
We ask this through Christ our Lord.
℟. **Amen.**
→ No. 32, p. 70

Optional Solemn Blessings, p. 92, and Prayers Over the People, p. 99

"Zacchaeus, hurry down. I mean to stay at your house today."

NOVEMBER 9

DEDICATION OF ST. JOHN LATERAN

(32nd SUNDAY IN ORDINARY TIME)

ENTRANCE ANT. Rv 21, 2   [The New Jerusalem]

I saw the holy city, new Jerusalem, coming down from God out of heaven, like a bride adorned in readiness for her husband. → No. 2, p. 10

OPENING PRAYER   [A Temple of People]

God our Father,
from living stones, your chosen people,
you built an eternal temple to your glory.
Increase the spiritual gifts you have given to your
   Church,
so that your faithful people may continue to grow
into the new and eternal Jerusalem.
We ask this . . . for ever and ever. R̸. **Amen.** ↓

OR   [A Church of People]

Father,
you called your people to be your Church.

494

As we gather together in your name,
may we love, honor, and follow you
to eternal life in the kingdom you promise.
Grant this through our Lord Jesus Christ, your Son
who lives and reigns with you and the Holy Spirit,
one God, for ever and ever. ℟. **Amen.** ↓

Other readings may also be chosen.

READING I 2 Chr 5, 6-10. 13—6, 2   [The Lord's Dwelling]

The cloud of God's Presence, which filled the temple of Solomon, is a reminder that in order to pray we must enter that "cloud" and put aside all distraction.

A reading from the second book of Chronicles

KING Solomon and the entire community of Israel gathered about him before the ark were sacrificing sheep and oxen so numerous that they could not be counted or numbered. The priests brought the ark of the covenant of the Lord to its place beneath the wings of the cherubim in the sanctuary, the holy of holies of the temple. The cherubim had their wings spread out over the place of the ark, sheltering the ark and its poles from above. The poles were long enough so that their ends could be seen from that part of the holy place nearest the sanctuary; however, they could not be seen beyond. The ark has remained there to this day. There was nothing in it but the two tablets which Moses put there on Horeb, the tablets of the covenant which the Lord made with the Israelites at their departure from Egypt.

When the trumpeters and singers were heard as a single voice praising and giving thanks to the Lord, and when they raised the sound of the trumpets, cymbals and other musical instruments to "give thanks to the Lord, for he is good, for his mercy endures forever," the building of the Lord's temple was filled with a cloud. The priests could not continue to minister because of the cloud, since the Lord's glory filled the house of God.

Then Solomon said: "The Lord intends to dwell in the dark cloud. I have truly built you a princely house and dwelling, where you may abide forever."—The word of the Lord. ℟. **Thanks be to God.** ↓

RESPONSORIAL PSALM Ps 84   [Yearning for God's Dwelling]

℟. **How lovely is your dwel-ling-place, Lord, might-y God!**

My soul yearns and pines
for the courts of the Lord.
My heart and my flesh
cry out for the living God.—℟.

Even the sparrow finds a home,
and the swallow a nest
in which she puts her young—
Your altars, O Lord of hosts,
my king and my God!—℟.

Happy they who dwell in your house!
continually they praise you.
Happy the men whose strength you are!
They go from strength to strength.—℟.

I had rather one day in your courts
than a thousand elsewhere;
I had rather lie at the threshold of the house of my
God
than dwell in the tents of the wicked.—℟. ↓

℟. Or: **Here God lives among his people.** ↓

READING II 1 Cor 3, 9-13. 16-17   [God's Building]
    Paul elaborates on the temple figure, of which your parish church is a sign. God's people can only be a solid building, in which the Spirit of God dwells, if it is built on the solid foundation that is Christ.

A reading from the first letter of Paul
to the Corinthians

YOU are God's building. Thanks to the favor God
showed me I laid a foundation as a wise master-
builder might do, and now someone else is building
upon it. Everyone, however, must be careful how he
builds. No one can lay a foundation other than the one
that has been laid, namely Jesus Christ. If different
ones build on this foundation with gold, silver, precious stones, wood, hay or straw, the work of each
will be made clear. The Day will disclose it. That day
will make its appearance with fire, and fire will test
the quality of each man's work.

Are you not aware that you are the temple of God,
and that the Spirit of God dwells in you? If anyone de-
stroys God's temple, God will destroy him. For the
temple of God is holy, and you are that temple.—The
word of the Lord. ℟. **Thanks be to God.** ↓

GOSPEL Lk 19, 1-10   [The Lord's Saving Presence]
Alleluia (2 Chr 7, 16)

℟. **Alleluia.** I have chosen and sanctified this house,
says the Lord,
that my name may remain in it for all time. ℟. **Alleluia.** ↓

The story of Zacchaeus shows that we must accept the
Lord into our inner "house" by bearing fruits of true repentance. He will then come to our "house" and impart to us
his saving grace, the principle of our salvation.

℣. The Lord be with you. ℟. **And also with you.**
✝ A reading from the holy gospel according to Luke.
℟. **Glory to you, Lord.**

ENTERING Jericho, Jesus passed through the city.
There was a man there named Zacchaeus, the
chief tax collector and a wealthy man. He was trying
to see what Jesus was like, but being small of stature,

was unable to do so because of the crowd. He first ran
on in front, then climbed a sycamore tree which was
along Jesus' route, in order to see him. When Jesus
came to the spot he looked up and said, "Zacchaeus,
hurry down. I mean to stay at your house today." He
quickly descended, and welcomed him with delight.
When this was observed, everyone began to murmur,
"He has gone to a sinner's house as a guest." Zacchaeus stood his ground and said to the Lord: "I give half
my belongings, Lord, to the poor. If I have defrauded
anyone in the least, I pay him back fourfold." Jesus
said to him: "Today salvation has come to this house,
for this is what it means to be a son of Abraham. The
Son of Man has come to search out and save what was
lost."—The gospel of the Lord. ℟. **Praise to you, Lord
Jesus Christ.**   → No. 14, p. 18

PRAYER OVER THE GIFTS   [Answered Prayers]

Lord, receive our gifts.
May we who share this sacrament
experience the life and power it promises,
and hear the answer to our prayers.
We ask this in the name of Jesus the Lord. ℟. **Amen.** ↓

PREFACE (P 53)   [A House of Prayer]

℣. The Lord be with you. ℟. **And also with you.**
℣. Lift up your hearts. ℟. **We lift them up to the Lord.**
℣. Let us give thanks to the Lord our God. ℟. **It is
right to give him thanks and praise.**

Father, all-powerful and ever-living God,
we do well always and everywhere to give you
    thanks.
Your house is a house of prayer,
and your presence makes it a place of blessing.
You give us grace upon grace
to build the temple of your Spirit,
creating its beauty from the holiness of our lives.

Your house of prayer
is also the promise of the Church in heaven.
Here your love is always at work,
preparing the Church on earth
for its heavenly glory
as the sinless bride of Christ,
the joyful mother of a great company of saints.
Now, with the saints and all the angels
we praise you for ever.   → No. 23, p. 23

COMMUNION ANT. 1 Pt 2, 5   [A Spiritual House]
**Like living stones let yourselves be built on Christ as
a spiritual house, a holy priesthood.** ↓

PRAYER AFTER COMMUNION [Temple of God's Presence]
Father,
you make your Church on earth
a sign of the new and eternal Jerusalem.
By sharing in this sacrament
may we become the temple of your presence
and the home of your glory.
Grant this in the name of Jesus the Lord.
℟. **Amen.**   → No. 32, p. 70

Optional Solemn Blessings, p. 92, and Prayers Over the People, p. 99

NOVEMBER 16

33rd SUNDAY IN ORDINARY TIME

ENTRANCE ANT. Jer 29, 11. 12. 14   **[God Hears Us]**

The Lord says: my plans for you are peace and not disaster; when you call to me, I will listen to you, and I will bring you back to the place from which I exiled you. → No. 2, p. 10

OPENING PRAYER   **[Faithful Service]**

Let us pray
  [that God will help us to be faithful]
Father of all that is good,
keep us faithful in serving you,
for to serve you is our lasting joy.
We ask this through our Lord Jesus Christ, your Son,
who lives and reigns with you and the Holy Spirit,
one God, for ever and ever. ℟. **Amen.** ↓

ALTERNATIVE OPENING PRAYER   **[God's Truth]**

Let us pray
  [with hearts that long for peace]

500

Father in heaven,
ever-living source of all that is good,
from the beginning of time you promised man salvation
through the future coming of your Son, our Lord
　　Jesus Christ.
Help us to drink of his truth
and expand our hearts with the joy of his promises,
so that we may serve you in faith and in love
and know for ever the joy of your presence.
We ask this through Christ our Lord. ℟. **Amen.** ↓

READING I Dn 12, 1-3　　　　　　[The Last Judgment]

　　Daniel describes events that will occur at the end of the
　　world. It will be a time of distress, but the just will live for-
　　ever in glory while others shall endure horror and disgrace.

　　A reading from the book of the prophet Daniel

AT that time there shall arise
　Michael, the great prince,
　　guardian of your people;
It shall be a time unsurpassed in distress
　　since nations began until that time.
At that time your people shall escape,
　　everyone who is found written in the book.
Many of those who sleep
　　in the dust of the earth shall awake;
Some shall live forever,
　　others shall be an everlasting horror and disgrace.
But the wise shall shine brightly
　　like the splendor of the firmament,
And those who lead the many to justice
　　shall be like the stars forever.
The word of the Lord. ℟. **Thanks be to God.** ↓

RESPONSORIAL PSALM Ps 16　　　　[God Our Hope]

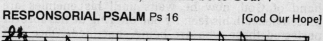

℟. Keep me safe, O　God;　you　are my hope.

O Lord, my allotted portion and my cup,
   you it is who hold fast my lot.
I set the Lord ever before me;
   with him at my right hand I shall not be disturbed.

℞. **Keep me safe, O God;**
   you are my hope.

Therefore my heart is glad and my soul rejoices,
   my body, too, abides in confidence;
Because you will not abandon my soul to the nether
   world,
   nor will you suffer your faithful one to undergo corruption.

℞. **Keep me safe, O God;**
   you are my hope.

You will show me the path to life,
   fullness of joys in your presence,
   the delights at your right hand forever.

℞. **Keep me safe, O God;**
   you are my hope. ↓

READING II Heb 10, 11-14. 18   [Jesus in Glory]

> **Jesus, unlike the other priests, offered only one sacrifice
> for sin and took his place forever at God's right hand. He
> has perfected those who are being sanctified.**

A reading from the letter to the Hebrews

EVERY other priest stands ministering day by day,
and offering again and again those same sacrifices
which can never take away sins. But Jesus offered one
sacrifice for sins and took his seat forever at the right
hand of God; now he waits until his enemies are
placed beneath his feet. By one offering he has forever
perfected those who are being sanctified. Once sins
have been forgiven, there is no further offering for
sin.—The word of the Lord. ℞. **Thanks be to God.** ↓

GOSPEL Mk 13, 24-32   [The Last Judgment]
Alleluia (Lk 21, 36)
℟. **Alleluia.** Be watchful, pray constantly,
that you may be worthy to stand before the Son of
   Man. ℟. **Alleluia.** ↓

> Jesus tells about the end of the world—the darkening of
> the sun, moon and stars. Then the Son of Man will come in
> glory. Learn from the signs of the fig tree. No one knows
> the exact time of this happening.

℣. The Lord be with you. ℟. **And also with you.**
✤ A reading from the holy gospel according to Mark.
℟. **Glory to you, Lord.**

JESUS said to his disciples: "During that period after
trials of every sort the sun will be darkened, the
moon will not shed its light, stars will fall out of the
skies, and the heavenly hosts will be shaken. Then
men will see the Son of Man coming in the clouds
with great power and glory. He will dispatch his messengers and assemble his chosen from the four winds,
from the farthest bounds of earth and sky. Learn a
lesson from the fig tree. Once the sap of its branches
runs high and it begins to sprout leaves, you know
that summer is near. In the same way, when you see
these things happening, you will know that he is near,
even at the door. I assure you, this generation will not
pass away until all these things take place. The heavens and the earth will pass away, but my words will
not.

"As to the exact day or hour, no one knows it, neither the angels in heaven nor even the Son, but only
the Father."—The gospel of the Lord. ℟. **Praise to you,
Lord Jesus Christ.**   → No. 14, p. 18

PRAYER OVER THE GIFTS   [Eternal Life]

Lord God,
may the gifts we offer

increase our love for you
and bring us to eternal life.
We ask this in the name of Jesus the Lord.
℟. **Amen.**   ➙ No. 21, p. 22 (Pref. P 29-36)

COMMUNION ANT. Ps 73, 28   [Hope in God]

**It is good for me to be with the Lord and to put my
hope in him.** ↓

OR Mk 11, 23. 24   [Believing Prayer]

**I tell you solemnly, whatever you ask for in prayer,
believe that you have received it, and it will be yours,
says the Lord.** ↓

PRAYER AFTER COMMUNION   [Growth in Love]

Father,
may we grow in love
by the eucharist we have celebrated
in memory of the Lord Jesus,
who is Lord for ever and ever.
℟. **Amen.**   ➙ No. 32, p. 70

Optional Solemn Blessings, p. 92, and Prayers Over the People, p. 99

"My kingdom does not belong to this world."

NOVEMBER 23
Last Sunday in Ordinary Time
CHRIST THE KING

ENTRANCE ANT. Rv 5, 12; 1, 6   **[Christ's Glory]**
**The Lamb who was slain is worthy to receive
strength and divinity, wisdom and power and honor:
to him be glory and power for ever.** → No. 2, p. 10

OPENING PRAYER   **[King of the Universe]**
Let us pray
   [that all men will acclaim Jesus as Lord]
Almighty and merciful God,
you break the power of evil
and make all things new
in your Son Jesus Christ, the King of the universe.
May all in heaven and earth acclaim your glory
and never cease to praise you.
We ask this . . . for ever and ever. ℟. **Amen.** ↓

ALTERNATIVE OPENING PRAYER   **[Spiritual Kingdom]**
Let us pray
   [that the kingdom of Christ
   may live in our hearts and come to our world]

505

Father all-powerful, God of love,
you have raised our Lord Jesus Christ from death to life,
resplendent in glory as King of creation.
Open our hearts,
free all the world to rejoice in his peace,
to glory in his justice, to live in his love.
Bring all mankind together in Jesus Christ your Son,
whose kingdom is with you and the Holy Spirit,
one God, for ever and ever. ℟. **Amen.** ↓

READING I Dn 7, 13-14   **[Everlasting Kingship]**

    **Daniel foresees the coming of the Son of Man. He receives
    all honor and glory. All peoples of every nation serve him.
    His kingship shall last forever.**

    A reading from the book of the prophet Daniel

A S the visions during the night continued, I saw
  One like a son of man coming,
   on the clouds of heaven;
When he reached the Ancient One
   and was presented before him,
He received dominion, glory, and kingship;
   nations and peoples of every language serve him.
His dominion is an everlasting dominion
   that shall not be taken away,
   his kingship shall not be destroyed.
The word of the Lord. ℟. **Thanks be to God.** ↓

RESPONSORIAL PSALM Ps 93   **[The Lord Is King]**

℟. **The Lord is king; he is robed in maj-es-ty.**

The Lord is king, in splendor robed;
   robed is the Lord and girt about with strength.

℟. **The Lord is king;
   he is robed in majesty.**

And he has made the world firm,
  not to be moved.
Your throne stands firm from of old;
  from everlasting you are, O Lord.

℟. **The Lord is king;**
  he is robed in majesty.

Your decrees are worthy of trust indeed;
  holiness befits your house,
    O Lord, for length of days.

℟. **The Lord is king;**
  he is robed in majesty. ↓

READING II Rv 1, 5-8   [The Alpha and the Omega]
  By the shedding of his blood, Jesus has made us a royal
  nation of priests to serve God. The Lord God is the Alpha
  and Omega—the beginning and the end. He is Almighty.

A reading from the book of Revelation

JESUS Christ is the faithful witness, the first-born
  from the dead and ruler of the kings of earth. To
him who loves us and freed us from our sins by his
own blood, who has made us a royal nation of priests
in the service of his God and Father—to him be glory
and power forever and ever! Amen.
See, he comes amid the clouds!
  Every eye shall see him,
  even of those who pierced him.
All the peoples of the earth
  shall lament him bitterly.
  So it is to be! Amen!
  The Lord God says, "I am the Alpha and the Omega,
the One who is and who was and who is to come, the
Almighty!"—The word of the Lord. ℟. **Thanks be to**
God. ↓

GOSPEL Jn 18, 33-37   [Christ's Kingdom]
Alleluia (Mk 11, 10)
℟. **Alleluia.** Blessed is he who inherits the kingdom of
  David our father;

blessed is he who comes in the name of the Lord. ℟.
Alleluia. ↓

> Before Pilate, Jesus admits that he is a king but that his
> kingdom is not of this world. Jesus says that he came into
> the world to testify to the truth.

℣. The Lord be with you. ℟. **And also with you.**
✚ A reading from the holy gospel according to John.
℟. **Glory to you, Lord.**

PILATE said to Jesus: "Are you the king of the
Jews?" Jesus answered, "Are you saying this on
your own, or have others been telling you about me?"
"I am no Jew!" Pilate retorted. "It is your own people
and the chief priests who have handed you over to me.
What have you done?" Jesus answered:
  "My kingdom does not belong to this world.
  If my kingdom were of this world,
  my subjects would be fighting
  to save me from being handed over to the Jews.
  As it is, my kingdom is not here."
At this Pilate said to him, "So, then, you are a king?"
Jesus replied:
  "It is you who say I am a king.
  The reason I was born,
  the reason why I came into the world,
  is to testify to the truth.
  Anyone committed to the truth hears my voice."
The gospel of the Lord. ℟. **Praise to you, Lord Jesus
Christ.**   → No. 14, p. 18

PRAYER OVER THE GIFTS   [Unity and Peace]

Lord,
we offer you the sacrifice
by which your Son reconciles mankind.
May it bring unity and peace to the world.
We ask this through Christ our Lord. ℟. **Amen.** ↓

PREFACE (P 51)   [Marks of Christ's Kingdom]

℣. The Lord be with you. ℟. **And also with you.**

℣. Lift up your hearts. ℟. **We lift them up to the Lord.**

℣. Let us give thanks to the Lord our God. ℟. **It is right to give him thanks and praise.**

Father, all-powerful and ever-living God,
we do well always and everywhere to give you thanks.
You anointed Jesus Christ, your only Son, with the oil
   of gladness,
as the eternal priest and universal king.
As priest he offered his life on the altar of the cross
and redeemed the human race
by this one perfect sacrifice of peace.
As king he claims dominion over all creation,
that he may present to you, his almighty Father,
an eternal and universal kingdom:
a kingdom of truth and life,
a kingdom of holiness and grace,
a kingdom of justice, love, and peace.
And so, with all the choirs of angels in heaven
we proclaim your glory
and join in their unending hymn of praise:

→ No. 23, p. 23

COMMUNION ANT. Ps 29, 10-11   [Gift of Peace]

The Lord will reign for ever and will give his people the gift of peace. ↓

PRAYER AFTER COMMUNION   [Joy of Christ's Kingdom]

Lord,
you give us Christ, the King of all creation,
as food for everlasting life.
Help us to live by his gospel
and bring us to the joy of his kingdom,
where he lives and reigns for ever and ever.
℟. **Amen.**   → No. 32, p. 70

Optional Solemn Blessings, p. 92, and Prayers Over the People, p. 99

"Pray constantly . . . to escape whatever is in prospect, and to stand secure before the Son of Man."

YEAR C
NOVEMBER 30
1st SUNDAY OF ADVENT

ENTRANCE ANT. Ps 25, 1-3   **[Hope]**

To you, my God, I lift my soul, I trust in you; let me never come to shame. Do not let my enemies laugh at me. No one who waits for you is ever put to shame.

→ No. 2, p. 10 (Omit Gloria)

OPENING PRAYER   **[Welcome for Christ]**

Let us pray
   [that we may take Christ's coming seriously]
All-powerful God,
increase our strength of will for doing good
that Christ may find an eager welcome at his coming
and call us to his side in the kingdom of heaven,
where he lives and reigns with you and the Holy Spirit,
one God, for ever and ever. ℟. **Amen.** ↓

ALTERNATIVE OPENING PRAYER   **[Longing for Christ]**

Let us pray
   [in Advent time
   with longing and waiting
   for the coming of the Lord]

510

Father in heaven,
our hearts desire the warmth of your love
and our minds are searching for the light of your Word.
Increase our longing for Christ our Savior
and give us the strength to grow in love,
that the dawn of his coming
may find us rejoicing in his presence
and welcoming the light of his truth.
We ask this in the name of Jesus the Lord. ℟. **Amen.** ↓

READING I Jer 33, 14-16   [The Lord's Messiah]

Jeremiah reveals the promise of the Lord made to the House of Israel. A shoot from David shall do what is right and just. Judah and Jerusalem shall be safe.

A reading from the book of the prophet Jeremiah

THE days are coming, says the Lord, when I will fulfill the promise I made to the house of Israel and Judah. In those days, in that time, I will raise up for David a just shoot; he shall do what is right and just in the land. In those days Judah shall be safe and Jerusalem shall dwell secure; this is what they shall call her: "The Lord our justice."—The word of the Lord. ℟. **Thanks be to God.** ↓

RESPONSORIAL PSALM Ps 25   [Eye on God]

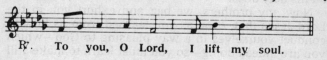

℟.   To you, O Lord, I lift my soul.

Your ways, O Lord, make known to me;
    teach me your paths,
Guide me in your truth and teach me,
    for you are God my savior,
    and for you I wait all the day.

℟. **To you, O Lord, I lift my soul.**

Good and upright is the Lord;
  thus he shows sinners the way.
He guides the humble to justice,
  he teaches the humble his way.

R). **To you, O Lord, I lift my soul.**

All the paths of the Lord are kindness and constancy
    toward those who keep his covenant and his de-
    crees.
The friendship of the Lord is with those who fear him,
  and his covenant, for their instruction.

R). **To you, O Lord, I lift my soul.** ↓

READING II 1 Thes 3, 12—4, 2   [Lives Pleasing to God]

Paul prays that the Lord will increase his love among the
Thessalonians. In turn they must live a life pleasing to God
so that they may progress in the way of perfection.

A reading from the first letter of Paul
to the Thessalonians

MAY the Lord increase you and make you over-
flow with love for one another and for all, even
as our love does for you. May he strengthen your
hearts, making them blameless and holy before our
God and Father at the coming of our Lord Jesus with
all his holy ones.

Now, my brothers, we beg and exhort you in the
Lord Jesus that, even as you learned from us how to
conduct yourselves in a way pleasing to God—which
you are indeed doing—so you must learn to make still
greater progress. You know the instructions we gave
you in the Lord Jesus.—The word of the Lord. R).
Thanks be to God. ↓

GOSPEL Lk 21, 25-28. 34-36   [Prayerful Vigilance]
Alleluia (Ps 85, 8)
R). **Alleluia.** Lord, let us see your kindness,
and grant us your salvation. R). **Alleluia.** ↓

Jesus tells his disciples that there will be signs for his second coming. The sun, moon, stars, anguish among people, fright—these will warn of his coming. They should watch, pray and stand secure before the Son of Man.

℣. The Lord be with you. ℟. **And also with you.**

✛ A reading from the holy gospel according to Luke.
℟. **Glory to you, Lord.**

JESUS said to his disciples: "There will be signs in the sun, the moon and the stars. On the earth, nations will be in anguish, distraught at the roaring of the sea and the waves. Men will die of fright in anticipation of what is coming upon the earth. The powers in the heavens will be shaken. After that, men will see the Son of Man coming on a cloud with great power and glory. When these things begin to happen, stand up straight and raise your heads, for your ransom is near at hand.

"Be on guard lest your spirits become bloated with indulgence and drunkenness and worldly cares. The great day will suddenly close in on you like a trap. The day I speak of will come upon all who dwell on the face of the earth, so be on the watch. Pray constantly for the strength to escape whatever is in prospect, and to stand secure before the Son of Man."—The gospel of the Lord. ℟. **Praise to you, Lord Jesus Christ.**   → No. 14, p. 18

PRAYER OVER THE GIFTS   [Promise of Eternal Life]

Father,
from all you give us
we present this bread and wine.
As we serve you now,
accept our offering
and sustain us with your promise of eternal life.
Grant this through Christ our Lord.
℟. **Amen.**   → No. 21, p. 22 (Pref. P 1)

COMMUNION ANT. Ps 85, 13   [A New World]

The Lord will shower his gifts, and our land will yield its fruit. ↓

PRAYER AFTER COMMUNION   [Love for Heaven]

Father,
may our communion
teach us to love heaven.
May its promise and hope
guide our way on earth.
We ask this through Christ our Lord.
℟. **Amen.**   → No. 32, p. 70

Optional Solemn Blessings, p. 92, and Prayers Over the People, p. 99

*"He went about the entire region of the Jordan
proclaiming a baptism of repentance."*

DECEMBER 7

2nd SUNDAY OF ADVENT

ENTRANCE ANT. See Is 30, 19. 30   [Lord of Salvation]

**People of Zion, the Lord will come to save all nations,
and your hearts will exult to hear his majestic voice.**
→ No. 2, p. 10 (Omit Gloria)

OPENING PRAYER   [Receiving Christ]

Let us pray
  [that nothing may hinder us
  from receiving Christ with joy]
God of power and mercy,
open our hearts in welcome.
Remove the things that hinder us from receiving
  Christ with joy,
so that we may share his wisdom
and become one with him
when he comes in glory,
for he lives and reigns with you and the Holy Spirit,
one God, for ever and ever. R̸. **Amen.** ↓

ALTERNATIVE OPENING PRAYER   [Christ's Wisdom]

Let us pray
  [in Advent time
  for the coming Savior to teach us wisdom]
Father in heaven,
the day draws near when the glory of your Son
will make radiant the night of the waiting world.
May the lure of greed not impede us from the joy
which moves the hearts of those who seek him.
May the darkness not blind us
to the vision of wisdom
which fills the minds of those who find him.
We ask this in the name of Jesus the Lord. R̸. **Amen.** ↓

READING I Bar 5, 1-9   [God's Favor on Jerusalem]

**Baruch tells Jerusalem of God's favor. God will gather the
people together that Israel may grow secure in the glory of
God. He leads in joy, mercy and justice.**

A reading from the book of the prophet Baruch

JERUSALEM, take off your robe of mourning and
  misery;
  put on the splendor of glory from God forever:

Wrapped in the cloak of justice from God,
  bear on your head the mitre
  that displays the glory of the eternal name.
For God will show all the earth your splendor:
  you will be named by God forever
  the peace of justice, the glory of God's worship.
Up, Jerusalem! stand upon the heights;
  look to the east and see your children
Gathered from the east and the west
  at the word of the Holy One,
  rejoicing that they are remembered by God.
Led away on foot by their enemies they left you:
  but God will bring them back to you
  borne aloft in glory as on royal thrones.
For God has commanded
  that every lofty mountain be made low,
And that the age-old depths and gorges
  be filled to level ground,
  that Israel may advance secure in the glory of God.
The forests and every fragrant kind of tree
  have overshadowed Israel at God's command;
For God is leading Israel in joy
  by the light of his glory,
  with his mercy and justice for company.
The word of the Lord. ℟. **Thanks be to God.** ↓

RESPONSORIAL PSALM Ps 126 [The Lord's Wonders]

℟. The Lord has done great things for us; we are filled with joy.

When the Lord brought back the captives of Zion,
  we were like men dreaming.
Then our mouth was filled with laughter,
  and our tongue with rejoicing.

℟. **The Lord has done great things for us;**
  we are filled with joy.

Then they said among the nations,
  "The Lord has done great things for them."
The Lord has done great things for us;
  we are glad indeed.

℟. **The Lord has done great things for us;**
  we are filled with joy.

Restore our fortunes, O Lord,
  like the torrents in the southern desert.
Those that sow in tears
  shall reap rejoicing.

℟. **The Lord has done great things for us;**
  we are filled with joy.

Although they go forth weeping,
  carrying the seed to be sown,
They shall come back rejoicing,
  carrying their sheaves.

℟. **The Lord has done great things for us;**
  we are filled with joy. ↓

READING II Phil 1, 4-6. 8-11   [Cooperating with Joy]

Paul rejoices in the progress of faith among the Philippians. He is sure that God who began this good work will help it grow. Paul prays that their love may even more abound that they may be rich in harvest.

A reading from the letter of Paul
to the Philippians

IN every prayer I utter, I rejoice as I plead on your behalf at the way you have all continually helped promote the gospel from the very first day.

I am sure of this much: that he who has begun the good work in you will carry it through to completion, right up to the day of Christ Jesus. God himself can testify how much I long for each of you with the affection of Christ Jesus! My prayer is that your love may more and more abound, both in understanding and

wealth of experience, so that with a clear conscience
and blameless conduct you may learn to value the
things that really matter, up to the very day of Christ.
It is my wish that you may be found rich in the harvest of justice which Jesus Christ has ripened in you,
to the glory and praise of God.—The word of the Lord.
℟. **Thanks be to God.** ↓

GOSPEL Lk 3, 1-6 [Prepare for the Lord]
Alleluia (Lk 3, 4. 6)
℟. **Alleluia.** Prepare the way for the Lord,
make straight his paths:
all mankind shall see the salvation of God.
℟. **Alleluia.** ↓

Luke outlines some historical facts at the time of John the
Baptizer's preaching. It is the fulfillment of the prophecy of
Isaiah. John prepares the way for the Lord.

℣. The Lord be with you. ℟. **And also with you.**
✝ A reading from the holy gospel according to Luke.
℟. **Glory to you, Lord.**

IN the fifteenth year of the rule of Tiberius Caesar,
when Pontius Pilate was procurator of Judea, Herod
tetrarch of Galilee, Philip his brother tetrarch of the
region of Ituraea and Trachonitis, and Lysanias
tetrarch of Abilene, during the high-priesthood of
Annas and Caiaphas, the word of God was spoken to
John son of Zechariah in the desert. He went about
the entire region of the Jordan proclaiming a baptism
of repentance which led to the forgiveness of sins, as
is written in the book of the words of Isaiah the
prophet:

"A herald's voice in the desert, crying,
'Make ready the way of the Lord,
 clear him a straight path.
Every valley shall be filled
 and every mountain and hill shall be leveled.

The windings shall be made straight
  and the rough ways smooth,
    and all mankind shall see the salvation of God.' "
The gospel of the Lord. R̸. **Praise to you, Lord Jesus
Christ.**
                                          → No. 14, p. 18

PRAYER OVER THE GIFTS   [Our Offering]

Lord,
we are nothing without you.
As you sustain us with your mercy,
receive our prayers and offerings.
We ask this through Christ our Lord.
R̸. **Amen.**   → No. 21, p. 22 (Pref. P 1)

COMMUNION ANT. Bar 5, 5; 4, 36   [Coming Joy]

**Rise up, Jerusalem, stand on the heights, and see the
joy that is coming to you from God.** ↓

PRAYER AFTER COMMUNION   [Wise Judgment]

Father,
you give us food from heaven.
By our sharing in this mystery,
teach us to judge wisely the things of earth
and to love the things of heaven.
Grant this through Christ our Lord.
R̸. **Amen.**   → No. 32, p. 70

Optional Solemn Blessings, p. 92, and Prayers Over the People, p. 99

*"Rejoice O highly favored daughter!
The Lord is with you."*

DECEMBER 8

IMMACULATE CONCEPTION

ENTRANCE ANT. Is 61, 10   [Mary's Joy in the Lord]

I exult for joy in the Lord, my soul rejoices in my God;
for he has clothed me in the garment of salvation and
robed me in the cloak of justice, like a bride adorned
with her jewels.   → No. 2, p. 10

OPENING PRAYER   [Living in God's Presence]

Let us pray
  [that through the prayers of the sinless Virgin Mary,
  God will free us from our sins]
Father,
you prepared the Virgin Mary
to be the worthy mother of your Son.
You let her share beforehand
in the salvation Christ would bring by his death,
and kept her sinless from the first moment of her conception.
Help us by her prayers
to live in your presence without sin.
We ask this through our Lord Jesus Christ, your Son,

who lives and reigns with you and the Holy Spirit,
one God, for ever and ever. ℟. **Amen.** ↓

ALTERNATIVE OPENING PRAYER [Mary's Faith and Love]

Let us pray

[on this feast of Mary
who experienced the perfection
of God's saving power]

Father,
the image of the Virgin is found in the Church.
Mary had a faith that your Spirit prepared
and a love that never knew sin,
for you kept her sinless from the first moment of her
    conception.
Trace in our actions the lines of her love,
in our hearts her readiness of faith.
Prepare once again a world for your Son
who lives and reigns with you and the Holy Spirit,
one God, for ever and ever. ℟. **Amen.** ↓

READING I Gn 3, 9-15. 20   [Promise of the Redeemer]

In the Garden, humankind enjoys an intimacy with God. It
is disrupted by sin, and the free and happy relationship between humankind and God is broken.

A reading from the book of Genesis

AFTER Adam had eaten of the tree the Lord God
called to the man and asked him, "Where are
you?" He answered, "I heard you in the garden; but I
was afraid, because I was naked, so I hid myself."
Then he asked, "Who told you that you were naked?
You have eaten, then, from the tree of which I had forbidden you to eat!" The man replied, "The woman
whom you put here with me—she gave me fruit from
the tree, and so I ate it." The Lord God then asked the
woman, "Why did you do such a thing?" The woman
answered, "The serpent tricked me into it, so I ate it."
    Then the Lord God said to the serpent:

"Because you have done this, you shall be banned
   from all the animals
   and from all the wild creatures;
On your belly shall you crawl,
   and dirt shall you eat
   all the days of your life.
I will put enmity between you and the woman,
   and between your offspring and hers;
He will strike at your head,
   while you strike at his heel."

The man called his wife Eve, because she became
the mother of all the living.—The word of the Lord. ℟.
Thanks be to God. ↓

RESPONSORIAL PSALM Ps 98   [God's Salvation]

℟. **Sing to the Lord a new song, for he has done marvelous deeds.**

Sing to the Lord a new song,
   for he has done wondrous deeds;
His right hand has won victory for him,
   his holy arm.

℟. **Sing to the Lord a new song,
   for he has done marvelous deeds.**

The Lord has made his salvation known:
   in the sight of the nations he has revealed his justice.
He has remembered his kindness and his faithfulness
   toward the house of Israel.

℟. **Sing to the Lord a new song,
   for he has done marvelous deeds.**

All the ends of the earth have seen
   the salvation by our God.
Sing joyfully to the Lord, all you lands;
   break into song; sing praise.

℟. **Sing to the Lord a new song,
   for he has done marvelous deeds.** ↓

READING II Eph 1, 3-6. 11-12   [God's Saving Plan]

God is praised for revealing his plan of salvation. Whatever God wills he works effectively and surely to accomplish. Let us make his will our will.

A reading from the letter of Paul to the Ephesians

PRAISED be the God and Father of our Lord Jesus Christ, who has bestowed on us in Christ every spiritual blessing in the heavens! God chose us in him before the world began, to be holy and blameless in his sight, to be full of love; likewise he predestined us through Christ Jesus to be his adopted sons—such was his will and pleasure—that all might praise the divine favor he has bestowed on us in his beloved.

In him we were chosen; for in the decree of God, who administers everything according to his will and counsel, we were predestined to praise his glory by being the first to hope in Christ.—The word of the Lord. ℟. **Thanks be to God.** ↓

GOSPEL Lk 1, 26-38   [Mary's Great Holiness]
Alleluia (Lk 1, 28)

℟. **Alleluia.** Hail, Mary, full of grace, the Lord is with you;

blessed are you among women. ℟. **Alleluia.** ↓

Mary has received a promise of supreme grace and blessing and accepts it in faith, assenting to God's Word with her "Amen."

℣. The Lord be with you. ℟. **And also with you.**

✝ A reading from the holy gospel according to Luke.
℟. **Glory to you, Lord.**

THE angel Gabriel was sent from God to a town of Galilee named Nazareth, to a virgin betrothed to a man named Joseph, of the house of David. The virgin's name was Mary. Upon arriving, the angel said to her: "Rejoice, O highly favored daughter! The Lord is with you. Blessed are you among women." She was deeply troubled by his words, and wondered what his greeting meant. The angel went on to say to her: "Do not fear, Mary. You have found favor with God. You shall conceive and bear a son and give him the name Jesus. Great will be his dignity and he will be called Son of the Most High. The Lord God will give him the throne of David his father. He will rule over the house of Jacob forever and his reign will be without end."

Mary said to the angel, "How can this be since I do not know man?" The angel answered her: "The Holy Spirit will come upon you and the power of the Most High will overshadow you; hence, the holy offspring to be born will be called Son of God. Know that Elizabeth your kinswoman has conceived a son in her old age; she who was thought to be sterile is now in her sixth month, for nothing is impossible with God."

Mary said: "I am the maidservant of the Lord. Let it be done to me as you say." With that the angel left her.—The gospel of the Lord. ℟. **Praise to you, Lord Jesus Christ.**　　　　　　　　→ No. 14, p. 18

PRAYER OVER THE GIFTS　　　[Helped by Mary's Prayers]

Lord,
accept this sacrifice
on the feast of the sinless Virgin Mary.
You kept her free from sin
from the first moment of her life.
Help us by her prayers,
and free us from our sins.
We ask this in the name of Jesus the Lord. ℟. **Amen.** ↓

PREFACE (P 58)　　　　　　　　[Mary Our Advocate]

℣. The Lord be with you. ℟. **And also with you.**
℣. Lift up your hearts. ℟. **We lift them up to the Lord.**
℣. Let us give thanks to the Lord our God. ℟. **It is right to give him thanks and praise.**

Father, all-powerful and ever-living God,
we do well always and everywhere to give you
    thanks.
You allowed no stain of Adam's sin
to touch the Virgin Mary.
Full of grace, she was to be a worthy mother of your
    Son,
your sign of favor to the Church at its beginning,
and the promise of its perfection as the bride of
    Christ, radiant in beauty.
Purest of virgins, she was to bring forth your Son,
the innocent lamb who takes away our sins.
You chose her from all women to be our advocate
    with you
and our pattern of holiness.
In our joy we sing to your glory
with all the choirs of angels: → No. 23, p. 23

COMMUNION ANT.   [All Honor to Mary]

**All honor to you, Mary! From you arose the sun of
justice, Christ our God.** ↓

PRAYER AFTER COMMUNION   [Free from Sin]

Lord our God,
in your love, you chose the Virgin Mary
and kept her free from sin.
May this sacrament of your love
free us from our sins.
Grant this through Christ our Lord.
℟. **Amen.**   → No. 32, p. 70

Optional Solemn Blessings, p. 92, and Prayers Over the People, p. 99

"John preached the good news to the people."

DECEMBER 14

3rd SUNDAY OF ADVENT

ENTRANCE ANT. Phil 4, 4. 5   [Mounting Joy]

Rejoice in the Lord always; again I say, rejoice! The Lord is near. → No. 2, p. 10 (Omit Gloria)

OPENING PRAYER   [Joy of Salvation]

Let us pray
   [that God will fill us with joy
   at the coming of Christ]
Lord God,
may we, your people,
who look forward to the birthday of Christ
experience the joy of salvation
and celebrate that feast with love and thanksgiving.
We ask this . . . for ever and ever. ℟. **Amen.** ↓

ALTERNATIVE OPENING PRAYER   [Joy and Hope]

Let us pray
   [this Advent
   for joy and hope in the coming Lord]
Father of our Lord Jesus Christ,
ever faithful to your promises
and ever close to your Church:

the earth rejoices in hope of the Savior's coming
and looks forward with longing
to his return at the end of time.
Prepare our hearts and remove the sadness
that hinders us from feeling the joy and hope
which his presence will bestow,
for he is Lord for ever and ever. ℟. **Amen.** ↓

READING I Zep 3, 14-18   [Joy Over the Mighty Savior]

**Zephaniah writes that Israel should shout for joy. Her King,
the Lord, is in her midst. The Lord is a mighty savior. Israel
should not be discouraged.**

A reading from the book of the prophet Zephaniah

SHOUT for joy, O daughter Zion!
sing joyfully, O Israel!
Be glad and exult with all your heart,
  O daughter Jerusalem!
The Lord has removed the judgment against you,
  he has turned away your enemies;
The King of Israel, the Lord, is in your midst,
  you have no further misfortune to fear.
On that day, it shall be said to Jerusalem:
  Fear not, O Zion, be not discouraged!
The Lord, your God, is in your midst,
  a mighty savior;
He will rejoice over you with gladness
  and renew you in his love.
He will sing joyfully because of you,
  as one sings at festivals.
The word of the Lord. ℟. **Thanks be to God.** ↓

RESPONSORIAL PSALM Is 12   [Joy Over the Holy One]

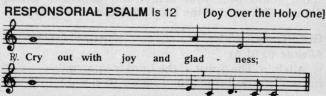

℟. Cry out with joy and glad - ness;

for among you is the great and Holy One of Is - ra - el.

God indeed is my savior;
  I am confident and unafraid.
My strength and my courage is the Lord,
  and he has been my savior.
With joy you will draw water
  at the fountain of salvation.—R̷.

Give thanks to the Lord, acclaim his name;
  among the nations make known his deeds,
  proclaim how exalted is his name.—R̷.

Sing praise to the Lord for his glorious achievement;
  let this be known throughout all the earth.
Shout with exultation, O city of Zion,
  for great in your midst
  is the Holy One of Israel!—R̷.↓

READING II Phil 4, 4-7   **[Rejoice in the Lord]**

Christians should rejoice in the Lord. They should take their prayers and petitions to him. God will watch over his children.

A reading from the letter of Paul
to the Philippians

REJOICE in the Lord always! I say it again. Rejoice! Everyone should see how unselfish you are. The Lord himself is near. Dismiss all anxiety from your minds. Present your needs to God in every form of prayer and in petitions full of gratitude. Then God's own peace, which is beyond all understanding, will stand guard over your hearts and minds, in Christ Jesus.—The word of the Lord. R̷. **Thanks be to God.** ↓

GOSPEL Lk 3, 10-18   **[Majesty of the Messiah]**
Alleluia (Is 61, 1)
R̷. **Alleluia.** The Spirit of the Lord is upon me;
he sent me to bring Good News to the poor. R̷. **Alleluia.** ↓

John preached a law of sharing. He baptized and admonished all to be just and loving and to pray. John tells the people about the majesty of the Messiah.

℣. The Lord be with you. ℟. **And also with you.**

✝ A reading from the holy gospel according to Luke.
℟. **Glory to you, Lord.**

THE crowds asked John, "What ought we to do?" In reply he said, "Let the man with two coats give to him who has none. The man who has food should do the same."

Tax collectors also came to be baptized, and they said to him, "Teacher, what are we to do?" He answered them, "Exact nothing over and above your fixed amount."

Soldiers likewise asked him, "What about us?" He told them, "Do not bully anyone. Denounce no one falsely. Be content with your pay."

The people were full of anticipation, wondering in their hearts whether John might be the Messiah. John answered them all by saying: "I am baptizing you in water, but there is one to come who is mightier than I. I am not fit to loosen his sandal strap. He will baptize you in the Holy Spirit and in fire. His winnowing-fan is in his hand to clear his threshing floor and gather the wheat into his granary, but the chaff he will burn in unquenchable fire." Using exhortations of this sort, he preached the good news to the people.—The gospel of the Lord. ℟. **Praise to you, Lord Jesus Christ.**

→ No. 14, p. 18

PRAYER OVER THE GIFTS [Continual Sacrifice]

Lord,
may the gift we offer in faith and love
be a continual sacrifice in your honor
and truly become our eucharist and our salvation.
Grant this through Christ our Lord.
℟. **Amen.** → No. 21, p. 22 (Pref. P 1 or 2)

COMMUNION ANT. See Is 35, 4   [Trust in God]

Say to the anxious: be strong and fear not, our God will come to save us. ↓

PRAYER AFTER COMMUNION   [Preparation for Christ]

God of mercy,
may this eucharist bring us your divine help,
free us from our sins,
and prepare us for the birthday of our Savior,
who is Lord for ever and ever.
℟. **Amen.**   → No. 32, p. 70

Optional Solemn Blessings, p. 92, and Prayers Over the People, p. 99

"Blessed are you among women and blessed is the fruit of your womb."

DECEMBER 21

4th SUNDAY OF ADVENT

ENTRANCE ANT. Is 45, 8   [The Advent Plea]

Let the clouds rain down the Just One, and the earth bring forth a Savior.   → No. 2, p. 10 (Omit Gloria)

OPENING PRAYER   [From Suffering to Glory]

Let us pray
     [as Advent draws to a close,
     that Christ will truly come into our hearts]

Lord,
fill our hearts with your love,
and as you revealed to us by an angel
the coming of your Son as man,
so lead us through his suffering and death
to the glory of his resurrection,
for he lives and reigns with you and the Holy Spirit,
one God, for ever and ever. R̷. **Amen.** ↓

ALTERNATIVE OPENING PRAYER   [Operative Faith]

Let us pray
   [as Advent draws to a close
   for the faith that opens our lives
   to the Spirit of God]
Father, all-powerful God,
your eternal Word took flesh on our earth
when the Virgin Mary placed her life
at the service of your plan.
Lift our minds in watchful hope
to hear the voice which announces his glory
and open our minds to receive the Spirit
who prepares us for his coming.
We ask this through Christ our Lord. R̷. **Amen.** ↓

READING I Mi 5, 1-4   [The Messiah from Bethlehem]

Micah speaks of the glory of Bethlehem, a lone town
among the people of Judah. From Bethlehem shall come
forth the promised one who shall stand firm and strong in
the Lord.

A reading from the book of the prophet Micah

THUS says the Lord:
   You, Bethlehem-Ephrathah,
  too small to be among the clans of Judah,
From you shall come forth for me
  one who is to be ruler in Israel;
Whose origin is from of old,
  from ancient times.

(Therefore the Lord will give them up, until the time
   when she who is to give birth has borne,
And the rest of his brethren shall return
   to the children of Israel.)
He shall stand firm and shepherd his flock
   by the strength of the Lord,
   in the majestic name of the Lord, his God;
And they shall remain, for now his greatness
   shall reach to the ends of the earth;
   he shall be peace.
The word of the Lord. ℟. **Thanks be to God.** ↓

RESPONSORIAL PSALM Ps 80   [Turn to the Lord]

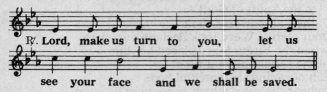

℟. **Lord, make us turn to you, let us
see your face and we shall be saved.**

O shepherd of Israel, hearken,
   from your throne upon the cherubim, shine forth.
Rouse your power,
   and come to save us.

℟. **Lord, make us turn to you,
   let us see your face and we shall be saved.**

Once again, O Lord of hosts,
   look down from heaven, and see;
Take care of this vine,
   and protect what your right hand has planted
   [the son of man whom you yourself made strong].

℟. **Lord, make us turn to you,
   let us see your face and we shall be saved.**

May your help be with the man of your right hand,
   with the son of man whom you yourself made
      strong.

Then we will no more withdraw from you;
  give us new life, and we will call upon your name.

R℘. **Lord, make us turn to you,**
  let us see your face and we shall be saved. ↓

READING II Heb 10, 5-10   [Doing God's Will]

Jesus said the sacrifices, sin offerings and holocausts did not delight the Lord. But he has come to do the will of God—to establish a second covenant.

A reading from the letter to the Hebrews

O N coming into the world Jesus said:
  "Sacrifice and offering you did not desire,
  but a body you have prepared for me;
Holocausts and sin offerings you took no delight in.
Then I said, 'As is written of me in the book,
  I have come to do your will, O God.' "
First he says,
"Sacrifices and offerings, holocausts and sin offerings
  you neither desired nor delighted in."
(These are offered according to the prescriptions of the law.) Then he says,
  "I have come to do your will."
In other words, he takes away the first covenant to establish the second.

  By this "will," we have been sanctified through the offering of the body of Jesus Christ once for all.—The word of the Lord. R℘. **Thanks be to God.** ↓

GOSPEL Lk 1, 39-45   [The Visitation]
Alleluia (Lk 1, 38)
R℘. **Alleluia.** I am the servant of the Lord:
may his will for me be done. R℘. **Alleluia.** ↓

Mary went to visit Elizabeth who was also blessed by the Holy Spirit. Elizabeth greeted Mary: "Blessed are you among women and blessed is the fruit of your womb."

℣. The Lord be with you. ℟. **And also with you.**

✝ A reading from the holy gospel according to Luke.

℟. **Glory to you, Lord.**

MARY set out, proceeding in haste into the hill country to a town of Judah, where she entered Zechariah's house and greeted Elizabeth. When Elizabeth heard Mary's greeting, the baby stirred in her womb. Elizabeth was filled with the Holy Spirit, and cried out in a loud voice: "Blessed are you among women and blessed is the fruit of your womb. But who am I that the mother of my Lord should come to me? The moment your greeting sounded in my ears, the baby stirred in my womb for joy. Blessed is she who trusted that the Lord's words to her would be fulfilled."—The gospel of the Lord. ℟. **Praise to you, Lord Jesus Christ.**   → No. 14, p. 18

PRAYER OVER THE GIFTS   [Power of the Spirit]

Lord,

may the power of the Spirit,

which sanctified Mary the mother of your Son,

make holy the gifts we place upon this altar.

Grant this through Christ our Lord.

℟. **Amen.**   → No. 21, p. 22 (Pref. P 1)

COMMUNION ANT. Is 7, 14   [The Virgin-Mother]

The Virgin is with child and shall bear a son, and she will call him Emmanuel. ↓

PRAYER AFTER COMMUNION   [Growth in Holiness]

Lord,

in this sacrament

we receive the promise of salvation;

as Christmas draws near

make us grow in faith and love

to celebrate the coming of Christ our Savior,

who is Lord for ever and ever.

℟. **Amen.**   → No. 32, p. 70

Optional Solemn Blessings, p. 92, and Prayers Over the People, p. 99

The Word is made flesh.

DECEMBER 25

CHRISTMAS

VIGIL MASS

ENTRANCE ANT. See Ex 16, 6-7   [Glory of God]
**Today you will know that the Lord is coming to save
us, and in the morning you will see his glory.**

→ No. 2, p. 10

OPENING PRAYER   [Welcoming Christ]
Let us pray
  [that Christmas morning will find us at peace]
God our Father,
every year we rejoice
as we look forward to this feast of our salvation.
May we welcome Christ as our Redeemer,
and meet him with confidence when he comes to be
    our judge,
who lives and reigns with you and the Holy Spirit,
one God, for ever and ever. ℟. **Amen.** ↓

535

ALTERNATIVE OPENING PRAYER [Answering Lord's Call]

Let us pray
  [and be ready to welcome the Lord]
God of endless ages, Father of all goodness,
we keep vigil for the dawn of salvation
and the birth of your Son.
With gratitude we recall his humanity,
the life he shared with the sons of men.
May the power of his divinity
help us answer his call to forgiveness and life.
We ask this through Christ our Lord. R̯. **Amen.** ↓

READING I Is 62, 1-5   [Bride of God]

Isaiah speaks of human misery but hope lives in the human
race because of the promises of God. Isaiah reinforces that
hope, saying that God shall rejoice in his creation.

A reading from the book of the prophet Isaiah

FOR Zion's sake I will not be silent,
  for Jerusalem's sake I will not be quiet,
Until her vindication shines forth like the dawn
  and her victory like a burning torch.
Nations shall behold your vindication,
  and all kings your glory;
You shall be called by a new name
  pronounced by the mouth of the Lord.
You shall be a glorious crown in the hand of the Lord,
  a royal diadem held by your God.
No more shall men call you "Forsaken,"
  or your land "Desolate,"
But you shall be called "My Delight,"
  and your land "Espoused."
For the Lord delights in you,
  and makes your land his spouse.
As a young man marries a virgin,
  your Builder shall marry you;
And as a bridegroom rejoices in his bride

so shall your God rejoice in you.
The word of the Lord. ℟. **Thanks be to God.** ↓

RESPONSORIAL PSALM Ps 89   [God's Eternal Goodness]

℟. For ev - er I will sing the good-ness of the Lord.

I have made a covenant with my chosen one,
    I have sworn to David my servant:
Forever will I confirm your posterity
    and establish your throne for all generations.

℟. **For ever I will sing the goodness of the Lord.**

Happy the people who know the joyful shout;
    in the light of your countenance, O Lord, they walk.
At your name they rejoice all the day,
    and through your justice they are exalted.

℟. **For ever I will sing the goodness of the Lord.**

He shall say of me, "You are my father,
    my God, the Rock, my savior."
Forever I will maintain my kindness toward him,
    and my covenant with him stands firm.

℟. **For ever I will sing the goodness of the Lord.** ↓

READING II Acts 13, 16-17. 22-25   [The History of Salvation]

Jesus is the New Man who will fulfill every wish of his
Father. Jesus is the Savior of Israel.

A reading from the Acts of the Apostles

[W]HEN Paul came to Antioch Pisidia, he entered
the synagogue there] and motioning to them
for silence, he began: "Fellow Israelites and you
others who reverence our God, listen to what I have to
say! The God of the people Israel once chose our fathers. He made this people great during their sojourn
in the land of Egypt, and 'with an outstretched arm' he
led them out of it. God raised up David as their king;

on his behalf he testified, 'I have found David son of
Jesse to be a man after my own heart who will fulfill
my every wish.'

"According to his promise, God has brought forth
from this man's descendants Jesus, a savior for Israel.
John heralded the coming of Jesus by proclaiming a
baptism of repentance to all the people of Israel. As
John's career was coming to an end, he would say,
'What you suppose me to be I am not. Rather, look for
the one who comes after me. I am not worthy to un-
fasten the sandals on his feet.' "—The word of the
Lord. ℟. **Thanks be to God.** ↓

GOSPEL Mt 1, 1-25 or 1, 18-25   [Jesus, God-with-Us]
Alleluia

℟. **Alleluia.** Tomorrow the wickedness of the earth
   will be destroyed:
the Savior of the world will be our king. ℟. **Alleluia.** ↓

> This genealogy reveals both the good and the evil persons
> who are in Jesus' bloodline of descent; he is a true repre-
> sentative of humanity with all its saints and sinners.
> Joseph's struggle reminds us how much of human life is
> burdensome and often not clear to us. It is this perplexity
> that impels us to seek our answers in faith.

[If "Short Form" is used, omit indented text in brackets.]

℣. The Lord be with you. ℟. **And also with you.**
✠ A reading from the holy gospel according to Matthew. ℟. **Glory to you, Lord.**

[A FAMILY record of Jesus Christ, son of
David, son of Abraham. Abraham was the
father of Isaac, Isaac the father of Jacob. Jacob
the father of Judah and his brothers.
Judah was the father of Perez and Zerah, whose
   mother was Tamar.
Perez was the father of Hezron,
Hezron the father of Ram.

Ram was the father of Amminadab,
Amminadab the father of Nahshon,
Nahshon the father of Salmon.
Salmon was the father of Boaz, whose mother was Rahab,
Boaz was the father of Obed, whose mother was Ruth.
Obed was the father of Jesse,
Jesse the father of King David.
David was the father of Solomon, whose mother had been the wife of Uriah.
Solomon was the father of Rehoboam,
Rehoboam was the father of Abijah,
Abijah the father of Asa.
Asa was the father of Jehoshaphat,
Jehoshaphat the father of Joram,
Joram the father of Uzziah.
Uzziah was the father of Jotham,
Jotham the father of Ahaz,
Ahaz the father of Hezekiah.
Hezekiah was the father of Manasseh,
Manasseh the father of Amos,
Amos the father of Josiah.
Josiah become the father of Jechoniah and his brothers at the time of the Babylonian exile.
After the Babylonian exile
Jechoniah was the father of Shealtiel,
Shealtiel the father of Zerubbabel.
Zerubbabel was the father of Abiud,
Abiud the father of Eliakim,
Eliakim the father of Azor.
Azor was the father of Zadok,
Zadok the father of Achim,
Achim the father of Eliud.
Eliud was the father of Eleazar,
Eleazar the father of Matthan,
Matthan the father of Jacob.

Jacob was the father of Joseph the husband of Mary.

It was of her that Jesus who is called the Messiah was born.

Thus the total number of generations is:

from Abraham to David, fourteen generations;

from David to the Babylonian captivity, fourteen generations;

from the Babylonian captivity to the Messiah, fourteen generations.]

Now this is how the birth of Jesus Christ came about. When his mother Mary was engaged to Joseph, but before they lived together, she was found with child through the power of the Holy Spirit. Joseph her husband, an upright man unwilling to expose her to the law, decided to divorce her quietly. Such was his intention when suddenly the angel of the Lord appeared in a dream and said to him: "Joseph, son of David, have no fear about taking Mary as your wife. It is by the Holy Spirit that she has conceived this child. She is to have a son and you are to name him Jesus because he will save his people from their sins." All this happened to fulfill what the Lord had said through the prophet:

"The virgin shall be with child
and give birth to a son,
and they shall call him Emmanuel,"

a name which means "God with us." When Joseph awoke he did as the angel of the Lord had directed him and received her into his home as his wife. He had no relations with her at any time before she bore a son, whom he named Jesus.—The gospel of the Lord. ℟. **Praise to you, Lord Jesus Christ.**

➙ No. 14, p. 18

In the profession of faith, all genuflect at the words, and became man.

PRAYER OVER THE GIFTS   [Beginning of Redemption]

Lord,
as we keep tonight the vigil of Christmas,
may we celebrate this eucharist
with greater joy than ever
since it marks the beginning of our redemption.
We ask this in the name of Jesus the Lord.
℟. **Amen.**   → No. 21, p. 22 (Pref. P 3-5)

When Eucharistic Prayer I is used, the special Christmas form of In union with the whole Church *is said.*

COMMUNION ANT. See Is 40, 5   [God's Saving Power]

The glory of the Lord will be revealed, and all mankind will see the saving power of God. ↓

PRAYER AFTER COMMUNION   [New Birth]

Father,
we ask you to give us a new birth
as we celebrate the beginning
of your Son's life on earth.
Strengthen us in spirit
as we take your food and drink.
Grant this through Christ our Lord.
℟. **Amen.**   → No. 32, p. 70

Optional Solemn Blessings, p. 92, and Prayers Over the People, p. 99

MASS AT MIDNIGHT

ENTRANCE ANT. Ps 2, 7   [Son of God]

The Lord said to me: You are my Son; this day have I begotten you.

OR   [True Peace]

Let us all rejoice in the Lord, for our Savior is born to the world. True peace has descended from heaven.

→ No. 2, p. 10

OPENING PRAYER   [Eternal Joy]

Let us pray
  [in the peace of Christmas midnight
  that our joy in the birth of Christ
  will last for ever]
Father,
you make this holy night radiant
with the splendor of Jesus Christ our light.
We welcome him as Lord, the true light of the world.
Bring us to eternal joy in the kingdom of heaven,
where he lives and reigns with you and the Holy Spirit,
one God, for ever and ever. ℟. **Amen.** ↓

ALTERNATIVE OPENING PRAYER   [Joy and Hope]

Let us pray
  [with joy and hope
  as we await the dawning of the Father's Word]
Lord our God,
with the birth of your Son,
your glory breaks on the world.
Through the night hours of the darkened earth
we your people watch for the coming of your promised Son.
As we wait, give us a foretaste of the joy that you will
  grant us
when the fullness of his glory has filled the earth,
who lives and reigns with you for ever and ever.
℟. **Amen.** ↓

READING I Is 9, 1-6   [The Messiah's Kingdom]

   **The Messiah is a promise of peace for the world. His reign
   shall be vast and filled with justice. The power of God is
   revealed through the weakness of humans.**

   A reading from the book of the prophet Isaiah

THE people who walked in darkness
  have seen a great light;

Upon those who dwelt in the land of gloom
  a light has shone.
You have brought them abundant joy
  and great rejoicing,
As they rejoice before you as at the harvest,
  as men make merry when dividing spoils.
For the yoke that burdened them,
  the pole on their shoulder,
And the rod of their taskmaster
  you have smashed, as on the day of Midian.
For every boot that tramped in battle,
  every cloak rolled in blood,
  will be burned as fuel for flames.
For a child is born to us, a son is given us;
  upon his shoulder dominion rests.
They name him Wonder-Counselor, God-Hero,
  Father-Forever, Prince of Peace.
His dominion is vast
  and forever peaceful,
From David's throne, and over his kingdom,
  which he confirms and sustains
By judgment and justice,
  both now and forever.
The zeal of the Lord of hosts will do this!
The word of the Lord. ℟. **Thanks be to God.** ↓

RESPONSORIAL PSALM Ps 96   [Bless the Lord]

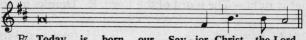

℟. **Today is born our Sav-ior, Christ, the Lord.**

Sing to the Lord a new song;
  sing to the Lord, all you lands.
Sing to the Lord; bless his name.

℟. **Today is born our Savior, Christ the Lord.**

Announce his salvation, day after day.
  Tell his glory among the nations;

Among all peoples, his wondrous deeds.

R̸. **Today is born our Savior, Christ the Lord.**

Let the heavens be glad and the earth rejoice;
  let the sea and what fills it resound;
  let the plains be joyful and all that is in them!
Then shall all the trees of the forest exult.

R̸. **Today is born our Savior, Christ the Lord.**

They shall exult before the Lord, for he comes;
  for he comes to rule the earth.
He shall rule the world with justice
  and the peoples with his constancy.

R̸. **Today is born our Savior, Christ the Lord.** ↓

READING II Ti 2, 11-14   [Salvation for All]

God offers salvation to all people. His way asks us to reject
worldly desires—to live temperately and justly. He even
asked his only Son to sacrifice himself to redeem us.

A reading from the letter of Paul to Titus

THE grace of God has appeared, offering salvation
to all men. It trains us to reject godless ways and
worldly desires, and to live temperately, justly, and
devoutly in this age as we await our blessed hope, the
appearing of the glory of the great God and of our
Savior Christ Jesus. It was he who sacrificed himself
for us, to redeem us from all unrighteousness and to
cleanse for himself a people of his own, eager to do
what is right.—The word of the Lord. R̸. **Thanks be to
God.** ↓

GOSPEL Lk 2, 1-14   [Birth of Christ]
Alleluia

R̸. **Alleluia.** Good News and great joy to all the world:
today is born our Savior, Christ the Lord. R̸. **Alleluia.** ↓

Caesar Augustus desired a world census. Joseph and Mary
go to Bethlehem where Jesus, the Lord of the universe, is
born in a stable. Glory to God and peace on earth!

℣. The Lord be with you. ℟. **And also with you.**

✝ A reading from the holy gospel according to Luke.

℟. **Glory to you, Lord.**

IN those days Caesar Augustus published a decree ordering a census of the whole world. This first census took place while Quirinius was governor of Syria. Everyone went to register, each to his own town. And so Joseph went from the town of Nazareth in Galilee to Judea, to David's town of Bethlehem—because he was of the house and lineage of David—to register with Mary, his espoused wife, who was with child.

While they were there the days of her confinement were completed. She gave birth to her first-born son and wrapped him in swaddling clothes and laid him in a manger, because there was no room for them in the place where travelers lodged.

There were shepherds in the locality, living in the fields and keeping night watch by turns over their flock. The angel of the Lord appeared to them, as the glory of the Lord shone around them, and they were very much afraid. The angel said to them: "You have nothing to fear! I come to proclaim good news to you—tidings of great joy to be shared by the whole people. This day in David's city a savior has been born to you, the Messiah and Lord. Let this be a sign to you: in a manger you will find an infant wrapped in swaddling clothes." Suddenly, there was with the angel a multitude of the heavenly host, praising God and saying,

"Glory to God in high heaven,
   peace on earth to those on whom his favor
   rests."

The gospel of the Lord. ℟. **Praise to you, Lord Jesus Christ.**

→ No. 14, p. 18

In the profession of faith, all genuflect at the words, and became man.

PRAYER OVER THE GIFTS   [Become Like Christ]

Lord,
accept our gifts on this joyful feast of our salvation.
By our communion with God made man,
may we become more like him
who joins our lives to yours,
for he is Lord for ever and ever.
R̸. **Amen.**   → No. 21, p. 22 (Pref. P 3-5)

When Eucharistic Prayer I is used, the special Christmas form of In union with the whole Church *is said.*

COMMUNION ANT. Jn 1, 14   [Glory of Christ]

The Word of God became man; we have seen his glory. ↓

PRAYER AFTER COMMUNION   [Following Christ]

God our Father,
we rejoice in the birth of our Savior.
May we share his life completely
by living as he has taught.
We ask this in the name of Jesus the Lord.
R̸. **Amen.**   → No. 32, p. 70

Optional Solemn Blessings, p. 92, and Prayers Over the People, p. 99

MASS AT DAWN

ENTRANCE ANT. See Is 9, 2. 6; Lk 1, 33   [Prince of Peace]

A light will shine on us this day, the Lord is born for us: he shall be called Wonderful God, Prince of peace, Father of the world to come; and his kingship will never end.   → No. 2, p. 10

OPENING PRAYER   [Light of Faith]

Let us pray
   [that the love of Christ
   will be a light to the world]

Father,
we are filled with the new light
by the coming of your Word among us.
May the light of faith
shine in our words and actions.
Grant this through our Lord Jesus Christ, your Son,
who lives and reigns with you and the Holy Spirit,
one God, for ever and ever. R̲). **Amen.** ↓

ALTERNATIVE OPENING PRAYER   [Christ's Peace]

Let us pray
  [for the peace
  that comes from the Prince of Peace]
Almighty God and Father of light,
a child is born for us and a son is given to us.
Your eternal Word leaped down from heaven
in the silent watches of the night,
and now your Church is filled with wonder
at the nearness of her God.
Open our hearts to receive his life
and increase our vision with the rising of dawn,
that our lives may be filled with his glory and his
    peace,
who lives and reigns for ever and ever. R̲). **Amen.** ↓

READING I Is 62, 11-12   [The Savior's Birth]

Isaiah foretells the birth of the Savior who will come to
Zion. These people will be called holy and they shall be redeemed.

A reading from the book of the prophet Isaiah

SEE, the Lord proclaims
  to the ends of the earth:
Say to daughter Zion,
  your savior comes!
Here is his reward with him,
  his recompense before him.
They shall be called the holy people,

the redeemed of the Lord,
and you shall be called "Frequented,"
  a city that is not forsaken.
The word of the Lord. ℟. **Thanks be to God.** ↓

RESPONSORIAL PSALM Ps 97   [Be Glad in the Lord]

    ℟. **A light will shine on us this day: the Lord is born for us.**

The Lord is king; let the earth rejoice;
  let the many isles be glad.
The heavens proclaim his justice,
  and all peoples see his glory.

℟. **A light will shine on us this day:**
  the Lord is born for us.

Light dawns for the just;
  and gladness, for the upright of heart.
Be glad in the Lord, you just,
  and give thanks to his holy name.

℟. **A light will shine on us this day:**
  the Lord is born for us. ↓

READING II Ti 3, 4-7   [Saved by God's Mercy]

  Christians are saved not because of their own merits but
because of the mercy of God. We are saved through baptism and renewal in the Holy Spirit.

    A reading from the letter of Paul to Titus

WHEN the kindness and love of God our Savior appeared, he saved us, not because of any righteous
deeds we had done, but because of his mercy. He
saved us through the baptism of new birth and renewal by the Holy Spirit. This Spirit he lavished on us
through Jesus Christ our Savior, that we might be jus-
tified by his grace and become heirs, in hope of eternal
life.—The word of the Lord. ℟. **Thanks be to God.** ↓

GOSPEL Lk 2, 15-20   [Jesus, the God-Man]
Alleluia

℟. **Alleluia.** Glory to God in heaven,
peace and grace to his people on earth. ℟. **Alleluia.** ↓

> The shepherds, the poor of the people of God, come to pay
> homage to Jesus. Mary ponders and prays over the great
> event of God becoming one of us.

℣. The Lord be with you. ℟. **And also with you.**
✚ A reading from the holy gospel according to Luke.
℟. **Glory to you, Lord.**

WHEN the angels had returned to heaven, the
shepherds said to one another: "Let us go over to
Bethlehem and see this event which the Lord has
made known to us." They went in haste and found
Mary and Joseph, and the baby lying in the manger;
once they saw, they understood what had been told
them concerning this child. All who heard of it were
astonished at the report given them by the shepherds.

Mary treasured all these things and reflected on
them in her heart. The shepherds returned, glorifying
and praising God for all they had heard and seen, in
accord with what had been told them.—The gospel of
the Lord. ℟. **Praise to you, Lord Jesus Christ.**

→ No. 14, p. 18

In the profession of faith, all genuflect at the words, and became man.

PRAYER OVER THE GIFTS   [Gift of Divine Life]

Father,
may we follow the example of your Son
who became man and lived among us.
May we receive the gift of divine life
through these offerings here on earth.
We ask this in the name of Jesus the Lord.
℟. **Amen.**   → No. 21, p. 22 (Pref. P 3-5)

*When Eucharistic Prayer I is used, the special Christmas
form of* In union with the whole Church *is said.*

COMMUNION ANT. See Zec 9, 9   [The Holy One]

**Daughter of Zion, exult; shout aloud, daughter of
Jerusalem! Your King is coming, the Holy One, the
Savior of the world.** ↓

PRAYER AFTER COMMUNION   [Riches Revealed in Christ]

Lord,
with faith and joy
we celebrate the birthday of your Son.
Increase our understanding and our love
of the riches you have revealed in him,
who is Lord for ever and ever.
℟. **Amen.**   → No. 32, p. 70

Optional Solemn Blessings, p. 92, and Prayers Over the People, p. 99

MASS DURING THE DAY

ENTRANCE ANT. Is 9, 6   [The Gift of God's Son]

**A child is born for us, a son given to us; dominion is
laid on his shoulder, and he shall be called Wonder-
ful-Counselor.**   → No. 2, p. 10

OPENING PRAYER   [Share in Christ's Glory]

Let us pray
   [for the glory promised by the birth of Christ]
Lord God,
we praise you for creating man,
and still more for restoring him in Christ.
Your Son shared our weakness:
may we share his glory,
for he lives and reigns with you and the Holy Spirit,
one God, for ever and ever. ℟. **Amen.** ↓

ALTERNATIVE OPENING PRAYER   [People of Light]

Let us pray
[in the joy of Christmas
because the Son of God lives among us]
God of love, Father of all,
the darkness that covered the earth
has given way to the bright dawn of your Word made
flesh.
Make us a people of this light.
Make us faithful to your Word,
that we may bring your life to the waiting world.
Grant this through Christ our Lord. R̸. **Amen.** ↓

READING I Is 52, 7-10   [Your God Is King]

**God shows salvation to all people. He brings peace and
good news. He comforts his people and redeems them.**

A reading from the book of the prophet Isaiah

HOW beautiful upon the mountains
are the feet of him who brings glad tidings,
Announcing peace, bearing good news,
    announcing salvation, and saying to Zion,
    "Your God is King!"
Hark! Your watchmen raise a cry,
    together they shout for joy,
For they see directly, before their eyes,
    the Lord restoring Zion.
Break out together in song,
    O ruins of Jerusalem!
For the Lord comforts his people,
    he redeems Jerusalem.
The Lord has bared his holy arm
    in the sight of all the nations;
All the ends of the earth will behold
    the salvation of our God.
The word of the Lord. R̸. **Thanks be to God.** ↓

RESPONSORIAL PSALM Ps 98   [Sing a New Song]

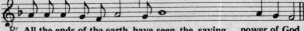

℟. All the ends of the earth have seen the saving power of God.

Sing to the Lord a new song,
  for he has done wondrous deeds;
His right hand has won victory for him,
  his holy arm.

℟. **All the ends of the earth have seen the saving power of God.**

The Lord has made his salvation known:
  in the sight of the nations he has revealed his justice.
He has remembered his kindness and his faithfulness
  toward the house of Israel.

℟. **All the ends of the earth have seen the saving power of God.**

All the ends of the earth have seen
  the salvation by our God.
Sing joyfully to the Lord, all you lands;
  break into song; sing praise.

℟. **All the ends of the earth have seen the saving power of God.**

Sing praise to the Lord with the harp,
  with the harp and melodious song.
With trumpets and the sound of the horn
  sing joyfully before the King, the Lord.

℟. **All the ends of the earth have seen the saving power of God.** ↓

READING II Heb 1, 1-6   [God Speaks through Jesus]

God now speaks through Jesus, his Son, who reflects his glory. The Son cleanses us from sin. Heaven and earth should worship him.

The beginning of the letter to the Hebrews

IN times past, God spoke in fragmentary and varied ways to our fathers through the prophets; in this, the final age, he has spoken to us through his Son, whom he has made heir of all things and through whom he first created the universe. This Son is the reflection of the Father's glory, the exact representation of the Father's being, and he sustains all things by his powerful word. When the Son had cleansed us from our sins, he took his seat at the right hand of the Majesty in heaven, as far superior to the angels as the name he has inherited is superior to theirs.

To which of the angels did God ever say,

"You are my son; today I have begotten you"?
Or again,

"I will be his father, and he shall be my son"?
And again when he leads his first-born into the world, he says,

"Let all the angels of God worship him."
The word of the Lord. ℞. **Thanks be to God.** ↓

GOSPEL Jn 1, 1-18 or 1, 1-5. 9-14   [The True Light]
Alleluia
℞. **Alleluia.** A holy day has dawned upon us.
Come, you nations, and adore the Lord.
Today a great light has come upon the earth. ℞. **Alleluia.** ↓

> John's opening words parallel the Book of Genesis. Jesus is the Word made flesh, the light of the world, who always was and will ever be.

[If the "Short Form" is used, the indented text in brackets is omitted.]

℣. The Lord be with you. ℞. **And also with you.**
✚ A reading from the holy gospel according to John.
℞. **Glory to you, Lord.**

IN the beginning was the Word;
the Word was in God's presence,

and the Word was God.
He was present to God in the beginning.
Through him all things came into being,
and apart from him nothing came to be.
Whatever came to be in him, found life,
life for the light of men.
The light shines on in darkness,
a darkness that did not overcome it.

> [There was a man named John sent by God,
> who came as a witness to testify to the light,
> so that through him all men might believe—
> but only to testify to the light, for he himself
> was not the light.]

The real light which gives light to every man was coming into the world.

> He was in the world,
> and through him the world was made,
> yet the world did not know who he was.
> To his own he came,
> yet his own did not accept him.
> Any who did accept him
> he empowered to become children of God.

These are they who believe in his name—who were begotten not by blood, nor by carnal desire, nor by man's willing it, but by God.

> The Word became flesh
> and made his dwelling among us,
> and we have seen his glory:
> the glory of an only Son coming from the Father,
> filled with enduring love.

> [John testified to him by proclaiming, "This is he of whom I said, 'The one who comes after me ranks ahead of me, for he was before me.'"
> Of his fullness
> we have all had a share—
> love following upon love.

For while the law was a gift through Moses, this enduring love came through Jesus Christ. No one has ever seen God. It is God the only Son, ever at the Father's side, who has revealed him.]

The gospel of the Lord. ℟. **Praise to you, Lord Jesus Christ.**   → No. 14, p. 18

In the profession of faith, all genuflect at the words, and became man.

PRAYER OVER THE GIFTS   [Peace and Praise]

Almighty God,
the saving work of Christ
made our peace with you.
May our offering today
renew that peace within us
and give you perfect praise.
We ask this in the name of Jesus the Lord.
℟. **Amen.**   → No. 21, p. 22 (Pref. P 3-5)

When Eucharistic Prayer I is used, the special Christmas form of In union with the whole Church *is said.*

COMMUNION ANT. Ps 98, 3   [God's Power]

All the ends of the earth have seen the saving power of God. ↓

PRAYER AFTER COMMUNION   [Children of God]

Father,
the child born today is the Savior of the world.
He made us your children.
May he welcome us into your kingdom
where he lives and reigns with you for ever and ever.
℟. **Amen.**   → No. 32, p. 70

Optional Solemn Blessings, p. 92, and Prayers Over the People, p. 99

"He went down with them then, and came to Nazareth and was obedient to them."

DECEMBER 28

HOLY FAMILY

ENTRANCE ANT. Lk 2, 16   [Jesus, Mary, and Joseph]

The shepherds hastened to Bethlehem, where they found Mary and Joseph, and the baby lying in a manger.   → No. 2, p. 10

OPENING PRAYER   [Peace in Families]

Let us pray
   [for peace in our families]
Father,
help us to live as the holy family,
united in respect and love.
Bring us to the joy and peace of your eternal home.
Grant this through our Lord Jesus Christ, your Son,
who lives and reigns with you and the Holy Spirit,
one God, for ever and ever. ℟. **Amen.** ↓

ALTERNATIVE OPENING PRAYER   [Value of Family Life]

Let us pray
   [as the family of God,
   who share in his life]

Father in heaven, creator of all,
you ordered the earth to bring forth life
and crowned its goodness by creating the family of
    man.
In history's moment when all was ready,
you sent your Son to dwell in time,
obedient to the laws of life in our world.
Teach us the sanctity of human love,
show us the value of family life,
and help us to live in peace with all men
that we may share in your life for ever.
We ask this through Christ our Lord. ℟. **Amen.** ↓

READING I Sir 3, 2-6. 12-14   [Duties toward Parents]

**Fidelity to God implies many particular virtues, and among
them Sirach gives precedence to duties toward parents. He
promises atonement for sin to those who honor their parents.**

A reading from the book of Sirach

THE Lord sets a father in honor over his children;
    a mother's authority he confirms over her sons.
He who honors his father atones for sins;
    he stores up riches who reveres his mother.
He who honors his father is gladdened by children,
    and when he prays he is heard.
He who reveres his father will live a long life;
    he obeys the Lord who brings comfort to his
    mother.
My son, take care of your father when he is old;
    grieve him not as long as he lives.
Even if his mind fail, be considerate with him;
    revile him not in the fullness of your strength.
For kindness to a father will not be forgotten,
    it will serve as a sin offering—it will take lasting
    root.
The word of the Lord. ℟. **Thanks be to God.** ↓

RESPONSORIAL PSALM Ps 128   [Happiness in Families]

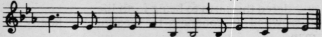

℟.   Hap - py are those who fear the Lord and walk in his ways.

Happy are you who fear the Lord,
  who walk in his ways!
For you shall eat the fruit of your handiwork;
  happy shall you be, and favored.—℟.

Your wife shall be like a fruitful vine
  in the recesses of your home;
Your children like olive plants
  around your table.—℟.

Behold, thus is the man blessed
  who fears the Lord.
The Lord bless you from Zion:
  may you see the prosperity of Jerusalem
  all the days of your life.—℟. ↓

READING II Col 3, 12-21   [Plan for Family Life]

Paul describes the life that Christians embrace through
their baptism. He stresses that they are entering the New
Israel, a new community of God's people, and that their relations to one another should reflect this. Paul's words are
a perfect plan for family life.

A reading from the letter of Paul to the Colossians

BECAUSE you are God's chosen ones, holy and
beloved, clothe yourselves with heartfelt mercy,
with kindness, humility, meekness, and patience. Bear
with one another; forgive whatever grievances you
have against one another. Forgive as the Lord has forgiven you. Over all these virtues put on love, which
binds the rest together and makes them perfect.
Christ's peace must reign in your hearts, since as
members of the one body you have been called to that

peace. Dedicate yourselves to thankfulness. Let the word of Christ, rich as it is, dwell in you. In wisdom made perfect, instruct and admonish one another. Sing gratefully to God from your hearts in psalms, hymns, and inspired songs. Whatever you do, whether in speech or in action, do it in the name of the Lord Jesus. Give thanks to God the Father through him.

You who are wives, be submissive to your husbands. This is your duty in the Lord. Husbands, love your wives. Avoid any bitterness toward them. You children, obey your parents in everything as the acceptable way in the Lord. And fathers, do not nag your children lest they lose heart.—The word of the Lord. ℟. **Thanks be to God.** ↓

GOSPEL Lk 2, 41-52   [Jesus Was Obedient to Them]
Alleluia (Col 3, 15. 16)

℟. **Alleluia.** May the peace of Christ rule in your hearts; and the fullness of his message live within you. ℟. **Alleluia.**

> Jesus and his parents go to Jerusalem for the Passover. Upon returning, Jesus is separated from them. Mary and Joseph find him in the temple teaching. When Mary asked why, Jesus replied that he must be doing his Father's work. Jesus returned with Mary and Joseph to Nazareth.

℣. The Lord be with you. ℟. **And also with you.**
✝ A reading from the holy gospel according to Luke.
℟. **Glory to you, Lord.**

THE parents of Jesus used to go every year to Jerusalem for the feast of the Passover, and when he was twelve they went up for the celebration as was their custom. As they were returning at the end of the feast, the child Jesus remained behind unknown to his parents. Thinking he was in the party, they continued their journey for a day, looking for him among their relatives and acquaintances.

Not finding him, they returned to Jerusalem in search of him. On the third day they came upon him in the temple sitting in the midst of the teachers, listening to them and asking them questions. All who heard him were amazed at his intelligence and his answers.

When his parents saw him they were astonished, and his mother said to him: "Son, why have you done this to us? You see that your father and I have been searching for you in sorrow." He said to them: "Why did you search for me? Did you not know I had to be in my Father's house?" But they did not grasp what he said to them.

He went down with them then, and came to Nazareth, and was obedient to them. His mother meanwhile kept all these things in memory. Jesus, for his part, progressed steadily in wisdom and age and grace before God and man.—The gospel of the Lord.
℟. **Praise to you, Lord Jesus Christ.** → No. 14, p. 18

PRAYER OVER THE GIFTS [Unite Our Families]

Lord,
accept this sacrifice
and through the prayers of Mary, the virgin Mother of God,
and of her husband, Joseph,
unite our families in peace and love.
We ask this in the name of Jesus the Lord.
℟. **Amen.** → No. 21, p. 22 (Pref. P 3-5)

When Eucharistic Prayer I is used, the special Christmas form of In union with the whole Church *is said.*

COMMUNION ANT. Bar 3, 38 [God with Us]
Our God has appeared on earth, and lived among men. ↓

PRAYER AFTER COMMUNION   [Strength for Families]

Eternal Father,
we want to live as Jesus, Mary, and Joseph,
in peace with you and one another.
May this communion strengthen us
to face the troubles of life.
Grant this through Christ our Lord.
℟. **Amen.**   ➜ No. 32, p. 70

Optional Solemn Blessings, p. 92, and Prayers Over the People, p. 99

THE LITURGICAL YEAR
AND THE HISTORY OF SALVATION

1. THE LITURGICAL YEAR

Every Sunday the Church keeps the memory of our Lord's Paschal Mystery. She sanctifies time, consecrates it to God, and as it were inserts us into the History of Salvation. Within the cycle of a year she unfolds the whole mystery of Christ—from His foreshadowings in the Old Testament to His majestic Life and Work in the New Testament.

Thus, the feasts of the Liturgical Year are first of all celebrations of the History of Salvation. The mysteries of our Salvation are to be honored not as something past but as something present, for while the act itself (e.g., Christ's birth, death, resurrection, ascension and the descent of the Holy Spirit) is past, its effects are present. Each feast puts before our mind the sign of some hidden sacred reality, which must be applied to us. We should celebrate the mysteries of our Salvation as happening now to us and we should undergo their mystical effect with an open heart. The best way to do so is by an active participation in Public Worship, aided by the Missal.

We can also be aided by the following summary of the major events of the History of Salvation.

2. ABRAHAM

a) The time around 1850 B.C. was a turning point in the long history of human beings. Almighty God interfered in the course of things and spoke to a man called Abraham. This man lived in what we call now the Fertile Crescent, i.e., the fertile countries along the Tigris and Euphrates rivers, the Jordan river and the Nile river, that surround the Syrian desert as a crescent. God gave the gift of faith to a simple bedouin, Abraham, who surrendered himself and his family entirely to God. Note that God blessed Abraham, promised to give the land of Canaan to his descendants, made a covenant (alliance) with him and wanted Abraham's faith to be sealed with a sign—circumcision (see Rm 4, 11). This is the first establishment of the Kingdom of God on this earth. Read: Gn 11, 27—12, 9; Gn 17, 1-14.

b) It is St. Paul who explains this simple beginning of God's dealings with humanity. Read: Gal 3, 16. 2629. 7-9; Rom 4, 18-25. The Church considers Abraham the Father of all the faithful.

c) During the time that the Kingdom of God was restricted to Abraham's carnal offspring, initiation into it was achieved by the sign of circumcision. Now that it is open to all, through Christ's Death and Resurrection, Baptism and Confirmation are the signs (sacraments) of initiation into God's people on earth. Read: Acts 15, 1-12; Col 2, 11-14.

3. PASSOVER AND EXODUS

a) "Abraham was the father of Isaac, Isaac the father of Jacob, Jacob the father of Judah and his brother" (Mt 1, 2). The clan of Jacob emigrated to Egypt where it later fell into slavery. However, God did not forget his chosen people. He bestowed a leader upon the people of Israel (Moses) who led them out of slavery in Egypt. This is called the Exodus.

Read: Gn 37; 41,37-46; 46,1-7. 28-34; Ex 1,1-14; 2, 1-21; 3, 1-14; 11; 12; 14, 10-31.

b) God's people was saved from bondage and evil by the Passover sacrifice and its Sacrificial Repast—which foreshadowed the perfect Sacrifice of Jesus Christ on the Cross. Because Jesus was man, he could offer a sacrifice. Because he was also God, his Sacrifice symbolized an infinitely perfect obedience and self-surrender and was worthy of God the father. We are saved from evil because of the blood of our Passover Lamb, Jesus Christ. We partake in this Sacrifice, made present to us under the signs of bread and wine, and eat the Sacrificial Repast. Read: Heb 10, 4-10; Mk 14, 12-16. 22-24; 1 Cor 5, 6-8.

4. GOD'S PROTECTION

a) Israel, God's people, went through the Red Sea and obtained their freedom from slavery in Egypt. Under the leadership of Moses they wandered in the desert for forty years and hoped to enter the Promised Land. Whatever they needed in the desert—water, meat and bread—they received through the prayer of Moses. Read: Ex 16, 4-15. 31-35; 17, 1-7.

b) We, who are the new people of God, obtained our freedom from the bondage of Satan by going through the water of Baptism (best symbolized in the ancient Church by immersion!). Under the leadership of Christ the Church passes through the desert of life, hoping to enter the Promised Land: heaven. All that the people need in order to reach their supreme goal is given through Christ, our Lord. Read: 1 Cor 10, 1-11; 2 Cor 5, 1-10; Jn 6, 48-71.

5. THE COVENANT

a) Moses ascended Mount Sinai as the mediator between God and the people. It was on this mountain that God proclaimed the Ten Commandments. The

Covenant of God with Abraham was then four hundred years old (see Gn 17, 1-8). It is a perpetual Covenant, unfolded gradually and consummated with the blood of sacrifice, which reaches its final perfection in its renewed form on Calvary. Read Ex 19, 1-8. 16-25; 20, 1-17; 24, 4-8.

b) The Mediator of the New Covenant is Jesus Christ. It is established on Calvary with all peoples of the world. The New Covenant is consummated with the Sacrifice of Christ's Precious Blood. Read Heb 3,1-6; 8, 6-13; Lk 22, 14-20.

6. FIRST FULFILLMENT OF GOD'S PROMISE

God promised Abraham to give the land of Canaan to his descendants (Gn 12, 7). God began to fulfill his promise when the Jews crossed the river Jordan at Jericho under the leadership of Joshua. He realized it under the kingship of David and of Solomon. This great kingdom, ever more idealized in Jewish history, was actually the Kingdom of God. The king was merely his representative and servant (2 Sm 7, 5). Since the kings were anointed to be king (2 Sm 5, 3) they were called: "The anointed of Yahweh," which means in Hebrew: "Mashiah." Hence the Bible speaks of the "Messiah" or "Christ" (from the Greek), being the king of the great Kingdom of God to come. But this first fulfillment of God's promise contained a further promise, namely, of the Universal Kingdom of God, the Church. God gradually revealed that David's kingdom merely prefigured this great Kingdom to come. Read: 2 Sm 5, 1-5; 7, 1-17 (esp. 12-16); Ps 71, 1-17; Lk 1, 31-33; Mk 1, 14-15; Mt 9, 35-38; Lk 22, 24-30; Jn 18, 33-38.

7. THE EXILE (BABYLONIAN CAPTIVITY)

a) Israel knew that all the blessings and promises of God depended on faithfulness to the Covenant. But

Israel was not faithful. God sent prophets to remind his people of the Covenant. He threatened them and finally had to punish them. Israel was carried away into exile. Read: 1 Kgs 19,1-4; 21; Am 3; Is 1,1-4; 5,17; Jer 2, 4-7; 6, 16-19; 15, 5-6; Bar 6, 1-6.

b) It was in the exile of Babylon that God's people started praying again. We should pray the psalms of God's chosen people and make them our prayer. Exile and punishment may be seen as separation from God, when we have sinned. We are now: Israel, House of Jacob, House of Judah, Zion or Jerusalem. Read: Ps 136, 1-6; 78; 41; 125; 135, 1-9. 26.

8. GOD'S PLAN OF SALVATION

a)) The wise men of Israel, moved by the Holy Spirit (Gn 1, 1—2, 7) tell us that God created everything. To make "everything" more understandable for the people of their time, they divided it up in six portions, calling them "days," in order to suggest that the Jews had six days to work and were supposed to rest on the Sabbath. Compare this story about creation with the lesson about it by St. Paul to the Athenians. Read: Gn 1, 1—2, 7; Acts 17, 22-34.

b) They give us God's plan: Human beings would share in God's own life. They would be only a little less than the angels (Ps 8, 6). They would live in happiness without pain, frustration, hard labor, or sickness and without dying would be admitted to see God in heaven. But this plan could not be realized, because Adam ate from the tree of knowledge of good and evil (committed sin). The Bible speaks of: "sin of the world" or simply: "sin." This is called "original sin"— the sinful condition in which all of us are born because of the sins of our first parents and everybody's sin. Read: Gn 1, 26-30; 2, 8-25.

c) God chose a people for himself. He began with Abraham. Patiently, he revealed his plans more clearly and finally established the Kingdom of God through Christ. God did not give up his original plan. He restored all things in Jesus. Read: Eph 1, 3-10.

9. PREPARATION

a) The punishment of the exile was the punishment of a loving Father. The prophet Ezekiel, who was with the exiled Jews in Babylon, taught them these things. This punishment was to cleanse the people from evil and to prepare them gradually for the coming of the Universal Kingdom of God with the true "Anointed," Jesus Christ. Read: Ez 36, 24-28. 33-38.

b) In the past centuries before the coming of Christ, the pious Jews, called "The Holy Remnant" or sometimes "The Poor of Yahweh," fostered that waiting and desire for the Kingdom of God. They knew their Bible and prayed. Their prayer should be our prayer during our celebration of Advent. Read: Gn 3, 14-15; Is 7, 14; 9, 1-7; 11, 1-9; 40, 1-11; 53, 1-7; Ps 21; Is 45, 8.

c) John the Baptist is the last of the prophets in the time of preparation. He introduced the Promised Messiah to his contemporaries. Read: Mt 3.

10. THE KINGDOM OF GOD IS AT HAND

a) When Jesus of Nazareth began preaching and establishing the Kingdom of God, he taught plainly: "I have come, not to abolish [the law and the prophets], but to fulfill them" (Mt 5, 17). The kingdom of David was only a first fulfillment of God's promise to Abraham. It contained a further promise, which has been fulfilled in the Kingdom of the Anointed of Yahweh par excellence: Christ Jesus. Read: Mk 1,14-22; Mt 5, 17-20; 4, 23-25; Jn 1, 35-51.

b) Christ Jesus explained that it was he of whom the prophets had spoken (see Jn 1,45) and he worked many miracles to manifest the glory and power of God in him. Read: Lk 4, 14-22; Mt 11, 16 and Is 35, 5 and 61, 1; Lk 18, 31-34; 24, 13-35 (esp.25-27); Jn 2, 1-12 (esp. 11); 11, 1-44 (esp. 42); 12, 37-43.

c) With both plain words and parables Jesus explained the nature of the Kingdom and what it means to us. It is a universal Kingdom for all people of faith, who are henceforth the real children of Abraham (see Gal 3, 7). It is a people cleansed from iniquity (see Eph 5, 25-27) and sharing God's life as originally planned by him (see No. 8b). Read: Mt 22,1-4; 21, 33-43; Jn 10, 11-16; 15, 1-11; 3, 1-6; Mt 13.

d) Jesus established a hierarchy of bishops to rule the Kingdom, to teach and to distribute God's blessings in his name, while he resides in heaven, sitting at God's right hand, i.e., as Man sharing power with God, being King and High Priest, interceding for us at God's throne (see Heb 7, 25). Read: Mt 28, 16-20; Lk 10, 1-16 (esp.16); Jn 20, 19-23; Mt 16, 13-20; Jn 21, 15-17; 1 Cor 11, 23-26 (esp. 24).

e) The gradually more perfect realization of the Kingdom in every person follows the universal law of birth and growth: Through pain and death to life everlasting! But it is worthwhile to give up everything to gain it. Read: Jn 12, 20-26; Mt 10, 16-20; Lk 22, 15-30; 12, 22-34; 18, 18-30; 24, 25-27.

11. THE UNIVERSAL CHURCH

The History of our Salvation began with Abraham, reached a peak in the Death and Resurrection of our Lord and became complete with the descent of the Holy Spirit. But it goes on. Christ leads the Church through the Holy Spirit (see Jn 14, 16 and Mt 10, 20). He continues to teach us and to bless us through holy Signs, the Sacraments. And our grateful answer to God by good behavior is possible only with the help of Christ. Read: Acts 8, 26-40; 8, 14-17; 2, 42-47; 2 Tim 1, 6-9; Eph 5, 22-33; Rm 8, 26.

12. THE FINAL FULFILLMENT

When Christ Jesus established the Kingdom of God, the promise to Abraham was fulfilled. God's original plan was restored in human beings. Sin and evil were defeated. Human beings shared in God's life. But like David's kingdom (see No. 6) this first fulfillment contains a promise, namely, the glorious Kingdom of God in the future world. This will be realized when Jesus will surrender the Kingdom to the Father and God will be all in all. Read: Mt 25, 33-46; 1 Cor 15, 22-28; Rv 21, 1-4; Ti 2, 11-15; Mt 6, 10.

CATECHISM OF THE CATHOLIC CHURCH: AN OVERVIEW

To mark the twentieth anniversary of the closing of the Second Vatican Council, Pope John Paul II convoked an extraordinary Synod of Bishops to study the teachings of the Council and make appropriate recommendations to ensure that its purposes would be fulfilled to the maximum degree.

During that convocation the Synod Fathers declared: "Very many have expressed the desire that a Catechism or compendium of all Catholic doctrine regarding faith and morals be composed, that it might be, as it were, a point of reference for the catechisms or compendiums that are prepared in various regions. The presentation of doctrine must be biblical and liturgical. It must be sound doctrine suited to the present life of Christians."

Pope John Paul II was enthusiastic in his support of this proposal, considering it as "fully responding to a real need of the universal Church and of the particular Churches."

According to the Pope in his Apostolic Constitution *Fidei Depositum* to mark the publication of the *Catechism of the Catholic Church,* the Catechism took six years to bring to completion, the main work being entrusted to a commission of twelve cardinals and bishops, assisted by an editorial committee of seven diocesan bishops who are experts in theology and catechesis. It was formally issued in its original French form by John Paul II on December 8, 1992. The English Edition appeared in June 1994.

Therefore, the *Catechism of the Catholic Church* clearly has its basic roots in the Second Vatican Council, as can be seen from the fact that about eighty percent of the citations from conciliar sources are from the documents of Vatican II.

USE OF THE CATECHISM

The Catechism encompasses more than eight hundred pages, and after the introductory Apostolic Constitution on the publication of the *Catechism of the Catholic Church*, and a Prologue that discusses the purpose of man, the value of catechesis, the people for whom the Catechism is intended, the structure of the work, and practical directions for its use, the Catechism itself is divided into four major Parts—Part One: The Profession of Faith; Part Two: The Celebration of the Christian Mystery; Part Three: Life in Christ; Part Four: Christian Prayer.

Each of these four Parts is divided into Sections, with the Sections further subdivided into Chapters and articles.

It could well serve as a textbook for various college courses in religion and the Catholic Church, but those whose education ceased somewhere along the high school level will find it pondersome and a difficult read. It is must reading for the clergy and others in religious life and education as they seek to fulfill their responsibility to expound upon and defend Catholic belief, whether in the pulpit, in the classroom, or in authorship.

All this being said, this Catechism is a monumental accomplishment crafted with care and intelligence and scholarship and love, another step in the on-going process of the last thirty years to modernize the Church while continuing to maintain the ancient truths whose essence can never be changed.

PART ONE: THE PROFESSION OF FAITH

Revelation

Part One is the longest of the four Parts. The opening sections deal with the longing of man for God and how God responds to that desire through his revelation that serves as a beacon of light that clearly reveals the path of salvation to man.

Jesus Christ as the Son of God is then shown to be the major source of the truths of divine revelation, which were transmitted by him to his apostles, and then by them and their successors through the teaching authority of the Church. Such revelation is contained in the Tradition of the Church, which the apostles received from the teaching of Jesus and through the inspiration of the Holy Spirit, and also in Sacred Scripture, comprising both the Old and the New Testaments, of which God himself is considered to be the actual author inasmuch as he inspired its human authors. All forty-six books of the Old Testament and all twenty-seven books of the New Testament are accepted by the Church as inspired teaching.

Faith

By far the greatest portion of Part One is devoted to a discussion of faith, going back in history to Abraham who was the father of all believers and whose faith and trust in God was so strong that he stood ready to obey God's command to sacrifice his only son, the beloved Isaac. The Blessed Virgin Mary is depicted as the one who most perfectly embodies the obedience of faith. And after stressing the necessity to believe not just in God the Father, but in Jesus Christ and the Holy Spirit, and describing faith as a grace and a totally human and free act in which we must persevere if we are to achieve eternal life, there follows a lengthy and detailed exposition of the Apostles' Creed, with an in-depth discussion of each of its twelve articles of Catholic faith.

The Triune God

The first article alone, "I believe in God, the Father almighty, creator of heaven and earth," consumes more than fifty pages of the Catechism, with special emphasis upon belief in *one* God, who has existed from eternity, merciful and gracious, and whom Sacred Scripture describes by the terms truth and love.

The coverage of that first article then moves on to the mystery of the Blessed Trinity, Father, Son, and Holy Spirit, and the development of the dogma of the Trinity, the essence of what is meant by the term "almighty" in reference to God, the creation of the world, the existence and the purpose of angels, the creation of man and the fall from grace of Adam and Eve in the Garden of Eden with its consequences for humanity, the fall of the angels, and the doctrine of original sin.

The material just described in part from the first article of the Apostles' Creed has been the subject of intensive study and prayerful contemplation by saints, fathers and doctors of the Church, clergy and laity, even atheists and those of limited education. Faithful observance of the truths explicitated in that first article alone would seem sufficient to ensure the leading of a way of life that would almost guarantee one's entrance into the companionship of God for eternity.

Jesus Christ, Son of God, and Redeemer

Articles 2 through 7 of the Apostles' Creed deal with Jesus Christ, with painstaking detail over nearly seventy pages, from his incarnation and birth until his death, resurrection, and ascension. Obviously here the Blessed Virgin Mary is covered from every aspect, including those that have been a source of contention and bitter disagreement with some other Christian and non-Christian religions, in particular the Immaculate Conception by which Mary was born without the stain of original sin in virtue of her pre-eminent role as the mother of the Savior, the manner in which she conceived while remaining a virgin, her complete submission to the will of God, and her perpetual virginity.

The treatise on the life of Christ begins with a discussion of why the Son of God became man, his incarnation, his simultaneous status as true God and true man, his human will, and the extent of his human knowledge. After a short section on the birth, infancy, and formative years of Jesus, the Catechism moves on to his baptism, the temptations to which he was subjected, the transfiguration, and his establishment of the Church by entrusting the keys of the kingdom to Simon Peter.

This treatise concludes with Jesus' messianic entrance into Jerusalem, his agony in the garden of Gethsemani, his trial, death, and burial, and his post-resurrection appearances before his ascension into heaven, where he sits at the right hand of the Father and will come again at the end of the world to judge the living and the dead.

The Spirit and the Church

The section on the Creed concludes with an exhaustive discussion on the Holy Spirit, about whom pre-Vatican II Catholics had only a hazy perception, the origin, foundation, and mission of the Roman Catholic Church, the Church in its role as the body of Christ, the bride of Christ, and the temple of the Holy Spirit, the distinctive marks that identify the true Church— one, holy, catholic, and apostolic—the relation of the Church to non-Christians, the possibility of salvation outside the Church, the jurisdiction of the Church in the forgiveness of sins, death and the resurrection of the body, the particular and final judgments, heaven, hell, and purgatory, and everlasting life.

PART TWO: THE CELEBRATION OF
THE CHRISTIAN MYSTERY

Part Two is essentially concerned with the liturgy of the Church as effected by the roles of the Father, the Son, and the Holy Spirit. Section One treats the celebration of the liturgy, with a discussion of such topics as signs and symbols, words and actions, singing and music, holy images, the liturgical seasons, the liturgical year, the primacy of the Lord's day, and the Liturgy of the Hours.

Full, Conscious, and Active Participation

It stipulates that the celebrating assembly is the community of the baptized who are consecrated to be a spiritual house and a holy priesthood that they may offer spiritual sacrifices. This "common priesthood" is that of Christ the sole priest, in which all his members participate. Mother Church earnestly desires that all the faithful should be led to that full, conscious, and active participation in liturgical celebrations which is demanded by the very nature of the liturgy, and to which the Christian people have a right and an obligation by reason of their Baptism.

In liturgical celebrations each person, minister or layman, who has an office to perform, should carry out all and only those parts which pertain to his office by the nature of the rite and the norms of the liturgy.

Baptism

Section Two deals with the seven sacraments of the Church, which are familiar to all practicing Catholics and play an essential role in their spiritual lives. Chapter One of this Section covers the sacraments of Christian initiation—Baptism, Confirmation, and the Eucharist. Baptism is seen as being prefigured in the Old Covenant, and Jesus himself, having willed to submit himself to a rite of Baptism administered by John the Baptist, commanded his apostles: "Go therefore and make disciples of all nations, baptizing them in the name of the Father and of the Son and of the Holy Spirit, teaching them to observe all that I have commanded you" (Matthew 28:19-20).

Baptism itself removes the stain of original sin and forgives all personal sins as well that have been committed prior to the reception of the sacrament. It is necessary for salvation, but it still holds true that even without the formal ritual of Baptism those who give their lives for the faith and those who lack sufficient knowledge of the Church but strive to do God's will can be saved—the categories known as Baptism of blood and Baptism of desire.

While a priest is the ordinary minister of Baptism, in cases of necessity any person can baptize who uses the proper form with the proper intention. As for those children who die without having received Baptism, the Church has not provided a definitive answer but advises that we simply trust in the mercy of God and pray for their salvation.

Confirmation

The second sacrament of initiation is Confirmation, which can be received by any baptized Catholic, and in some areas is administered right after Baptism. Generally administered by a bishop, except in cases of necessity, its purpose is to effect the increase and deepening of baptismal grace through the reception of the full outpouring of the Holy Spirit, as occurred in the case of the apostles on Pentecost, and as related in the Acts of the Apostles when Peter and John laid their hands on those in Samaria who had been baptized in the name of the Lord Jesus, and who then received the Holy Spirit (Acts 8:14-17).

Eucharist

The third and final sacrament of initiation is the Holy Eucharist, instituted by Jesus Christ at the Last Supper when he gave his apostles his Body and his Blood and instructed them to continue this practice: "And he took bread, and when he had given thanks he broke it and gave it to them, saying, 'This is my body which is given for you. Do this in remembrance of me.' And likewise the cup after supper, saying, 'This cup which is poured out for you is the New Covenant in my blood'" (Luke 22:19-20).

The liturgical celebration of the Eucharist, also known as the Holy Sacrifice of the Mass, comprises the Liturgy of the Word and the Liturgy of the Eucharist. The former basically is made up of readings from the Old and the New Testaments and a homily by the celebrant, while the latter includes what in former days were designated as the Offertory, the Consecration, and the Communion.

However, unlike former times, the Mass is now much more designed as a communal celebration at which those in attendance unite with the others who are present and symbolically with all other Catholics throughout the world in an act of unified worship.

Penance

Chapter Two deals with the sacraments of healing: Penance and Anointing of the Sick.

Jesus Christ himself instituted the sacrament of Penance when he appeared to his apostles after his resurrection: "He breathed on them, and said to them: 'Receive the Holy Spirit. If you forgive the sins of any, they are forgiven; if you retain the sins of any, they are retained'" (John 19:22-23). Human beings of their very nature are weak, and they tend to fail in their religious life many times. However, if they turn to God with a firm resolution to amend their lives and confess their sins to a priest who has been authorized by the Church to administer this sacrament, they will receive forgiveness through God's infinite mercy.

Penitents must have contrition or true sorrow for their failings and fulfill any penance that the confessor deems appropriate. In thus being reconciled with the Church, they are also reconciled with God, although they may still have to undergo temporal punishment for their sins after their death. However, by means of indulgences the faithful can obtain either partial or total remission of the temporal punishment due to sin both for themselves and also for the souls in Purgatory.

Anointing of the Sick

The sacrament of the Anointing of the Sick was known as Extreme Unction in pre-Vatican II days. Although then it was basically reserved for those in serious danger of death, now it is offered to those who are approaching that condition, whether from sickness or old age. Its foundation can be traced to the New Testament Letter of James: "Is any among you sick? Let him call for the presbyters of the Church, and let them pray over him, anointing him with oil in the name of the Lord; and the prayer of faith will save the sick man, and the Lord will raise him up; and if he has committed sins, he will be forgiven" (James 5:14-15).

In addition to the sacrament of the Anointing of the Sick, the Church will also include reception of the Eucharist as viaticum to those whose life is drawing to a close. However, even if viaticum is not offered, only a priest or a bishop can administer the sacrament of the Anointing of the Sick.

Holy Orders

Chapter Three deals with the final two sacraments, Holy Orders and Matrimony. The sacrament of Holy Orders was prefigured in the Old Testament in the priesthood of Aaron and the service of the Levites and the priesthood of Melchizedek. There are three degrees of this sacrament—episcopal ordination, the ordination of priests, and the ordination of deacons. Ordination itself can be administered solely by a bishop, and only a baptized man can validly receive sacred ordination.

Matrimony

As for Matrimony, Jesus Christ raised marriage to the dignity of a sacrament, and one that is indissoluble, when he said: "Therefore what God has joined together, let no man put asunder" (Matthew 19:6). And the apostle Paul adds: "Husbands, love your wives, as Christ loved the church and gave himself up for her, that he might sanctify her. For this reason a man shall leave his father and mother and be joined to his wife, and the two shall become one" (Ephesians 5:25-26). While the bride and groom confer the sacrament on each other, the celebration of marriage generally takes place during Mass in the presence of a priest as the official witness.

For a marriage to be valid, the contracting parties must be free of coercion or serious fear, and not be impeded by any natural or ecclesiastical law. Other areas dealt with are mixed marriages, unity and indissolubility of marriage, fidelity of conjugal love, and openness to bringing children into the world.

Sacramentals and Funerals

Sacramentals and popular piety are also treated, as are Christian funerals and the proper manner of celebrating such funerals.

PART THREE: LIFE IN CHRIST

Part Three consumes almost two hundred pages that deal with two major sections: Man's Vocation: Life in the Spirit, and The Ten Commandments.

The Beatitudes and the Virtues

In regard to man's vocation, a wide variety of topics are covered: the dignity of the human person as created in the image of God, our life as affected by the beatitudes, human freedom, the morality and immorality of human actions, the formation of conscience, the problems raised by an erroneous conscience, the cardinal virtues (prudence, justice, fortitude, and temperance), the theological virtues (faith, hope, and charity), the gifts of the Holy Spirit (wisdom, understanding, counsel, fortitude, knowledge, piety, and fear of the Lord), and the fruits of the Holy Spirit (charity, joy, peace, patience, kindness, goodness, generosity, gentleness, faithfulness, modesty, self-control, and chastity).

Sin

In opposition to these are sins, whether mortal or venial. The catechism carefully distinguishes between the two and restates the ancient formula in regard to mortal sin that requires grave matter, and is committed with deliberate consent and full knowledge that the act is seriously wrong.

The Law of Love

The final chapter ideals with moral law and grace, comparing and contrasting the law of the Old Testament with the law of the Gospel, centered in the command of Jesus Christ to love one another as he has loved us, and also discusses the role of the Church as the teacher and arbiter of moral life.

The Ten Commandments

Section Two covers exhaustively every aspect of the Ten Commandments revealed by God to his people through Moses. Those commandments were the essential law for the Israelites. They continued to be such for the early Church and remain so for Catholics today— and will so remain valid for all future generations.

First Commandment

The first commandment states: "I am the Lord your God; you shall not have strange gods before me." As such, to him is due adoration, prayer, sacrifice, and submission to his will while defending the right to freedom of religion and avoiding superstition, idolatry, divination, magic, simony, sacrilege, and other practices encouraged by an atheistic and agnostic world.

Second Commandment

The second commandment, "You shall not take the name of the Lord your God in vain," prescribes respect for the name of the Lord and forbids its abuse and careless use, while condemning blasphemy, false oaths, and perjury.

Third Commandment

The third commandment, "Remember to keep holy the Lord's day," requires Catholics to fulfill the obligation to mark the day of the resurrection by their attendance at the Sunday Eucharist. Those who deliberately fail to observe this obligation are guilty of a grave sin.

Fourth Commandment

The fourth commandment, "Honor your father and your mother," goes essentially and significantly further than those words imply, for our obligations in this regard must be toward not only our parents but all other relatives and those who are deserving of our respect—church authority, government officials, law enforcement personnel, clergy, teachers, and all other individuals of this kind.

And while children have duties and responsibilities toward their parents, it must not be forgotten that parents have solemn duties and responsibilities toward their children, involving their physical well-being and their education, particularly in a moral sense.

Fifth Commandment

The fifth commandment, "You shall not kill," clearly has become an increasingly major issue in the last two decades of this century. Obviously the killing of another human being is innately wrong, but the Catechism makes it clear that such killing may be done in a legitimate act of defense, whether of oneself, or one's family and friends, or one's country.

Also affirmed is the right and duty of legitimate public authority "to punish malefactors by means of penalties commensurate with the gravity of the crime, not excluding, in cases of extreme gravity, the death penalty." The Catechism also condemns abortion, euthanasia, and suicide.

Sixth and Ninth Commandments

The sixth commandment, "You shall not commit adultery," and the ninth commandment, "You shall not covet your neighbor's wife," are treated separately in the Catechism, but both are concerned with immorality, which in secular society seems to have become the rule rather than the exception. All human beings of their very nature are required to be chaste in their own thoughts and actions and to respect the bodily integrity of others. Explicitly condemned are acts of lust, masturbation, fornication, pornography, prostitution, and rape. Those who are homosexual in nature are forbidden to engage in any kind of homosexual activity, although it is stressed that compassion must be shown to those so afflicted. Adultery, polygamy, divorce, and incest are also condemned.

Seventh and Tenth Commandments

The seventh commandment, "You shall not steal," and the tenth commandment, "You shall not covet your neighbor's goods," are also treated separately but again deal with similar themes. Involved is more than simply the outright theft of the money or the property of another. Other acts that contravene the intent of these laws would include deliberate retention of goods that have been lent or objects that have been lost, paying unjust wages to employees, and business fraud.

The Catechism also upholds the right of workers to have recourse to a strike, the necessity to practice social justice, the support of organizations devoted to charitable causes and the alleviation of poverty and disease, and the imitation of Christ in his love for the poor.

Eighth Commandment

The eighth commandment, "You shall not bear false witness against your neighbor," condemns perjury, rash judgment, detraction, and calumny, not only by individuals but also by nations and organizations. The social communications media, with their tremendous power to affect public opinion, must particularly strive to be scrupulously fair and truthful in their dissemination and assessment of the news.

PART FOUR: CHRISTIAN PRAYER

Part Four is the final major division of the Catechism. The custom of raising one's mind and heart to God in prayer can be traced through Sacred Scripture back to the earliest chapters of the Old Testament, and in the New Testament Jesus and Mary have been our primary teachers in this regard.

Types of Prayer

Among the various kinds of prayer, those which are most frequently used are the prayer of blessing and adoration, the prayer of petition, the prayer of intercession, the prayer of thanksgiving, and the prayer of praise. In its mode of expression, it can be vocal prayer, contemplative prayer, and meditation.

The Petitions of the Lord's Prayer

In the final section, the Catechism gives an exhaustively detailed treatment of each of the themes of the Lord's Prayer, more familiarly termed the Our Father, with its various petitions that discuss such topics as the fatherhood of God, the necessity of our praise directed toward him, the coming of the kingdom, obedience to the will of God, the deeper meaning of our daily bread, the forgiving of the sins of our neighbors against us and the hope that our trespasses against them will also be forgiven, and the difficulties of avoiding evil and overcoming temptation.

A BOOK FOR EVERY HOME

There was a great deal of anticipation prior to the publication of the Catechism, and the interest shown by both Catholics and those of other religious denominations was to be expected. What was not anticipated was the tremendous worldwide interest that has made this Catechism a best-seller. It clearly belongs on the bookshelf of every Catholic home.

Saint Joseph
HYMNAL

Praise My Soul, The King of Heaven

F. Lyte

John Goss

1. Praise my soul, the King of hea-ven; To his feet thy
2. Praise him for his grace and fa-vor To his children
3. Fa-ther-like he tends and spares us; Well our feeble
4. An-gels help us to a-dore him; You be-hold him

1. tri-bute bring; Ran-somed healed, re-stored, for-giv-en
2. in dis-tress; Praise him still the same as ev-e.
3. frame he knows; In his hand he gen-tly bears us,
4. face to face; Sun and moon, bow down be-fore him,

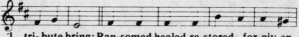

1. Ev-er-more his prais-es sing: Al-le-lu-ia!
2. Slow to chide, and swift to bless: Al-le-lu-ia!
3. Res-cues us from all our foes: Al-le-lu-ia!
4. Dwell-ers all in time and space. Al-le-lu-ia!

1. Al-le-lu-ia! Praise the ev-er-last-ing King.
2. Al-le-lu-ia! Glo-rious in his faith-ful-ness.
3. Al-le-lu-ia! Wide-ly yet his mer-cy flows.
4. Al-le-lu-ia! Praise with us the God of grace.

A Mighty Fortress Is Our God

Cyr de Brant

M. Luther

1. A might-y for-tress is our God, A bul-wark nev-er fail - ing, Our help-er he a - bove the flood Of earth - ly woe pre - vail - ing. The earth and rag - ing sea, Re-lease their pow - ers free; God wat-ches from the height and shields us with his

2. Here Crys-tal ri-vers flow a - long, Their brac-ing wa-ters swell - ing; A ci - ty where there is no wrong Where God and saints are dwell - ing. If kings and ru - lers rage, And man his wars will wage, God is our hope and shield. Just rea - son ne'er to

3. Thy ways and works, Cre - a - tor, Lord, Make days of peace a - chiev - ing. Thy might-y voice can still the sword And ways of wrath pre - vail - ing. With faith and trust in God, Who rules by might and rod, No man need ev - er fear, The God of Hosts is

586

1. might.	The	God	of	Hosts	pro –	tects	us.
2. yield.	O	God	of	Hosts	sus –	tain	us.
3. near.	O	God	of	Hosts	de –	fend	us.

Praise God from Whom All Blessings Flow

3

1. Praise God, from whom all blessings flow;
   Praise him, all creatures here below;
   Praise him above, ye heav'nly host:
   Praise Father, Son, and Holy Ghost.

2. All people that on earth do dwell.
   Sing to the Lord with cheerful voice;
   Him serve with mirth, his praise forth tell,
   Come ye before him and rejoice.

3. Know that the Lord is God indeed:
   Without our aid he did us make;
   We are his flock, he doth us feed,
   And for his sheep he doth us take.

4. O enter then his gates with praise,
   Approach with joy his courts unto;
   Praise, laud, and bless his name always,
   For it is seemly so to do. Amen.

Faith of Our Fathers

4

1. Faith of our fathers! living still,
   In spite of dungeon, fire, and sword:
   O how our hearts beat high with joy,
   Whene'er we hear that glorious word!

   Refrain: Faith of our fathers holy faith,
   We will be true to thee till death.

2. Faith of our fathers! We will love
   Both friend and foe in all our strife,
   And preach thee too, as love knows how,
   By kindly words and virtuous life.

3. Faith of our fathers! Mary's prayers
   Shall keep our country close to thee:
   And through the truth that comes from God.
   O we shall prosper and be free.

5

Praise to the Lord

1. Praise to the Lord,
    The almighty, the King of creation;
   O my soul, praise him,
    For he is our health and salvation;
   Hear the great throng,
    Joyous with praises and song,
   Sounding in glad adoration.

2. Praise to the Lord,
    Who doth prosper thy way and defend thee;
   Surely his goodness
    And mercy shall ever attend thee;
   Ponder anew
    What the almighty can do,
   Who with his love doth befriend thee.

3. Praise to the Lord,
    O let all that is in me adore him!
   All that hath breath join
    In our praises now to adore him!
   Let the "Amen"
    Sung by all people again
   Sound as we worship before him. Amen.

6

God Father Praise and Glory

1. God Father, praise and glory
    Thy children bring to thee.
   Good will and peace to mankind
    Shall now forever be.

Refrain: O most Holy Trinity,
        Undivided Unity; Holy God,
           Mighty God, God immortal be adored.

2. And thou, Lord Coeternal,
    God's sole begotten Son;
   O Jesus, King anointed,
    Who hast redemption won. *Refrain*

3. O Holy Ghost, Creator,
    Thou gift of God most high;
   Life, love and sacred Unction
    Our weakness thou supply. *Refrain*

Now Thank We All Our God 7

1. Now thank we all our God,
   With heart and hands and voices,
Who wondrous things hath done,
   In whom his world rejoices;
Who from our mother's arms
   Hath blessed us on our way
With countless gifts of love,
   And still is ours today.

2. All praise and thanks to God,
   The Father now be given,
The Son, and him who reigns
   With them in highest heaven,
The one eternal God
   Whom earth and heav'n adore;
For thus it was, is now,
   And shall be ever more.

The Church's One Foundation 8

1

The Church's one foundation
Is Jesus Christ her Lord.
She is his new creation,
By water and the Word;
From heav'n he came and sought her,
To be his holy bride;
With his own blood he bought her,
And for her life he died.

2

Elect from ev'ry nation,
Yet one o'er all the earth.
Her charter of salvation,
One Lord, one faith, one birth;
One holy Name she blesses,
Partakes one holy food;
And to one hope she presses,
With ev'ry grace endued.

3

Mid toil and tribulation,
And tumult of her war.
She waits the **consummation**
Of peace for evermore;
Till with the vision glorious
Her loving eyes are blest,
And the great Church victorious
Shall be the Church at rest.

589

9

O King of Might and Splendor

Dom Gregory Murray, O.S.B.

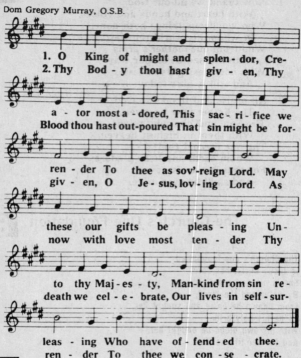

1. O King of might and splen - dor, Cre -
a - tor most a - dored, This sac - ri - fice we
ren - der To thee as sov'-reign Lord. May
these our gifts be pleas - ing Un -
to thy Maj - es - ty, Man-kind from sin re -
leas - ing Who have of - fend - ed thee.

2. Thy Bod - y thou hast giv - en, Thy
Blood thou hast out-poured That sin might be for-
giv - en, O Je - sus, lov - ing Lord. As
now with love most ten - der Thy
death we cel - e - brate, Our lives in self - sur -
ren - der To thee we con - se - crate.

Praise the Lord of Heaven

Praise the Lord of Heaven,
   Praise Him in the height.
Praise Him all ye angels,
Praise Him stars and light;
   Praise Him skies and waters
   which above the skies
When His word commanded,
   Mighty did arise,

Praise Him man and maiden,
   Princes and all kings,
Praise Him hills and mountains,
   All created things;
Heav'n and earth He fashioned
   mighty oceans raised;
This day and forever
His name shall be praised.

Alleluia! Alleluia! Hearts and Voices

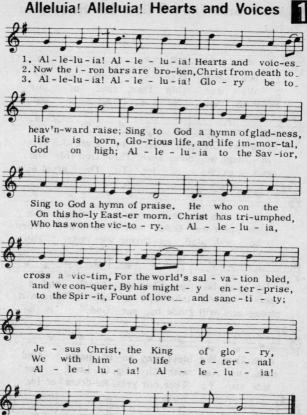

1. Al - le - lu - ia! Al - le - lu - ia! Hearts and voic-es
2. Now the i - ron bars are bro-ken, Christ from death to
3. Al - le - lu - ia! Al - le - lu - ia! Glo - ry be to

heav'n-ward raise; Sing to God a hymn of glad-ness,
life is born, Glo-rious life, and life im-mor-tal,
God on high; Al - le - lu - ia to the Sav-ior,

Sing to God a hymn of praise. He who on the
On this ho-ly East-er morn. Christ has tri-umphed,
Who has won the vic-to - ry. Al - le - lu - ia,

cross a vic-tim, For the world's sal - va - tion bled,
and we con-quer, By his might - y en - ter - prise,
to the Spir-it, Fount of love and sanc - ti - ty;

Je - sus Christ, the King of glo - ry,
We with him to life e - ter - nal
Al - le - lu - ia! Al - le - lu - ia!

Now is ris - en from the dead.
By his re - sur - rec - tion rise.
To the Tri - une Ma - jes - ty.

12 We Praise Thee O God Our Redeemer

Ps. 26:12
Tr. Julia B. Cady

E. Kremser

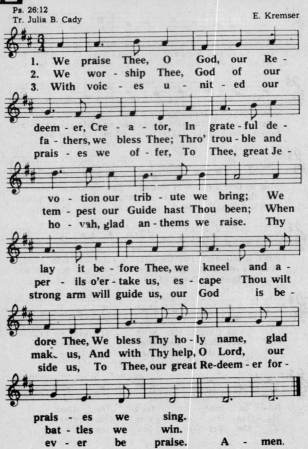

1. We praise Thee, O God, our Re-deem-er, Cre-a-tor, In grate-ful de-vo-tion our trib-ute we bring; We lay it be-fore Thee, we kneel and a-dore Thee, We bless Thy ho-ly name, glad prais-es we sing.

2. We wor-ship Thee, God of our fa-thers, we bless Thee; Thro' trou-ble and tem-pest our Guide hast Thou been; When per-ils o'er-take us, es-cape Thou wilt make us, And with Thy help, O Lord, our bat-tles we win.

3. With voic-es u-nit-ed our prais-es we of-fer, To Thee, great Je-ho-vah, glad an-thems we raise. Thy strong arm will guide us, our God is be-side us, To Thee, our great Re-deem-er for-ev-er be praise. A-men.

Rejoice, the Lord is King

13

C. Wesley, alt.

J. Darwall, 1770

1. Re - joice, the Lord is King! Your Lord and King a-
2. The Lord, the Sav-ior reigns, The God of truth and
3. His king-dom can-not fail; He rules o'er earth and

1. dore! Let all give thanks and sing, And tri-umph
2. love, When he had purged our stains, He took his
3. heav'n; The King of vic-t'ry hail, all praise to

Refrain

1. ev - er - more. Lift up your heart! Lift
2. seat a - bove.
3. Christ be giv'n.

up your voice! Re-joice! a - gain I say 're - joice!

We Gather Together

14

(Same Melody as Hymn No. 12)

1. We gather together to ask the Lord's blessing;
   He chastens and hastens his will to make known;
   The wicked oppressing now cease from distressing:
   Sing praises to his name; he forgets not his own.

2. Beside us to guide us, our God with us joining,
   Ordaining, maintaining his kingdom divine;
   So from the beginning the fight we were winning:
   Thou Lord, wast at our side: all glory be thine.

3. We all do extol thee, thou leader triumphant,
   And pray that thou still our defender wilt be.
   Let thy congregation escape tribulation:
   Thy name be ever praised! O Lord, make us free!

15 Lord, Dismiss Us with Thy Blessing

1. Lord dis-miss us with thy bless-ing;
2. Thanks to thee and a-dor-a-tion
3. O when, Lord, thy love shall call us,

1. Fill our hearts with joy and peace;
2. For the scrip-tures' joy-ful sound,
3. From this world of strife a-way

1. May we all, thy love pos-sess-ing,
2. May the fruit of thy re-demp-tion
3. Let not fear of death ap-pall us

1. Tri-umph in re-deem-ing grace: O re-fresh us,
2. In our hearts and lives a-bound; Ev-er faith-ful,
3. Glad thy sum-mons to o-bey: May we ev-er

1. O re-fresh us, and the world its tur-moil cease.
2. ev-er faith-ful to the ways of truth be found.
3. May we ev-er reign with thee in end-less day.

16 Holy, Holy, Holy

1. Holy, holy, holy! Lord God almighty.
   Early in the morning our song shall rise to thee:
   Holy, holy, holy! Merciful and mighty.
   God in three persons, blessed Trinity.

2. Holy, holy, holy! Lord God almighty.
   All thy works shall praise thy name in earth and
       sky and sea;
   Holy, holy, holy! Merciful and mighty,
   God in three persons, blessed Trinity.

3. Holy, holy, holy! All thy saints adore thee,
   Praising thee in glory, with thee to ever be;
   Cherubim and Seraphim, falling down before thee,
   Which wert and art and evermore shall be.

To Jesus Christ, Our Sovereign King 17

1. To Jesus Christ, our sov'reign King,
   Who is the world's Salvation,
   All praise and homage do we bring
   And thanks and adoration.

2. Your reign extend, O King benign,
   To ev'ry land and nation;
   For in your kingdom, Lord divine,
   Alone we find salvation.

3. To you and to your Church, great King,
   We pledge our heart's oblation;
   Until before your throne we sing
   In endless jubilation.

   Refrain:

   Christ Jesus, Victor! Christ Jesus, Ruler!
   Christ Jesus, Lord and Redeemer!

Father, We Thank Thee 18

1. Father, we thank thee who has planted
      The Holy Name within our hearts,
   Knowledge and faith and life immortal
      Jesus thy Son to us imparts.
   Thou, Lord, didst make all for thy pleasure,
      Didst give man food for all his days.
   Giving in Christ the Bread eternal;
      Thine is the power, be thine the praise.

2. Watch o'er thy Church, O Lord, in mercy,
      Save it from evil, guard it still,
   Perfect it in thy love, unite it,
      Cleansed and conformed, unto thy will.
   As grain, once scatter'd on the hillside,
      Was in this broken bread made one,
   So from all lands thy Church be gather'd
      Into thy Kingdom by the Son. Amen.

595

19 Crown Him with Many Crowns

1. Crown him with many crowns,
   The Lamb upon his throne;
   Hark how the heav'ly anthem drowns
   All music but its own;

   Awake my soul, and sing
   Of him who died for thee,
   And hail him as thy matchless King
   Through all eternity.

2. Crown him of lords the Lord,
   Who over all doth reign,
   Who once on earth, the incarnate Word,
   For ransomed sinners slain,

   Now lives in realms of light,
   Where saints with angels sing
   Their songs before him day and night,
   Their God, Redeemer, King.

20 O Perfect Love

1. O perfect love, all human thought transcending,
   Lowly we kneel in prayer before thy throne,
   That theirs may be the love that knows no ending,
   Whom thou for evermore dost join in one.

2. O perfect Life, be thou their full assurance
   Of tender charity and steadfast faith,
   Of patient hope, and quiet, brave endurance,
   With child-like trust that fears not pain nor death.

21 On Jordan's Bank

1. On Jordan's bank the Baptist's cry
   Announces that the Lord is nigh
   Awake and hearken, for he brings
   Glad tidings of the King of Kings.

2. Then cleansed be ev'ry breast from sin;
   Make straight the way of God within,
   Oh, let us all our hearts prepare
   For Christ to come and enter there.

The Coming of Our God

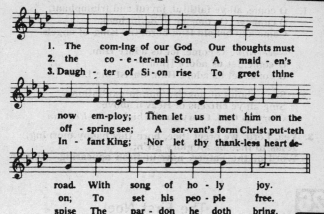

22

1. The com-ing of our God   Our thoughts must
2. the   co-e-ter-nal Son   A   maid-en's
3. Daugh-ter of Si-on rise   To   greet   thine

now em-ploy;   Then let us   met him on the
off-spring see;   A ser-vant's form Christ put-teth
In-fant King;   Nor let thy thank-less heart de-

road. With   song   of   ho-ly   joy.
on;   To   set   his   peo-ple   free.
spise   The   par-don   he   doth   bring.

O Come, O Come, Emmanuel

John M. Neale, Tr.   Melody adapted by T. Helmore

O come, O come, Emmanuel,
And ransom captive Israel,
That mourns in lowly exile here,
Until the Son of God appear.

Refrain: Rejoice! Rejoice! O Israel,
To thee shall come Emmanuel.

Come, Thou Long Expected Jesus

1. Come, thou long expected Jesus,
Born to set thy people free;
From our sins and fears release us,
Let us find our rest in thee.

2. Israel's strength and consolation,
Hope of all the earth thou art;
dear desire of every nation,
Joy of every longing heart.

3. Born thy people to deliver,
Born a child and yet a king.
Born to reign in us for ever,
Now thy gracious kingdom bring.

25 O Come, All Ye Faithful

1. O come, all ye faithful, joyful and triumphant,
   O come ye, O come ye to Bethlehem;
   Come and behold Him born, the King of angels.

   —*Refrain:* O come, let us adore Him,
   O come, let us adore Him,
   O come, let us adore Him, Christ the Lord.

2. Sing, choirs of angels. Sing in exultation,
   Sing all ye citizens of Heav'n above;
   Glory to God, Glory to the highest. —*Refrain*

3. Yea, Lord, we greet thee, born this happy morning,
   Jesus to thee be all glory giv'n;
   Word of the Father, now in flesh appearing.—Refrain

26 The First Noel

1. The first Noel the angel did say,
   Was to certain poor shepherds in fields as they lay;
   In fields where they lay keeping their sheep
   On a cold winter's night that was so deep.

   —*Refrain:* Noel, Noel, Noel, Noel,
   Born is the King of Israel.

2. They looked up and saw a star,
   Shining in the east, beyond them far,
   And to the earth it gave great light,
   And so it continued both day and night. —*Refrain*

4. This star drew nigh to the northwest,
   O'er Bethlehem it took its rest,
   And there it did stop and stay,
   Right over the place where Jesus lay. *Refrain*

5. Then entered in those wise men three,
   Full reverently upon their knee,
   And offered there, in his presence,
   Their gold and myrrh and frankincense. *Refrain*

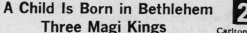

A Child Is Born in Bethlehem
Three Magi Kings

27

Carlton

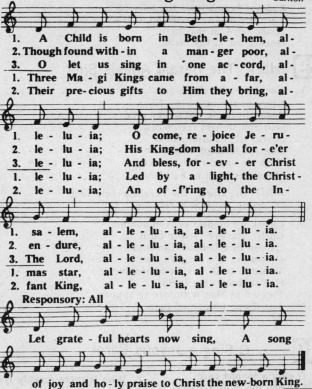

1. A Child is born in Beth - le - hem, al -
2. Though found with - in a man - ger poor, al -
3. O let us sing in one ac - cord, al -
1. Three Ma - gi Kings came from a - far, al -
2. Their pre - cious gifts to Him they bring, al -

1. le - lu - ia; O come, re - joice Je - ru -
2. le - lu - ia; His King - dom shall for - e'er
3. le - lu - ia; And bless, for - ev - er Christ
1. le - lu - ia; Led by a light, the Christ -
2. le - lu - ia; An of - f'ring to the In -

1. sa - lem, al - le - lu - ia, al - le - lu - ia.
2. en - dure, al - le - lu - ia, al - le - lu - ia.
3. The Lord, al - le - lu - ia, al - le - lu - ia.
1. mas star, al - le - lu - ia, al - le - lu - ia.
2. fant King, al - le - lu - ia, al - le - lu - ia.

Responsory: All

Let grate - ful hearts now sing, A song

of joy and ho - ly praise to Christ the new-born King.

Silent Night

28

Silent night, holy night!
 All is calm, all is bright.
'Round yon Virgin Mother and
 Child,
 Holy Infant so tender and mild:
Sleep in heavenly peace,
 Sleep in heavenly peace!

Silent night, holy night!
 Shepherds quake at the sight!
Glories stream from heaven afar,
 Heav'nly hosts sing Alleluia:
Christ, the Savior is born,
 Christ, the Savior is born!

599

3. Silent night, holy night,
   Son of God, lov's pure light
   Radiant beams from thy holy face,
   With the dawn of redeeming grace,
   Jesus, Lord, at thy birth,
   Jesus Lord, at thy birth.

29 Hark! The Herald Angels Sing

1. Hark! The herald angels sing,
   Glory to the new-born King.
   Peace on earth, and mercy mild
   God and sinners reconciled."
   Joyful all ye nations rise,
   Join the triumph of the skies,
   With th' angelic host proclaim,
   "Christ is born in Bethlehem."

   —*Refrain.* Hark! The herald angels sing,
   "Glory to the new-born King."

2. Christ, by highest heaven adored,
   Christ, the everlasting Lord,
   Late in time behold Him come,
   Off-spring of a virgin's womb,
   Veiled in flesh, the God-head see;
   Hail th' incarnate Deity!
   Pleased as Man with men to appear,
   Jesus, our Immanuel here! —*Refrain.*

30 O Sing a Joyous Carol

O sing a joyous carol
  Unto the Holy Child,
And praise with gladsome
    voices
  His mother undefiled.
Our gladsome voices greeting
  Shall hail our Infant King;
And our sweet Lady listens
  When joyful voices sing.

2. Who is there meekly lying
    In yonder stable poor?
Dear children, it is Jesus;
  He bids you now adore.
Who is there kneeling by him
  In Virgin beauty fair?
It is our Mother Mary,
  She bids you all draw near.

Joy to the World

31

Joy to the world! The Lord is come;
  Let earth receive her King;
Let every heart prepare him room,
  And heav'n and nature sing,
And heav'n and nature sing,
  And heaven, and heaven and
    nature sing.

Joy to the world! the Savior reigns;
  Let men their songs employ,
While fields and floods,
  Rocks, hills, and plains,
Repeat the sounding joy,
  Repeat the sounding joy,
Repeat, repeat the sounding joy.

O Come Little Children

32

O come little children, O come one and all
Draw near to the crib here in Bethlehem's stall
And see what a bright ray of heaven's delight,
Our Father has sent on this thrice holy night.

He lies there, O Children, on hay and straw,
Dear Mary and Joseph regard Him with awe,
The shepherds, adoring, how humbly in pray'r
Angelical choirs with song rend the air.

O children bend low and adore Him today,
O lift up your hands like the shepherds, and pray
Sing joyfully children, with hearts full of love
In jubilant song join the angels above.

A Great and Mighty Wonder

A great and mighty wonder!
A full and holy cure!
The Virgin bears the Infant
With Virgin honor pure!

  Refrain:
  Repeat the hymn again!
  To God on high be glory,
  And peace on earth to men.

The Word becomes incarnate,
And yet remains on high;
And cherubim sing anthems
To shepherds from the sky Refrain:

34 Good Christian Men Rejoice

Tr. John Mason Neale

German

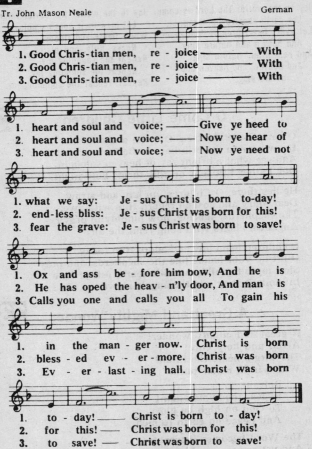

1. Good Chris-tian men, re - joice ———— With
2. Good Chris-tian men, re - joice ———— With
3. Good Chris-tian men, re - joice ———— With

1. heart and soul and voice; ———— Give ye heed to
2. heart and soul and voice; ———— Now ye hear of
3. heart and soul and voice; ———— Now ye need not

1. what we say: Je - sus Christ is born to-day!
2. end-less bliss: Je - sus Christ was born for this!
3. fear the grave: Je - sus Christ was born to save!

1. Ox and ass be - fore him bow, And he is
2. He has oped the heav - n'ly door, And man is
3. Calls you one and calls you all To gain his

1. in the man - ger now. Christ is born
2. bless - ed ev - er - more. Christ was born
3. Ev - er - last - ing hall. Christ was born

1. to - day! ——— Christ is born to - day!
2. for this! ——— Christ was born for this!
3. to save! ——— Christ was born to save!

602

Angels We Have Heard on High

1. Angels we have heard on high,
   Sweetly singing o'er our plains,
   And the mountains in reply
   Echoing their joyous strains.

   Refrain: **Gloria in excelsis Deo.** (Repeat)

2. Shepherds, why this **jubilee,**
   Why your rapturous song **prolong?**
   What the gladsome tidings be
   Which inspire your heav'nly song? —*Refrain*

3. Come to Bethlehem and see
   Him whose birth the angels sing;
   Come, adore on bended knee
   Christ the Lord, the new-born King. —*Refrain*

Away in a Manger

36

1. Away in a manger, no crib for his bed,
   The little Lord Jesus laid down his sweet head.
   The stars in the bright sky looked down where he lay,
   The little Lord Jesus asleep on the hay.

2. The cattle are lowing, the baby awakes,
   But little Lord Jesus no crying he makes.
   I love thee, Lord Jesus! Look down from the sky,
   And stay by my side until morning is nigh.

3. Be near me Lord Jesus, I ask thee to stay
   Close by me forever, and love me I pray
   Bless all the dear children in thy tender care,
   And fit us for heaven to live wth thee there.

O Little Town of Bethlehem

O little town of Bethlehem,
How still we see thee lie!
Above the deep and dreamless sleep
The silent stars go by;
Yet in the dark streets shineth
The everlasting Light;
The hopes and fears of all the years
Are met in thee tonight.

For Christ is born of Mary,
And gathered all above,
While mortals sleep, the angels keep
Their watch of wondering love.
O morning stars, together
Proclaim the holy birth!
And praising sing to God the King
And peace to men on earth.

O holy Child of Bethlehem!
Descend on us we pray;
Cast out our sin, and enter in,
Be born in us today.
We hear the Christmas angels,
The great glad tidings tell;
O come to us, abide with us,
Our Lord Emmanuel.

38   What Child Is This

What child is this, who laid to rest,
On Mary's lap is sleeping?
Whom angels greet with anthem's sweet,
While shepherds watch are keeping?

Refrain. This, this is Christ the King,
whom shepherds guard and angels sing:
Haste, haste to bring him laud,
The Babe, the Son of Mary.

Why lies he in such mean estate
Where ox and ass are feeding?
Good Christian fear, for sinner's here
The silent Word is pleading:

So bring him incense, gold, and myrrh,
Come peasant, king to own him,
The King of kings salvation brings,
Let loving hearts enthrone him.

As with Gladness Men of Old

1. As with gladness men of old
   Did the guiding star behold,
   As with joy they hailed its light,
   Leading onward, beaming bright,
   So, most gracious Lord, may we
   Evermore beled to thee.

2. As with joyful steps they sped
   To that lowly manger bed,
   There to bend the knee before
   him, whom heav'n and earth adore,
   So may we, our worship pay.
   For the blessing of this day.

40

We Three Kings

1. We three kings of Orient are
   Bearing gifts we traverse afar,
   Field and fountain, moor and mountain,
   Following yonder Star.

   Refrain: O Star of wonder, Star of night,
   Star with royal beauty bright,
   Westward leading, still proceeding,
   Guide us to thy perfect light,

2. Born a king on Bethlehem's plain,
   Gold I bring to crown Him again,
   King forever, ceasing never,
   Over us all to reign. —*Refrain*

3. Frankincense to offer have I
   Incense owns a Deity high,
   Prayer and praising, all men raising.
   Worship Him, God most High. —*Refrain*

4. Myrrh is mine, its bitter perfume
   Breathes a life of gathering gloom:
   Sorrowing, sighing, bleeding, dying.
   Sealed in the stone-cold tomb. —*Refrain*

5. Glorious now behold Him arise,
   King and God and Sacrifice,
   Alleluia, Alleluia,
   Earth to the heavens replies. —*Refrain*

41   Of the Father's Love Begotten

1. Of the Father's love begotten
   Ere the worlds began to be,
   He is Alpha and Omega,
   He the source, the ending He,
   Of the things that are, that have been
   And that future years shall see,
   Refrain: Ever more and ever more.

2. O that birth for ever blessed,
   When the Virgin, full of grace,
   By the Holy Ghost conceiving,
   Bore the Savior of our race;
   And the Babe, the world's Redeemer,
   First reveal'd His sacred face. *(Refrain)*

42   To the Name

1. To the name that brings salvation
   Honor worship let us pay,
   Which for many a generation
   Had in God's fore-knowledge lay,
   But with holy exultation
   We may sing aloud today.

2. 'Tis the name for adoration
   'Tis the name of victory
   'Tis the name for meditation
   In this vale of misery,
   'Tis the name of veneration
   By the citizens on high.

43   Holy God, We Praise Thy Name

1. Holy God, we praise Thy Name!
     Lord of all, we bow before Thee!
   All on earth Thy sceptre claim,
     All in heaven above adore Thee.
   Infinite Thy vast domain,
     Everlasting is Thy reign. *Repeat last two lines*

2. Hark! the loud celestial hymn,
     Angel choirs above are raising;
   Cherubim and seraphim,
     In unceasing chorus praising,
   Fill the heavens with sweet accord!
     Holy, holy, holy Lord! *Repeat last two lines*

606

Lord, Who throughout These 40 Days

44

1. Lord, who throughout these forty days
   For us did fast and pray,
   Teach us with you to mourn our sins,
   And close by you to stay.

2. And through these days of penitence,
   And through your Passiontide,
   Yea, evermore, in life and death,
   Jesus! with us abide.

3. Abide with us, that so, this life
   Of suff'ring over past,
   An Easter of unending joy
   We may attain at last! Amen.

When I Behold the Wondrous Cross **45**

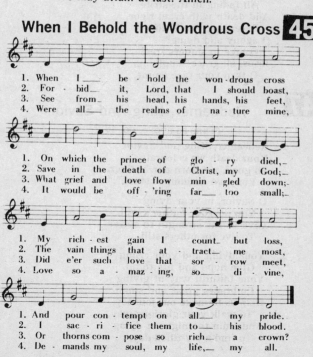

1. When I ___ be - hold the won - drous cross
2. For - bid ___ it, Lord, that I should boast,
3. See from ___ his head, his hands, his feet,
4. Were all ___ the realms of na - ture mine,

1. On which the prince of glo - ry died,—
2. Save in the death of Christ, my God;
3. What grief and love flow min - gled down;
4. It would be off - 'ring far ___ too small;—

1. My rich - est gain I count but loss,
2. The vain things that at - tract ___ me most,
3. Did e'er such love that sor - row meet,
4. Love so a - maz - ing, so di - vine,

1. And pour con - tempt on all ___ my pride.
2. I sac - ri - fice them to ___ his blood.
3. Or thorns com - pose so rich ___ a crown?
4. De - mands my soul, my life, ___ my all.

46   O Sacred Head Surrounded

1. O sacred Head surrounded
     By crown of piercing thorn!
   O bleeding Head, so wounded,
     Reviled, and put to scorn!
   Death's pallid hue comes ov'r you,
     The glow of life decays,
   Yet angel hosts adore you,
     And tremble as they gaze.

2. I see your strength and vigor
     All fading in the strife,
   And death with cruel rigor,
     Bereaving you of life.
   O agony and dying!
     O love to sinners free!
   Jesus, all grace supplying,
     O turn your face on me.

47   Redeemer, King And Savior

(Tune as above, no. 46)

1. Redeemer, King and Savior
   Your death we celebrate
   So good, yet born our brother,
     You live in human state.

   O Savior, in your dying
     You do your Father's will,
   Give us the strength to suffer
     To live for others still.

2. Your dying and your rising
     Give hope and life to all.
   Your faithful way of giving
     Embraces great and small.
   Help us to make our journey,
     To walk your glorious way,
   And from the night of dying
     To find a joy-filled day.

Where Charity and Love Prevail

1. Where char - i - ty and love pre - vail
2. With grate - ful joy and ho - ly fear
3. For - give we now each oth - er's faults
4. Let strife a - mong us be un - known,
5. Let us re - call that in our midst
6. No race nor creed can love ex - clude

1. There God is ev - er found;
2. His char - i - ty we learn;
3. As we our faults con - fess;
4. Let all con - ten - tion cease;
5. Dwells God's be - got - ten Son;
6. If hon - ored be God's Name;

1. Brought here to - geth - er by Christ's love
2. Let us with heart and mind and soul
3. And let us love each oth - er well
4. Be his the glo - ry that we seek,
5. As mem - bers of his Bod - y joined
6. Our broth - er - hood em - brac - es all

1. By love are we thus bound.
2. Now love him in re - turn.
3. In Chris - tian ho - li - ness.
4. Be ours his ho - ly peace.
5. We are in him made one.
6. Whose Fa - ther is the same.

O Faithful Cross

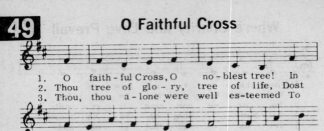

1. O faith-ful Cross, O no-blest tree! In
2. Thou tree of glo-ry, tree of life, Dost
3. Thou, thou a-lone were well es-teemed To

all the woods there's none like thee! No earth-ly
mark the world's most might-y strife. For once had
bear the Lamb who man re-deemed; Thy spread-ing

groves, no shad-y bowers. Pro-duce such leaves, such
been the sigh of shame, For Je-sus now the
arms, like bal-ance true; Weighed out the price for

fruit, such flowers. Sweet are the nails and sweet the
world doth claim. Lo, from the cross, his al - tar
sin-ners due. And on thy al - tar, meek-ly

wood That bears a load so sweet, so good!
throne, He gent - ly draws and rules his own.
laid, The Lamb of God a - tone-ment made.

50 O God, Our Help in Ages Past

1.

O God, our help in ages past,
 Our hope for years to
 come,
Our shelter from the stormy
 blast,
 And our eternal home.

2.

Under the shadow of Thy
 throne,
Thy saints have dwelt
 secure.
Sufficient is Thine arm
 alone,
 And our defense is sure.

3.

A thousand ages in Thy
 sight,
Are like an evening gone:
Short as the watch that
 ends the night,
 Before the rising sun.

4.

O God, our help in ages past,
 Our hope for years to
 come,
Be Thou our guide while
 troubles last,
 And our eternal home.

I. Watts.

610

Were You There

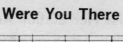

1. Were you there when they cru - ci - fied my
2. Were you there when they nailed him to the
3. Were you there when they laid him in the

1. Lord? Were you there when they
2. tree? Were you there when they
3. tomb? Were you there when they

1. cru - ci - fied my Lord?
2. nailed him to the tree?
3. laid him in the tomb?

Oh _____

Some-times it caus - es me to

trem - ble, trem - ble, trem - ble,

1. Were you
2. Were you
3. Were you

1. there when they cru - ci - fied my Lord?
2. there when they nailed him to the tree?
3. there when they laid him in the tomb?

52 At the Cross Her Station Keeping

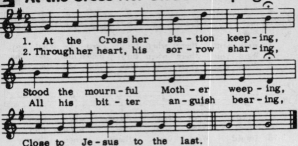

1. At the Cross her sta-tion keep-ing,
2. Through her heart, his sor-row shar-ing,

Stood the mourn-ful Moth-er weep-ing,
All his bit-ter an-guish bear-ing,

Close to Je-sus to the last.
Now at length the sword has passed. A - men.

3 Oh, how sad and sore distressed
Was that Mother highly blessed
of the sole begotten One!

4 Christ above in torment hangs,
She beneath beholds the pangs
Of her dying, glorious Son.

5 Is there one who would not weep
'Whelmed in miseries so deep
Christ's dear Mother to behold?

6 Can the human heart refrain
From partaking in her pain,
In that mother's pain unto'd?

7 Bruised, derided, cursed, defiled,
She beheld her tender Child,
All with bloody scourges rent.

8 For the sins of His own nation
Saw Him hang in desolation
Till His spirit forth He sent.

9 O sweet Mother! fount of love,
Touch my spirit from above,
Make my heart with yours accord.

10 Make me feel as you have felt,
Make my soul to glow and melt
With the love of Christ, my Lord.

11 Holy Mother, pierce me through,
In my heart each wound renew
Of my Savior crucified

12 Let me share with you His pain,
Who for all our sins was slain,
Who for me in torments died.

13 Let me mingle tears with you
Mourning Him Who mourned for me,
All the days that I may live.

14 By the Cross with you to stay,
There with you to weep and pray,
Is all I ask of you to give.

15 Virgin of all virgins blest!
Listen to my fond request
Let me share your grief divine.

16 Let me, to my latest breath
In my body bear the death
Of that dying Son of yours.

17 Wounded with His every wound,
Steep my soul till it has swooned
In His very blood away.

18 Be to me, O Virgin, nigh,
Lest in flames I burn and die,
In His awful judgment day.

19 Christ, when You shall call me hence,
Be Your Mother my defense,
Be Your Cross my victory

20 While my body here decays,
May my soul Your goodness praise,
Safe in heaven eternally,
Amen Alleluia

612

Jesus Christ Is Risen Today

53

1. Jesus Christ is ris'n today, **alleluia!**
   Our triumphant holy day, **alleluia.**
   Who did once upon the cross, **alleluia!**
   Suffer to redeem our loss, alleluia.

2. Hymns of praise then let us sing, **alleluia!**
   Unto Christ our heav'nly King, **alleluia!**
   Who endured the cross and grave, **alleluia.**
   Sinners to redeem and save, **alleluia!**

3. Sing we to our God above, **alleluia!**
   Praise eternal as his love, **alleluia!**
   Praise him, all ye heav'nly host, **alleluia.**
   Father, Son and Holy Ghost, **alleluia!**

At the Lamb's High Feast We Sing

1. At the Lamb's high feast we sing
   Praise to our victor'ous King,
   Who has washed us in the tide
   Flowing from his pierced side;
   Praise we him whose love divine
   Gives the guests his Blood for wine,
   Gives his Body for the feast,
   Love the Victim, Love the Priest,

2. When the Paschal blood is poured,
   Death's dark Angel sheathes his sword;
   Israel's hosts triumphant go
   Through the wave that drowns the foe
   Christ, the Lamb whose Blood was shed,
   Paschal victim, Paschal bread;
   With sincerity and love
   Eat we Manna from above.

All Glory, Laud and Honor

Tr. John Mason Neale, 1851   Melchior Teschner, pub. 1615

1. All glo-ry, laud, and hon--or To thee, Re-deem-er, King! To whom the lips of chil-dren Made glad ho-san-nas ring. ★
3. The com-pa-ny of an--gels Are prais-ing thee on high; And mor-tal men and all things Cre-a-ted make re-ply. ★
5. To thee be-fore thy Pas--sion They sang their hymns of praise: To thee, now nigh ex-alt-ed, Our mel-o-dy we raise. ★

2. Thou art the King of Is-ra-el, Thou Dav-id's roy-al Son, Who in the Lord's Name com-est, The King and Bless-ed One. ★
4. The peo-ple of the He-brews With palms be-fore thee went: Our praise and prayer and an-thems Be-fore thee we pre-sent. ★
6. Thou didst ac-cept their prais-es: Ac-cept the praise we bring, Who in all good de-light-est, thou good and gra-cious King. ★

★ Refrain: after each stanza except the first.

614

Christ the Lord Is Risen Today

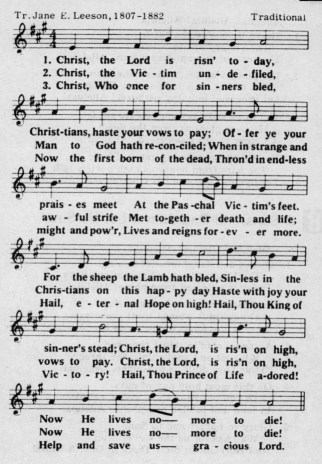

Tr. Jane E. Leeson, 1807–1882

Traditional

1. Christ, the Lord is risn' to-day,
2. Christ, the Vic-tim un-de-filed,
3. Christ, Who once for sin-ners bled,

Christ-tians, haste your vows to pay; Of-fer ye your
Man to God hath re-con-ciled; When in strange and
Now the first born of the dead, Thron'd in end-less

prais-es meet At the Pas-chal Vic-tim's feet.
aw-ful strife Met to-geth-er death and life;
might and pow'r, Lives and reigns for-ev-er more.

For the sheep the Lamb hath bled, Sin-less in the
Chris-tians on this hap-py day Haste with joy your
Hail, e-ter-nal Hope on high! Hail, Thou King of

sin-ner's stead; Christ, the Lord, is ris'n on high,
vows to pay. Christ, the Lord, is ris'n on high,
Vic-to-ry! Hail, Thou Prince of Life a-dored!

Now He lives no— more to die!
Now He lives no— more to die!
Help and save us— gra-cious Lord.

57   The Strife is O'er

Alleluia! Alleluia! Alleluia!

1. The strife is o'er, the battle done!
    The victory of life is won!
    The song of triumph has begun! Alleluia!

2. The powers of death have done their worst,
    But Christ their legions has dispersed;
    Let shouts of holy joy outburst! Alleluia!

3. The three sad days are quickly sped,
    He rises glor'ous from the dead;
    All glory to our risen Head! Alleluia!

4. He closed the yawning gates of hell;
    The bars from heaven's high portals fell;
    Let hymns of praise His triumph tell! Alleluia!

58   O Sons and Daughters, Let Us Sing!

Alleluia! Alleluia! Alleluia!

1. O sons and daughters, let us sing!
    The King of heav'n, the glorious King,
    Today is ris'n and triumphing. Alleluia!

2. On Easter morn, at break of day,
    The faithful women went their way
    To seek the tomb where Jesus lay. Alleluia!

3. An angel clad in white they see,
    Who sat and spoke unto the three,
    "Your Lord doth go to Galilee." Alleluia!

4. On this most holy day of days,
    To you our hearts and voice we raise,
    In laud and jubilee and praise. Alleluia!

5. Glory to Father and to Son,
    Who has for us the vict'ry won
    And Holy Ghost; blest Three in One. Alleluia!

Christ the Lord Is Risen Again

59

1. Christ the Lord is ris'n a - gain!
2. He who gave for us his life,
3. He who bore all pain and loss

Christ has bro - ken ev - 'ry chain!
Who for us en - dured the strife,
Com - fort - less up - on the Cross,

Hark, the an - gels shout for joy,
Is our Pas - chal Lamb to - day!
Lives in glo - ry now on high,

Sing - ing ev - er - more on high, —
We too sing for joy and say, —
Pleads for us and hears our cry, —

Al - le - lu - ia, Al - le - lu -

SING WE TRIUMPHANT HYMNS OF PRAISE

60

1. Sing we triumphant hymns of praise
   To greet our Lord these festive days.
   Alleluia, alleluia!
   Who by a road before untrod
   Ascended to the throne of God.
   Alleluia, alleluia, alleluia, alleluia.

2. In wond'ring awe His faithful band
   Upon the Mount of Olives stand.
   Alleluia, alleluia!
   And with the Virgin Mother see
   Their Lord ascend in majesty.
   Alleluia, alleluia, alleluia, alleluia.

617

61   All Hail, Adored Trinity

All hail, adored Trinity;
All hail, eternal Unity,
O God the Father, God the Son,
And God the Spirit, ever One.

2. Three Persons praise we evermore,
And One, Eternal God adore;
In thy sure mercy ever kind,
May we our true protection find.

3. O Trinity! O Unity!
Be present as we worship thee;
And with the songs the angels sing
Unite the hymns of praise we bring.

62   Lift Up, Ye Princes of the Sky

1. Lift up, ye prin - ces of the sky; Lift
2. Lift up your por - tals, lift them high; Ye

1. up your por - tals, lift them high; And
2. prin - ces of the con - quered sky, And

1. you, O ev - er - last - ing gates, Back
2. you, O ev - er - last - ing gates, Back

1. on your gold - en hin - ges fly, For
2. on your gold - en hin - ges fly, For

1. lo, the King of glo - ry waits To
2. lo, the King of glo - ry waits The

1. en - ter in with vic - to - ry.
2. Lord of hosts, the Lord most high.

Come, Holy Ghost, Creator Come  63

1. Come, Holy Ghost, Creator come From thy bright heav'n ly throne, Come take pos ses sion of our souls, And make them all thy own.

2. Thou who art called the Par a clete, Best gift of God a bove, The liv ing spring, the liv ing fire, Sweet unc tion and true love.

3. O guide our minds with thy bless'd light With love our hearts in flame; And with thy strength which ne'er de cays, Con form our mor tal frame.

4. All glo ry to the Fa ther, be, With her co e qual Son; The same to thee, great Par a clete, While end less a ges run.

Creator Spirit, Lord of Grace 64

Creator Spirit, Lord of Grace
Make thou our hearts thy dwelling place
And with thy might celestial, aid
The souls of those whom thou hast made.

O too our souls thy light impart;
And give thy love to every heart;
Turn all our weakness into might,
O thou the source of life and light.

To God the Father let us sing
To God the Son, our risen king;
And equally with thee adore
The Spirit, God forevermore.

65 Come Down, O Love Divine

1. Come down, O Love divine,
   Seek thou this soul of mine, And
   visit it with thine own ardour glowing;
   O Comforter, draw near, Within my
   heart appear, And kindle it, thy
   holy flame bestowing.

2. O let it freely burn,
   Till earthly passions turn To
   dust and ashes in its heat consuming;
   And let thy glorious light Shine ever
   on my sight, And clothe me round, the
   while my path illuming.

3. And so the yearning strong,
   With which the soul will long, Shall
   far out-pass the pow'r of human telling;
   For none can guess its grace, Till he be-
   come the place Where-in the Holy
   Spirit makes his dwelling.

620

Come Holy Ghost, Creator Blest

66

1. Come, Holy Ghost, Creator blest,
   And in our hearts take up thy rest;
   Come with thy grace and heav'nly aid
   To fill the hearts which thou hast made,
   To fill the hearts which thou hast made.

2. O Comforter, to thee we cry,
   Thou heav'nly gift of God most high;
   Thou fount of life and fire of love
   And sweet anointing from above,
   And sweet anointing from above.

3. Praise we the Father, and the Son,
   And the blest Spirit with them one;
   And may the Son on us bestow
   The gifts that from the Spirit flow,
   The gifts that from the Spirit flow.

O God of Loveliness

67

1. O God of loveliness, O Lord of Heav'n above,
   How worthy to possess my heart's devoted love!
   So sweet Thy Countenance, so gracious to behold,
   That one, and only glance to me were bliss untold.

2. Thou are blest Three in One, yet undivided still;
   Thou art that One alone whose love my heart can fill,
   The heav'ns and earth below, were fashioned by Thy
       Word;
   How amiable art Thou, my ever dearest Lord!

3. O loveliness supreme, and beauty infinite
   O everflowing Stream, and Ocean of delight;
   O life by which I live, my truest life above,
   To You alone I give my undivided love.

68

O Jesus, Joy of Loving Hearts

1. O Je - sus, joy of lov - ing hearts, The
2. We taste and eat, O Liv - ing _ Bread, And
3. Your truth un-changed has ev - er _ stood, You

fount of life, the joy of men, From
long to feast up - on you still; We
save all them who on you call; To

all the plea - sures earth im - parts, We _
drink of you, the Foun - tain - head Our _
them that seek, You are all good To _

turn, un - filled, to you a - gain.
thirst - ing _ souls a - gain you _ fill.
them that _ find, you are their _ all.

Jesus, Highest Heaven's Completeness

1. Jesus, highest heaven's completeness,
   Name of music to the ear,
   To the lips surpassing sweetness,
   Wine the fainting heart to cheer.

2. Eating thee (you) the soul may hunger,
   Drinking still a thirst may be,
   But for earthly food no longer
   Nor for any stream but thee (you).

3. Jesus, all delight exceeding,
   Only hope of hearts distressed,
   Weeping eyes and spirits bleeding
   Find in thee a place to rest.

When Morning Gilds the Skies

E. Caswall, Tr.

Traditional

1. When morning gilds the skies My
2. Be this, while life is mine, My
3. To God, the Word, on high The
4. Let earth's wide circle round In

1. heart awaking cries; May Jesus Christ be
2. canticle divine; May Jesus Christ be
3. hosts of angels cry; May Jesus Christ be
4. joyful song resound; May Jesus Christ be

1. praised! Alike at work and prayer To
2. praised! Be our eternal song, Through
3. praised! Let nations too upraise Their
4. praised! Let air, and sea, and sky, Through

1. Jesus I repair: May Jesus Christ be
2. all the ages long. May Jesus Christ be
3. voice in hymns of praise: May Jesus Christ be
4. depth and height reply May Jesus Christ be

1. praised! May Jesus Christ be praised!
2. praised! May Jesus Christ be praised!
3. praised! May Jesus Christ be praised!
4. praised! May Jesus Christ be praised!

71 How Blessed We Are

How bless'd are we who share this Bread, the
Oh Lord, we eat this Bread of Life, the

Flesh and Blood of Christ our Lord. May
Bread you give to faith-ful sons. The

love u-nite us grate-ful-ly, As
peace of Christ, your Son is ours u-

sons of God who live in peace.
nit-ing us who do your will.

72 Word of God to Earth Descending

Word of God to earth descending
Hastes his mission to fulfill
See his hands himself bestowing
In the hallowed Bread and Wine.

Holy Body, Blood all precious
Giv'n by Him to be our food
With them both he doth refresh us
Form'd like him from flesh and blood.

Mighty Victim, earth's salvation
Heav'nly gates unfolding wide
Help thy people in temptation,
Feed them from thy bleeding side.

Loving Shepherd of Your Sheep 73

1. Lov - ing Shep - herd of your sheep,
2. Lov - ing Shep - herd you did give,
3. Lov - ing Shep - herd ev - er near,

Keep us Lord in safe - ty keep;
Your own life that we might live;
Teach us still your voice to hear;

Noth - ing can your pow'r with - stand,
May we love you day by day,
Suf - fer not our steps to stray

None can pluck us from your hand.
Glad - ly your sweet Will o - bey.
From the straight and nar - row way.

Good Shep - herd, shield us.
Good Shep - herd, lead us.
Good Shep - herd, guide us.

In the Lord's Atoning Grief 74

1. In the Lord's atoning grief
   Be our rest and sweet relief;
   Deep within our hearts we'll store
   Those dear pains and wrongs he bore.

2. Thorns and cross and nail and spear,
   Wounds that faithful hearts revere,
   Vinegar and gall and reed.
   And the pang his soul that freed.

3. Crucified we thee adore,
   Thee with all our hearts implore;
   With the saints our soul unite.
   In the realms of heav'nly light.

75 Let All Mortal Flesh Keep Silence

Gerald Moultrie

French, Traditional

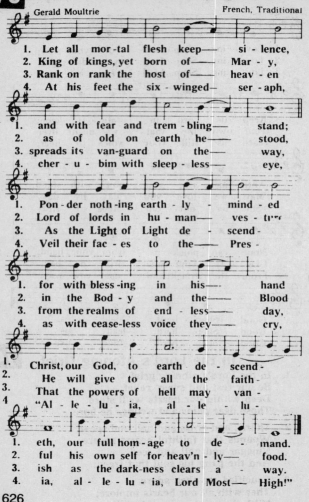

1. Let all mor-tal flesh keep si-lence,
2. King of kings, yet born of Mar-y,
3. Rank on rank the host of heav-en
4. At his feet the six-winged ser-aph,

1. and with fear and trem-bling stand;
2. as of old on earth he stood,
3. spreads its van-guard on the way,
4. cher-u-bim with sleep-less eye,

1. Pon-der noth-ing earth-ly - mind-ed
2. Lord of lords in hu-man ves-ture
3. As the Light of Light de-scend-
4. Veil their fac-es to the Pres-

1. for with bless-ing in his hand
2. in the Bod-y and the Blood
3. from the realms of end-less day
4. as with cease-less voice they cry,

1. Christ, our God, to earth de-scend-
2. He will give to all the faith-
3. That the powers of hell may van-
4. "Al-le-lu-ia, al-le-lu-

1. eth, our full hom-age to de-mand.
2. ful his own self for heav'n-ly food.
3. ish as the dark-ness clears a-way.
4. ia, al-le-lu-ia, Lord Most High!"

626

O Lord, I Am Not Worthy

76

1. O Lord, I am not worthy,
   That thou should come to me,
   But speak the word of comfort
   My spirit healed shall be.

2. And humbly I'll receive thee,
   The bridegroom of my soul,
   No more by sin to grieve thee
   Or fly thy sweet control.

3. O Sacrament most holy,
   O Sacrament divine,
   All praise and all thanksgiving
   Be every moment thine.

To Christ the Prince of Peace

J. S. Bach
E. Caswell, Tr.
Arr. Cyr de Brant

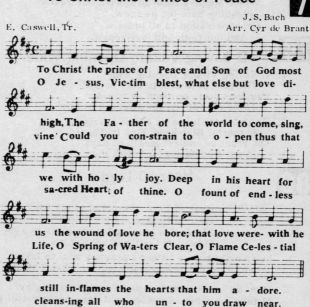

To Christ the prince of Peace and Son of God most
O Je - sus, Vic-tim blest, what else but love di-

high, The Fa - ther of the world to come, sing,
vine Could you con-strain to o - pen thus that

we with ho - ly joy. Deep in his heart for
sa-cred Heart of thine. O fount of end - less

us the wound of love he bore; that love were- with he
Life, O Spring of Wa-ters Clear, O Flame Ce-les - tial

still in-flames the hearts that him a - dore.
cleans-ing all who un - to you draw near.

78   Lord, Accept the Gifts

1. Lord, accept the gifts we offer
   At this Eucharistic Feast.
   Bread and wine to be transformed now
   Through the action of thy priest.
   Take us, too, O Lord, transform us;
   Be thy grace in us increased.

2. May our souls be pure and spotless
   As the Hosts of wheat so fine;
   May all stain of sin be crushed out
   Like the grape that form the wine:
   As we, too, become partakers
   In this sacrifice divine.

3. Take our gifts, almighty Father,
   Living God, eternal, true,
   Which we give through Christ, our Savior,
   Pleading here for us anew.
   Grant salvation to all present
   And our faith and love renew.

79   O Saving Victim, Opening Wide

1. O Saving Victim, opening wide
   The gate of heav'n to man below!
   Our foes press on from ev'ry side:
   Thine aid supply, thy strength bestow.

2. To thy great name be endless praise,
   Immortal God-head, One in Three;
   Oh, grant us endless length of days
   In our true native land with thee. Amen.

80   Hear, O Lord

Refrain: Hear, O Lord, the sound of my call;
   Hear, O Lord, and have mercy.
   My soul is longing for the glory of you.
   O hear, O Lord, and answer me.

1. Ev'ry night before I sleep I pray my soul to take,
   Or else I pray that loneliness is gone when I awake.

2. Why do I no longer feel like I've a place to stay?
   O take me where someone will care, so fear will go
   away.

Sing My Tongue the Savior's Glory

1. Sing my tongue, the Savior's glory,
   Of his flesh the mystr'y sing;
   Of the Blood all price exceeding,
   Shed by our immortal King,
   Destined for the world's redemption,
   From a noble womb to spring.

2. Of a pure and spotless Virgin
   Born for us on earth below,
   He, as Man, with man conversing,
   Stayed, the seeds of truth to sow;
   Then he closed in solemn order
   Wondrously his life of woe.

3. On the night of that Last Supper,
   Seated with his chosen band,
   He the Paschal victim eating,
   First fulfils the Law's command;
   Then as food to his Apostles
   Give himself with his own Hand.

4. Word made flesh the bread of nature
   By his word to Flesh he turns;
   Wine into his blood he changes
   What though sense no change discerns?
   Only he the heart in earnest,
   Faith her lesson quickly learns.

   (Tantum ergo)

5. Down in adoration falling
   Lo! the sacred Host we hail
   Lo! o'er ancient forms departing,
   Newer rites of grace prevail;
   Faith for all defects supplying,
   Where the feeble senses fail.

6. To the Everlasting Father,
   And the Son who reigns on high,
   With the Holy Ghost proceeding
   Forth from each eternally
   Be salvation honor, blessing,
   Might, and endless majesty. Amen.

Sing of Mary, Pure and Lowly

Trier, 1695

1. Sing of Ma - ry, pure and low - ly,
2. Sing of Je - sus; son of Ma - ry,
3. Glo - ry be to God the Fa - ther,

Vir - gin - moth - er un - de - filed,
In the home at Na - za - reth.
Glo - ry be to God the Son;

Sing of God's own Son most ho - ly,
Toil and la - bor can - not wea - ry
Glo - ry be to God the Spir - it;

Who be - came her lit - tle child.
Love en - dur - ing un - to death.
Glo - ry to the Three in One.

Fair - est child of fair - est moth - er,
Con - stant was the love he gave her,
From the heart of bless - ed Ma - ry,

God the Lord who came to earth,
Though he went forth from her side,
From all saints the song as - cends,

Word made flesh, our ve - ry broth - er,
Forth to preach, and heal, and suf - fer,
And the Church the strain re - ec - hoes

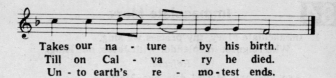

Takes our na - ture by his birth.
Till on Cal - va - ry he died.
Un - to earth's re - mo - test ends.

The God Whom Earth and Sea and Sky 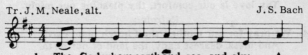 **83**

Tr. J. M. Neale, alt.   J. S. Bach

1. The God whom earth and sea and sky   A-
2.   O Moth-er blest! the chos-en shrine, Where-
3. Blest in the mes-sage Gab-riel brought; Blest
4.   O Lord, the Vir-gin born, to thee   E-

dore and laud and mag-ni-fy, Whose
in the Ar-chi-tect di-vine, Whose
by the work the Spir-it wrought; Most
ter-nal praise and glo-ry be, Whom

might they own, whose praise they tell,   In
hand con-tains the earth and sky, Vouch-
blest, to bring to hu-man birth The
with the Fa-ther we a-dore And

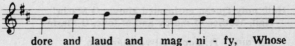

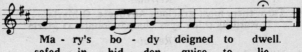

Ma - ry's bo - dy deigned to dwell.
safed in hid-den guise to lie.
long de-stred of all the earth.
Ho - ly Ghost for ev - er - more.

631

Immaculate Mary

1. Immaculate Mary, thy praises we sing,
   Who reignest in splendor with Jesus, our King.
   Refrain:
   Ave, ave, ave, Maria! Ave, ave, Maria!

2. In heaven, the blessed thy glory proclaim,
   On earth, we thy children invoke thy fair name.
   Refrain:

3. Thy name is our power, thy virtues our light,
   Thy love is our comfort, thy pleading our might.
   Refrain:

4. We pray for our mother, the Church upon earth;
   And bless, dearest Lady, the land of our birth.
   Refrain:

85 # Hail, Holy Queen Enthroned Above

   Hail, holy Queen enthroned above, O Maria!
   Hail, Mother of mercy and of love, O Maria!

   Refrain: Triumph, all ye cherubim,
               Sing with us, ye seraphim,
               Heav'n and earth resound the hymn.
               Salve, salve, salve Regina.

2. Our life, our sweetness here below, O Maria!
   Our hope in sorrow and in woe, O Maria!
   Refrain:

3. To thee we cry, poor sons of Eve, O Maria!
   To thee we sigh, we mourn, we grieve, O Maria!
   Refrain:

4. Turn, then, most gracious Advocate, O Maria!
   Toward us thine eyes compassionate, O Maria!
   Refrain:

5. When this our exile's time is o'er, O Maria!
   Show us thy Son for evermore, O Maria!
   Refrain:

Joseph, Be Our Guide

86

1. Jo - seph, be our guide and pat - tern,
2. Faith - ful to the guid - ing vi - sion,
3. Lead - ing them through man - y dan - gers
4. Work - man skilled with saw and ham - mer,
5. Train - ing Christ, the grow - ing Mas - ter,

1. Faith - ful to your sa - cred trust,
2. Lis - t'ning to the an - gel's word;
3. To the home in Na - za - reth,
4. Strong to earn the dai - ly bread,
5. In the skil - ful use of tools;

1. Strong pro - tec - tor of the Vir - gin
2. Shield - ing Mar - y from all slan - der,
3. Hum - bly for their needs pro - vid - ing
4. From the gifts of God cre - at - ing
5. Teach - ing him, the world's Re - deem - er,

1. And the in - fant, Je - sus Christ.
2. Guard - ing Christ, the lit - tle Lord.
3. In your wise and stead - fast faith.
4. Use - ful things to meet man's need.
5. Craft - man's love of wood and nails.

1. Jo - seph, firm and faith - ful; guide us,
2. Jo - seph, true and trust - ing, guide us,
3. Jo - seph, brave, o - be - dient, guide us,
4. Jo - seph, strong and stead - fast, guide us,
5. Jo - seph, hum - ble, help - ful, guide us,

1. Jo - seph, walk the way with us.

87 Ye Watchers and Ye Holy Ones

Athelstan Riley, 1858-1945

Cologne, 1623

1. Ye watch-ers and ye ho-ly ones, Bright ser-aphs, cher-u-bim, and thrones, Raise the glad strain, al-le-lu-ia! Cry out, do-min-ions, prince-doms, powers, Vir-tues, arch-an-gels, an-gels' choirs,

2. Re-spond, ye souls in end-less rest, Ye pa-tri-archs and proph-ets blest, Al-le-lu-ia, al-le-lu-ia! Ye ho-ly twelve, ye mar-tyrs strong, All saints, tri-umph-ant, raise the song: Al-le-lu-ia,

3. O friends, in glad-ness let us sing, All heav-en's an-thems ech-o-ing, Al-le-lu-ia, al-le-lu-ia! To God the Fa-ther, God the Son, And God the Spir-it, Three in one,

al-le-lu-ia, al-le-lu-ia, al-le-lu-ia, al-le-lu-ia!

634

For All the Saints

88

William W. How
Moderately, in unison

R. Vaughan Williams, 1872-1958

1. For all the saints,
who from their labors rest,
Who Thee by faith
before the world confessed,
Thy Name, O Jesus, be for ever blest.
Alleluia, alleluia!

2. O blest communion!
fellowship divine!
We feebly struggle,
they in glory shine;
Yet all are one in Thee, for all are Thine.
Alleluia, alleluia!

3. From earth's wide bounds,
from ocean's farthest coast,
Through gates of pearl streams
in the countless host,
Singing to Father, Son and Holy Ghost.
Alleluia, alleluia!

The King of Glory

89

W. F. Jabusch

Israeli Folksong

Ref.: The King of Glory comes, the nation rejoices;
Open the gates before him, lift up your voices.

1. Who is the King of Glory; how shall we call him?
He is Emmanuel, the promised of ages.

2. In all of Galilee, in city or village,
He goes among his people curing their illness.

3. Sing them of David's Son, our Savior and brother;
In all of Galilee was never another.

4. He gave his life for us, the lamb of salvation,
He took upon himself the sins of the nation.

5. He conquered sin and death, he truly has risen,
And he will share with us his heavenly vision.

Recorded on LP "Songs of Good News. © Copyright 1969 by ACTA
Foundations, 4848 N. Clark St., Chicago, Ill.

90 Glorious God

By Sebastian Temple

Glorious God, King of creation,
We praise You, We bless You,
   We worship You in song,
Glorious God, in adoration, at Your feet we belong.

Refrain:
Lord of Life, Father Almighty, Lord of Hearts,
Christ the King, Lord of Love, Holy Spirit,
To whom we homage bring.

Glorious God, magnificent, holy,
We love You, Adore You, and come to You in prayer.

Glorious God, mighty eternal,
We sing your praise ev'rywhere.

© 1967 Franciscan Communications Center. Reprinted with permission.

91 Peace Prayer of St. Francis

Make me a channel of your peace
Where there is hatred, let me bring you love.
Where there is injury, your pardon, Lord.
And where there's doubt, true faith in you.

Make me a channel of your peace.
Where there's despair in life, let me bring hope.
Where there is darkness only light.
And where there's sadness ever joy.

O Master, grant that I may never seek.
So much to be consoled as to console.
To be understood as to understand.
To be loved, as to love, with all my soul.

Make me a channel of your peace.
It is in pardoning that we are pardoned.
In giving to all men that we receive.
And in dying that we're born to eternal life.

© 1967 Franciscan Communications Center. Reprinted with permission.

For All the Love

92

(Use the same melody as "For All the Saints")

For all the love that in our life abounds,
For all the beauty that this world surrounds,
For music which so joyfully resounds,
Alleluia, Alleluia.

For all the love of family and friends,
And for the love which God in mercy sends,
For all the love toward other he intends,
Alleluia, Alleluia.

For all God's love to bless their vows today,
For all the love to guide them on their way,
For all his love and joy and peace we pray,
Alleluia, Alleluia.

Creighton Lacey

Accept, O Lord

93

Mrs. A. C. Marshall, 1973

Charlotte Hay

1. Ac - cept, O Lord from grate-ful hearts Our
2. We join our hands, our voi - ces raise, Be -
3. On high the host of an - gels song, Both

thanks for gifts__ thy love im - parts; For
fore thy throng__ to sing thy praise; One
heav'n and earth__ with joy now ring. From

this good life we with thee share, And
fam - i - ly whom thou hast made, Thy
Par - a - dise thy saints give hymn, With

broth - er man, for whom we care.
whole cre - a - tion, here ar - ranged.
love that time nor space can dim.

94   With Hearts Renewed

1. With hearts renewed by living faith,
   We lift our thoughts in grateful prayer
   To God our gracious Father.
   Whose plan it was to make us sons
   Through His own Son's redemptive death
   That rescued us from darkness.

   Refrain: Lord God, Savior, gives us strength
              To mould our hearts in your true lifeness.
              Sons and servants of our Father.

2. So rich God's grace in Jesus Christ,
   That we are called as sons of light
   To bear the pledge of glory.
   Through Him in Whom all fullness dwells.
   We offer God our gift of self
   In union with the spirit.

   Refrain: Lord God, Savior, gives us strength . . .

95   Praise the Lord

Praise the Lord for He is glorious,
never shall His promise fail.
God has made His saints victorious,
sin and death shall not prevail.
Praise the God of our salvation;
Hosts on high His power proclaim;
Heav'n and earth and all creation,
Praise and magnify His name.

Worship, honor, glory, blessing,
Lord, we offer unto Thee;
Young and old Thy praise expressing,
In glad homage bend the knee.
All the saints in heaven adore Thee,
We would bow before Thy throne;
As thine angels serve before Thee,
so on earth Thy will be done.

That All Be One

S. Somerville - J. Ritchie

96

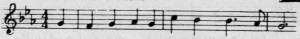

1. That all be one in you, O Lord, we pray,
2. When we are gath-ered for the Eu - char -ist,

That Christ-ians all be joined in one true fold; O
Re - mind us of the words you ut-tered then-Your

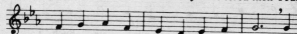

heal the sad di - vis-ions in your Church, Re-
prayer of u - ni - ty and peace and love, The

store the Faith kept.. by your saints of old, Good
one-ness sym - bo - lized by bread and wine. So

Shep-herd of the sheep, re-make us one, All
may we all one bread, one Bod - y be, Through

broth-ers born for you, God's on - ly Son.
this blest sac -ra- ment of u - ni - ty. A-men.

3. Let charity direct our thoughts and deeds,
   Let your love for all men be in our heart;
   So Shall we truly your disciples be,
   So for our sep'rate brethren do our part.
   Teach us our common Father all to own.
   Your holy people in one only home.

639

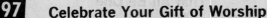

97 Celebrate Your Gift of Worship

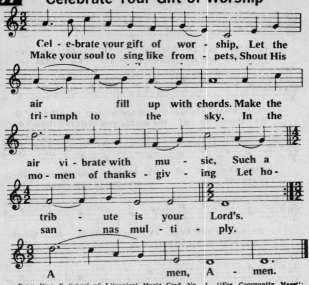

Cel - e-brate your gift of wor - ship, Let the
Make your soul to sing like from - pets, Shout His

air fill up with chords. Make the
tri - umph to the sky. In the

air vi - brate with mu - sic, Such a
mo - men of thanks - giv - ing Let ho -

trib - ute is your Lord's.
san - nas mul - ti - ply.

A men, A - men.

From Pius X School of Liturgical Music Card No. 1—"For Community Mass":
copyright © 1964 and 1965 by McLaughlin and Reilly Co., Evanston, Illinois.

98 America the Beautiful

O beautiful for spacious skies,
For amber wave of grain,
For purple mountain majesties
Above the fruited plain.
America! America! God shed his grace on thee.
And crown thy good with brotherhood
From sea to shining sea.

2. O beautiful for pilgrim feet
Whose stern impassioned stress
A thoroughfare for freedom beat
Across the wilderness.
America America! God mend thy ev'ry flaw,
Confirm thy soul in self control,
Thy liberty in law.

640

America

99

1.
My country, 'tis of thee,
Sweet land of liberty,
Of thee I sing;
Land where my fathers died,
Land of the pilgrim's pride
From ev'ry mountainside
Let freedom ring.

My native country, thee,
Land of the noble free,
Thy name I love;
I love thy rocks and rills,
Thy woods and templed hills;
My heart with rapture thrills
Like that above.

3.
Our father's God, to thee,
Author of liberty,
To thee we sing;
Long may our land be bright
With freedom's holy light,
Protect us by thy might,
Great God, our King.

Battle Hymn of the Republic

1. Mine eyes have seen the glory of the coming of the Lord;
He is trampling out the vintage where the grapes of wrath are stored;
He hath loosed the fateful lightning of his terrible swift sword:
His truth is marching on.

Refrain:

Glory, Glory, hallelujah! Glory, glory, hallelujah!
Glory, glory, hallelujah! His truth is marching on.

2. He has sounded forth the trumpet that shall never call retreat;
He is sifting out the hearts of men before his judgment seat;
O be swift my soul to answer him; be jubilant, my feet!
Our God is marching on! —*Refrain*

3. In the beauty of the lilies Christ was born across the sea,
With a glory in his bosom that transfirgures you and me;
As he died to make men holy, let us die to make men free,
While God is marching on. —*Refrain*

Amazing Grace

1. Amazing grace! how sweet the sound
   That saved a wretch like me!
   I once was lost, but now am found,
   Was blind, but now I see.

2. 'Twas grace that taught my heart to fear,
   And grace my fears relieved;
   How precious did that grace appear
   The hour I first believed!

3. Through many dangers, toils, and snares,
   I have already come;
   'Tis grace hath brought me safe thus far,
   And grace will lead me home.

4. The Lord has promised good to me,
   His word my hope secures;
   He will my shield and portion be,
   As long as life endures.

5. Yea, when this flesh and heart shall fail,
   And mortal life shall cease,
   I shall possess, within the veil,
   A life of joy and peace.

102

Lord Who at Cana's Wedding Feast

1. Lord who at Cana's wedding feast
   Did as a guest appear,
   Though dearer far than earthly guest,
   We ask thy presence here,
   For holy you indeed did prove
   This sacrament to be,
   Proclaim it as a bond of love
   For all mankind to see.

2. This holy vow that man can make,
   The golden thread of life,
   The bond that none should dare to break,
   The bond of man and wife;
   Which blest by you whate'er befalls
   No evil can destroy,
   This blessing, Lord, when one recalls,
   Can heighten every joy.

Gift of Finest Wheat

Omer Westendorf   Robert E. Kreutz

103

Refrain: You satisfy the hungry heart
With gift of finest wheat;
Come give to us, O saving Lord,
The bread of life to eat.

1. As when the shepherd calls his sheep,
They know and hear his voice;
So when you call your fam'ly, Lord,
We follow and rejoice.

2. When joyful lips we sing to you
Our praise and gratitude,
That you should count us worthy, Lord,
To share this heav'nly food.

3. Is not the cup we bless and share
The blood of Christ out-poured?
Do not one cup, one loaf, declare
Our oneness in the Lord?

4. The myst'ry of your presence, Lord,
No mortal tongue can tell:
Who all the world cannot contain
Comes in our hearts to dwell.

5. You give yourself to us, O Lord;
Then selfless let us be,
To serve each other in your name.
In truth and charity.

Christ Our Victor

104

Refrain: Christ our Victor,
Christ our Ruler,
Christ our Lord and Savior.

May good and blessed times come to us;
May Christ's peace be upon us;
May the kingdom of Christ come!

To Thee O Christ Eternal King;
To Thee O blest Redeemer
Let us sing our endless praises.

Praise be to the Father and to the Son
And to the holy Spirit
Let our praises be forever.

105

Whatsoever You Do

Refrain:

Whatsoever yo do to the least of my brothers
That you do unto me.

When I was hungry you gave me to eat.
When I was thirsty you gave me to drink.
Now enter into the home of my Father.

When I was homeless you opened your door.
Whn I was naked you gave me your coat.
Now enter into the home of my Father.

When I was weary you helped me find rest.
When I was anxious you calmed all my fears.
Now enter into the home of my Father.

When in prison you came to my cell.
When on a sick bed you cared for my needs.
Now enter into the home of my Father.

In a strange country you made me at home.
Seeking employment you found me a job.
Now enter into the home of my Father.

Hurt in a battle you bound up my wounds.
Searching for kindness you held out your hands.
Now enter into the home of my Father.

When I was aged you bothered to smile.
When I was resless you listened and cared.
Now enter into the home of my Father.

When I was laughed at you stood by my side.
When I was happy you shared in my joy.
Now enter into the home of my Father.

106

Blest Are the Pure in Heart

Blest are the pure in heart,
For they shall see our God;
The secret of the Lord is theirs,
Their soul is Christ's abode.

2. The Lord, who left the heav'ns
Our life and peace to bring,
To dwell in lowliness with men,
Their pattern and their King.

TREASURY OF PRAYERS

MORNING PRAYERS

Most holy and adorable Trinity, one God in three Persons, I praise you and give you thanks for all the favors you have bestowed upon me. Your goodness has preserved me until now. I offer you my whole being and in particular all my thoughts, words and deeds, together with all the trials I may undergo this day. Give them your blessing. May your Divine Love animate them and may they serve your greater glory.

I make this morning offering in union with the Divine intentions of Jesus Christ who offers himself daily in the holy Sacrifice of the Mass, and in union with Mary, his Virgin Mother and our Mother, who was always the faithful handmaid of the Lord.

Glory be to the Father, and to the Son, and to the Holy Spirit. Amen.

Prayer for Divine Guidance through the Day

Partial indulgence (No. 21) *

Lord, God Almighty, you have brought us safely to the beginning of this day. Defend us today by your mighty power, that we may not fall into any sin, but that all our words may so proceed and all our thoughts and actions be so directed, as to be always just in your sight. Through Christ our Lord. Amen.

* The indulgences quoted in this Missal are taken from the 1968 Vatican edition of the "Enchiridion Indulgentiarum" (published by Catholic Book Publishing Co.).

Partial indulgence (No. 1)

Direct, we beg you, O Lord, our actions by your holy inspirations, and carry them on by your gracious assistance, that every prayer and work of ours may begin always with you, and through you be happily ended. Amen.

NIGHT PRAYERS

I adore you, my God, and thank you for having created me, for having made me a Christian and preserved me this day. I love you with all my heart and I am sorry for having sinned against you, because you are infinite Love and infinite Goodness. Protect me during my rest and may your love be always with me. Amen.

Eternal Father, I offer you the Precious Blood of Jesus Christ in atonement for my sins and for all the intentions of our Holy Church.

Holy Spirit, Love of the Father and the Son, purify my heart and fill it with the fire of your Love, so that I may be a chaste Temple of the Holy Trinity and be always pleasing to you in all things. Amen.

Plea for Divine Help

Partial indulgence (No. 24)

Hear us, Lord, holy Father, almighty and eternal God; and graciously send your holy angel from heaven to watch over, to cherish, to protect, to abide with, and to defend all who dwell in this house. Through Christ our Lord. Amen.

PRAYERS BEFORE HOLY COMMUNION

Act of Faith

Lord Jesus Christ, I firmly believe that you are present in this Blessed Sacrament as true God and true Man, with your Body and Blood, Soul and Divinity. My Redeemer and my Judge, I adore your Divine Majesty together with the angels and saints. I believe, O Lord; increase my faith.

Act of Hope

Good Jesus, in you alone I place all my hope. You are my salvation and my strength, the Source of all good. Through your mercy, through your Passion and Death, I hope to obtain the pardon of my sins, the grace of final perseverance and a happy eternity.

Act of Love

Jesus, my God, I love you with my whole heart and above all things, because you are the one supreme Good and an infinitely perfect Being. You have given your life for me, a poor sinner, and in your mercy you have even offered yourself as food for my soul. My God, I love you. Inflame my heart so that I may love you more.

Act of Contrition

O my Savior, I am truly sorry for having offended you because you are infinitely good and sin displeases you. I detest all the sins of my life and I desire to atone for them. Through the merits of your Precious Blood, wash from my soul all stain of sin, so that, cleansed in body and soul, I may worthily approach the Most Holy Sacrament of the Altar.

PRAYERS AFTER HOLY COMMUNION

Act of Faith

Jesus, I firmly believe that you are present within me as God and Man, to enrich my soul with graces and to fill my heart with the happiness of the blessed. I believe that you are Christ, the Son of the living God!

Act of Adoration

With deepest humility, I adore you, my Lord and God; you have made my soul your dwelling place. I adore you as my Creator from whose hands I came and with whom I am to be happy forever.

Act of Love

Dear Jesus, I love you with my whole heart, my whole soul, and with all my strength. May the love of your own Sacred Heart fill my soul and purify it so that I may die to the world for love of you, as you died on the Cross for love of me. My God, you are all mine; grant that I may be all yours in time and in eternity

Act of Thanksgiving

From the depths of my heart I thank you, dear Lord, for your infinite kindness in coming to me. How good you are to me! With your most holy Mother and all the angels, I praise your mercy and generosity toward me, a poor sinner. I thank you for nourishing my soul with your Sacred Body and Precious Blood. I will try to show my gratitude to you in the Sacrament of your love, by obedience to your holy commandments, by fidelity to my duties, by kindness to my neighbor and by an earnest endeavor to become more like you in my daily conduct.

Act of Offering

Jesus, you have given yourself to me, now let me give myself to you; I give you my body, that it may be chaste and pure. I give you my soul, that it may be free from sin. I give you my heart, that it may

IN LOVING MEMORY OF

Mary Elizabeth Cowan

Feb 13, 1910 - Oct 27, 1996

For to His angels
He's given a command
to guard you in all of your ways.
And he will raise you up
on eagles wings,
bear you on the breath of dawn,
make you shine like the sun
and hold you in the palm of
His hand.
Straub's Funeral Home
Camas, Washington

always love you. I give you every thought, word, and deed of my life, and I offer all for your honor and glory.

Prayer to Christ the King

O Christ Jesus, I acknowledge you King of the universe. All that has been created has been made for you. Exercise upon me all your rights. I renew my baptismal promises, renouncing Satan and all his works and pomps. I promise to live a good Christian life and to do all in my power to procure the triumph of the rights of God and your Church.

Divine Heart of Jesus, I offer you my poor actions in order to obtain that all hearts may acknowledge your sacred Royalty, and that thus the reign of your peace may be established throughout the universe. Amen.

Indulgenced Prayer before a Crucifix

Look down upon me, good and gentle Jesus, while before your face I humbly kneel, and with a burning soul pray and beseech you to fix deep in my heart lively sentiments of faith, hope and charity, true contrition for my sins, and a firm purpose of amendment, while I contemplate with great love and tender pity your five wounds, pondering over them within me, calling to mind the words which David, your prophet, said of you, my good Jesus: "They have pierced my hands and my feet; they have numbered all my bones" (Ps 21, 17-18).

A plenary indulgence is granted on each Friday of Lent and Passiontide to the faithful, who after Communion piously recite the above prayer before an image of Christ crucified; on other days of the year the indulgence is *partial. (No. 22).*

Prayer to Mary

O Jesus living in Mary, come and live in your servants, in the spirit of your holiness, in the fullness of your power, in the perfection of your ways, in the truth of your mysteries. Reign in us over all adverse powers by your Holy Spirit, and for the glory of the Father. Amen.

Anima Christi

Partial indulgence (No. 10)

Soul of Christ, sanctify me.
Body of Christ, save me.
Blood of Christ, inebriate me.
Water from the side of Christ, wash me.
Passion of Christ, strengthen me.
O good Jesus, hear me.
Within your wounds hide me.
Separated from you let me never be.
From the malignant enemy, defend me.
At the hour of death, call me.
And close to you bid me.
That with your saints I may be
Praising you, for all eternity. Amen.

THE SCRIPTURAL WAY OF THE CROSS

The Way of the Cross is a devotion in which we accompany, in spirit, our Blessed Lord in his sorrowful journey to Calvary, and devoutly meditate on his suffering and death.

A plenary indulgence is granted to those who make the Way of the Cross. (No. 63)

1. Jesus Is Condemned to Death — God so loved the world that he gave his only-begotten Son to save it (John 3, 16).

2. Jesus Bears His Cross— If anyone wishes to come after me, let him deny himself, and take up his cross daily (Luke 9, 23).

3. Jesus Falls the First Time—The Lord laid upon him the guilt of us all (Isaiah 53, 6).

4. Jesus Meets His Mother—Come, all you who pass by the way, look and see whether there is any suffering like my suffering (Lam. 1, 13).

5. Jesus Is Helped by Simon—As long as you did it for one of these, the least of my brethren, you did it for me (Matt. 25, 40).

6. Veronica wipes the Face of Jesus—He who sees me, sees also the Father (John 14, 9).

7. Jesus Falls a Second Time—Come to me, all you who labor and are burdened, and I will give you rest (Matt. 11, 28)

8. Jesus Speaks to the Women—Daughters of Jerusalem, do not weep for me, but weep for yourselves and for your children (Luke 23, 2).

9. Jesus Falls a Third Time—Everyone who exalts himself shall be humbled, and he who humbles himself shall be exalted (Luke 14, 11).

10. Jesus Is Stripped of His Garments — Every one of you who does not renounce all that he possesses cannot be my disciple (Luke 14, 33).

11. Jesus Is Nailed to the Cross — I have come down from heaven, not to do my own will, but the will of him who sent me (John 6, 38).

12. Jesus Dies on the Cross — He humbled himself, becoming obedient to death, even to death on a cross. Therefore God has exalted him (Phil. 2, 8-9).

13. Jesus Is Taken Down from the Cross — Did not the Christ have to suffer those things before entering into his glory? (Luke 24, 26).

14. Jesus Is Placed in the Tomb — Unless the grain of wheat falls into the ground and dies, it remains alone. But if it dies, it brings forth much fruit (John 12, 24-25).

STATIONS
of the
CROSS

1. Jesus is Condemned to Death
O Jesus, help me to appreciate Your sanctifying grace more and more.

2. Jesus Bears His Cross
O Jesus, You chose to die for me. Help me to love You always with all my heart.

3. Jesus Falls the First Time
O Jesus, make me strong to conquer my wicked passions, and to rise quickly from sin.

4. Jesus Meets His Mother
O Jesus, grant me a tender love for Your Mother, who offered You for love of me.

STATImport
STATIONS
of the
CROSS

5. Jesus is Helped by Simon

O Jesus, like Simon lead me ever closer to You through my daily crosses and trials.

6. Jesus and Veronica

O Jesus, imprint Your image on my heart that I may be faithful to You all my life.

7. Jesus Falls a Second Time

O Jesus, I repent for having offended You. Grant me forgiveness of all my sins.

8. Jesus Speaks to the Women

O Jesus, grant me tears of compassion for Your sufferings and of sorrow for my sins.

STATIONS
of the
CROSS

9. Jesus Falls a Third Time

O Jesus, let me never yield to despair. Let me come to You in hardship and spiritual distress.

10. He is Stripped of His Garments

O Jesus, let me sacrifice all my attachments rather than imperil the divine life of my soul.

11. Jesus is Nailed to the Cross

O Jesus, strengthen my faith and increase my love for You. Help me to accept my crosses.

12. Jesus Dies on the Cross

O Jesus, I thank You for making me a child of God. Help me to forgive others.

STATIONS
of the
CROSS

13. Jesus is Taken down from the Cross

O Jesus, through the intercession of Your holy Mother, let me be pleasing to You.

14. Jesus is Laid in the Tomb

O Jesus, strengthen my will to live for You on earth and bring me to eternal bliss in heaven.

Prayer after the Stations

JESUS, You became an example of humility, obedience and patience, and preceded me on the way of life bearing Your Cross. Grant that, inflamed with Your love, I may cheerfully take upon myself the sweet yoke of Your Gospel together with the mortification of the Cross and follow You as a true disciple so that I may be united with You in heaven. Amen.

THE HOLY ROSARY

Prayer before the Rosary

QUEEN of the Holy Rosary, you have deigned to come to Fatima to reveal to the three shepherd children the treasures of grace hidden in the Rosary. Inspire my heart with a sincere love of this devotion, in order that by meditating on the Mysteries of our Redemption which are recalled in it, I may be enriched with its fruits and obtain peace for the world, the conversion of sinners and of Russia, and the favor which I ask of you in this Rosary. (*Here mention your request.*) I ask it for the greater glory of God, for your own honor, and for the good of souls, especially for my own. Amen.

The Five Joyful Mysteries

1. The Annunciation
For the love of humility.

2. The Visitation
For charity toward my neighbor.

4. The Presentation
For the virtue of obedience.

3. The Nativity
For the spirit of poverty.

5. Finding in the Temple
For the virtue of piety.

The Five
Sorrowful
Mysteries

3. Crowning with Thorns
For moral courage.

1. Agony in the Garden
For true contrition.

4. Carrying of the Cross
For the virtue of patience.

2. Scourging at the Pillar
For the virtue of purity.

5. The Crucifixion
For final perseverance.

The Five

Glorious

Mysteries

1. The Resurrection
For the virtue of faith.

2. The Ascension
For the virtue of hope.

4. Assumption of the B.V.M.
For devotion to Mary.

3. Descent of the Holy Spirit
For love of God.

5. Crowning of the B.V.M.
For eternal happiness.

PRAYER TO ST. JOSEPH

O Blessed St. Joseph, loving father and faithful guardian of Jesus, and devoted spouse of the Mother of God, I beg you to offer God the Father his divine Son, bathed in blood on the Cross. Through the holy Name of Jesus obtain for us from the Father the favor we implore.

FOR THE SICK

Father, your Son accepted our sufferings to teach us the virtue of patience in human illness. Hear the prayers we offer for our sick brothers and sisters. May all who suffer pain, illness or disease realize that they are chosen to be saints, and know that they are joined to Christ in his suffering for the salvation of the world, who lives and reigns with you and the Holy Spirit, one God, for ever and ever.

FOR RELIGIOUS VOCATIONS

Father, you call all who believe in you to grow perfect in love by following in the footsteps of Christ your Son. May those whom you have chosen to serve you as religious provide by their way of life a convincing sign of your kingdom for the Church and the whole world.

FOR THE ASSEMBLY OF NATIONAL LEADERS

Father, you guide and govern everything with order and love. Look upon the assembly of our national leaders and fill them with the spirit of your wisdom. May they always act in accordance with your will and their decisions be for the peace and well-being of all.

PRAYER OF A FAMILY

God of goodness and mercy, to your fatherly protection we commend our family, our household and all that belongs to us. We entrust all to your love and keeping. Fill our home with your blessings as you filled the holy house of Nazareth with your presence.

Above all else, keep far from us the stain of sin. We want you alone to rule over us. Help each one of us to obey your holy laws, to love you sincerely and to imitate your example, the example of Mary, your mother and ours, and the example of your holy guardian, saint Joseph.

Lord, preserve us and our home from all evils and misfortunes. May we be ever resigned to your divine will even in the crosses and sorrows which you allow to come to us.

Finally, give all of us the grace to live in perfect harmony and love toward our neighbor. Grant that every one of us may deserve by a holy life the comfort of your holy sacraments at the hour of death.

Bless this house, God the Father, who created us, God the Son, who suffered for us upon the cross, and God the Holy Spirit, who sanctified us in baptism. May the one God in three divine persons preserve our bodies, purify our minds, direct our hearts and bring us all to everlasting life.

Glory be to the Father, glory be to the Son, glory be to the Holy Spirit! Amen.

PRAYER FOR HEALTH

O Sacred Heart of Jesus, I come to ask of Your infinite mercy the gift of health and strength that I may serve You more faithfully and love You more sincerely than in the past. I wish to be well and strong if this be Your good pleasure and for Your greater glory. Filled with high resolves and determined to perform my tasks most perfectly for love of You, I wish to be enabled to go back to my duties.

PRAYER FOR PEACE AND JOY

Jesus, I want to rejoice in You always. You are near. Let me have no anxiety, but in every concern by prayer and supplication with thanksgiving I wish to let my petitions be made known in my communing with God.

May the peace of God, which surpasses all understanding, guard my heart and my thoughts in You.

PRAYER TO KNOW GOD'S WILL

God the Father of our Lord Jesus Christ, the Author of glory, grant me spiritual wisdom and revelation. Enlighten the eyes of my mind with a deep knowledge of You and Your holy will. May I understand of what nature is the hope to which You call me, what is the wealth of the splendor of Your inheritance among the Saints, and what is the surpassing greatness of Your power toward me.

PRAYER FOR CIVIL AUTHORITIES

Almighty and everlasting God, You direct the powers and laws of all nations; mercifully regard those who rule over us, that, by Your protecting right hand, the integrity of religion and the security of each country might prevail everywhere on earth. Through Christ our Lord. Amen.

PRAYER TO ST. JOSEPH

Guardian of virgins, and holy father Joseph, to whose faithful custody Christ Jesus, innocence itself, and Mary, Virgin of virgins, were committed; I beg you, by these dear pledges, Jesus and Mary, that, being preserved from all uncleanness, I may with spotless mind, pure heart and chaste body, ever serve Jesus and Mary most chastely all the days of my life. Amen.

THE TEN COMMANDMENTS

1. I, the Lord, am your God. You shall not have other gods besides Me.
2. You shall not take the Name of the Lord, your God, in vain.
3. Remember to keep holy the sabbath day.
4. Honor you father and your mother.
5. You shall not kill.
6. You shall not commit adultery.
7. You shall not steal.
8. You shall not bear false witness against your neighbor.
9. You shall not covet your neighbor's wife.
10. You shall not covet anything that belongs to your neighbor.

THE GREAT COMMANDMENT

You shall love the Lord your God with your whole heart, and with your whole soul, and with all your mind. This is the greatest and the first commandment. And the second is like it: you shall love your neighbor as yourself.
—Mt 22, 37

NEW RITE OF PENANCE

(Extracted from the Rite of Penance)

Texts for the Penitent

The penitent should prepare for the celebration of the sacrament by prayer, reading of Scripture, and silent reflection. The penitent should think over and should regret all sins since the last celebration of the sacrament.

RECEPTION OF THE PENITENT

The penitent enters the confessional or other place set aside for the celebration of the sacrament of penance. After the welcoming of the priest, the penitent makes the sign of the cross saying:

In the name of the Father, and of the Son, and of the Holy Spirit. Amen.

The penitent is invited to have trust in God and replies:

Amen.

READING OF THE WORD OF GOD

The penitent then listens to a text of Scripture which tells about God's mercy and calls man to conversion.

CONFESSION OF SINS AND ACCEPTANCE OF SATISFACTION

The penitent speaks to the priest in a normal, conversational fashion. The penitent tells when he or she last celebrated the sacrament and then confesses his or her sins. The penitent then listens to any advice the priest may give and accepts the satisfaction from the priest. The penitent should ask any appropriate questions.

PRAYER OF THE PENITENT AND ABSOLUTION

Prayer

Before the absolution is given, the penitent expresses sorrow for sins in these or similar words:

My God,
I am sorry for my sins with all my heart.
In choosing to do wrong
and failing to do good,
I have sinned against you
whom I should love above all things.
I firmly intend, with your help,
to do penance,
to sin no more,
and to avoid whatever leads me to sin.
Our Savior Jesus Christ
suffered and died for us.
In his name, my God, have mercy.

OR:

> Remember, Lord, your compassion and mercy which you
>   showed long ago.
> Do not recall the sins and failings of my youth.
> In your mercy remember me, Lord, because of your
>   goodness.

OR:

> Wash me from my guilt
> and cleanse me of my sin.
> I acknowledge my offense;
> my sin is before me always.

OR:

> Father, I have sinned against you
> and am not worthy to be called your son.
> Be merciful to me, a sinner.

OR:

> Father of mercy,
> like the prodigal son
> I return to you and say:
> "I have sinned against you
> and am no longer worthy to be called your son."
> Christ Jesus, Savior of the world,
> I pray with the repentant thief
> to whom you promised Paradise:
> "Lord, remember me in your kingdom."
> Holy Spirit, fountain of love,
> I call on you with trust:
> "Purify my heart,
> and help me to walk as a child of light."

OR:

> Lord Jesus,
> you opened the eyes of the blind,
> healed the sick,
> forgave the sinful woman,
> and after Peter's denial confirmed him in your love.
> Listen to my prayer,
> forgive all my sins,
> renew your love in my heart,
> help me to live in perfect unity with my fellow Christians
> that I may proclaim your saving power to all the world.

OR:

> Lord Jesus;
> you chose to be called the friend of sinners.
> By your saving death and resurrection
> free me from my sins.
> May your peace take root in my heart

and bring forth a harvest
of love, holiness, and truth.

OR:

Lord Jesus Christ,
you are the Lamb of God;
you take away the sins of the world.
Through the grace of the Holy Spirit
restore me to friendship with your Father,
cleanse me from every stain of sin
and raise me to new life
for the glory of your name.

OR:

Lord God,
in your goodness have mercy on me:
do not look on my sins,
but take away all my guilt.
Create in me a clean heart
and renew within me an upright spirit.

OR:

Lord Jesus, Son of God,
have mercy on me, a sinner.

ABSOLUTION

*If the penitent is not kneeling, he or she bows his or her
head as the priest extends his hands (or at least extends his
right hand).*

God, the Father of mercies,
through the death and resurrection of his Son
has reconciled the world to himself
and sent the Holy Spirit among us
for the forgiveness of sins;
through the ministry of the Church
may God give you pardon and peace,
and I absolve you from your sins
in the name of the Father, and of the Son,
and of the Holy Spirit. Amen.

PROCLAMATION OF PRAISE OF GOD AND DISMISSAL

Penitent and priest give praise to God.

Priest: Give thanks to the Lord, for he is good.
Penitent: His mercy endures for ever.

Then the penitent is dismissed by the priest.

Form of Examination of Conscience

This suggested form for an examination of conscience should be completed and adapted to meet the needs of different individuals and to follow local usages.

In an examination of conscience, before the sacrament of penance, each individual should ask himself these questions in particular:

1. What is my attitude to the sacrament of penance? Do I sincerely want to be set free from sin, to turn again to God, to begin a new life, and to enter into a deeper friendship with God? Or do I look on it as a burden, to be undertaken as seldom as possible?

2. Did I forget to mention, or deliberately conceal, any grave sins in past confessions?

3. Did I perform the penance I was given? Did I make reparation for any injury to others? Have I tried to put into practice my resolution to lead a better life in keeping with the Gospel?

Each individual should examine his life in the light of God's word.

I. The Lord says: "You shall love the Lord your God with your whole heart."

1. Is my heart set on God, so that I really love him above all things and am faithful to his commandments, as a son loves his father? Or am I more concerned about the things of this world? Have I a right intention in what I do?

2. God spoke to us in his Son. Is my faith in God firm and secure? Am I wholehearted in accepting the Church's teaching? Have I been careful to grow in my understanding of the faith, to hear God's word, to listen to instructions on the faith, to avoid dangers to faith? Have I been always strong and fearless in professing my faith in God and the Church? Have I been willing to be known as a Christian in private and public life?

3. Have I prayed morning and evening? When I pray, do I really raise my mind and heart to God or is it a matter of words only? Do I offer God my difficulties, my joys, and my sorrows? Do I turn to God in time of temptation?

4. Have I love and reverence for God's name? Have I offended him in blasphemy, swearing falsely, or taking his name in vain? Have I shown disrespect for the Blessed Virgin Mary and the saints?

5. Do I keep Sundays and feast days holy by taking a full part, with attention and devotion, in the liturgy, and especially in the Mass? Have I fulfilled the precept of annual confession and of communion during the Easter season?

6. Are there false gods that I worship by giving them greater attention and deeper trust than I give to God: money, superstition, spiritism, or other occult practices?

II. The Lord says: "Love one another as I have loved you."

1. Have I a genuine love for my neighbors? Or do I use them for my own ends, or do to them what I would not want done to myself? Have I given grave scandal by my words or actions.?

2. In my family life, have I contributed to the well-being and happiness of the rest of the family by patience and genuine love? Have I been obedient to parents, showing them proper respect and giving them help in their spiritual and material needs? Have I been careful to give a Christian upbringing to my children, and to help them by good example and by exercising authority as a parent? Have I been faithful to my husband/wife in my heart and in my relations with others?

3. Do I share my possessions with the less fortunate? Do I do my best to help the victims of oppression, misfortune, and poverty? Or do I look down on my neighbor, especially the poor, the sick, the elderly, strangers, and people of other races?

4. Does my life reflect the mission I received in confirmation? Do I share in the apostolic and charitable works of the Church and in the life of my parish? Have I helped to meet the needs of the Church and of the world and prayed for them: for unity in the Church, for the spread of the Gospel among the nations, for peace and justice, etc.?

5. Am I concerned for the good and prosperity of the human community in which I live, or do I spend my life caring only for myself? Do I share to the best of my ability in the work of promoting justice, morality, harmony, and love in human relations? Have I done my duty as a citizen? Have I paid my taxes?

6. In my work or profession am I just, hard-working, honest, serving society out of love for others? Have I paid a fair wage to my employees? Have I been faithful to my promises and contracts?

7. Have I obeyed legitimate authority and given it due respect?

8. If I am in a position of responsibility or authority, do I use this for my own advantage or for the good of others, in a spirit of service?

9. Have I been truthful and fair, or have I injured others by deceit, calumny, detraction, rash judgment, or violation of a secret?

10. Have I done violence to others by damage to life or limb, reputation, honor, or material possessions? Have I involved them in loss? Have I been responsible for advising an abortion or procuring one? Have I kept up hatred for others? Am I estranged from others through

quarrels, enmity, insults, anger? Have I been guilty of refusing to testify to the innocence of another because of selfishness?

11. Have I stolen the property of others? Have I desired it unjustly and inordinately? Have I damaged it? Have I made restitution of other people's property and made good their loss?

12. If I have been injured, have I been ready to make peace for the love of Christ and to forgive, or do I harbor hatred and the desire for revenge?

III. Christ our Lord says: "Be perfect as your Father is perfect."

1. Where is my life really leading me? Is the hope of eternal life my inspiration? Have I tried to grow in the life of the Spirit through prayer, reading the word of God and meditating on it, receiving the sacraments, self-denial? Have I been anxious to control my vices, my bad inclinations and passions, e.g., envy, love of food and drink? Have I been proud and boastful, thinking myself better in the sight of God and despising others as less important than myself? Have I imposed my own will on others, without respecting their freedom and rights?

2. What use have I made of time, of health and strength, of the gifts God has given me to be used like the talents in the Gospel? Do I use them to become more perfect every day? Or have I been lazy and too much given to leisure?

3. Have I been patient in accepting the sorrows and disappointments of life? How have I performed mortification so as to "fill up what is wanting to the sufferings of Christ"? Have I kept the precept of fasting and abstinence?

4. Have I kept my senses and my whole body pure and chaste as a temple of the Holy Spirit consecrated for resurrection and glory, and as a sign of God's faithful love for men and women, a sign that is seen most perfectly in the sacrament of matrimony? Have I dishonored my body by fornication, impurity, unworthy conversation or thoughts, evil desires or actions? Have I given in to sensuality? Have I indulged in reading, conversation, shows, and entertainments that offend against Christian and human decency? Have I encouraged others to sin by my own failure to maintain these standards? Have I been faithful to the moral law in my married life?

5. Have I gone against my conscience out of fear or hypocrisy?

6. Have I always tried to act in the true freedom of the sons of God according to the law of the Spirit, or am I the slave of forces within me?

HYMN INDEX

WHY . . . You should have a
MISSAL . . . of Your OWN!

AT MASS . . . for complete participation and understanding

- ✔ TO RECITE or SING . . . your parts with understanding and devotion.
- ✔ TO LISTEN . . . attentively to the Word of God.
- ✔ TO UNITE . . . with the prayers of the priest.
- ✔ TO HOLD . . . attention and increase your devotion.
- ✔ TO HELP . . . during short periods recommended for personal prayer.

AT HOME . . . to guide your Christian Life and personal spiritual reading

- ✔ TO PREPARE . . . yourself for Mass by reading over the texts and helpful commentary.
- ✔ TO SEE . . . the liturgical year as a whole.
- ✔ TO GUIDE . . . your life in the spirit of the liturgy.
- ✔ TO MODEL . . . your prayers on liturgical sources.
- ✔ TO MEDITATE . . . often on the Word of God.

IDEAL GIFT   New American Bible